D1522062

# Constructing Black Selves

# NATION OF NEWCOMERS

## Immigrant History as American History

Matthew Frye Jacobson and Werner Sollors
GENERAL EDITORS


*Beyond the Shadow of Camptown:*
*Korean Military Brides in America*
Ji-Yeon Yuh

*Feeling Italian:*
*The Art of Ethnicity in America*
Thomas J. Ferraro

*Constructing Black Selves:*
*Caribbean American Narratives and the Second Generation*
Lisa D. McGill

LISA D. McGILL

# Constructing
# Black Selves

## Caribbean American
## Narratives and the
## Second Generation

NEW YORK UNIVERSITY PRESS
New York and London

NEW YORK UNIVERSITY PRESS
New York and London
www.nyupress.org

Library of Congress Cataloging-in-Publication Data
McGill, Lisa D.
Constructing Black selves : Caribbean American narratives and the second generation
/ Lisa D. McGill.
p. cm. — (Nation of newcomers)
Includes bibliographical references and index.
ISBN–13: 978–0–8147–5691–1 (acid-free paper)
ISBN–10: 0–8147–5691–3 (acid-free paper)
1. Caribbean Americans—Intellectual life.   2. Children of immigrants—United
States—Intellectual life.   3. Caribbean Americans—Race identity.   4. African
Americans—Relations with Caribbean Americans.   5. Ethnicity—United States.
6. African diaspora.   7. Caribbean Americans—Social conditions.   8. Children of
immigrants—United States—Social conditions.   9. Performing arts—Social
aspects—United States.   10. American literature—Caribbean American authors—
History and criticism.   I. Title.   II. Series.
E184.C27M33     2005
700'.89'960729—dc22          2005011452

Manufactured in the United States of America
10 9 8 7 6 5 4 3 2 1

For Chad, Camryn, Cayla, and Chloé

*the next generation*

# CONTENTS

# ACKNOWLEDGMENTS

In researching and writing this book, I benefited from the personal and professional support, advice, and scholarship of several colleagues and friends. I owe a particular thanks to Hazel Carby, who first shepherded this project as a dissertation in the American Studies Program at Yale University. Hazel's work, enthusiasm, and mentoring were very important to my graduate school career. I am also grateful for the intellectual support of Michael Denning, Robert Stepto, and Matthew Jacobson. They were always willing to offer insights and direction as my project evolved over the years. Matthew Jacobson was especially helpful in pushing me to explore immigrant cultural history as I revised the manuscript.

I am indebted to Patricia Pessar, who agreed to do an independent study course on Dominican immigrants with me in my first year of graduate school. Her intellectual prodding from the beginning helped me conceptualize a project that considered the connections between migration and cultural studies. She has continued to help me think critically about race, gender, and migration.

Further, I want to express my gratitude to teenagers and cultural workers from La Alianza Dominicana, Dominican 2000, and L.E.A.P for sharing their time and thoughts with me for my last chapter. I have always thought of myself more as a practitioner of community building than as a pure academic. I have made an attempt to create a bridge between my academic specialization and my commitment to be a change agent in urban communities. I am sincerely grateful to my former students from Latino Youth Development in New Haven, Connecticut, who always made my scholarship on second-generation Caribbean youth in the United States seem worthwhile.

There really is no way to even begin to thank my husband, Jay Readey, and the McGill family. Jay, Rose, Michael, Lorraine, Linda, Camryn, Cayla, and Chloé encouraged me, provided emotional sustenance, and initiated ordinary conversation to give me much-needed breaks from this study. My son, Chad, entered this world to challenge my time-management skills and completion goals but provided good company and irreplaceable laughter as I wrote to finish up and he flipped through books patiently.

# Introduction

In 1993, the sociologists Alejandro Portes and Min Zhou introduced their study of the new second generation with the rap of "Herbie," a Haitian American who rhymed:

> My name is Herb
> and I'm not poor;
> I'm the Herbie that you're looking for,
> like Pepsi,
> a new generation
> of Haitian determination—
> I'm the Herbie that you're looking for.[1]

Portes and Zhou explained that Herbie's rap, "Straight Out of Haiti," illuminated the dilemma of assimilation for post-1965 immigrant youth. As Portes and Zhou saw it, Herbie was caught in the cultural conundrum of other second generationers in the 1990s. He, like most in his peer group, had at least three assimilation possibilities:

> One of them replicate[d] the time-honored portrayal of growing acculturation and parallel integration into the white middle-class; a second

le[d] straight in the opposite direction to permanent poverty and assimilation into the underclass; still a third associate[d] rapid economic
advancement with deliberate preservation of the immigrant community's values and tight solidarity.[2]

Herbie's fate, Portes and Zhou warned, depended on what choices he
made as a black immigrant especially. Was his hip-hop braggadocio a
sign that he had fallen victim to "adopting the outlooks and cultural
ways of the native-born," meaning the urban African American population? Had he found a way to "retain [his] ethnic identity by cloaking it
in black American cultural forms?"[3] Or could he, despite the lure of
urban African American culture, still find a way to maintain "the immigrant community's values" and attain the American dream?

Current debates over the assimilation of second-generation Caribbean
immigrants have revitalized contemporary discussions of migration to
the United States. Children born to parents who emigrated from
Caribbean islands have been the topic of recent inquiries about the political and social formations of West Indian and Latino communities in
American cities. Appearing in the 1990s, Portes and Zhou's article—
along with the works of Ruben Rumbaut (1991) and Mary C. Waters
(1996; 1999)—sought to challenge the straight-line models of generational assimilation into white America, models that had dominated immigration scholarship since the mid-twentieth century.[4] Scholars such as
Portes and Zhou, Rumbaut, and Waters recognized the limitations of previous models suggested by Marcus Lee Hansen (1938), William Lloyd
Warner and Leo Srole (1945), and others—scholars who often focused
their research exclusively on European immigrants.[5] Contemporary social scientists realized that, as products of the migration patterns that developed after changes in U.S. immigration policy in 1965, which encouraged an increase in migration from non-European countries, recent immigrants and their children raised complex questions about America as
the proverbial melting pot, while they experienced varied integration
processes in the United States.

Despite the attention given to Caribbean immigrants and their negotiations of African American cultural forms in postwar America, there has
yet to be an in-depth analysis of the ways in which cultural production
becomes a site of cultural engagement between Caribbean second gener-

ationers and African Americans in the twentieth century. *Constructing Black Selves* is that study. Portes, Zhou, Waters, and others warn that the cultural practices of hip hop might prove inimical to the class aspirations of post-1965 immigrant parents, but they never consider what these cultural practices afford Caribbean American youth who try to locate themselves ethnically and racially in African America, American society, and even immigrant enclaves. Herbie's rap, "Straight Out of Haiti," may not articulate the prospects of his social mobility in America, but it does identify a cultural self imagined, created, and re-created through cultural production. That Herbie linguistically and culturally employs African American hip hop to talk about being "straight out of Haiti" suggests the complexities of representing Caribbean American identity. Portes and Zhou insinuate that immigrants such as Herbie often attempt to "cloak" their immigrant identities in urban African American styles like hip hop.[6] However, Herbie's rap, as I argue about other cultural works in this study, intimates another reality: a dialogue taking place between Caribbean American youth and the African American community. "Straight Out of Haiti" uses the language of rap to negotiate and perform racial and ethnic identities in the United States.

*Constructing Black Selves* focuses on the cultural narratives of second-generation Caribbean immigrants like Herbie in the post–World War II era. It departs from the aforementioned studies in the social sciences with its interdisciplinary focus and emphasis on performance and cultural production. From the release of Harry Belafonte's *Calypso* in 1956, discussed in the first chapter, to *Proyecto Uno*'s merengue hip hop of the late 1990s, examined in the final chapter, the cultural texts of Caribbean second generationers have emerged in relation to the influx of Caribbean immigrants to the United States since World War II. Giving primacy to the narratives created by artists and intellectuals, this study examines the ways in which different media—music, literature, autobiography, and film—provide one means to explore the formation of Caribbean American identity for second-generation immigrants.

This study does not attempt to provide comprehensive analyses of Caribbean American immigrants. Instead, by looking at various representations of Caribbean American identity in the cultural productions of the singer-actor Harry Belafonte, the writers Paule Marshall, Audre Lorde, and Piri Thomas, and the merengue hip-hoppers of *Proyecto Uno*, it both considers and asks questions regarding how second generationers perform and construct relationships to a parent culture on one hand and American cultures on the other. I begin with the questions that have confounded the most recent studies of twentieth-century black immigrants to the United States: how do Caribbean immigrants negotiate languages of race and ethnicity in American social and cultural politics? As black immigrants, into which America do they assimilate? I show that cultural production serves as an apt site for an investigation of discourses on racialized, ethnic, and American identity constructions. My analysis illuminates the ways in which Caribbean second generationers use literature, music, and other expressive forms as vehicles to explore interactions with white America, African America, and parent Caribbean cultures.

This project differs from recent migration scholarship in the social sciences, which often focuses on the disparities between African American and Caribbean identities in the United States. Here, I separate myself from scholars who often (mis)use new models of immigrant identities—transnationalism, pan-Caribbeanness, and ethnic culturalism—to negate the significance of dialogues between native-born and immigrant black populations.[7] It is not that I challenge the models themselves. In fact, I employ them in my analyses of cultural texts, and I recognize their importance to the study of Caribbean American cultural formation. However, in an attempt to differentiate between black immigrant and African American identities in recent migration studies, several social scientists' employments of these models often conceal more than they reveal about the construction of Caribbean American identity for children of immigrants. Their suggestion of an either/or paradigm for black immigrants often limits our understanding of the ways in which Caribbean Americans' independence from and engagement with African Americans have not been, nor need not be, mutually exclusive. The cultural dialogue between Caribbean Americans and African Americans provides one of the most robust ways to analyze the participation of second-generation immigrants in American society.

Further, *Constructing Black Selves* fills a glaring gap in the study of black immigrants, especially of the second generation, in contemporary literary and cultural studies. While social scientists often focus on the perceived differences between black Caribbean immigrants and African

Americans after World War II, literary and cultural theorists instead oversimplify the similarities between these ethnicities as represented in the works of several artists and intellectuals featured here. Their Caribbean heritage and second-generation identity often serve as an ancillary feature, not a subject of examination itself, when anthologized in cultural compilations or studied in the African American canon. Very rarely does one find a course of study that concentrates on the formation of *Caribbean American* identity, even in its relationship with African America. The works of West Indian second generationers such as Audre Lorde and Paule Marshall are usually confined to African American literature classes, for example, or to literary and cultural studies focused on the Caribbean diaspora.

The connection between African American and black Latino cultural production suffers even more in the humanities. Artists and intellectuals who are black, Latino, and of the second generation are seldom studied for their participation in both Latino and African American cultural movements. The 1960s and early 1970s marked a moment when artists such as Piri Thomas, Felipe Luciano, and Sandra María Esteves were discussed and anthologized in black American collections and scholarly publications; however, the celebration of those connections was short-lived. Most of those who identify as Latinos of African heritage have been widely discussed as seminal figures in the U.S. Latino culture industry. But, they have not received adequate attention for the role that they have played in articulating the experiences of black and second-generation immigrants in the United States. *Constructing Black Selves* thus employs the cultural texts of black West Indian and Latino second generationers to push the boundaries of immigration scholarship in the social sciences as it engages the humanities to consider Caribbean American cultures in more meaningful ways.

## Theorizing Black Immigrant Cultures in the United States

"Our choices became clear," writes Evelio Grillo in his memoir *Black Cuban, Black American*, "to swim in black American society or drown in the Latin ghettoes of New York City, never to be an integral part of American life." He continues:

> This is why the experience of black Cubans who joined with black Americans is so different from that of black Cubans who remained loosely tethered to white Cuban society. Integration presented us with simple options: join the black American society, with its rich roots deep in this country, or have no American roots at all.[8]

Grillo's story represents one seldom told about the black and immigrant experience in the United States. Grillo, the son of black Cuban immigrants, came of age in the 1930s and 1940s at the height of academic and popular debates on assimilation, cultural pluralism, and American civic nationalism. His was a lived experience virtually invisible to those most concerned with the massive waves of European immigrants as American citizens, commentators, and politicians grappled with the impact that twentieth-century immigration would have on the American way of life.

Grillo was born into a world where, between 1900 and 1930, there were at least 18.6 million immigrants to the United States. At least 6.7 million of these immigrants were from European countries; 2.5 million from Canada, Newfoundland, and Mexico; and approximately 683,000 from Asia. During this period, the Caribbean islands sent approximately 305,871 immigrants to the United States—primarily to urban centers such as New York. By 1940, the black foreign-born population had risen from 20,336 in 1900 to 83,941.[9]

America's response to this intense immigration varied. Leading educators such as Ellwood Cubberley, of Stanford University, felt that immigrant children would be a debilitating presence in American society as adults if they were not Americanized properly to understand American social, political, and cultural values. The National Education Association in the 1890s and Cubberley in the early 1900s were very vocal about their belief that this Americanization was the responsibility of the public school systems. Nativists such as Madison Grant and Harry Laughlin purported that most of the nonwhite, non-Protestant immigrants could not be assimilated and should thus be barred from entering the country. This sentiment and subsequent advocacy by the Ku Klux Klan, the Immigration Restriction League, and other nativist groups led to the most stringent immigration laws in American history. Progressive intellectuals such as Horace Kallen and Ralph Bourne outwardly validated the survival of ethnic traditions and customs among immigrant groups, suggesting that Americanization, in its contemporary context, was not only impossible but ill advised.[10]

Evelio Grillo entered Xavier University, a Louisiana institution dedicated to the higher education of African Americans, in 1937—the same year that the historian Marcus Hansen shared his oft-quoted thesis, "what the son wishes to forget the grandson wishes to remember," with the Augustana Historical Society in Rock Island, Illinois.[11] Marcus Hansen's speech, like most discussions of the time, focused on the assimilation process for white immigrants and their future generations. Hansen postulated that children of immigrants often chose to relinquish their ethnic heritage to become a part of mainstream American culture. Their offspring, however, were proud of their ethnic background, seldom had an inferiority complex, and were thus more willing to explore the contributions of the immigrant ancestors to the fabric of American life. Although his speech emphasized third-generation identity in his attempts to mobilize the Swedish American "grandsons" to whom he was speaking, it was his notion of second-generation identity that resonated with postwar scholars attempting to understand the generational assimilation processes for immigrants to the United States.

I highlight Evelio Grillo's narrative by way of introduction because the glaring absence of stories like his defines a central problem in early-twentieth-century scholarship on immigration. Not only were stories of black immigrants virtually untold; they were also undervalued in the emerging examination of American ethnicity. What is most obvious about several of the debates between 1900 and 1940—Hansen's included —is that very few paid attention to the experiences of West Indians and other black immigrants from Caribbean islands. When discussions about assimilation and American's black population arose, scholars concentrated primarily on native-born blacks and the prospects of their acculturation in cities such as Chicago, St. Louis, Boston, and New York.

Ira D. A. Reid's 1939 study, *The Negro Immigrant: His Background, Characteristics, and Social Adjustment,* stands out as one of the very few in-depth documentations of black immigrants in the United States during this time. It is by far one of the best studies prior to the postwar era, especially given its understanding of the push and pull factors that influenced immigration, as well as the assimilation processes of immigrants from not only the West Indies but the Spanish and French Caribbean islands, as well.[12] Another notable exception, although not entirely focused on black immigrants, is Lawrence Chenault's book, *The Puerto Rican Migrant in New York City,* published in the same year. This study on Puerto Ricans in New York predates several books in the 1950s that began to more closely examine the role that race, especially African heritage, played in the assimilation of black and mixed-race Puerto Ricans who migrated to major American cities.[13]

The story of Grillo and those featured in the works of Reid and Chenault suggested what most immigration scholars in the first half or more of the twentieth century clearly were not ready to acknowledge: that a growing, although largely unrecognized, transculturation was taking place between native-born blacks and black immigrants, as well as between black immigrants and the larger American society. Theirs was just the beginning of what others would learn was the undeniable presence and influence of the black foreign-born and their children in postwar America. It was an influence that Americans would increasingly be forced to face as changes in the second half of the twentieth century led to much more globalized economies and cultures, with increased movements of people and capital despite the boundaries of nation-states in the Western hemisphere.

This early oversight suggestively reflected the cultural biases of the institutions, academics, and American citizens who were most concerned with defining American nationalism through whiteness at the time. Problematic on its own, I argue that it also points to a larger issue: Early immigration scholarship in the social sciences was built on an unstable foundation that severely hindered the growth of the field after 1965, when American migration was at a height not reached since the turn of the nineteenth century. Migration to the United States in the first half of the twentieth century was greatly limited by immigration quotas in the 1920s, the Great Depression, and then World War II.[14] However, the Hart-Celler Immigration Reform Act of 1965 changed all of that, opening the doors to blacks and other immigrants of color from non-European countries.

Although the intricacies of U.S. immigration law changes are beyond the scope of this discussion, one of the unexpected outcomes of the 1965 Act and its subsequent amendments was that Asian, Latin American, and Caribbean countries became the major sources of immigrants to the United States after 1965. Between 1971 and 1985, for example, Mexico and the Philippines became the countries with the greatest numbers of immigrants to the United States, averaging 64,817 and 38,759 people per year, respectively. They were followed by South Korea, with 29,198, and Vietnam, with 27,637 immigrants on average per year.[15]

The newly formed microstates in the Anglo Caribbean, no longer under British rule, sent roughly 40,000 people each year to major American cities between 1966 and 1984. Jamaica alone sent approximately 16,170 annually between 1971 and 1985. The Spanish Caribbean island of Cuba sent approximately 22,384 immigrants to American shores each year, while the Dominican Republic was the donor country for an average of 16,845 immigrants annually. Its neighboring country, Haiti, sent approximately 6,840 immigrants per year during this period.[16]

This influx was influenced not only by a change in U.S. immigration policy that supported outmigration from former European colonies in the Western Hemisphere but, in some cases, by the restrictions Britain imposed on immigration from its former colonies in 1962. Great Britain's own xenophobia about blacks from the English-speaking islands forced several former British subjects to look beyond the mother country for better opportunities. Many settled in the United States. Furthermore, revolutionary struggles and political overthrows in the Caribbean basin became a major supply of both legal and illegal immigrants, refugees, and exiles. Fidel Castro rose to leadership in Cuba in 1959. The Dominican Republic was faced with the death of Rafael Trujillo Molina and, subsequently, a loosening of its own emigration policies. Several refugees from Haiti left that small island to escape the political repressions of the Duvalier regime. All of these realities served as push factors that brought Caribbean immigrants to American cities.[17]

America was not quite ready for this unexpected population growth, and it was especially surprised by the demographic shift spawned by changes in U.S. immigration policies. Immigrants from countries in the Caribbean and elsewhere altered the face of America at a time when

America was undergoing its own struggles for civil rights, identity consciousness, and racial equality for native-born people of color who had been historically disenfranchised and marginalized in the United States. The arrival of blacks and other immigrants of color after 1965 was concomitant with the U.S. civil rights and ethnic consciousness movements of the late 1950s through the early 1970s. This reality had a significant impact on those with a history in America and on those immigrants and their children who were just beginning to adjust to life in the United States.

Unfortunately, at a time when race and ethnicity took center stage in American popular life, the presence of black immigrant cultures was largely absent from the limelight of public discussion in the 1960s and 1970s. American immigration scholars seemed handicapped by a legacy left them by Hansen and others from an earlier generation and ill equipped to even capture the transformations taking place among the native-born immigrants of color and a second generation of immigrants coming of age at this volatile time in American history. Immigrants of color and their second generation—especially those like Belafonte, Marshall, and Lorde, all of whom had parents who migrated to the U.S. in the 1920s and 1930s—were often trailblazers in challenging America's monolithic and provincial view of itself in the 1960s and 1970s. However, both public discourse and emerging scholarly debates focused primarily on racial minorities with a long history in the United States, or, to the contrary, on white America's mixed responses to its own ethnic diversity during this consciousness-raising era.

Mary Waters, in an attempt to understand this cultural moment, explains:

> These debates were all based on an assumption—only sometimes made explicit—that what happened to white immigrants from Europe would provide a model or a comparison point for the experience of other ethnic and racial groups. In fact, the models of assimilation and cultural pluralism used by American sociologists were developed based on the experiences of these European groups—and especially important in these models is the concept of movement through generations. The further removed in generations from the earlier immigrants, the more assimilated the descendants would be. Thus the de-

bate that began in the 1960s and 1970s about the relative importance
of ethnicity for groups of European origin had a great deal of significance.[18]

Waters notes that whatever the terminology used—melting pot, cultural
pluralism, new ethnicity—a new field of inquiry arose in response to the
implicit need to come to terms with the post-1965 migration increase
from non-European countries. These very obvious changes to the face of
America raised the bar for postmodern immigration studies, forcing
scholars to question more critically the prevailing notion of generational
assimilation.

Doing so may have fueled a new interest in the revival of white ethnic
consciousness, but it did little to build the body of literature on or even
public awareness about black immigrants. Blacks from the Caribbean
were clearly recognized as a major piece of the puzzle, if only covertly.
The sheer numbers of blacks coming from English-, French-, and Span-
ish-speaking countries not only influenced African America; they also
became a salient reminder for scholars of immigration and the average
American citizen that race and ethnicity were not one and the same.
Some studies by scholars such as Nathan Glazer and Daniel Patrick
Moynihan (1963) and Ulf Hannerz (1976) made gestures toward acknowledging the presence of black immigrants when they referenced the
possibilities for integration for American blacks.[19] Few, if any, made the
leap to closely examine how the question of generational assimilation,
which had arguably defined the first half of the twentieth century, could
find some answers by placing black immigrants at the center and not the
periphery of scholarly enterprise.

It was not until the mid-1980s that social scientists began to seriously
consider the assimilation processes and social formation of the black foreign-born and the second generation. This moment was an important one
for the field, because, although problematic in its own way, it challenged
the exclusive nature by which American immigration studies had been
traditionally defined. From the start, these scholars were confronted
with the limitation of frameworks established by Hansen in the 1930s, as
well as by Joshua Fishman, Vladimir Nahirny, and Oscar Handlin in the
1960s. They found that, although these earlier frameworks might have
been useful in considering the white ethnic population of the twentieth

century, they did little to address the increasingly global world in which black immigrants operated and the undeniable role both race and ethnicity played in the ways black immigrants experienced both home and host societies.[20] Theorizations on ethnic identity and generational assimilation processes into the American mainstream were challenged and then revamped by new frameworks on transnationalism, pan-Caribbeanness, and postmodern notions of diasporic identities.

These new studies changed the tone of discussions in the mid-1980s and 1990s and had a critical impact on shaping the direction of immigration scholarship at the dawn of the twenty-first century. First, scholars during these two decades were able to document the ways in which black immigrants were deeply influenced by what happened both in American cities and in their island communities, with whose people, politics, and culture they maintained contact. In their 1994 study on immigrants from Grenada and St. Vincent, for instance, Linda Basch, Nina Glick Schiller, and Cristina Szanton Blanc smartly surmised that what traditionally fell under the study of "ethnicity" in the United States must be complicated by these "transmigrants" who "rework[ed] different hegemonic constructions of identity developed in their home and new nation-state(s)" to participate in a transnational sphere.[21] Patricia Pessar and Sherry Grasmuck similarly underscored the importance of the social networks at play in the Dominican exodus to New York City. They examined the ways in which social relations "organized and directed by the circulation of labor, capital, goods" and so forth strengthened migrants' social ties to the Dominican Republic, even if economic realities had them situated in the United States.[22]

Second, and perhaps most useful, some social scientists began to consider the nuanced differences between race and ethnicity for black immigrants. Race has often been accepted as the defining factor—the master status—that helped explain housing discrimination, labor participation, and the ease or difficulty with which blacks negotiated American social life.[23] Debates about race went to the heart of debates about post-1965 immigrants. Questions resounded about whether recent immigrants of color, especially black immigrants, would suffer the same fate disproportionately experienced by native-born blacks or whether they would find or create opportunities for attaining the American dream. Scholars began to test the limits of America's racial codes, attempting to determine whether race or ethnicity was more critical in influencing the assimilation possibilities for foreign-born blacks and their children.

Although these scholars' conclusions may have differed in details, most began to show an emerging, and disappointing, trend in immigration studies. Several suggested that ethnicity, and not race, was the defining factor in understanding Caribbean American adjustment in the United States. Scholars such as Milton Vickerman (1999) argued that West Indian immigrants often tried to steer clear of conceptualizations of blackness in the United States, for example, using West Indian ethnicity as an indicator of class to avoid association with native-born blacks. Basch et al. (1994) concluded that transnational identities allowed black immigrants to eschew the racial politics of the United States and that West Indians preferred a transnational identity that afforded a cultural capital not supposedly provided by an African American one. Philip Kasinitz (1992) suggested that West Indians created a pan-ethnic identity in the United States that allowed them to supersede participation in African American identity politics. With the freedom to explore ethnic versus racial allegiances in the post-1965 era, according to these scholars, West Indians chose to see themselves as distinct from the African American population.

Although many of these studies gave voice and legitimacy to a growing Caribbean population in U.S. cities, several also silenced an important discussion around blackness and the transculturation between Caribbean blacks from the Spanish-, French-, and English-speaking islands and African Americans since 1965. For example, the recent emphasis on transnationalism and pan-ethnic Caribbean identity prematurely suggests that Caribbean immigrants construct black identities mostly outside African American political and social spheres. This new direction of black immigrant studies leaves questions unanswered about what Earl Lewis calls the "practice of writing African peoples into a history of overlapping diasporas" in the United States.[24] Caribbean immigrants may live in ethnic enclaves and participate in culturally defined activities on a day-to-day basis; yet, they constantly, if only subconsciously, negotiate their relationship with blackness as defined in the American milieu. In short, they are in ever-changing, always active discourse with African American culture and cultural expression. This reality is particularly true for the second generation.

If postwar Caribbean immigrants live mostly outside African America, what accounts for the rise in arts festivals that celebrate the African diaspora in major urban cities? Why the focused attention on black Caribbean and African American fusions in popular urban media for music, business, and film? Why the number of Caribbean immigrants and their children who continue to participate in historically African American institutions and organizations? Why the concern over the choices of the Caribbean second generation?

Social scientists are right to argue that the second (and future) generation(s) will provide the litmus test for understanding the assimilation processes for black immigrants. However, they are often blinded by a one-sided focus on economic mobility, or at least the corollary, how these second generationers self-identify (as immigrant, as African American, as part of the American mainstream) and the prospect for their class status in the United States. The growing sense that contact with African American culture means arrested development for the second and future generations of Caribbean immigrants at best simply denies the regenerative influence that African American culture has had on other cultures in the diaspora and at worst falsely suggests that American racism and unwillingness to fully accept racial minorities may be the true hindrances to black immigrants' attaining American ideals of success. Social scientists have thus gone from turning a blind eye to the differences between African American and Caribbean immigrants—not seeing Caribbean immigrants as a legitimate subject of examination in the quest to understand American ethnics—to devaluing the constant interchange between Caribbean immigrants and blacks native to the United States.

## Constructing Black Selves

Against these recent trends in reading Caribbean American identity, I argue that the second-generation artists and intellectuals discussed in *Constructing Black Selves* make blackness an attractive and useful site for self-discovery. The use of blackness is a focal point of this book, which engages the term as it is used in migration studies while seeking to un-

derstand the political, social, and cultural meanings of blackness suggested by second-generation immigrants in postwar America.[25] For these
artists and intellectuals, representations of blackness demand negotiations of African American *and* Caribbean identities, although these negotiations are fraught with the tensions of narrating racial, ethnic, and
gendered selves to an American public. The fear of African Americanization often constructed in literatures of the social sciences undermines
the voices of second-generation artists, like those examined here, who
work through and in between the Caribbean and African America to explore their relationships to their parent cultures, African Americans, and
other populations in the United States and beyond.

Further, I suggest that the black immigrant experience and the performance of culture are intimately linked. When Portes and Zhou use
Herbie's rap "Straight Out of Haiti" as a signifier of Herbie's conundrum,
they rightly suggest that this young artist's choice of expression comes
about not just because he is black but, more tellingly, because he is
black, immigrant, and of the second generation. Although flawed on various levels, scholarship by Portes, Zhou, Kasinitz, and others has been
very successful at acknowledging the multiplicity of black ethnicities in
the United States and their cultural expressions. The recognition of this
multiplicity—arguably not yet understood in a sustained way in black
cultural studies—is at the heart of my work.

If *Constructing Black Selves* has an implicit, overarching critique of
contemporary scholarship from literary and cultural studies, it is that
cultural critics seldom push their thinking to really examine this difference in black experiences. Acknowledging that some of the richest theorizing on ethnicity emanates most recently from the humanities, I also
suggest that humanists who write on and research black culture are either often unaware of or not concerned with the cutting-edge work of
ethnic populations in disciplines of the social sciences or unwilling to
look beyond what have become canonized understandings of U.S. black
literary and cultural traditions.

Part of the problem lies in what I see as the reluctance to have one's
scholarship in the humanities too closely associated with the social sciences in a post-1960s, post–identity politics era. Ethnic and cultural
studies, in many ways, developed as a product of the consciousness-raising of students, alumni, and scholar-activists on many college campuses

across the country in the 1960s and early 1970s. There was much public debate about the validity of departments, programs, and areas of inquiry dedicated to the study of people of color and other marginalized groups. As Thomas Ferraro points out in *Ethnic Passages,* an examination of twentieth-century white immigrant writers, the words "ethnic" and "literature," when juxtaposed, were and continue to be pejoratively read as oxymoronic by more than a few. Consequently, scholars in these fields too often struggle with the question of how to validate ethnic literature and cultural production as artistic, while exploring the sociological undercurrents frequently evidenced in works by ethnic artists and intellectuals.

Leading associations such as the Society for the Study of Multi-Ethnic Literature in the United States (MELUS) and the Modern Language Association (MLA), for example, have attempted to deal with this question at least since the early 1980s by promoting the message that ethnic literature is in fact *American* literature. MLA, through its Committee on Literature and Languages of America, understands American literature as a "patchwork quilt" and argues that literary criticism should be based on a model that celebrates the multiracial heritage of the United States and not just its European influences.[26] MELUS similarly suggests that one of the inherent values of ethnic literature is that it forces us to rethink our definition of U.S. mainstream literature. Since 1973, it has made a commitment to expanding understandings of American literature and asserts this commitment as the bedrock of its constitution and by-laws. In recent years, this public message from both associations has been supported by the studies of scholars such as William Boelhower, Mary Dearborn, Werner Sollors, and others who have tried to establish the relationship between ethnic literature and what academia has traditionally identified as quintessentially American about works that make up the mainstream literary canon.[27]

Except for the theoretical frameworks developed by scholars such as Ferraro and Sollors, or, more recently, young scholars such as Heather Hathaway (1999), there are very few literary and cultural studies that acknowledge the value of creating a discourse with the social sciences as a means of providing a new and important way to examine cultural narratives written and performed by ethnic populations. This unwillingness to cross academic borders has particular implications for understanding the cultural production of black West Indian and Latino immigrants of the second generation in the twentieth century. In an attempt to legitimate them as part of an American—and, in some cases, an African American—cultural canon, contemporary literary and cultural criticisms seldom deal with the impact of the immigrant experience itself. More often than not, immigrants are simply reduced to ethnics—despite generational differences, their arrival during different immigration phases, and the uniqueness of the host communities in which they settle.

Dearborn (1986) thus discusses Zora Neale Hurston as part of an African American tradition and makes only a peripheral nod to her West Indian background and its influence on her writing. The actors Harry Belafonte and Sidney Poitier are featured as important to creating a new image for blacks after World War II in Daniel Leab's comprehensive work on blacks in film; yet, their second-generation identities are never carefully examined for how they shaped Belafonte's and Poitier's lives both on and off the screen. Audre Lorde is heralded for her contributions to the feminist, African American, and Caribbean aesthetics by gifted cultural critics as varied as AnaLouise Keating, Claudine Raynaud, and Chinosole. But, unfortunately, few have taken the time to carefully consider how her experience as a child of black immigrants influenced not only her work but the ties she established to multiple communities throughout her life. In essence, the immigrant impulse in several bodies of scholarship featuring black immigrants of the second generation is simply an anecdotal provocation in the task of deconstructing tropes and giving close textual readings of literature, music, and other narratives in the American culture industry. The study makes the important claim that the performative value of blackness in Caribbean American cultural production does not supersede the import of immigrant identity construction as explored by Harry Belafonte, Paule Marshall, Audre Lorde, Piri Thomas, and the hip-hoppers of *Proyecto Uno*.

This book thus engages in conversation with cultural critics whose work explores linkages between ethnicity, identity politics, and the performance of culture, scholars such as Frances Aparicio, Hazel Carby, Juan Flores, Robin Kelley, George Lipsitz, and the social scientist Paul Gilroy. Although several of these scholars do not focus on the intersections between black, immigrant, and generational identities specifically, all have pushed the boundaries of academic silos to make much-needed connections between lived experience and the culture industry of blacks, Latinos, and other people of color. From Frances Aparicio and Hazel Carby's scholarship on gender and class to Paul Gilroy's work on ethnicity and the black diaspora, the work of these scholars stands as a constant and important reminder of the ways in which literature, music, film, and autobiography can become sites for exploring and working through issues of race, gender, sexuality, and class. Beyond its individual merits, their scholarship presents tools on which I often rely or theoretical frameworks with which I am often in dialogue as I explore the cultural production of black Latino and West Indian immigrants of the second generation after World War II.

## Framing Narratives

*Constructing Black Selves* focuses on the period after World War II, when Caribbean American communities of size and distinct identity were taking form in urban enclaves. The first easily identifiable population of second-generation immigrants, with parents who migrated from the Caribbean around the 1920s, was nurtured and influenced by the emerging black cultures in the United States. These second generationers were also deeply affected by the growing number of black immigrants to the United States after 1965—the same time that America was undergoing a cultural metamorphosis that would change future race relations. Thus, starting in the postwar era allows this study to both examine some of the first cultural expressions of second-generation artists from the late 1940s through the early 1960s and connect these earlier cultural texts with works subsequently produced by second-generation immigrants in the late twentieth century. It further provides the chance to explore how second-generationers constantly reinvented and renegotiated their identities in relation to America's changing cultural landscape during the Civil Rights era, the consciousness movements of the 1960s and 1970s, and the increasingly globalized world at the turn of the century.

I must admit that, at the start of this project, I had not intended to engage a cultural history of social movements in the United States. As the project emerged, however, I recognized how important most of the leading social movements—Civil Rights, Black Power, Pan-Africanism, Feminism, Hip Hop—were to Belafonte, Marshall, Lorde, Thomas, and the members of *Proyecto Uno,* both as second-generation immigrants of African descent and as artists and intellectuals. The timing of these movements and their respective trajectories after World War II often reveal as much about the artists and their cultural productions as do their individual relationships with parent communities, white society, and African America. It is always a slippery slope to begin to discuss the impact of movements on people's identity politics, let alone the growth of their artistic consciousness. Yet, the postwar moment was a period of great change in America, and there were very few who were left unaffected by mass attempts to challenge white supremacy, gender norms, and sexual, racial, and class biases in concerted, strategic ways. Belafonte, Marshall, Lorde, Thomas, and even *Proyecto Uno* are not very different in that respect from most Americans who came of age after World War II.

Because it became increasingly difficult to talk about the cultural productions of the second-generation artists collected in this study without discussing the relevance of key social movements, these movements share a small part of the stage with my analyses of the actual works themselves. Several movements—especially those of import during the 1950s, 1960s, and 1970s—often find a place in my examination of multiple artists, many of whom are contemporaries of each other. True to the individual nature of identity construction, these artists often have very different responses to the ideological underpinnings of each cultural moment. For example, Marshall's response to the integrationist politics of the Civil Rights Movement does not mirror Belafonte's, although both make use of Caribbean cultures in their works. Audre Lorde's understanding of Pan-Africanism engages the mainstream Feminist Movement in ways that Marshall's does not, despite the presence of Africa as a central motif in their writings. Thus, even as I acknowledge that social and cultural movements are crucial to how these second generationers understand and explore Caribbean American identity in the narratives they produce, this study is careful to point out that each artist has his or her own unique response to these movements as a second generationer from a particular cultural and individual background. The works explored in this study are reflective of that uniqueness.

This project is deliberately bounded by chapter in its discussion of artists' negotiations of Caribbean and African American cultures. Harry Belafonte, Paule Marshall, Audre Lorde, Piri Thomas, and *Proyecto Uno,* of course, are not the only artists and intellectuals who could have been chosen for this study. Still, each employs black identities at various stages in the postwar period in ways that prove useful to an examination of second-generation identity, representation, and performance. Collectively, they provide a framework through which to map second-generation identity while analyzing ethnicity as it intersects with issues of race, gender, class, and sexuality.

These artists range in ethnic origin from the West Indies to the Spanish Caribbean islands, and their cultural texts create overlapping, yet often dissonant, dialogues with each other. Although I focus on negotiations of black identities, I have been careful to resist choosing artists who produce discourses in similar ways. My goal is not to establish a unified articulation of second-generation identity for Caribbean immigrants but to illustrate the ways in which multiple factors affect and underscore narrations of Caribbean American selves for second generationers.

The study begins by examining representations of Harry Belafonte's performative body in 1950s America. Born in New York to Jamaican and Martiniquan parents, Belafonte was one of the first second-generation West Indian immigrants to experience success as an American pop icon in the culture industry. Although questions remain about Belafonte's commodification in mass culture, I maintain that the emphasis on his body in the postwar period presents a provocative and discursive site for illuminating what was at stake in performances of racial and ethnic identities for black immigrants. Belafonte was successful as the "King of Calypso" at a moment when white Americans were becoming increasingly aware of West Indian cultures through music, films, and an increase in American tourism to Caribbean islands. Their engagement with Caribbean culture paralleled the growing tensions at home with African Americans after World War II. An analysis of Belafonte's performative body illustrates the challenges of participating in mainstream America for native-born and foreign blacks while asserting one's cultural and racial self. I argue that Belafonte invoked his Caribbean heritage to challenge the boundaries of black male citizenship in 1950s America.

Through performing a Caribbean identity, Belafonte altered mainstream imaginings of blacks in the United States at the dawn of the civil rights era.

The next chapter examines the literature and political activism of Paule Marshall, a second-generation immigrant of Barbadian descent. It focuses on the ideological crises of black and leftist politics that Paule Marshall explored in her fiction between 1959 and 1983. In contrast to Belafonte, Marshall provided an alternative stage for the examination of racial, ethnic, and gender locations. Belafonte's work suggests the importance of integration into American society, whereas Marshall's literature intimates the necessity of maintaining and preserving ties with black diasporic cultures. Here, I suggest that Marshall attempted to avoid assimilation into mainstream American culture by establishing links between Caribbeans and African Americans. I explore the ways in which Marshall established these ties by reconciling her leftist sensibilities with imaginings of an African diaspora in her work. Offering a close reading of her novel *Praisesong for the Widow* (1983), the chapter contends that Marshall used the Caribbean and African America as sites that enacted a turn away from the white American mainstream and a movement toward an African diasporic identity.

The third chapter considers Audre Lorde's use of Africa, building on the previous chapter's discussion of the African diaspora in Paule Marshall's literature. Reading Lorde after Marshall, I suggest that Africa and the African diaspora become imaginative *American* constructions for both of these women who are influenced by their affiliations with social and political consciousness movements in the United States. However, although Lorde employed tropes of Africa, she resisted the temptation to distance herself from American culture. For this Barbadian and Grenadian second generationer, Africa became an imagined stage for recuperating black and gender subject-positions during the Black Arts and Feminist Movements. Using African mythological figures, Lorde engaged racial, sexual, and cultural communities outside the Caribbean, African America, and the black diaspora. This chapter examines two of Lorde's writings: *The Black Unicorn* (1978), a collection of poetry, and *Zami* (1982), Lorde's "biomythography." It suggests that Lorde used tropes of Africa to validate a politically black and lesbian identity and to empower the political identities of others.

The final two chapters augment understandings of Caribbean American identity in the United States with their focus on second-generation immigrants of Latino parentage. With my analyses of Spanish Caribbean cultural productions, I hope to expand readings of black identity in the United States. The fourth and fifth chapters suggest that black identity is not just an issue for West Indian immigrants, who are often racialized as black. Understandings of black identity also inform the cultural representations of more ambiguously racialized immigrants, such as immigrants from Puerto Rico and the Dominican Republic.

The fourth chapter examines the 1967 autobiography *Down These Mean Streets,* by Piri Thomas, a Nuyorican writer. Piri Thomas's autobiography complicates Marshall's and Lorde's understandings of black identity by voicing the complex reality that their imaginings of blackness placed on Thomas's multiracial and masculine Caribbean self. The chapter posits that Piri Thomas's negotiation of black identity in *Down These Mean Streets* threatens the autobiographical self's identification as a Puerto Rican man. It illustrates how Thomas's account of his racial discovery as a black Puerto Rican reveals his fraught relationships with white America and African America, as well as with his native Hispanic community. Although Thomas attempts to embrace a black identity in his autobiography, he does so only to experience dislocation in the urban environment of New York and in the American South. His autobiography ultimately raises questions about the rigidity of racial constructs in post-1965 America.

The book culminates with an analysis of the merengue hip hop of *Proyecto Uno,* a group started by two Dominican second generationers in the late 1980s. The chapter illuminates the ways in which the negotiation of a black identity first presented by Thomas in *Down These Mean Streets* provided a language for subsequent Afro-Latino artists to more easily engage African American and Hispanic cultures. Further, this final chapter addresses the immigrant experience of the "new" second generation—that is, children of immigrants who came to the United States after 1965. While Belafonte, Marshall, Lorde, and Thomas were all children of first-generation immigrants who migrated to the United States in the 1920s and 1930s, the members of *Proyecto Uno* are part of the migration influx from the Caribbean islands after changes in U.S. immigration policy in 1965. By focusing on second-generation immigrant culture in the late twentieth century, I explore new developments in the performance and enunciation of Caribbean American identity.

The final chapter examines the hip-hop music of *Proyecto Uno* through an analysis of its lyrics, style, and performance. Linking the cultural history of Spanish Caribbean immigration with the development of second-generation Latino angst in American cities, the chapter uses contemporary gender and cultural theory to suggest the importance of providing alternative readings to the group's urban male braggadocio and chauvinistic image. Pushing the boundaries of cultural studies, the chapter argues that the lyrical play of *Proyecto Uno*'s songs reveals identity formations that illuminate negotiations of immigrant, island, and black diasporic cultures in the 1990s. It concludes that cultural practices of post-1965 immigrant children suggest new ways of understanding the interaction between Caribbean and African American cultures at the turn of the twenty-first century.

Because of their location within, outside, and between black cultural and ethnic communities, second-generation Caribbean Americans reveal multiple ways of exploring discourses of race and ethnicity in the United States. *Constructing Black Selves* is the first book to offer a sustained reading of second-generation Caribbean identity. It illustrates that cultural production reveals the ways in which people see themselves and want to be seen by others and, in doing so, provides an alternative lens for understanding the social formations of Caribbean cultures in the United States. Collectively, the subjects of the book—Harry Belafonte, Paule Marshall, Audre Lorde, Piri Thomas, and *Proyecto Uno*—raise the challenge of reconsidering the complexities of Caribbean American identity for second-generation immigrants and, by implication, for future Caribbean populations in the United States. Their stories have much to tell us about the ways in which second generationers of the twentieth century have used various devices and narratives for constructing black selves.

CHAPTER **1**

# Performing the Caribbean

Harry Belafonte and
the Black Male Body

"Can a Brother Get Some Love?"
*Essence* magazine asked in its February 2000 issue, featuring the late-twentieth-century African American male actors Morris Chestnut, Blair Underwood, and Mekhi Phifer on its cover. More than four decades after Harry Belafonte emerged as the first Negro matinee idol, *Essence,* in sarcastic fashion, quipped "Not in Hollywood" in its exposé on African American male sexuality on the silver screen. "Studios have never been interested in portraying Black men as fully realized sexual beings," the authors of the *Essence* article reflected. "That's why studios failed to capitalize on the huge appeal of leading men like Harry Belafonte in *Carmen Jones,* Billy Dee Williams in *Lady Sings the Blues* and Sidney Poitier in *Guess Who's Coming to Dinner?*"[1] In this article, black cultural critics illuminated the problems that contemporary black male actors faced in their attempts to explore sexual selves in the American culture industry. Critics linked the filmic woes of men such as Denzel Washington and Morris Chestnut to those of their black predecessors in earlier moments of the twentieth century.

This *Essence* cover story evoked the uniqueness of Harry Belafonte's career in the 1950s. Beyond making specific references to Belafonte as one of the first black male sex symbols in American cultural history, it revealed both Belafonte's success and failure as a 1950s cultural icon: he was the black male sex symbol before the surplus of black men in action and buddy films, the actor whose "radiant smile made our hearts leap" and "sultry, soul-stirring presence"[2] set the stage for Denzel Washington's and Morris Chestnut's new kind of magnetism in late-twentieth-century films such as *Mo' Better Blues* (1990) and *The Best Man* (1999). Yet, he, as the cover story intimated, was also the figure who reflected the limitations of placing black male bodies in American film, especially after World War II. On one level, he captured the gaze of the American public as calypso singer and crossover film star, initiating new tropes for African American images in the popular culture of the 1950s. On another level, his figure articulated contested social issues of race and gender played out in the popular media of music, film, and television in the postwar era. The trajectory of Belafonte's stardom between roughly 1956 and 1959 staged the contradictions of his diverse cultural and political functions at the height of his music and film career.

In this chapter, I explore representations of Belafonte's performative body in the 1950s through an examination of the calypso craze, started by the release of the album *Harry Belafonte—Calypso* in 1956 and Belafonte's role as David Boyeur in the 1957 film *Island in the Sun*. I argue that the iconization of his body—his Caribbean body in particular—elucidates sociocultural politics in the United States after World War II. The 1950s body of Harry Belafonte sat at the cusp of a performative past and future for African American men, pushing the cultural aperture established by the changing structures of American society after 1945. Belafonte's body acted as a tidal force for both asserting and demanding African American male citizenship that would later come to shape discourses around popular and political culture as television, radio programs, and films became fixtures of American life. His body in American mass culture created an outlet not yet fully imagined in the culture industry: the marketing of black male sexuality in the racially charged political landscape of American society after the war.[3]

This chapter first seeks to provide a critical analysis of the ways in which Belafonte's calypso image exploited a Caribbean heritage to both engage and challenge the anxieties of integration between African Americans and whites. Over the years, several critics have argued that Belafonte's calypso image severely sidetracked struggles in the 1950s, both on and off the screen, for African American citizenship.[4] For some, the tenor of these criticisms may have particular currency when juxtaposed with the harsh events of the decade: the "all deliberate speed" shenanigans of desegregating public schools; hard-fought challenges against Jim Crow in places like Montgomery, Alabama, and Little Rock, Arkansas; and the African American male lynchings that still occurred, although sporadically, in the deep South.

Here, I suggest that if most cultural critics simply read Belafonte's calypso image as a way for mainstream America to escape the reality of African American struggles in the 1950s, then they miss telling cues about how his image encouraged discursive spaces for protest and struggles against the status quo *within the African American culture industry*. As the *Essence* article suggested, Belafonte and his image have been embraced as part of African American historical memory, even despite disputes over their relevance. Although Belafonte made a calculated decision to position his Caribbean heritage as part of his commercial persona in the late 1950s, a more expansive look at his political, artistic, and personal affiliations suggests his intimate participation in African America not simply as the Caribbean Other but as one deeply committed to and part of the struggles African Americans faced.

The point of my analysis is not to be overly celebratory. Belafonte's success was never completely triumphant. It was severely hampered by white America's inability in the late 1950s to finally translate its adoration of the King of Calypso into an acceptance of African American male citizenship. America's flirtation with Belafonte really said as much about the uncertainties of the times and the mood of mainstream America as it did about Belafonte's talent itself. Caught in the whirlwind of the U.S. Supreme Court's decision in *Brown v. Board of Education* (1954), the emergence of charismatic black leaders such as the Reverend Dr. Martin Luther King, Jr., and the passing of the Civil Rights Act (1957), few white Americans knew what to make of African Americans' ever-increasing demands for civil rights. Some were sympathetic to the struggles of African Americans; others felt threatened by the push for an integrated society. Much of this social drama about the citizenship of African Americans resonated in America's fascination with Harry Belafonte as Calypso King.

This chapter further suggests that Belafonte's use of the Caribbean is the primary reason that this titillating discourse of sex, race, and integration was even allowed to take place. As I frame the discussion of Belafonte's performative career, I locate the importance of the Caribbean trope placed on his black male body especially. Belafonte's mother was part of the first wave of West Indian immigrants that came to the United States between 1900 and 1930. Born in the United States, Belafonte spent five of his childhood years in Jamaica, where his immigrant mother was raised. He often acknowledged the deep influence Caribbean culture had on his identity. The heightened emphasis given to Belafonte's Caribbean heritage with the release of *Harry Belafonte—Calypso* sought to authenticate the album's focus on the calypso island genre. At its release, *Harry Belafonte—Calypso* was promoted as "a truly mature gift; a really definitive work in the field of West Indian music."[5]

Belafonte's Caribbean heritage was used as a strategic cultural signifier that sought to push his career to new heights. The importance of his iconization after the release of *Harry Belafonte—Calypso* was not based on Belafonte's second-generation status or his Jamaican and Martiniquan ancestry per se. Instead, it was based on the ways in which the Caribbean persona was used to mainstream Belafonte as sexual icon. I argue that the Caribbean became the site of making Belafonte's—and, by extension, African American male—sexuality palatable to an American mainstream. The ideal of West Indian warmth engendered by his musical repertoire, and Belafonte's Caribbean otherness provided a means of exploring black male sexuality without fully alienating white America. The use of the Caribbean covertly staged a new militancy in the presentation of black male sexuality to an American public.

Finally, the chapter maintains that this commodified use of Caribbean heritage had particular advantages for Belafonte as a second-generation immigrant and black artist in the 1950s. I consider the ways in which Belafonte himself employed his Caribbean identity to gain his own sense of agency and to demand a sphere of resistance—if only through commercial success. While mediated by the influences of managers, promoters, and filmmakers, Belafonte's image became a tool by which he could challenge the status quo and create new opportunities for himself in a society that he felt was ill prepared to accept him as an equal. His live performances in particular and his attempts to use his celebrity to speak out on issues of civil rights are subtle utterances of this agency.

This chapter is divided into two sections. The first examines the marketing of Belafonte's Caribbean body in relation to the performative bodies of African American men in the film and music industry prior to Belafonte's success in 1956 and 1957. In the first section, I explore the narrativization of black male sexuality in popular media prior to Belafonte and the ways in which Belafonte's reign as King of Calypso revealed the seemingly contradictory spaces he occupied as the new symbol of black manhood in the United States. The second section gives a close reading of Belafonte's Caribbean body within a film narrative. It examines the body of Belafonte/Boyeur in Darryl Zanuck's film *Island in the Sun*. By analyzing Belafonte's Boyeur in *Island in the Sun,* I further suggest what his Caribbean body enabled for African American male images in popular culture, while also pointing to the limitations of his body as black sex icon in American popular culture of the 1950s.

## Calypso Harry: An American Icon

For decades, many Americans have associated calypso music with Harry Belafonte's yelp "Day-O!" from the "Banana Boat Song," featured on *Harry Belafonte—Calypso,* in 1956.[6] Despite the fact that this song was actually a rendition of a West Indian work song, not calypso music, and that Belafonte, even in 1956, warned that the *Calypso* album songs "weren't calypso at all—even though everybody seems to have hung that tag on them,"[7] America has had an endearing fascination with its Calypso King. Part of the fascination in 1956 and 1957 was that an American entertainer could bring folk music to a mass audience and become a million-dollar performer. *Harry Belafonte—Calypso* became the first LP by a single artist in American music history to sell more than a million copies—only to be challenged soon after by the gyrating Elvis Presley with his self-titled album *Elvis,* in 1956.

The music critic Craig Rosen observes in his study of *Billboard* hits that "[w]ith a total of 31 weeks at the summit, *Calypso* set the early standard as the [n]umber [o]ne album with the most weeks at the top."[8] Even with the rise of rock 'n' roll, which commanded its own place in American music history, Belafonte's Caribbean folk style soared in popularity between 1956 and 1957, keeping its momentum until the end of the decade. *Look* magazine, in its article "The Belafonte Boom," on August 21, 1956, observed, "Harry Belafonte breaks all the rules [and] becomes a national singing sensation."[9] The magazine noted, for instance, the attendance records Belafonte broke at Lewisohn Stadium, in New York, when he entertained an unprecedented 25,000 people in the arena. *Look* also observed that Belafonte was the "night-club singer most in demand," with his reported "$7,500 a week"[10] salary. The following year, the *Saturday Evening Post,* in its spread on Belafonte, reported, "Harry can now draw down $10,000 for a single concert."[11]

Belafonte, according to leading magazines such as *Variety* and *Cashbox,* also started the "calypsomania" that ensued in the late 1950s. Belafonte's signature song, "Banana Boat—Day-O," was considered "one of the top selling, most often played songs in the country" in 1957.[12] In a fan magazine dedicated especially to Belafonte, the journalist Robert Metz reported that because of Belafonte's success, calypso music was experiencing a second renaissance in northern cities like New York. Although calypso had been popular among the club set in New York in the 1930s and early 1940s, it now reached a new popularity with its crossover appeal. He wrote,

> Every Saturday night hundreds of fans—young and not-so-young—crowd into New York's Carnegie Hall for two shows featuring calypso singers, calypso dancers and the unique steel bands. The "concerts" have been selling out for eight months.[13]

By 1957, at least ten versions of "Marianne," a West Indian classic, were heard over the American airwaves over a two- to three-month span, mostly in response to the sales of *Calypso.* The actor Robert Mitchum and the writer Maya Angelou even tried to capitalize on the calypso craze, releasing "Calypso Is Like So" and "Miss Calypso," respectively, in 1957. The Kingston Trio first cut its teeth fashioning itself as a calypso group because of the success of Belafonte's album. Hollywood also tried to benefit from the craze with a film, *Calypso Joe,* in 1957, which featured calypsonians from Trinidad such as Duke of Iron and Lord Flea.

The Calypso King that *Time, Variety, Look,* and others reproduced in their feature stories indicated that America's fascination with Belafonte was about much more than *Calypso*'s songs. Between 1956 and 1957, single releases from *Harry Belafonte—Calypso* were pop charters, but none reached the number one spot as the entire album did. Although cultural critics and journalists were fascinated by Belafonte's success as a folk singer in a mass market, the tenor of their conversations about Belafonte as pop icon often worked on two levels instead: one focused on the use of his body in the performance of folk songs, while the other more overtly focused on the visual exposé of his body alone. Rarely did feature articles pay attention to his voice or to the songs' lyrical qualities. When songs such as "Day-O" and "Man Smart (Woman Smarter)" from *Calypso* and other albums were mentioned, critics usually did so to consider the function of his body as he explored the underlying meanings of folk music.

As the *New York Times* accounted for his success in 1959, for instance, Belafonte's performance "reveal[ed] the theatrical measure of the man." The journalist Emily Coleman reported, in December:

> [W]hen Harry Belafonte strides out of semi-darkness into the spotlight of stage center at the Palace Theatre, the total effect will be theatrical, but simple—deceptively simple. The open-necked cotton shirt he wears, the lights which bathe his easy grace, the projected scenery, the musical effects, none of this will be there just because of happenstance.[14]

Describing his stage performance on songs like "The Bald-headed Woman" and others, she added:

> With arms, shoulders and head, he shows that he's breaking rocks on a chain gang, singing of the bald-headed woman he doesn't want because she's so mean. In a spiritual like "Take My Mother Home," Belafonte does not move at all, but stands stone still in pin spot which lights only his head and shoulders. In the Mexican folk song "Cu Cu Ru Cu Cu Paloma," however, he is the male on the make, moving sinuously with catlike ease.[15]

To complete the narrative created by Coleman's discussion, the article featured a full-length picture of Belafonte in his usual costume—white shirt, black pants, and double-buckled leather belt—gripping a microphone. The caption read, "When the show is over, one finds it hard to remember anything in very much detail—or who else was on stage. The total impact is of Harry Belafonte alone."[16]

Similarly, in a *Look* article written three years before the *New York Times* feature on Belafonte, the focus on his body was even more fully realized. The pictorial of Belafonte in a variety of singing poses overshadowed the editorial; there was no byline for the feature story. In movie still frame, Belafonte stood in a series of pictures shot at a singing engagement at the Copacabana, in which his usual costume was altered slightly by the substitution of a striped shirt. The article noted,

> Harry Belafonte calls himself "an actor in song." In performance, he sways back and forth, almost in rock 'n' roll rhythm, his eyes seeing behind half-closed lids and a plaintive baritone voice pouring from his chest. He moves easily from song to song, varying pace and mood, and he uses his arms with a Barrymore's dramatic power. Often, his face is somber and intense. But at times, it lights up with an infectiously mischievous smile that captivates his audience, who can never anticipate what this remarkable entertainer will do next.[17]

The next year, in the *Saturday Evening Post,* the journalist Jeanne Van Holmes, almost in apologetic fashion, conceded: "Actually, it's not primarily vocal quality that Belafonte is seeking to get across to his audiences." She continued, quoting Belafonte: "'What I want to communicate,' [Belafonte] says, 'is the honest emotion of, for instance, some little guy in Haiti when he sings forth his harvest prayer of thanksgiving.'"[18] For most critics like Holmes and even for Belafonte's fans, he did not quite evoke that "honest emotion of . . . some little guy in Haiti" as he wished but, instead, something a bit more suggestive: the exploration of black masculinity through his sexual body, in repose or in performance. The suggestiveness of his sexual body, of course, was tempered by the "actor in song," who provided a pop-lite rendition of Caribbean and other folk musical genres.

That the popular media gazed so openly on black male sexuality suggests the shifts in American culture by 1956. That the gaze was tempered
by the exoticism of the Caribbean suggests the struggles at hand in embracing African American male citizenship on its own terms. White
America was still grappling with the growing and insistent demands of
African Americans following World War II during Belafonte's rise to
fame. On the one hand, some progress was evident. The campaigns of
black soldiers and war workers during and after the war provided a catalyst for the language of integrationist politics that would take form in
the decade of Belafonte's success. The stage often varied—urban riots,
NAACP legal battles, federal intervention, and nonviolent sit-ins—but
African Americans were becoming increasingly willing and able to orga-
nize against second-class citizenship.

On the other hand, resistance from white society was ever present. Although some whites were open to engaging African Americans as equals,
others were concerned that the push for integration was really more
about a desire for interracial marriage and race mixing than about civil
rights. The fascination with Belafonte's sexualized image came in the
years after Secretary of War Henry Stimson's very public support for the
continued segregation of the armed forces during World War II; he felt
that the war was being used by "radical [black] leaders" to obtain "in-
termarriages."[19] At least twenty-seven states had antimiscegenation laws
still on the books after 1955, despite the record gains made by blacks
after the war.[20] Belafonte, in fact, rose to fame in the shadow of the hang-
ing, in 1955, of Emmett Till, a black male youth from Chicago who dared
to whistle at a white female clerk in Mississippi. His murderers were later
acquitted by an all-white jury—a testament to the growing paranoia
about new black male freedoms in post–World War II America.

Suggestively, Belafonte's sexualized image was on a par with, and received as much attention as, the public displays of sexuality that were
slowly emerging in 1950s white America, especially in popular media. By
the mid-1950s, the television and motion picture industries were beginning to liberalize production codes that once had censored displays of
sexuality in films and television programs.[21] The "gentlemen's" magazine
Confidential went into circulation in 1951, followed by Playboy in 1953.
White female stars such as Marilyn Monroe and Carroll Baker began to

bare skin and to assert their sexuality in films such as the *Seven Year Itch* (1955) and *Baby Doll* (1956). White men also started to openly explore sexuality in the public sphere. Elvis Presley gyrated to the beat of African American music on the *Ed Sullivan Show* in 1956. As Steven Cohan notes in his study of white male stars in the 1950s, traditional understandings of American masculinity, upheld by images of the "Man in the Gray Flannel Suit" and the "Organizational Man," were often subverted by alternative masculinities performed through the sexualized bodies of young and white film stars such as Marlon Brando, James Dean, and Kirk Douglas.[22]

What was different about Belafonte's sexualized image, of course, was that its success relied heavily on a cultural distance from (African) American masculinity. Because of phallocentric fears of African American manhood, in particular, Belafonte's performance of a black Caribbean body afforded a sexual freedom not made available to his black American one. During Belafonte's rise to fame as Calypso King, however, there were multiple, and often conflicting, narratives at play. Mainstream America's flirtations with black male sexuality through Belafonte's body were limited to an act of distancing that the Caribbean afforded but were contingent on the proximity to African American culture that Belafonte's subject-position as second-generation immigrant and participant in African America demanded.

Despite most recent attempts to reconstruct Belafonte's ethnic identity through a post-1965 lens, Belafonte's image and Belafonte himself were always perceived by contemporaries as part of African America and its culture industry, even before his rise to fame in the mid-1950s. As a second-generation immigrant, at a time when Caribbean Americans were widely considered participants in African American culture, Belafonte developed both personal and artistic sensibilities in relation to the struggles of African Americans in the United States. He experienced Jim Crow in the U.S. Navy along with other black soldiers as they contemplated the wisdom of W. E. B. Du Bois. He was an avid student of African American folk music, spending an inordinate amount of time at the library for an untrained scholar. He cut his teeth as an actor in the American Negro Theater, where he befriended rising African American stars.[23] By the late 1940s and 1950s, not only did he see himself as part of the trajectory of

African American male performers, but also he was seen by both black and white audiences as part of the evolution of African American images on screen and in the entertainment world.

Except for the marginal success in the 1940s of Josh White, an African American folk singer whom Belafonte considered an early influence on his artistic style, in venues such as the Café Society, Belafonte, with his 1956 album, stood out as one of the first black stars to successfully undermine the desexualization of black manhood in a mainstream entertainment market. As Hazel Carby observes in *Race Men*, Paul Robeson, a noteworthy predecessor to Belafonte, had experienced crossover success in film, theater, and the music industry in the mid-1920s through the late 1930s, but he found it difficult to overcome prevailing white discourses of African American masculinity in his work. Robeson, like Belafonte, was popular with black and white consumers for his representations of the black folk in multiple media. Yet, even as he introduced narratives of black virility to films like *Emperor Jones* (1933) and on Broadway in roles like *Othello* (1943–1945), he also embodied the ever-present tensions associated with exploring black sexual beings in front of a white American public.[24]

Images that permeated the popular media, especially from the mid-nineteenth century on, often asserted pejorative paradigms of African American masculinity. Live performances of minstrel shows, as early as the 1840s, toured the country and often featured white men in blackface performing representations of black manhood and, as Eric Lott suggests in *Love and Theft: Blackface Minstrelsy and the American Working Class*, acting out their own anxieties about gender and race.[25] In these early forms of American popular entertainment, black men were impersonated as buffoons, comedic foil, or, in the tradition of the Uncle Tom character in Harriet Beecher Stowe's *Uncle Tom's Cabin* (1852), asexual, kindhearted men who maintained the social order of the Old South.

With the advent of motion pictures, another image of African American manhood emerged to augment the negative paradigms already working in the American popular sphere. Jester figures were joined by savage, rapist, and brute images of black men, and these began to dominate early-twentieth-century discourses of black masculinity. The film *The Birth of a Nation*, in 1915, was one of the first to canonize this inscription of African American manhood for a white American audience. The film portrayed blacks as threatening, uncontrollable, and lacking in leadership abilities, suggesting at the film's end the need for white hegemony over America's black population. In particular, the film located the menace of blackness through gender, especially in its imaginings of black manhood. Black men were sexual predators who wanted American citizenship only to satisfy their sexual desires for white women. Thought to be a classic by many scholars because of its revolutionary cutting techniques on film, *The Birth of Nation* announced, perpetuated, and maintained the racial and gender prejudices of white America in the early twentieth century.[26]

With the growing popularity of "talking" films after Al Jolson's *Jazz Singer,* in 1927, blacks began to receive less overtly racist, although by no means sympathetic, roles in motion pictures. As the film critic Daniel J. Leab has noted, blacks appeared in supporting parts as comedic foils, servants, or loyal sidekicks to white leading characters.[27] Explorations of personal lives, not to mention sexual lives, were out of the question for black male performers in the Hollywood movie industry. By the 1930s, actors such as Stepin Fetchit (né Lincoln Perry), in films such as *Judge Priest* (1934) and *One More Spring* (1935), and Bill "Bojangles" Robinson, with Shirley Temple in *The Littlest Rebel* (1935) and *Rebecca of Sunnybrook Farm* (1938), provided comic relief in mostly white-cast films and were very popular in these subservient roles.

Times looked like they were changing for African Americans and black artists in the 1940s, when Belafonte first started his career. This anticipation of change was marked as much by what was going on at home in the United States as by America's activities abroad. The United States entered World War II in 1941 in alliance with the Soviet Union and Britain to defeat the fascist governments of Germany and Italy and the nation of Japan. Black involvement became a significant, although contested, part of this effort. African Americans made notable progress during the war years. On the eve of the United States's entry into the war, the War Department made a commitment to draft African Americans to constitute approximately 10 percent of the total armed forces, equaling the percentage of the black population in the country. Blacks, often operating in segregated units, achieved several firsts in the fight against fascism: first trained aviation pilots, at Tuskegee; first admittances to the Marine Corps; and the first promotion of a black man to the rank of brigadier general.[28]

The war also provided the opportunity for several blacks, especially in the North, to secure better jobs and economic mobility for their families. Increased wartime production advanced blacks in several skilled positions in mechanics, shipbuilding, and other industries that supported wartime activity.[29] It also helped that President Franklin Delano Roosevelt, by executive order, established the Fair Employment Practices Commission (FEPC), in 1941, to police unfair practices and to address discrimination grievances. The increase in jobs and the relative job security encouraged southern blacks to move to northern cities, where they continued to face discrimination but also experienced the power of numbers by establishing voting blocs. According to John Hope Franklin, northern politicians often courted African American voters, and blacks began to exercise their ability to effect change and to demand better treatment through voting, advocacy, and collaboration. The importance of this moment was not lost on African Americans, who worked harder than ever to force white America to realize that the United States could not fight for democracy abroad without dealing with racial discrimination and inequality at home.

The unfortunate reality is that this progress immediately after the war had limited impact on the availability of new artistic opportunities for black male entertainers. Most white audiences were still more comfortable with blacks, especially black men, playing roles that supported their traditional subservience to the needs and pleasures of white consumers. When Belafonte first started as an entertainer in the late 1940s, the singers and musicians who were most popular with crossover audiences still fit within prevailing paradigms of black masculinity established prior to the war. Their crossover appeal was often defined by a refined, supper club image or by a more carnivalesque, comedic one. The entertainment industry provided a few of these entertainers with the opportunity to succeed with mainstream audiences, while being careful to regulate their and others' expressions of black masculinity, militancy, and full citizenship. And, although sexuality could be placed within representations of black womanhood, especially through the iconized bodies of songstresses like Lena Horne, whom *Life* magazine called the "season's top nightclub star," in 1948, it could not be staged through black male performances of sexual selves.[30]

The careers of two of the most popular entertainers during and after the war, Louis Jordan and Nat King Cole, illustrate the multiple and lingering paradigms against which Belafonte was working when *Harry Belafonte—Calypso* was introduced in 1956. Louis Jordan, one of the most popular black artists with crossover audiences in the 1940s, embodied the codification of the comedic on the bodies of African American men in mainstream consumer markets. With his jump blues, Jordan was most popular during and after World War II. He and his *Tympany Five* band had several pop and race chart hits that were million-copy sellers. Between 1943 and 1950, Jordan and his band had at least eighteen songs that were number one hits on the R&B ("race") charts, including "Choo Choo Ch'Boogie," "Saturday Night Fish Fry," and "Ain't Nobody Here but Us Chickens." One of his most popular songs with white audiences, "Is You Is or Is You Ain't My Baby," was in the Top Ten on both the pop and the race charts in 1944. It was so successful that Jordan performed it in the wartime movie *Follow the Boys* (1944).[31]

In musical performances, in movies, and in his songs, Louis Jordan created an atmosphere of good times, fun, and relaxation for an America experiencing World War II and its aftermath. He appeared in more than a dozen "soundies" played on jukeboxes across the country, which contributed to his growing popularity on the radio in white consumer markets. These soundies were produced by Astor Pictures, which later capitalized on Louis Jordan's popularity in both black and white markets to release shorts and full-length films, including *Caldonia* (1945), *Reet-Petite and Gone* (1947), and *Beware!* (1946). Jordan's performances in films varied in theme, but the shorts and movies always featured Jordan as the "jive"-talking black male decked out in zootsuit finery. Featured in colorful ensembles with a wide smile and welcoming body gestures in various mass media, Jordan encoded black masculinity with comedic levity and an unthreatening public image.

The other prevailing paradigm of black masculinity in the postwar era was evidenced on the body of Nat King Cole, who employed the supper club image for crossover appeal from the late 1930s until the mid-1950s. In 1946, songs such as "Christmas Song" and "Nature Boy" established Cole as a singer, even though he was a successful jazz pianist with the

Nat Cole Trio, which had started in 1938 and was popular in the 1940s.[32] With the release and success of "Christmas Song" and "Nature Boy," followed by "Mona Lisa," in 1950 and "Unforgettable," in 1951, Cole became one of the most, if not the most, popular African American entertainers of the postwar years. In 1956 and 1957, during the period that Belafonte's career was at its highest point, Nat King Cole was the first and only African American to have his own syndicated program on network television.[33]

Besides his extraordinary voice, the success of Nat King Cole was located in the easy, exterior image he presented to the American public. Always dressed in tuxedo suits, he conjured the aura of the classic dresser, the sophisticated African American man. In doing so, he became part of a continuum of African American male performers, including Duke Ellington, Cab Calloway and Sammy Davis, Jr., who provided an uncomplicated leisure for their crossover audiences, whom they often entertained in segregated settings. Cole always had a relaxed demeanor, and, as his biographer Leslie Gourse notes, his style suggested a sense of order and tranquility in a 1950s America on the brink of civil unrest.[34] Like that of Louis Jordan, ironically, his stylized persona perpetuated the limited roles that black men could occupy in the culture industry. His songs and his sultry voice, coupled with the ease in which he played the piano and provided a romantic atmosphere for white audiences, helped to maintain codings of black manhood that left private, sexual beings unexplored in popular culture.

While many fans wrongly assume that Belafonte started his career with *Calypso,* he actually started as a singer and actor in the 1940s, working within the same limitations that faced Jordan, Cole, and other African American contemporaries. Belafonte's stardom in 1956 and 1957 came on the heels of his relative success as a folk singer in a variety of media and performance venues. He had started off as a pop singer in the late 1940s at places like the Five O' Clock Club, in Florida, where he could not be on the street after dark, and debuted as a soloist in 1951 at the Village Vanguard, a night club in New York's Greenwich Village that regularly featured jazz musicians and folk artists. In the mid-1950s, Belafonte appeared on Broadway to perform folk songs in John Murray Anderson's *Almanac,* for which he received an Antoinette Perry (Tony) award, which, in turn, garnered him his first spot on the *Ed Sullivan Show*.[35] In 1955, he toured the country in *Three for Tonight,* a musical revue with the dance duo Marge and Gower Champion. He occasionally appeared on television specials such as the *Cavalcade of Stars,* in 1951, and in the all-Negro films *Bright Road* (1953) and *Carmen Jones* (1954). He also recorded the albums *Mark Twain* and *Belafonte* in 1954 and 1956, respectively.

The biographer Arnold Shaw points out that Belafonte's career began to blossom between 1955 and 1956 under the care of Jay Richard Kennedy, his new manager. Shaw argues, and I agree, that the shift in Belafonte's career corresponded with the addition of sex to his stage image. He notes,

> The truth is that Harry is not, and never was, a sexy singer. A dramatic singer, yes. A magician at evoking certain moods and emotions, yes. . . . What Harry sounds like and what he looks like are not the same thing. Kennedy apparently went to work on Harry's dress and manner. In this period Harry deserted the casual slacks and loose denims he had been wearing from Village days and donned tight, black mohair pants that emphasized every move he made. In place of the casual open shirt, Harry began wearing tailored silk shirts with a plunging neckline that almost exposed his navel. Accompanying the change in costume was a parallel emphasis in stance, gesture, and movement that could not fail to arouse the female libido.[36]

The sexualization of Belafonte's body happened in stages, but it was definitely an apparent part of his star image by 1956. Whether the change can be credited to Kennedy, who "went after the big spots for Harry," as Shaw contends, or to Belafonte is not as easy to determine. Yet, what is clear is that, before 1956, cultural critics rarely noted Belafonte's sex appeal, even when they applauded him for his theatrical performance. In *Cosmopolitan*'s March 1954 issue, for example, Jon Whitcomb reviewed *Almanac,* noting simply that "[Belafonte] has a way with folk songs, and a set of versatile vocal chords to make them interesting."[37] The only reference to his body is that he "is six-feet-two-and-a-half high." Commenting in his performance in *Three for Tonight, Life*'s review stated: "Whatever he sings—reverent spirituals or saucy folk songs—Belafonte holds his audience,"[38] while making no reference to the iconization of his body.

The most intriguing link between Belafonte's performative body and sex appeared with the inscriptions of Caribbeanness placed on his body in 1956. I would like to add to Shaw's observation that Belafonte's sexual body coincided with the emphasis on his Caribbean one. In short, I argue that he shed a performative African American identity from the late 1940s and early 1950s for the freedom availed through claiming a Caribbean self. The release of *Harry Belafonte—Calypso* artfully combined sex and a Caribbean trope to reimagine Belafonte for a consuming audience. Belafonte had always had calypso and other West Indian music as part of his folk repertoire. "Matilda, Matilda," a favorite in Belafonte's stage performances, was recorded as early as 1953. *Harry Belafonte—Calypso* was a by-product of an NBC television show sequence, "Holiday in Trinidad," that featured Belafonte in October 1955. However, *Harry Belafonte—Calypso* offered a sustained packaging of the Caribbean—from Belafonte's body to the songs—that proved a winning combination for the folk singer.

Before *Harry Belafonte—Calypso,* in 1956, and the subsequent release of the film *Island in the Sun* the following year, Belafonte's record sales were good, but not excellent—that is, not until the Caribbean motif was exploited by Belafonte, his manager, and RCA Victor. Both of his albums in the 1950s prior to *Calypso* did merit some attention. *Mark Twain,* first released in 1954, was not a pop charter until 1956, when Belafonte began to utilize his Caribbean persona in performances. In January 1956, and not in 1954, when it was first released, *Mark Twain* reached number three on the *Billboard* pop charts, remaining on the Top Forty charts for six weeks.[39] *Belafonte,* released right before *Calypso* in 1956, did hit number one, debuting on the charts in February of that year. Although it stayed on the Top Forty charts for sixty-two weeks, it was number one for only six weeks. In contrast, *Calypso,* which debuted in June 1956, held the number one spot for thirty-one weeks and remained on the Top Forty chart for seventy-two.[40] Moreover, only singles released between 1956 and 1957—at the height of the calypso craze—made *Cash Box*'s Top Forty charts for pop recordings.[41]

The album covers for *Mark Twain, Belafonte,* and *Harry Belafonte—Calypso* suggest the connection between the emergence of Belafonte's

Fig. 1. Album cover, "Mark Twain and Other Folk Favorites." Used courtesy of the RCA Music Group, a Unit of BMG.

Caribbean body and the increase in his popularity as an American sex icon. The differences in the three album covers between 1954 and 1956 are striking. Together, they highlight the changes in the presentation of his body when the Caribbean was used to promote him to the American mass market. Belafonte's *Mark Twain* offers one of the most graphic displays of America's, and the record industry's, phallocentric concerns with displaying the African American male body in a public sphere. *Mark Twain*'s cover art narrativizes the focus on the music as it simultaneously minimizes the importance of Belafonte's physique (see Figure 1). The star billing of the title song, "Mark Twain," especially when juxtaposed with the background head shot of Belafonte, suggests a covert attempt to subjugate the African American male body.

Fig. 2. Album cover, "Belafonte." Used courtesy of the RCA Music Group, a
Unit of BMG.

*Belafonte,* the album released right before *Calypso,* marks a drastic
change. Following the alterations to his performative body in 1955, the
album art reveals the emergent dialectic between sex and mood in the
iconization of his body on stage, in television spots, and in the growing
number of pictorials in the popular press (see Figure 2). This album
proved neither as provocative nor as successful as *Harry Belafonte—Calypso,* but it anticipated the winning combination of his sex appeal and
the performance of Caribbean cultural identity. The album art of *Belafonte* inverts the previous tensions around the spectacle of Belafonte's
black body on *Mark Twain,* and it re-envisions the exploration of black
male sexuality as public discourse. The close-up shot of Harry Bela-

fonte's body in soft pastel colors on the cover of *Belafonte* sets the stage for the power and agency of a sexual image evidenced with *Calypso*'s release.

*Harry Belafonte—Calypso* employs Belafonte's body again, but with very different results. The moody and rather melancholy Belafonte on the cover of *Belafonte* is replaced with the smiling, active figure on the *Calypso* cover (see Figure 3). Dressed in a lively, bright green shirt and black pants, Belafonte is featured against a bright red backdrop. His figure here is located in a performance, in contrast to his reposed figure on *Belafonte,* with his outstretched hands and full smile. The album art shows just enough of his lower torso to draw the gaze of the consumer downward, suggestively locating the fullness of his entire body. Unlike

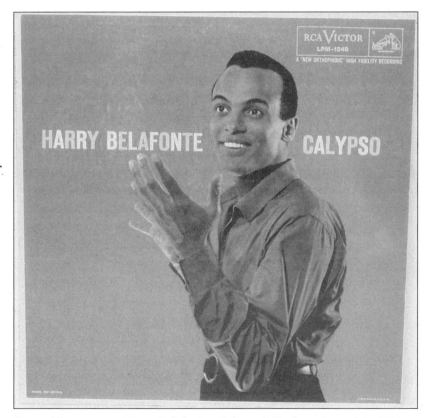

Fig. 3. Album cover, "Harry Belafonte—Calypso." Used courtesy of the RCA Music Group, a Unit of BMG.

his reposed figure on *Belafonte,* his image on *Calypso* suggests not danger but something else: an enticement, fun, and the potential voyeurisms of calypso. Further, although his body is just as imposing on both albums, the naming of Belafonte on the album cover is no longer center stage. "Harry Belafonte" and "Calypso" receive equal billing, creating a telling interconnectedness between Belafonte and the performance of a Caribbean self.

While cultural critics and the popular press emphasized Jordan's swinging tempo and Cole's perfect diction in the 1940s and early 1950s, they paid particular attention to the Caribbean ethos surrounding Belafonte by 1956. Given that Belafonte's career reached its highest peak after the release of the *Calypso* album, the nexus created by the marketing of his sex appeal and Caribbean otherness is quite telling. In *Look* magazine, on June 25, 1957, one female fan was most explicit about her attraction to the Calypso King. She told the journalist Jack Hamilton, "He's as handsome as sin and blessed with sufficient West Indian tradition to remind women of romance under an island sun. When he's on stage, he makes us feel like doing crazy things."[42] With Belafonte, white American women especially openly engaged and gazed upon black male sexuality in public discourses for perhaps the first time. Belafonte's body was not the "authentic" black folk body as Robeson's, for example, was narrativized during 1930s. Robeson's body evoked African nobility and slave labor; Belafonte's, instead, evoked the "sins," as the *Look* interviewee intimated, of sex in 1950s America. Further, his body demanded the intrigue and dangers of cross-racial sexual discovery, if only through performance. Yet, because of resistance to cross-racial sexual discovery, Belafonte's performative body was tempered by the notion of black male sexuality "under an *island* sun"—but not quite *in* the United States.

The number of debates over his body alone in the magazines and popular press of the late 1950s suggests the necessity of the Caribbean trope in his popularity as an (African) American sex icon. *Time,* featuring Belafonte on the cover in 1959, wrote that his background was "an arresting mixture of black and white ancestry, of Harlem harshness and the West Indian languor,"[43] while it discussed his success in film, television, and the music industry. In "The Girls Are Wild about Harry," an article from 1957, Hy Steirman reminded readers that Belafonte was of Jamaican and Martiniquan "extraction" and had spent several years in the

Caribbean islands. He talked about his ancestry as he, too, reasoned why female fans were so attracted to the Calypso King. He observed:

> His costumes underscore the virility that stands out in his appearance. His bright shirts have necklines that plunge almost to his navel, showing the big, powerful, tanned chest. His trousers are practically molded to his thighs, reacting to every muscular movement. His movements—as he slaps his thighs and clenches his fist—employ every exciting subtlety.[44]

The explicit sexual overtones of Steirman's reading presented, without question, a changing discourse around black male sexuality in America, if only through the language of a Caribbean Other.

The *Saturday Evening Post*'s article on Belafonte in 1957 is a significant record in this regard because it promotes Belafonte's sex appeal by attending to his skin color and Anglo features on one hand and his pan-ethnic Caribbean identity on the other. The author wrote that Belafonte "[i]s tall and slim, with clear features and gold-brown skin." She added, giving primacy to his West Indian heritage:

> Though Belafonte was born in New York City, his family is West Indian, and the West Indian influence has been strong in both his life and his folk songs. His mother was a Jamaican, his father a Martinique seaman. His paternal grandfather, a white French farmer, went to the West Indies and married a Haitian; his maternal grandfather, of African descent, married a white woman from England. Harry is half-white and half-Negro, but he considers himself a Negro.[45]

Here, Belafonte's body became a symbol of interracial sex (or, even more interesting, interracial marriage), which, then, created a discursive space for emerging discourses on integration in the United States. In part, he was the leading black performer at this cultural moment because his performative body imagined the possibilities of a new social formation between blacks and whites in the American nation-state. However, the author employed his mixed racial heritage of black and white, while backing away from the pejorative readings this heritage could possibly demand, especially for a consuming American audience still working through its own racial anxieties. Belafonte "considers himself a Negro," as the *Saturday Evening Post* consoled its readers. Despite the potentials of his claims to whiteness, in essence, he knew his place, which was a comforting appeal to whites.

America's fascination with interracial bodies in the postwar period amplified both its fear and its consideration of the prospect of integrating African Americans into the mainstream. Not only did African American artists and intellectuals employ interracial bodies to explore relationships between black and white communities, but also white popular media attempted cross-racial dialogues through mulatto or mixed-race figures. Most often these figures were African American women, who embodied America's often contested response to integration after World War II. Black actresses such as Nina Mae McKinney, Lena Horne, and Dorothy Dandridge enticed and disgusted American audiences with their light skin, their vivacious presences, and their ability to remind America of interracial sex, its potential, and, for some, its threats to white supremacy in the United States.[46]

Belafonte, however, provided one of the first instances of this fascination with interracial bodies written on a black man. His gender created a particular dynamic of its own. Beyond figures such as the predator, Silas Lynch, in *The Birth of a Nation,* in 1915, Belafonte presented one of the first examples of manhood—interracial manhood—used in discourses of integration and interracial sex in the popular media. Of course, he was unique because he was seen not as a predator but as a sex symbol. In fact, a reading of his popularity in 1956 and 1957 suggests that Belafonte engendered new "romances" with interracial identity in the white imagination at the dawn of the civil rights era.

The link Americans made among interracial bodies, interracial marriage, and integration was clear, as evidenced by the popular discussions of integration at the time. An October 17, 1958, Gallup poll showed that most whites, approximately 96 percent, disapproved of interracial marriage between blacks and whites.[47] According to the historian Renee Romano, most southern whites in particular were adamant campaigners against integration. In her study, Romano notes that, even by the late 1950s, whites feared that integration would lead to intermarriage, which would supposedly lead to the demise of the white race. Other whites, mostly northern and liberal, were willing to consider integration but

were torn on the subject of intermarriage. Questions regarding black
male and white female marriage drew raised eyebrows from some and
adamant disapproval from most.[48] As "half-white and half-Negro," Belafonte embodied these conflicts through his mixed heritage, but also
through the adulation young white women heaped on him for his good
looks, sleek frame, and sexy voice. Concerns and fascinations with his
interracial identity became even more charged when he divorced his
African American wife, Marguerite, in 1957, to marry Julie Robinson, a
white American dancer.[49]

Interestingly, the anxieties over interracial sex, African American
male sexuality, and integration were curbed by a Caribbean trope that
was not ethno-specific in the least but that instead, comprised a mixture
of Caribbean cultures. It did not matter that calypso music was actually
from Trinidad and that Belafonte, despite his Haitian, Jamaican, and
Martiniquan heritage, had spent only five of his formative years in Jamaica. The pan-ethnicity of his Caribbean persona further obfuscated
any real sense of calypso music and the ways in which it was connected
to particular cultural and political traditions in its place of origin.

Calypso, despite the American promotion of the calypso craze in the
1950s, was not new to the United States. The first calypso boom took
place in New York and other northern cities in the 1930s. Calypso singers
and calypsonians from Trinidad such as Sir Lancelot, Wilmoth Houdini,
and Roaring Lion entertained a somewhat visible, yet often disregarded,
West Indian immigrant population that had reached 98,620 by 1930.[50]
They also experienced some crossover success with white American audiences, performing in places such as the Village Vanguard and Carnegie
Hall. Yet, Sir Lancelot, Wilmoth Houdini, and Roaring Lion often worked
within the same paradigms of black masculinity as their African American counterparts while performing for a white clientele in the United
States.[51]

I want to be careful here to reinforce that America's fascination with
Belafonte's Caribbean image was underscored by the dialectical relationship he and his work had with African American cultural formation in
1956. That native calypsonians who were already touring and recording
in the United States did not experience overwhelming adulation suggests
that donning a Caribbean persona alone did not translate into the ability
to challenge white consuming gazes. Belafonte once confided, "There

were great calypsonians who could never see the light of day in this
country, because they were so distanced from this culture."[52] His statement suggests that the ability to use the Caribbean trope to explore black
male sexuality was intimately linked to his belongingness in the American body politic. Of course, the irony is that as a black man in the United
States, he was more than aware of the widely held belief that full citizenship was not available to him.

The evolution of Belafonte's calypso image paralleled his growing activism in African American political spheres. Known for his associations
with African American leftists prior to his reign as King of Calypso—an
affiliation rumored to have kept him partially blacklisted in the early
1950s—Belafonte became very active in African Americans' more vocal
and organized demands for civil rights. In 1950, prior to achieving stardom, he was seen walking a picket line to protest the criminal indictment
by the U.S. government of W. E. B. Du Bois, who was accused of being an
agent of the Soviet Union for circulating the Stockholm Appeal for peace
while in the United States. Du Bois had been Belafonte's idol since educated black soldiers introduced Belafonte to Du Bois's writings, including *Color and Democracy,* during his navy days.[53]

Belafonte was later courted privately by the young Reverend Dr. Martin Luther King, Jr., who wanted him to use his celebrity as a platform
for the emerging Civil Rights Movement, just before *Calypso* was released. As Taylor Branch observes, King approached Belafonte because
he felt that Belafonte cared about the struggles of African Americans, ir-
respective of what he did on stage, in movies, and on television. John
Kennedy, a senator and a young presidential aspirant, approached Belafonte during his reign as King of Calypso to help him attract the Negro
vote in preparation for the 1960 election. He felt that Belafonte's influence in African America could counter Jackie Robinson's endorsement
of Richard Nixon. Belafonte then introduced Kennedy to the potential of
King's leadership, and the resulting networks that linked celebrity, the
federal government, and grassroots organizers pushed a civil rights
agenda yet to be experienced in the United States. Belafonte's role in this
nexus surpassed mere celebrity endorsement, and the popular press eagerly followed this metanarrative of Belafonte's performance off-stage as
it simultaneously delighted in his performance of a Caribbean self.[54]

Thus, in the mid- to late 1950s, it was the Caribbeanization of Belafonte's body in the context of his black American identity that allowed for the exploration of black male sexuality in performances, on television, and finally in the film *Island in the Sun.* Calypso as a musical genre had had a notable following in American markets in the 1930s, but it had never approached the appeal it had in the 1950s when offered through the figure of Harry Belafonte. With the sexualization of Belafonte's Caribbean body in particular, white Americans could more easily engage their own fears of integration, which were often couched in troubling discourses of gender and race. Concerns over the demise of white cultural supremacy and the rise of racial amalgamation—especially in the South—were joined by more liberal discourses on the possibilities of a more inclusive America and the changing situatedness of African Americans in the cultural economy. Belafonte's sexual provocations, coupled with both the fears and intrigue of his black and white heritage, were displaced on a Caribbean body as they were worked through an American cultural framework. His Caribbean body served as the symbolic means of negotiating integration and even its dangers in American society.

By the mid-1950s, civil rights organizations such as the National Association for the Advancement of Colored People (NAACP) and the newly formed Southern Christian Leadership Council were deeply entrenched in advocating African Americans' rights for social justice and integration. The NAACP, for example, leveraged the gains made during World War II to strike at racial discrimination through strategic use of the legal system. Armed with its roster of roughly half a million black and white supporters, its legal battles were legendary. In 1952 alone, as John Hope Franklin observes, the NAACP challenged "separate but equal" by taking at least "five cases arising in South Carolina, Virginia, Kansas, Delaware, and the District of Columbia" to the U.S. Supreme Court.[55] Thurgood Marshall and other young talented lawyers argued test cases, such as *McLaurin v. Board of Regents* and *Sweatt v. Painter,* that provided early ammunition to illustrate the ways in which segregation was unconstitutional.[56] The NAACP had a major victory in 1954 in *Brown v. Board of Education of Topeka,* which overturned *Plessy v. Ferguson* (1896). In the landmark *Brown* case, the Court held that public school segregation was unlawful and that schools should be integrated with "all deliberate speed," creating a foundation for future challenges to segregation and other forms of institutionalized racism.

Blacks, including the politically active Belafonte, began to focus their energies on nonviolent, participatory forms of social protest, as well. Many African Americans successfully boycotted bus discrimination in Montgomery, Alabama, and introduced other Americans to the power of mass mobilization that could challenge the status quo under Jim Crow in the South. Led by the Reverend Dr. Martin Luther King, Jr., the 361-day boycott was able to force the hand of the officials who controlled Montgomery's city buses, which were officially integrated in December 1956, after the U.S. Supreme Court ruled that bus segregation, too, was unconstitutional. The success of the boycott helped inspire the modern civil rights struggle, and Dr. King was elected to lead the nascent Southern Christian Leadership Council in January 1957, less than a month after the boycott ended and the same year the U.S. Congress passed the Civil Rights Act to protect voting rights regardless of color, race, religion, or national origin. The desegregation efforts of the mid-1950s gave life to the 1960s "sit-ins" later organized by the Student Nonviolent Coordinating Committee, a student-based, interracial protest group supported heavily by Harry Belafonte, in states like North Carolina and Georgia, and the Congress of Racial Equality's (CORE) freedom rides to Alabama and Mississippi in 1961.

The deep South in particular did not seem quite ready for these changes. It did not go without notice, either, that Belafonte made a conscientious decision not to tour in the deep South between 1954 and 1962. After the U.S. Supreme Court decided that "separate but equal" was not legal, several states, including Mississippi, Virginia, Alabama, and Georgia, made every effort to defy the directive of the federal government.[57] In response to *Brown,* Tom P. Brady, a circuit court judge in Mississippi, wrote the infamous *Black Monday* (1955), a long diatribe against the desegregation of schools based on the "inherent deficiencies" of American blacks, suggesting once again that the desire for integration was about intermarriage.[58] The publication was widely celebrated and distributed by the Ku Klux Klan and the emerging White Citizens Council, both of which were interested in protecting their shared interest in white supremacy. In other places, state officials and public servants were more surreptitious in their efforts. They circumvented the Supreme Court decision through the loophole language of "all deliberate speed" and simply avoided any serious attempt to act on the law.

Little Rock, Arkansas, in 1957, became one of the worst examples of white southern resistance. Parents of white high schoolers and others harassed nine African American teenagers as they tried to enter Central High School and desegregate the all-white school. Governor Orval Faubus, a vocal opponent of desegregation, used his power as governor to have the state National Guard block the entry of these students. It was not until a federal judge intervened that Governor Faubus relented and had the guardsmen removed. To protect the civil rights of the students throughout the year, President Eisenhower was forced to nationalize the National Guard. In retaliation, public schools were closed in Little Rock in 1958 and 1959.[59]

Against this backdrop of tense relations between whites and African Americans, the Caribbean trope of Belafonte's performative body in the 1950s had its advantages. For middle- and upper-class America, Belafonte's body underscored ideals of the Caribbean as a particular topos of freedom and leisure, reminiscent of vacations spent in America's favorite playgrounds. Its cultural Otherness suggested the sensuality of a faraway place, where social and racial codes and decorum were different from those established in the United States. Sex could be written on Belafonte at this cultural moment because his sexuality did not suggest an immediate overthrow of the social order of American society. The Caribbean othering of Belafonte's body and "calypso" music partially removed Belafonte from the racial baggage of the United States and placed him and his audience in a new, although unexplored, field of cross-cultural politics.

As the Civil Rights Movement gained publicity on television with the bus boycott, led by King, in 1956, Americans were traveling to the Caribbean islands as never before. In 1947, approximately 500,000 Americans traveled outside the continental United States. A decade later, that number had almost tripled. In 1956, 1,318,000 Americans, according to *U.S. News & World Report*, traveled abroad.[60] Most traveled to European countries, but the second most frequent destination was the Caribbean archipelago. As early as 1952, despite America's concerns with the Cold War, a *Business Week* article headlined "Caribbean Gets Busier and Busier" featured the U.S. Virgin Islands, Puerto Rico, Jamaica, Trinidad, and Cuba as popular travel destinations. The business journal noted that the rise in travel to the Caribbean was due to special packages from agents and airlines and also a result of the development of a tourist industry, complete with first-class hotels, on the islands. Even during the economic recession of 1958, Americans took advantage of the proximity of the Caribbean islands, and the abundance of affordable packages, to spend their vacations close to home.[61]

In the 1950s, Haiti, Jamaica, and other exotic destinations were seen as places where Americans could escape their stressful lives and explore in voyeuristic fashion the simpler and "happy" lives of black peasants. A special pamphlet on "authentic calypso" in 1957 noted:

> To the native of the Indies calypso means unbridled happiness, a release from life's tensions and frustrations . . . rum and drums . . . dance and romance.
>
> To his North American counterpart, the tense, overworked businessman of our bustling metropoleis [sic], calypso can also offer a wonderful fount of relaxation.[62]

The dichotomy set up between the overworked, puritanical American and the romantic and free native became a signature part of advertising promotions for Caribbean vacations. Caribbean islands were promoted as places of "luxury and gay society," as one promotion on Nassau chimed in 1954,[63] or, as a *Look* article noted, as places where there was "little red tape" for American travelers—supposedly with regard to the need for passports, but suggestively for other cross-national indiscretions. Americans could thus experience lots of "dancers" and "voodoo drums," freedom and masquerading, all within the comfort of luxurious hotels designed to meet their every need.[64]

Not surprisingly, white Americans were often blind to—or unwilling to admit—the ways in which they discriminated against black West Indian immigrants in the United States. By the 1950s, foreign-born blacks, mostly from the West Indies, represented roughly 1 percent of the U.S. black population, although Caribbean migration to the United States had come to a virtual halt during the Great Depression and increased marginally to meet the demands of wartime industry during World War II. Before

1965, West Indian immigrants and their second generation in the United States were largely a disempowered group. Prior to 1965, as Philip Kasinitz, Irma Watkins-Owens, and others have noted, they were also very much a part of the African American community, despite interethnic conflicts.[65] White Americans saw primarily their race and categorized them as they did native-born blacks, with few exceptions. West Indian immigrants, despite their higher levels of education and access to skills in their home societies, often faced the same discrimination as African Americans in housing, employment, and the use of public facilities. This systematic racial discrimination occurred not just in the South but also in northern states like New York, where most West Indian immigrants settled.

Further, the tourist industry obscured the growing problems between the descendants of slaves and native white and colored elites in European colonies, problems that mirrored what was taking place in the United States. It often carted Americans off to resorts and sandy beaches where they did not experience much of the island cultures as lived by the majority of the native population or the employees who served them in hotels, resorts, and entertainment venues. The short-lived West Indies Federation was emerging in the 1950s and had as one of its goals the promotion of tourism for the West Indies.[66] This push for tourism as a lucrative industry, however, was undergirded by an attempt by black leadership in particular to move toward independence from European countries and away from British, French, American, and other Western imperialism.

In places like Trinidad, calypso became one of the primary languages for criticizing the Caribbean's relationship to the West. Although Caribbean music from the lips and body of Harry Belafonte provided a space for cross-cultural politics in the United States, the American consuming public often listened to Belafonte's calypso without fully acknowledging its political underpinnings in the mouths of the Caribbean folk. Despite the reality that calypso and other Caribbean musical genres were often entrenched in the political and ideological battles that permeated the Caribbean at the time, Americans often associated calypso solely with the tourist industry and West Indian carnivals or Mardi Gras. They were seldom cognizant of the ways in which Caribbean musical genres existed outside Western-influenced economies—that is, the tourist, music, and film industries—and within particular Caribbean cultural traditions that, in fact, challenged their consuming gazes.

The same year that Belafonte was crowned King of Calypso in the United States, Mighty Sparrow was officially crowned King of Calypso in Trinidad at the annual Carnival. Their signature songs are works in contrast. "Day-O" evokes a laborer's work in the banana plantations, and most of its lyrical content is hindered by Belafonte's overpowering presence when delivering the song. Mighty Sparrow became the "King of Calypso" with "Jean and Delilah," a song that discusses sex, romance, and their connection to the departure of the U.S. military from Trinidad. While Belafonte's "Day-O" never explores who is to blame for the laborers' plight, Mighty Sparrow, with his witty commentary, is much more explicit in "Jean and Delilah":

> It's the glamour boys again
> We are going to rule Port of Spain
> No more Yankees to spoil the fete
> Dorothy have to take what she get
> All of them used to make style
> Taking their two shilling with a smile
> No more Hotel and Simmonds bed
> By the sweat of thy brow thou shall eat bread[67]

"Jean and Delilah" is not only anti-imperialist; it is specifically anti-American. Belafonte's "Day-O," from the *Calypso* album, is much more subtle in its critique—if it is critical at all.[68] In "Day-O," Belafonte sings:

> Day-O, Day-O
> Daylight come and me wanna go home
> Day! Me say Day, me say Day, me say Day-O
> Daylight come and me wanna go home
> Work all night and a drink a rum
> Daylight come and me wanna go home
> Stock me banana until the morning come
> Daylight come and me wanna go home
> Come Mr. "Tally-man," tally me banana
> Daylight come and me wanna go home
> Come Mr. "Tally-man," tally me banana

> Flip six-foot, seven-foot, eight-foot bunch
> Daylight come and me wanna go home[69]

In an interview with Henry Louis Gates, Belafonte observed, of his popularity as King of Calypso,

> I think the whole thing came in a package that was quite comfortable
> —attractive, articulate. With all my passion, I've never driven people
> to extremes. And what they loved so much was "Banana Boat" and "Jamaica Farewell," and all that stuff.[70]

Not bringing people to extremes left little room for the works of calypsonians like Mighty Sparrow, who infused their art with more overt, and thus problematic, politics. Mighty Sparrow, although well known within the Caribbean American community, did not gain a following in the United States until the next decade. Belafonte was the only Calypso King around.

Regardless, Belafonte in the 1950s was unique because he and his promoters used America's imaginings of the Caribbean and America's contradictory discourses on integration to their advantages. Working within and through the framework on the culture industry, his performances of the Caribbean as a second-generation immigrant in particular showcased a challenge to the status quo, while not wholly forcing the issue of integration for the country's African American masses. His white audiences were able to engage his challenge, but only by first displacing it onto a Caribbean Other. Indeed, they were allowed to enjoy his performance of a Caribbean body without fully relinquishing their power over his black self.

For Belafonte, the spectacle of his Caribbean body in performance and photographs afforded a recuperation of the black male body in mass culture. This sense of agency was critical for a second-generation immigrant described by his biographer Arnold Shaw as being preoccupied with the race question as a youth. Of the young Harry, Shaw observes,

> He hated the daily reminder of life in the slums of Harlem. He hated
> the daily reminders of the humiliating status to which his skin color

reduced him. And he hated having to fight constantly to assert his simplest rights as a human being.[71]

The young Belafonte, prior to *Calypso,* was known to be very angry about American racism and the limitations he faced as both a man and an actor struggling to break into the industry. Hi first wife, Marguerite, as Shaw has stated, felt that his early anger while they were dating was often unchanneled, with no clear focus. Belafonte was always ready to "speak out" against American injustices, even it if it meant the occasional defacing of New York subway advertisements that marketed products exclusively to white Americans.[72]

Robin Kelley's work on zootsuiters and jukers is helpful here because it speaks to the transition afforded Belafonte by the use of a Caribbean body. Kelley notes the ways in which style and performance can be powerful forms of resistance for marginalized people, especially young black men in the United States.[73] Linda España-Maram makes a similar argument in her study of Filipino immigrant youth prior to 1965.[74] Just as "dressing up" became the culture of resistance for the zootsuiters and jukers of Kelley's study, the removal of clothing—the shedding of the trappings of traditional black male entertainment—presented a new disruption of the power over black male identity in the widespread multimedia of television and film. Belafonte claimed his Caribbean body and confronted the racial codes of American society by asserting its sexual presence. This assertion was a powerful statement for Belafonte who, even as an international star, still experienced Jim Crow while singing in American cities or attempting to find housing for his family in New York. Dress—or the lack thereof—became the means by which he articulated a new order for black male sexuality to an American public.

The popularity of songs like "Day-O," "Jamaica Farewell," and "Man Smart" should be considered with the significance of Belafonte's Caribbean body in mind. In a 1991 interview with the *New York Times,* Belafonte recalled that it was in itself a political act to bring Caribbean songs to the homogeneous culture of 1950s America. He stated,

I was absolutely amazed at the response to the music, especially that of white America. . . . I can't think of another music from an outside source that has impacted on the American popular music world so strongly. . . . Singing those songs was as political as one could get while still trying to sell something.[75]

I would argue that the political act really rested in the sexual confrontation explicit—or perhaps implicit—in the performance of "traditional" Caribbean songs. It was not simply the songs that undergirded the "Belafonte Boom" but, rather, the delivery of the songs explored through provocative stage, television, and public performances.

Live performance footage of the hit single "Day-O" reveals the power of sexuality and its packaging in the success of Belafonte's Caribbean image. This Afro-Caribbean work song was first popularized by the Tarriers, a folk trio that achieved moderate success with it in the United States and was then released, according to Craig Rosen, as a single from the *Calypso* album after the Tarriers's version had aroused some interest.[76] Belafonte's stage and television performances of the song were important to the single's rise to the number five spot on the pop charts. The combination of the initial song recognition and the intense power of Belafonte's sexualized and Caribbeanized image enabled the song to move up the charts like a bullet, establishing the song and subsequently the album as new favorites of the American mainstream.

Performances of "Day-O" provocatively accentuated Belafonte's use of his physique—even though "Day-O" is not characterized by a frenetic rhythm or sexually suggestive lyrics.[77] The guttural utterances of Belafonte's "Day-O" yelps and the intense, full force of his movements revealed not only the mood of the unfolding drama of West Indian laborers but also the orgasmic "play" of his own body, which became a site of work *and* sexual pleasure. With "Day-O," the work of Belafonte's Caribbean frame sat in contrast with the laboring of the West Indian banana boaters of whom he sang. His "working" of the body reclaimed the "play," or the diversions, of black male subjects, and it redefined the historical emphasis of black male bodies as objects or instruments of painstaking labor. In performance, the aura created by the stage lighting and shadows of pastel colors intensified the gesticulations of Belafonte's sexual enterprise. The framing of the body articulated a performative language that in many ways denied the work of the songs and identified the pleasure of the sexual terrain explored.

The performance of "Day-O" asserts a sexual pleasure that became even more effervescent with the performance of the fast-paced, polyrhythmic songs such as "Will His Love Be Like His Rum?," "Dolly Dawn," and "Man Smart (Woman Smarter)," all on the *Harry Belafonte—Calypso* album. In some ways, Belafonte's gregarious rapport with the audience freed its members of their sexual, cultural, and racial inhibitions, but it also made them a party to his own recuperation of the black male body for its own sake. The inviting nature of his gesticulating body encouraged what bell hooks terms the oppositional gaze, but it also warned of the danger of its captivating Caribbean form.[78] In a 1959 interview with *Time,* Belafonte attempted to explain this dialectic when he spoke of establishing a relationship with his audience. He asserted that his stage persona let his audience know that "I'll take no liberties with you and I hope you'll take none with me."[79] Yet, in the sociocultural moment of the 1950s, he did take those liberties—even as he challenged the audience's right to appropriate his performative self. The frenetic movement of his body offered a giving of himself to the audience, but also a giving of himself for the self, for the reclaiming of his own black manhood in the United States.

A prime example of this sexual energy in performances from the 1950s is evidenced in the live recordings of "Man Smart (Woman Smarter)," a stage favorite from the *Harry Belafonte—Calypso* album. Belafonte exerted his black male body as a means to reclaim control over its appropriation. At Carnegie Hall, in 1959, for example, his situatedness as storyteller allowed him to live out the drama of the piece, and Belafonte artistically used performance as a tool to create his own playground of self-fulfilling ecstasy:

> I say let us put a man and a woman together
> To find out which one is smarter. Heh!
> Some say man but I say no
> The women got the men beat
> They should know
>
> Uh, not me, heh, but the people they say
> The big man has always led woman astray
> But I say, please listen when I say

> She smarter than the man in every way.
> That's right, the woman is SMARTER
> That's right, the woman is SMARTER
> That's right, the woman is SMARTER
> That's right, That's right.[80]

For Belafonte, the Caribbean body, along with the delivery of the lyrics, became an instrument of self-articulation. Again, the "play[ing]" of the body from the onset of the music mirrored the syncopation of the Afro-Caribbean drumming, which underscored the melodic structure of the song. Intense facial expressions and smooth body gyrations enticed the audience members to experience his infectious joy. Belafonte held their gazes with his ever-moving form and thus *made* them act as participants in his dismantling of sexual and cultural norms. Moreover, Belafonte's own laughter unearthed the performative power of displaying black male virility on stage:

> You meet girl at a pretty dance,
> Thinking that you would stand a chance
> Take her home thinking she alone, heh, [laughter]
> Open the door you see her husband's at home

The mesmerizing tone of his West Indian lilt, which was even more pronounced when his own laughter set up the periodic punch lines, illuminated the ways in which Belafonte was performing for his own gratification. His ability to enjoy himself, regardless of the audience's antiphony, or, perhaps, in spite of it, insisted that he was in a performative world of his own making.

## Island in the Sun: Calypso in Motion (Pictures)

The political underpinnings of Belafonte's Caribbean body are most evident when Belafonte actually enters a larger narrative, namely the filmic one of the *Island in the Sun,* in 1957. Set in the fictional Caribbean island of Santa Marta, *Island in the Sun* worked through the Caribbeanization of

Belafonte's black male body to suggest the interconnectedness of race, sex, and power after World War II in the United States. Using Belafonte's calypso persona, *Island in the Sun* provided one of the best discursive spaces for exploring new representations of black masculinity on the silver screen and in the American culture industry in the 1950s.

*Island in the Sun* was a Darryl Zanuck film based on the 1955 best-selling novel by Alec Waugh. It was the first independent film produced by Zanuck, with Darryl Zanuck Productions, during his brief retirement from Twentieth Century Fox, the movie studio that collaborated with Zanuck to release *Island in the Sun* in 1957. Robert Rossen directed the film, and Alfred Hayes, best known for the Oscar-nominated film *Teresa* (1951), wrote the screenplay. The islands of Grenada and Barbados were the sites where *Island in the Sun* was filmed. The movie featured a star-studded cast of veteran and up-and-coming actors and actresses. The stars included Joan Fontaine, James Mason, Michael Rennie, and the newcomers Joan Collins and Dorothy Dandridge. Harry Belafonte co-starred as David Boyeur.

The film plot of *Island in the Sun* works on two levels. In the film, the well-established Fleury family lives through the transition of power from the colonial elite to the native black population in the fictional Santa Marta. The youngest members of the family, Maxwell (James Mason) and Jocelyn (Joan Collins), fall victim to a sense of social dislocation during the shift from white to black rule. They both feel they have no claim to England, since they have spent most of their lives in the Caribbean. They also feel that they no longer belong on the island with the impending self-government of blacks. Jocelyn has the opportunity to marry and thus to try to establish a place for herself, through a white husband, in British society. Maxwell feels limited by his marginal education in Santa Marta and the lack of power he commands in both Santa Marta and England. Maxwell vies for a seat in the local government against David Boyeur (Harry Belafonte), the black labor leader of Santa Marta, only to draw ridicule from Boyeur and his rather sizable political constituency.

The racy aspect of the plot involves various subplots of interracial romances, which build on the tensions between blacks and whites in Santa Marta. Euan Templeton (Stephen Boyd), who is the governor's son, and Jocelyn Fleury have an affair, only to discover that Jocelyn is pregnant and that she, unbeknownst to her, has a black forebear. Denis Archer

(John Justin), who is the governor's white aide, falls for Margot Seaton (Dorothy Dandridge), an upwardly mobile black woman, and they have a clandestine romance of their own. David Boyeur and Mavis Norman (Joan Fontaine), who is a white socialite, contemplate an affair as he serves as her guide to understanding the "real" Santa Marta, where the majority of the West Indian folk live. Boyeur finally decides that he cannot have a relationship with Mavis because too many problems would arise for a black man who loved a white woman. The film ends with the white men and "black" women[81]—Euan, Jocelyn, Denis, and Margot—leaving for a better and easier life as interracial couples in England. Boyeur and Mavis remain in Santa Marta, unable to fulfill their desires for each other.

   *Island in the Sun* relied on the spectacle of Belafonte's body to infuse value into the Boyeur character and the political and racially charged undercurrents of the film. As King of Calypso, he lent his presence to underscore the constructed Caribbean aura of *Island in the Sun,* which marketing blitzes in popular magazines, on the radio, and in newspaper advertisements promoted as offering "real" Caribbean locals and "real" shots of island topography from Grenada and Barbados. Belafonte's musical segment in the film was featured on the *Ed Sullivan Show* on June 9, 1957, the week of the film's release, to promote the movie. Radio stations, in conjunction with RCA Victor and Twentieth Century Fox, also declared the week of June 9 "Harry Belafonte—*Island in the Sun* Week." Most pop music disc jockeys in the country promoted *Island in the Sun* by playing Belafonte's songs written especially for the film—"Lead Man Holler" and "Island in the Sun"—as well as other songs from his still popular *Harry Belafonte—Calypso* album.

   Moreover, in an attempt to help national movie and radio vendors promote the movie, two pages in the press book of *Island in the Sun* were dedicated to the marketing appeal of Harry Belafonte and the "Belafonte Boom."[82] Not one of the other "stars" of the movie received such coverage. Belafonte was also featured exclusively on one of two prerecorded radio interviews. The first tape was a series of combined interviews with Mason, Collins, Fontaine, and Rennie. The other was a voiceover of just Belafonte discussing his two songs from the film and "put[ting] special emphasis on the influence of the British West Indies" on "his meteoric career."[83]

*Island in the Sun* capitalized on the popularity of Belafonte's heightened black sexuality in star form. To the film narrative, he brought the sexual language of his performative Caribbean body as created, marketed, and exploited in 1956. His Caribbean and sexual body narrativized by the star system set a critical tone for the film's controversial discourses of sex, integration, and political overthrow, even when the screenplay fell short of its highly touted combination of entertainment and sociological values. The meta-narrative of his black male body in the star system of the 1950s offered a particular threat to the mainstream world of the film and, by implication, the mainstream world of American social life.

Belafonte's Caribbean image and iconization as sex symbol did several things for the film's narrative structure. By offering a Caribbean authenticity to the film's production, it deflected the ways in which *Island in the Sun*'s race wars were really about the tensions between blacks and whites in the United States. Belafonte's Caribbean body, supported by his Calypso King reign, both located and dislocated the true cultural terrain of the film. Belafonte created a space for a filmic investigation of the "color problem" for the United States. Yet, he did so through a fictional island in the West Indies, thereby avoiding completely alienating most American spectators with the film's political and controversial message.

This is not to argue that the West Indian colonies were not having social problems of their own. Indeed, the Caribbean islands were experiencing a shift from rule by the colonial elite to black-led self-governance in the 1950s. In 1958, the West Indies Federation, which had been discussed and debated since the Montego Bay Conference, in 1947, was established by the British crown in collaboration with representatives from its islands, including Jamaica, Barbados, and Trinidad. The federation was a combination of federalism, with power shared between islands, and self-governance for each island. It was established with the help of Britain and without full separation from the colonial power. The Federation failed by 1962, and a series of independence movements by black Caribbean countries dominated the early part of the 1960s. Jamaica was the first to ask for independence, gaining it in 1962. Trinidad soon followed, along with other former colonies in the Federation; Guyana and Barbados achieved full independence in 1966.

Most Americans were familiar with the changes in the West Indies, but the racial tensions in *Island in the Sun* seemed to arouse more concerns about the social drama in southern states and northern cities unfolding right before their eyes on the nightly news, in the newspapers, and even in the films of the 1950s. Although popular magazines such as *Time* and *Newsweek* and business journals such as *Business Week* covered the conflicts within the West Indies Federation and the subsequent independence movements in the Caribbean, the area was still a very popular vacation spot for middle- and upper-class Americans, with the notable exceptions of Haiti, Cuba, and the Dominican Republic.[84] Boyeur's militancy in *Island in the Sun,* however, echoed the growing racial awareness and mobilizing of African Americans at home. With the assistance of civil rights organizations, black activists in the late 1950s, like the fictional Boyeur, dared to challenge white American authority in legal, social, educational, and political discourses.

As mentioned previously, the NAACP was victorious in *Brown v. Board of Education of Topeka* in 1954, which set the grounds for the desegregation of schools and other public facilities in the years that followed, notably, in 1957, in Little Rock, Arkansas. That same year, Martin Luther King, Jr., began a decade of demonstrations and marches for Negro civil rights before his assassination in 1968. For an American audience, Boyeur, then, presented the open and increasingly confrontational and institutionalized challenges made by African Americans against second-class citizenship across the country.

Although *Island in the Sun* was an independent film by Darryl Zanuck, it was a product of the American culture industry.[85] Darryl Zanuck had been the studio head at Warner Brothers, Fox, and Twentieth Century Fox, in Hollywood, before deciding to start his own production company. Zanuck prided himself on his ability to turn controversial films, especially those with historical American subjects, into box-office successes. "Controversial pictures, because they stir the public conscience and set people talking, even wrangling," he once reflected, "can be pretty good box office."[86] *Island in the Sun* was the first of Zanuck's independent ventures; however, before *Island in the Sun,* he had produced *Grapes of Wrath* (1940), *Wilson* (1944), *Gentleman's Agreement* (1947), and *Pinky* (1949) for major Hollywood studios.

Especially with films such as *Gentlemen's Agreement*, which won the Best Picture Oscar for its release year, and *Pinky*, Zanuck stood out as a producer willing to provide controversial representations of American ethnic and racial conflicts in post–World War II America.[87] *Gentlemen's Agreement* attempted to deal with anti-Semitism in the United States, not just in Hitler's fascist regime. Its plot revolved around the character of Philip Green, who posed as a Jewish man to research a newspaper piece on anti-Semitism, only to uncover the discrimination experienced by Jewish people in America.

*Pinky* was the story of a mulatto woman, played by the white actress Jeanne Craine, who "passed" for white in the North but later had to make a decision about her racial allegiance—whether to remain in the North and marry her white fiancé or return to the South to help her grandmother, played by Ethel Waters, and the black community in which she was raised. Both *Gentlemen's Agreement* and *Pinky* were part of an emerging genre of American films in the late 1940s and the 1950s that attempted, with some honesty, to explore the social realities of America's ethnic and racial minorities. As the black film critics Donald Bogle and Thomas Cripps have noted in their studies of film history, these films and others often focused on and contemplated the conflicts between mainstream society and its marginalized groups as they aspired to discourses of a more pluralist America after World War II.[88] African Americans, of course, were central to this genre, and films such as *Pinky*, in the late 1940s, along with 1950s films featuring mixed casts such as *No Way Out* (1950), were indicative of the emerging civil rights struggles that were taking center stage in the 1950s.

Like *Pinky* and *Gentlemen's Agreement*, *Island in the Sun*, as a postwar cultural production on race, held true to its controversial appeal. However, its box office pull was amplified by Belafonte's performance of black masculinity and sexuality as a challenge to white (male) hegemony. Racialized sex became the site through which discourses of American citizenship took place. Not only did *Island in the Sun* "set people talking" and going to the box office; it also managed to offend several groups in the South. Segregationist groups campaigned to stop its release in American cities, even asking the Defense Department to refuse to show the film to the American military.[89] In South Carolina, there was discussion about passing a bill that would fine theaters $5,000 for showing the film.

Darryl Zanuck issued a counterattack of his own. He agreed to pay any fines levied against theaters for showing *Island in the Sun*. Further, in a strategic gesture, Zanuck offered this to the press: "The problems that arise in the British West Indies because of racial issues are not at all comparable to the color problem in the United States today."[90] The movie seemed more about the United States than ever before.

What is ironic, but perhaps predictable, is that the campaign against the movie identified solely the racial crossing placed on the body of Harry Belafonte as David Boyeur. The highly eroticized bodies of the African American actress Dorothy Dandridge and even Joan Collins, who played the mulatta role, were mere backgrounds against the body of what Americans seemed to fear most: an assertive and sexual black man. Controversy surrounded the body of Belafonte in ways not imagined on the bodies of Joan Collins and Dorothy Dandridge, who also blurred the racial and sexual boundaries of American social decorum.

Joan Fontaine, in her autobiography *No Bed of Roses,* revealed that she received hundreds of letters at her residence regarding her character's sexual flirtations with Boyeur on screen. Hate letters varied from "How far into the slime will the race-mixers sink?"[91] as reported in *Look,* to "If you're so hard up that you have to work with a nigger . . ."[92] followed by the usual expletives. Fontaine received hate letters that were not sent to her white male counterpart, John Justin, who in the final version of the film is actually seen caressing Dorothy Dandridge, his black love interest, on screen. The disproportionate focus on the white woman/black male paradigm became so apparent that eventually Belafonte received a gag order from Zanuck and Twentieth Century Fox, both of which asked him to refrain from mentioning Fontaine's name or the Boyeur/Mavis affair in any statements to the press.

The controversy about Belafonte's body, then, reveals that the film was not just about the race question in the United States but specifically about the race question as posed through the body of a black man. Although David Boyeur is considered a minor character in *Island in the Sun,* with Belafonte listed as merely a co-star, Boyeur and Belafonte are central to the extra- and intertextual dialogues of integration and racial conflicts in the film. Boyeur's radical politics as the Negro labor leader center him as essential to the unfolding of the plots and subplots. The interweaving of the multiple plots in *Island in the Sun* is sustained, if problematically, by Boyeur's presence in the lives of the main characters. He is present even in his absence: the whites—especially the governor, the Fleurys, and the American journalist—discuss, contemplate, and worry about his power in Santa Marta even when he is not around. They consider him smart, assertive, intriguing, yet dangerous. For black and white Santa Martans, he is the symbol of the impending changes in the social order, the ultimate challenge to the racial and gender status quo. Perhaps most suggestive, for the white elite he also signifies the eroticized evils of black male power unleashed in white society.

The pivotal characterization of Boyeur had specific results in a film that institutionalizes Belafonte's sexual body. As Boyeur, Belafonte engages new ways of (re)presenting black masculinity on screen. Belafonte/Boyeur asserts a black screen image that works against previous narrativizations of black men in popular media, but especially in the movie industry. He is sexual, militant, and vocal. His body signifies on stereotypical constructions of black masculinity—as comedic foils, servants, and sexual predators—that had been a part of the American imagination in film since *The Birth of a Nation,* in 1915.

Also, Belafonte's body in *Island in the Sun* inverted Belafonte's film persona as it simultaneously worked to invert the historical film personae of black men. Before *Island in the Sun,* Belafonte, in *Bright Road* and *Carmen Jones,* had suffered the sexual, cultural, and gender limitations of black men on screen in the first half of the twentieth century. He was the soft-spoken and asexualized principal in *Bright Road.* He was the sexually impotent, yet irresponsible black man in the urban world of *Carmen Jones.*

However, in *Island in the Sun,* Belafonte's body is unique because, while working within the integrationist framework of 1940s and 1950s films, it interrogated the framework at the same time. As with other black male bodies such as Sidney Poitier's and Juano Hernandez's in *No Way Out* (1950) and *Trial* (1955), Belafonte's body sought to assert black humanity, namely the right to gain American citizenship because of one's decency, unselfishness, and commitment to the American ideal.[93] On another, and more controversial, level, though, his body did not ask for civil rights—like the others—but demanded them. Belafonte's body threatened the societal repercussions whites would experience if they did not acknowledge black humanity and address the second-class citizenship of blacks in American society.

Here, to explore my point of Belafonte/Boyeur's centrality to the film's narrative, I want to offer a close textual reading of two key scenes in the film. Both scenes provide Belafonte/Boyeur's most sustained performances in *Island in the Sun*. Most important, when read together, they help identify the power located in Belafonte's body on screen. In the first scene, Boyeur is with his love interest, Mavis, in the all-black environment of the fishing dock in Santa Marta. Boyeur and Mavis participate in the fishing ritual of the black folk, who welcome Boyeur as one of their own. The second scene features Boyeur in a confrontation with the rising symbol of white cultural supremacy on the island, Maxwell Fleury. Maxwell Fleury is attempting to maintain white power through electoral politics, only to be confronted in a public forum by Boyeur and his black supporters.

The first scene, which I henceforth refer to as the "Lead Man Holler" scene, utilizes Belafonte's singing celebrity as it explores new inscriptions of black masculinity in *Island in the Sun*. The scene is a work scene, and, because of this, it surreptitiously displaces the working trope often written on the bodies of black men in popular American media in the first half of the twentieth century. At the onset of the singing sequence, Belafonte/Boyeur's pristine, tailored white shirt and sharing of the symbolic coconut with Mavis separates Belafonte/Boyeur from the workers, even as he vicariously participates in the act of their labor. He enjoys the communal experiences on the dock, but the workers' ragged, heat-stricken images reveal that Belafonte/Boyeur is not situated as an integral part of the painstaking work for daily survival. The dichotomy apparent between the black laborers and Belafonte/Boyeur both disrupts and provides a confluence between the past and the present: the laborers evoke the real and performative history of black men; Boyeur's presence suggests opportunities for a new and different role for blacks in an integrated society. The working bodies of the laborers heighten the flirtations of Belafonte/Boyeur's own body and the ways in which it asserts new utterances of black manhood in the United States.

Like other songs in Belafonte's stage and television performances, "Lead Man Holler" reworks the historicity of black men in American popular culture because Belafonte/Boyeur's body becomes a site for erotic pleasure and not work.[94] The scene asserts Boyeur/Belafonte's sexuality and thus challenges the construction of black men's narrativizations in public media as mere servants and comedic foils. Belafonte/Boyeur is strategically positioned with his white female friend *above* the actual work site of the West Indian laborers. The shots and countershots, which juxtapose Belafonte/Boyeur's performative lead and the actual work of the dock workers, elucidate the ways in which Belafonte/Boyeur's body asserts a playful sexuality for the erotic gaze of the consuming public. Pictured in a white silk shirt and blue cotton pants, Belafonte/Boyeur's body encourages the recognition of the ways in which this body is different from those of the men calling the boats to shore. The cuts from one image to the other (versus a panning technique to frame all the action taking place) add to the focus on Belafonte/Boyeur's sexual body in the scene. The adoring gaze of Mavis further draws attention to the body's provocations as Belafonte dramatizes the work taking place below.

When read alongside the film image of an earlier crossover star such as Paul Robeson in *Showboat* (1936), the significance of "Lead Man Holler" and Belafonte's role in *Island in the Sun* becomes apparent.[95] "Lead Man Holler" revises the celebrated "Ole Man River" sequence of Paul Robeson in *Showboat,* as well as performances by other black male entertainers prior to Belafonte in *Island in the Sun*. I am suggesting not that "Lead Man Holler" sought to deconstruct the working body of Paul Robeson in particular but, rather, that it was used to dismantle the master-servant and often asexual paradigms that circumscribed the bodies of Paul Robeson and others. The new envisioning of black manhood with Belafonte's Boyeur sits in direct contrast to the subservience of characters like Robeson's Joe—Joe has to succumb to manual labor; Boyeur rises above it.

Although Belafonte and actors such as Robeson both brought a particular star quality to their films, the disparities in their film images, especially in crossover films such as *Island in the Sun* and *Showboat,* are evidenced by disparate narratives established in these respective musical sequences. In "Lead Man Holler," Belafonte/Boyeur emerges as an autonomous and sexual black being, whereas in "Ole Man River," Robeson/Joe is emasculated by a labor that denies him his personhood. The cameras of both mises-en-scène suggestively create a shot/countershot effect, both of which establish the proprietor of the black male body. The pre–World War II imagining of black masculinity asserts that Joe has given the power over his body to enslavement on the dock. The countershots of Joe's toil flashed as he sings "Ole Man River" suggest the ongoing, never-ending cycle of his pain. The framing of his body on screen, which later incorporates the framing of other workers, elucidates that his body is a site of manual labor from which he has no respite.

In the "Lead Man Holler" scene's new imaginings of black manhood, however, the black male prototype lays claim to his body and the ritual of his body's labor. Paul Robeson's Joe is searching for pleasure—to be like the Ole Man River. Belafonte's Boyeur claims this pleasure through the work of his body as he performs "Lead Man Holler." The scene's portrayal of black male power asserts a liberation for Belafonte/Boyeur and even the dock workers, rescripting the angst experienced by Joe on the dock. Belafonte/Boyeur claims authority over the black male body and, in turn, undermines hierarchical structures of race and gender in American society.

The inversion of the working trope in "Lead Man Holler" foreshadows the most dramatically intense scene in *Island in the Sun,* in which Belafonte/Boyeur's sexual body translates into a political one. The mounting tensions between Boyeur and Fleury culminate at a pre-election event where Fleury stages a platform for his bid for a seat on the legislative council. The beginning of the scene artfully frames the black masses and their duplicitous merrymaking against the nervous, lone white figures of Fleury and others who attempt to re-establish institutionalized power through the electoral support of the island's black populace. These dialectical images of blacks, who are in control, and whites, who lack a sense of control, unveil the dawning of a new era of black political power, even before Boyeur's body arrests Fleury's in a public sphere.

Boyeur emerges from the crowd, and his body becomes the film's index of black protest. Attempting to support the integrity of the political process, Boyeur stands out as the voice of reason, the one who can successfully channel the masses' demonstration against Fleury's attempts to use blacks for political gain. Yet, too, the camera's tracking of Belafonte/Boyeur's body as he moves from the masses to occupy Fleury's space suggests the ways in which he stands apart from the black folk. As with the "Lead Man Holler" scene, he presents a continuum and a disruption, the past and the present. The crowd, despite its disapproval of

Fleury, remains at a distance. Belafonte/Boyeur steps from the crowd and alone usurps Fleury's spatial domain.

Finally allowed to speak, Fleury addresses the crowd:

> Many of you out there know me. You've cut my sugarcane and harvested my coffee crop. And yet I have not known you, and in this I failed—as I have in other things. To deny this would be to deny truth. I will speak to you tonight only in truth. I've passed you in the fields or in the cocoa sheds and you've been just a name or a face or a number in a book. And I've lived in a world through which you've moved as only shadows to be feared or ignored. I've now lived in the two worlds of Santa Marta. I know how they think, how they feel.[96]

Fleury himself becomes the muted "shadow" image as the camera is preoccupied with Belafonte's body, which is surrounded and embraced by the black Caribbean folk. As the camera captures Fleury's back and side profiles during the speech, its emphasis on Belafonte/Boyeur's body conjures the emerging encroachment of black power in the social, cultural, and political lives of the white mainstream. The movie audience hears Fleury's words, which almost seem dubbed in the scene, but the audience is consumed by the image of Belafonte/Boyeur. Belafonte/Boyeur— here in his crisp white shirt and tan, snug-fitting pants—stands as the focal image and the source of true power. With the support of the black masses, he represents the ultimate challenge to Fleury's attempt to maintain white control in Santa Marta.

Further, sex and power coalesce in the black male posturing that ensues. Belafonte/Boyeur completely invades Fleury's platform and confines him and his white supporters to the stage. Fleury is flustered and trapped. Belafonte/Boyeur remains in control even though he exercises his anger at whites. Standing *between* white and black Santa Martans, he holds his audience captive as he openly confronts Fleury in front of others. His body, as much as his words, becomes the catalyst for this confrontation. Here, the camera shots offer a prolonged focus on Belafonte/Boyeur alone: the shots maintain the audience's desire for Belafonte's sexual body as they contribute to inscriptions of political insurgency placed on the character's body, as well. Belafonte/Boyeur's arm movements and stance, reminiscent of Belafonte in concert, insinuate black male aggressiveness, playing into whites' sexual and political anxieties regarding black masculinity. Belafonte/Boyeur demands his power on screen and in the white imagination, and the fear of Boyeur as a synecdochic (film) representation of black male power is finally realized.

Of course, the syntax embedded in the final scene of *Island in the Sun* disrupts any effective reconstruction of black male identity imagined in the 1957 film. For all of its good intentions, *Island in the Sun* did not live up to its media hype as a daring and innovative film on race in Western societies. At the close of the film, Boyeur is rendered racially and sexually impotent: he and Mavis are unable to create a life together in Santa Marta or elsewhere, while the "black" female characters and their white lovers are allowed to do so at the film's conclusion. Mavis asks, "In a girl's case does it work the other way around? . . . when it's the other way around, does it make any difference?" Boyeur responds in the affirmative, breaking his relationship with Mavis, and then walks off alone to the movie's theme song, "Island in the Sun."

Joan Fontaine writes in her autobiography that her character Mavis and Boyeur did initially exchange a kiss at the end of the film. According to Fontaine, Darryl Zanuck edited the kiss because he "felt that it was too soon to tackle the race question with honesty."[97] Ironically, although Belafonte's character, Boyeur, was touted as revisionary, issues were still left unresolved concerning the presence of black male sexuality on the American screen. Even with the political, cultural, and social potency placed on Belafonte's body in this film, he as his character was still not permitted to touch Ms. Fontaine as Mavis. In 1957, their bodies could be close, but not intimate.

The iconization of Belafonte's Caribbean body in the 1950s did not erase the fact that most white Americans feared black masculinity in the culture industry and in American social life. Hollywood, the record industry, and white American audiences valued Belafonte for his sexual provocations, but they also feared him for the political challenges his black male body demanded in the postwar era. By 1959, Belafonte could not maintain the music and film success experienced during the calypso craze. He tried to re-invent himself by abandoning the calypso image, starting an independent film company, in 1959, to advance African American images, and focusing on African American folk genres such as spirituals, jazz, and blues. He, in turn, did not appear in a major Holly-wood film between 1960 and 1969. His albums of the 1960s, such as *Midnight Special* (1962), *The Many Moods of Belafonte* (1963), and *In My Quiet Room* (1966), although moderately successful, never achieved the heights of *Harry Belafonte—Calypso*. Hollywood, record moguls, and the American public seemed reluctant to fully embrace a sexually suggestive and politically vocal Belafonte, especially when Belafonte used his celebrity to become a leader in the Civil Rights Movement and a spokesperson for human rights at the dawn of the 1960s.

The Caribbean body of Harry Belafonte was ironically replaced by that of another Caribbean American, Sidney Poitier, who, as Thomas Cripps argues, "lent [himself] to a gentle politics of the center."[98] Belafonte exited the role of American cultural icon and Negro matinee idol, and Sidney Poitier entered to create an entire genre of films that explored less confrontational imaginings of black manhood in the 1960s. Belafonte, however, opened the way for the new inscriptions of African American masculinity simmering behind Poitier's relaxed, middle-class image, which dominated the next decade. Belafonte's struggles within the culture industry epitomized the successes and the failures of exploring black male sexual beings in American popular culture—issues still relevant for African American male artists such as Denzel Washington today. At the end of the twentieth century, Harry Belafonte recalled that his days as King of Calypso were a "big scam." He added, "My good friend and mentor Paul Robeson once told me, 'Harry, get them to sing your song, and they'll want to know who you are.'"[99] As a second-generation immigrant and black man who attempted to show America who he was, Belafonte saw calypso as one of the ultimate means for challenging the American public to construct, celebrate, and demand the legitimacy of a black male self in 1950s America.

# CHAPTER 2

# "All o' We Is One"

Paule Marshall,
Black Radicalism,
and the African Diaspora
in *Praisesong for the Widow*

If the Caribbean (body) was used by Harry Belafonte to engage white American racial and gender discourses in the mid-twentieth century, it was used by his contemporary Paule Marshall to disengage from white American society. In the previous chapter, I argued that Harry Belafonte employed the Caribbean as a site for confronting the racial and gender prejudices experienced in the United States. In this chapter, I turn to the Barbadian second generationer Paule Marshall, who uses the Caribbean in her fiction for other, almost antithetical, purposes. Mediating her own conceptualization of race, class, and gender, Marshall locates the Caribbean in relation to African America, renarrativizing the cultural differences between West Indians and African Americans that Belafonte's Caribbean body might demand. Marshall's work does not displace an African American self for a Caribbean one; instead, it evokes and establishes the African American and Caribbean communities' relationship to each other. Marshall's literature suggests a black cultural and political sphere beyond the integrationist yearnings of Belafonte's *Calypso,* imagining an African diaspora through which blacks can recuperate racial and gender selves that challenge loyalties to the Western nation-state.

It has become commonplace to critically examine Marshall's literary oeuvre for her portrayal of black women in both Caribbean and African American cultural landscapes.[1] Her first novel, *Brown Girl, Brownstones* (1959), was well received by black, feminist, and Third World scholars for its lyrical imaginings of the intersection of ethnicity, gender, and class in American society.[2] First published in 1959, it focused on Caribbean, immigrant, and female subjects within the black urban community of Brooklyn and was heralded for challenging the prevailing discourses in the African American literary canon, which often focused on black male individualism and black men's confrontations with mainstream America. In 1969, scholars and reviewers also celebrated *The Chosen Place, The Timeless People* for the attention it paid to postcolonial Caribbean peoples after their independence from European control.[3] Later, they recognized *Praisesong for the Widow* (1983) and *Daughters* (1991) for the ways in which these novels creatively envisioned black female characters who had cultural ties to black communities in both the West Indies and the United States.[4]

Absent from the growing body of scholarship on Marshall's literature, however, is a consideration of the ways in which Marshall's use of Caribbean and African American cultures is linked to her participation in activist-artist groups in the United States such as the Harlem Writers' Guild and the Association of Artists for Freedom and to the ties she had to the American left.[5] Except for James C. Hall, scholars often read the political nature of her work in terms of a diasporic communal vision outside the sociocultural freedom movements of the period and outside the framework of her participation in those movements.[6] For some critics, especially Caribbean literary critics and black feminists, she becomes the alternative to the parochialism of black cultural nationalism in which two of her books emerged. For example, Lean'tin Bracks and Stelamaris Coser rightly connect Marshall to Alice Walker, Toni Morrison, Gayle Jones, and others who reclaim power for black women through the folk vernacular and ritual.[7] Sabine Brock argues that the movements, or "efforts to create a space for women to move," evidenced in Marshall's work are symbolic of her extratextual goal of escaping white American discourses and engendering a creative space for black women to find selfhood.[8] Melvin Rahming, the author of *The Evolution of the West Indian's Image in the Afro-American Novel*, even suggests that Marshall's use of black women in specifically black cultures reflects the "essential 'West Indianness' of the author."[9]

In this chapter, I examine Marshall's use of black women in Caribbean and American diasporic spaces within a larger framework that discusses the importance of her political activism at the time she was writing her novels *Brown Girl, Brownstones, The Chosen Place, The Timeless People,* and *Praisesong for the Widow.* Although readings by Davies, Coser, Rahming, and others are both helpful and insightful, they limit an understanding of Marshall's relationship to black cultural nationalism and the African American left during the late 1950s and 1960s, especially as this relationship helped to fashion her use of black women and the African diaspora in her novels between 1959 and 1983. Marshall's novels not only pose questions and answers about black women's selfhood in specifically black communities but, when extrapolated, also do the same for the development of Marshall's political consciousness as a second-generation Caribbean immigrant. Her novels between 1959 and 1983 elicit the contradictions and tensions of her own political situatedness in the civil rights and emerging Black Power era. Was she an integrationist, and thus in alliance with the American left-wing politics of the 1950s and 1960s? Or was she a black cultural nationalist, even though leaders of the Black Arts Movement such as Larry Neal were critical of her work? Her fiction at this historical juncture, I contend, became the creative sphere through which she sought to both resolve these questions and create a vision of community for African diasporic people—Caribbean and African American—who permeated her novels and short fiction.

Further, I suggest that Marshall's literary imaginings of the interconnectedness between Caribbean and African American people were deeply influenced by her personal journey as a second-generation immigrant. Marshall, against the generational paradigm established by Hansen in 1937, saw her Barbadian heritage as a cultural tap root. It not only shaped her literary style but provided sustenance as she began to find her sense of belongingness in the United States and in her various travels to places in the African diaspora. Marshall equally claimed the African American community as her own. Growing up in Brooklyn, she experienced and became a part of the day-to-day rhythms of the black native born. Later, she was very active in social justice struggles often associated with African Americans. Even after 1965, the period that Basch,

Kasinitz, and other social scientists often identify as the point of demarcation between native black and U.S. immigrant communities, Marshall resisted pressures to simply choose one community; instead, she affirmed her birthright to both. Marshall's emerging politicism created an imperative that Caribbean (immigrant) and African American communities recognize their shared interests and join together to challenge white hegemony and thus preserve the best parts of themselves.

The first section of the chapter examines Marshall's participation in the Harlem Writers' Guild and the Association of Artists for Freedom, as well as her connection with the black journal *Freedomways* at the time she was writing *Brown Girl, Brownstones* and *The Chosen Place, The Timeless People*. I argue that her participation in these artistic-political realms undergirded the tensions in her work, specifically through the ways in which she began to demand a discursive space outside white cultural hegemony for her characters, her readers, and African diasporic people. As Harold Cruse and even contemporary cultural historians such as Alan Wald and Michael Denning have explored, the relationships of several black intellectuals to the white American left and an emerging black nationalist community were embedded in the conflicts that warring ideologies posed for black writers and artists with whom Marshall was politically allied, people such as Ossie Davis, Ruby Dee, LeRoi Jones, Lorraine Hansberry, and John O. Killens.[10] In this section, I illustrate the ways in which Marshall's novels negotiate these conflicts and suggestively embody the growing disaffection with integrationist politics apparent in her work.

Next, I argue that Marshall's use of African American and Caribbean cultures in her literature imagines a recuperation of a black diasporic identity as a source of spiritual and political power for blacks. Marshall's understanding of the black diaspora evolves over time in her work but is essentially characterized by its location outside Western culture, by its foundation in black cultural traditions, and by the social, cultural, and political interconnectedness it encourages between black ethnic populations. I examine how this understanding of blackness becomes a useful site for self-discovery as Marshall affirms her second-generation identity and gives voice to her belongingness in both African American and Caribbean communities.

To illustrate the interdependence among Marshall's political activism, her use of Caribbean and African American cultures, and her (re)construction of a black diaspora, I finally turn to a close reading of *Praisesong for the Widow*, situating it as the master narrative that enacts the possibilities of a diasporic identity for blacks as imagined by Marshall at that particular stage of her literary career.[11] In *Praisesong for the Widow*, Marshall builds on previous critiques of Western and bourgeois cultures in *Brown Girl, Brownstones* and *The Chosen Place, The Timeless People* to establish ties between West Indians and African Americans. Marshall's political envisioning of black people outside the Western nation-state is romanticized in *Praisesong for the Widow* through the literary trope of diaspora, which seeks to link black female subjects—and black people—to black ancestral spaces and thus to one another.

## Political (En)visions: American Left or Black Cultural Nationalism?

On Monday, June 22, 1964, the *New York Post* columnist James Wechsler wrote "Sound Barrier," an article describing the "debacle" of a debate between "white liberals" and "black militants" at a symposium titled "The Black Revolution and the White Backlash," sponsored by the Association of Artists for Freedom. The debate had taken place the previous week, on June 15, at Town Hall, in New York, and was promoted as a dialogue across racial lines about the civil rights struggles in the United States. Confused by the "bewildering aspects of the meeting," Wechsler shared with his readers:

> These lines are not written easily; they were set down several days after the evening in the hope that passage of time might diminish the heat and perhaps throw some retroactive light on a dismal evening spent on a platform at Town Hall. . . . All of us on the platform had voiced a clear commitment in the civil rights battle; yet the evening was dominated by an atmosphere of adversary relationship between the "white" liberals—Charles Silberman of Fortune . . . , David

Susskind, who technically occupied the role of moderator, and myself
—and Negro participants—Ossie Davis, Lorraine Hansberry, Ruby
Dee, John Killens, Paule Marshall, LeRoi Jones.[12]

Advertised heavily in the leftist journal *National Guardian*, the debate
was one of the first events sponsored by the Association of Artists for
Freedom, a group that included Louis Lomax, LeRoi Jones, Ruby Dee,
Ossie Davis, James Baldwin, John O. Killens, Lorraine Hansberry, and
Paule Marshall.[13] Developed in response to the racially motivated church
bombing that killed four black children in Birmingham, Alabama, in
September 1963, the Association planned to create a platform for discussing social reform and charting a new course for the Negro freedom
movements. The 1964 symposium offered an introduction to the newly
organized group of black artists and to what the American public could
expect from them in the future.

Part of Wechsler's chagrin, as he explained in his columns on both
June 22 and June 23, was the tenor of the discussion with black intellectuals with whom he had previously "ha[d] an instinctive sense of fra-
ternity."[14] What he had thought would be "basically communicative discussion" between political allies quickly turned into a serious political
divide between white panelists who were in favor of leading civil rights
organizations such as the NAACP and the Southern Christian Leadership
Conference (SCLC), led by integrationists such as Martin Luther King,
Jim Farmer, Roy Wilkins and A. Philip Randolph,[15] and the "black radical intellectuals"[16] of the Association, who supported the newly popular political current that favored black-only alliances. Wechsler noted
that he felt the "personification of the white liberal devil"[17] as members
of the Association harangued both white liberals for dominating civil
rights organizations and current black leaders for allowing whites to gain
control over the freedom movement. Wechsler felt that the Association
members were mistakenly giving "credence to the doctrines of the separatists"[18] through their own new militant stance. He lamented that they
were demeaning the progress made by civil rights leaders at the national
and legislative levels.

What Wechsler witnessed, and was perhaps unable to properly articulate in 1964, was the changing tide of black political activism in the
African American community and also in the Negro left in the 1950s and

1960s. The Association was a group whose members were often affiliated with the American left community, the Communist Party, and/or organizations that had left-wing political leanings. The battles waged in June 1964, then, suggest not only the larger battles waged against civil rights leaders, as Wechsler insisted, but also emerging battles concerning the "Negro Question" within the leftist movement. Wechsler was tellingly confused by, and thus gave special coverage to, the new militant stance of the black intellectuals; without question, he paid particular attention to the group's youngest members, LeRoi Jones, who "expressed disgust at the time being wasted in discussion"[19] with white liberals, and Paule Marshall, who was seen as the most militant voice in the symposium.

Wechsler used Paule Marshall's comments to sum up what he felt was the Association's basic platform. He wrote:

> For the underlying thrust of almost everything said by the Negro panelists and their remarks varied in tone but not direction—was that the time had come to repudiate the spirit and strategy of the nonviolence movement and to create, in Miss Marshall's words, "a nationwide organization far more militant than any that exists."[20]

Paule Marshall's remarks on a "militant" and "nationwide organization," in fact, were much more detailed than Wechsler was willing to concede. Marshall had commented:

> This is not to say that I personally reject nonviolence as a method of struggle, but I am coming more and more to the conclusion that there is a need now for the establishment of a nationwide organization that is far more militant than any today. An organization with its base in the South where the potential political power of the Negro lies, with its roots reaching down into the mass of the Negro community, an organization with a well-planned and sustained program of action . . . an organization, finally, which is totally committed to the liberation of the black man in America by whatever means prove the most effective. Most important, this organization must be fully independent. By this, I mean that it should not have to look for its financial support from the very sources it is working to overcome. Rather, it must be both financed and led by the black man himself.[21]

Considering Marshall's comments, Wechsler's concerns with the political stance of "Negro radicals" raised the concerns prevalent among other white liberals regarding what they saw as the artists' endorsement of militancy and even rebellion as means for civil rights. Marshall, along with Jones, stood out in the debates as the new, disconcerting voices of the Negro left, their comments tied to the growing political angst of black "separatists" emerging in the 1960s. When asked by a white liberal about the best ways to follow the emerging Negro leadership, for example, Marshall responded that he should go "into the white community and there try to change them,"[22] suggesting the extent to which she had begun to embrace black-only organizing. In addition, she saw the ongoing tension between Association members and the liberals at Town Hall as an example of "how impossible right now it is to carry on a dialogue with a white man, and that he is not ready."[23]

The relatively older members of the Association—Ossie Davis, Ruby Dee, Lorraine Hansberry, and the usually radical John O. Killens—seemed far less militant than Marshall and Jones, even as they inveighed against white liberals. John O. Killens introduced the Association by remarking that "the role of the Negro artists and intellectuals in the Civil Rights struggle was not in conflict with the official civil rights organizations."[24] Ruby Dee remarked that she did not "believe in violence" and that "violence is no answer."[25] She also proposed a conversation on socialism, because, as she argued, "the enemy are the people who have taken what we have invented in the factory and claimed that it is theirs."[26] Lorraine Hansberry observed that "radicalism" was in order, and she conceded that "[r]adicalism is not alien to this country, neither black nor white, and we have a very great tradition of white radicalism in the United States."[27] Ossie Davis added that, although he felt that a change needed to be made in civil rights organizations, problems existed not simply "because of race" but because there was not "full employment" in urban and southern areas where blacks resided.[28]

The lack of cohesiveness in the political stances of the Association members, as well as the obvious vacillations in their relationships to white liberalism, can be explained by two shifts in the Civil Rights Movement: a public endorsement of integrationist organizations in 1957 by the Communist Party, with which most of the Association members were affiliated,[29] and the burgeoning discourse of separatism among younger blacks like Marshall and Jones that replaced the integrationist politics of the civil rights organizations that had dominated the post–World War II era. Before the Communist Party's decision to actively work with groups such as the NAACP, SCLC, and the Urban League, the American left had often had a tenuous relationship with civil rights organizations. These organizations historically had reservations about the Communist Party's goals of working outside American democratic structures. Further, they were not impressed with early attempts by the Comintern, in 1930, to create a "Negro Nation" in the Black Belt, seeing it as a sign of separatist politics and thus not in harmony with their goals of integrating blacks into the American mainstream.[30]

Committed to the Negro class struggle, however, American Communists began making serious efforts to strengthen their political ties with major black leaders as early as 1935.[31] To do this, they had to look outside the leftist community and to create alliances with powerful groups such as the NAACP and the Urban League. Although the Party had dropped the "Negro Nation" platform, hoping to appease potential black allies outside the Party, it made a commitment to continue its fight within a "united front" for civil rights. In 1957, the American Communist Party took an even bolder step to court integrationist organizations. At its national convention, members decided that, in the Party's efforts to contribute to the fight for Negro rights, it would no longer promote "separate organizations," which had been a long-standing part of its platform.[32]

The Party's new commitment to curtailing the promotion of "separate organizations" and its support of moderate organizations such as the Urban League, NAACP, and SCLC had perplexing implications for black leftists in the Association of Artists for Freedom. First, as the Town Hall debate revealed, Association members had several problems with the direction, or lack thereof, of those organizations. Most of their comments suggested that the prevalence of white domination in the leading civil rights organizations made them ineffective in addressing the concerns of the black masses. According to Marshall, Davis, Dee, Hansberry, and others, a much more radical approach was needed to respond to the new violence coming to a head in American cities. It also did not help that the Association had approached the NAACP the previous year about a boycott during the Christmas season to protest the Birmingham bombings.[33]

The request for help, as perhaps evidenced by the attacks on the NAACP in June 15, 1964, was denied.

For most members of the Association, the new platform of the American left also raised concerns regarding the role black people would play in their own struggles for social and economic liberation. These black radicals, for the most part, were strong supporters of integration. Yet, they had traditionally participated in white leftist organizations *and* predominantly black groups such as the Committee for the Negro Arts and the Harlem Writers' Guild. The Committee for the Negro Arts was a theater group founded by Rosa Guy after the Communist-affiliated American Negro Theatre, in which young actors like Harry Belafonte participated, became defunct. Its goal was to provide and expand the opportunities for blacks in theater. There was, however, a tension apparent in the need to balance the nurturing of black ethnic arts and the attempt to integrate black actors and playwrights into the larger community of American theater.[34]

In 1951, Guy also started the Harlem Writers' Guild with John Henrik Clarke, John O. Killens, and Walter Christmas, all of whom were reportedly affiliated with white left-wing organizations. Led by John O. Killens, the Guild was a writers' workshop created, according to founding member Rosa Guy, to "project . . . the life, the style, the dialogue, the type of writing, [the] expression that could only come from the black experience in the United States."[35] When the group was started, Walter Christmas was the only member to have published a book, *The Boy Who Painted Christ Black,* which was self-published in 1948. However, John O. Killens soon published *Youngblood* (1954), which became an inspiration to other authors who were convening and sharing their work. Rosa Guy estimates that more than half of the most influential black writers in the second half of the twentieth century were members of the Harlem Writers' Guild at some point in their careers.[36] Members during the 1950s and 1960s included Julian Mayfield, Audre Lorde, John Henrik Clarke, Sylvester Leaks, Lonnie Elder, Louise Meriwether, and Paule Marshall.[37]

Marshall's and Jones's ambivalence toward white leftists and liberals at the Town Hall debate in June 1964 added another dimension to the growing tensions between African America and the American left. The *National Guardian,* which had advertised the debate since May, ironically headlined its report on the debate the "Negro Revolution and the White Backlash—*A Confrontation*."[38] For younger radicals like Paule Marshall and LeRoi Jones, the left's shift toward supporting integrationist and moderate groups such as the NAACP caused a further sense of disillusion with the white left. LeRoi Jones soon shed his name and leftist white alliances to become Imamu Amiri Baraka. By 1965, after the death of Malcolm X, he made alliances with black nationalist organizations and led the Black Arts Movement, which grew out of the black militancy of the 1960s.

Paule Marshall did not sever ties with black left-wing organizations, but her work evolved to first embrace and resolve the tensions between her leftist and nationalist political alliances. The Harlem Writers' Guild of the 1950s had been the creative and intellectual community that had helped her write *Brown Girl, Brownstones,* which tellingly echoed the American left's concern with materialism, capitalism, and the lumpen proletariat. Yet, by 1961, Marshall's work began to further develop the connections that she as a second generationer made between black diasporic populations, even as her creative enterprise continued to have an anticapitalist slant. Before the Town Hall debate in 1964, she released *Soul Clap Hands and Sing* (1961), a collection of short stories that figuratively traveled through the West Indies to the continental United States and back to the Caribbean and Luso-America. The novellas of *Soul Clap Hands and Sing* were loosely interconnected by the unhappy experiences of their black subjects, who mistakenly lived their lives through the prism of Western culture. In 1962, she also did a "story-essay" for "The American Female" supplement on black women published by *Harper's* magazine.[39] The story was entitled "Reena," and it featured a young woman of African American and West Indian heritage as the title character, revealing the new terms on which Marshall was constructing a black political and literary vision.

What perhaps made Marshall's public comments at "The Black Revolution and the White Backlash" debate in 1964 so volatile was that she called for a black nationalism, reminiscent of Garveyism, that alienated more traditional black and white leftists and the white liberals who had convened at Town Hall. Marshall was very familiar with Marcus Garvey and his "Back-to-Africa" movement; the Barbadian women whom she had creatively fictionalized as early as 1959 in *Brown Girl, Brownstones* were avid Garvey followers. These women were part of the first migration wave of West Indian immigrants who came to the United States in the early 1900s, mostly in the 1920s, from islands such as Barbados, Jamaica, and Grenada. Many Barbadians, as Imra Watkins-Owens has noted, first worked in various capacities on the U.S.-sponsored Panama Canal project before sojourning to the United States. The influx of black Caribbean immigrants between 1900 and 1930 led to a 232 percent increase in the U.S. black foreign-born population, compared to a 30.6 percent increase during the same years in the white foreign-born group.[40]

Marshall's Barbadian mother, with other black immigrant and African American women, participated in Garvey's Nurse's Brigade and his spectacular parades of the 1920s. Although Marshall was born in 1929, two years after Garvey was deported from the United States to Jamaica, Marshall still identified Garvey as having had an enormous impact on her personal and political development. Speaking of Garvey, she once recalled:

> Because of their [the Barbadian women's] constant reference to him, he became a living legend for me, so that although, when I was a little girl, he had been stripped of his power and was an old man living out his days in obscurity in England, he was still an impressive figure, a Black radical and freedom fighter whose life and example had more than a little to do with moving me toward what I see as an essentially political perspective in my work.[41]

Marcus Garvey had long been a problematic figure to both the American left and integrationist organizations. He was a first-generation Caribbean immigrant who organized the United Negro Improvement Association (UNIA), a self-contained organization that promoted black economic and social advancement. The UNIA was started in his home country of Jamaica and then transported to Harlem in 1916 with the goal of utilizing America's black population to promote the "general uplift of the Negro peoples of the world."[42] Garvey criticized Communists for trying to encourage blacks to ally with whites on the basis of a class struggle, observing that "the Negro will always suffer from the prejudices of the dominant whites."[43] In turn, the American left saw Garvey and the power of his organization in New York as threats to its goals of uniting blacks and whites against capitalist structures. Garvey was equally threatening to black and white integrationists who encouraged blacks to stake their political, social, and economic futures in the United States and not Africa. His black nationalist movement challenged both the left and integrationist movements' attempts to mobilize blacks along class or national lines, respectively.

However, Garvey's "Back-to-Africa" movement, his Black Star Line project, and the "great Garvey Parades"[44] continued to shape the politics of African Americans and Caribbean Americans like Marshall, even after Garvey was deported from the United States for mail fraud in 1927. Marshall's response to Garvey was rooted in her second-generation status as a child of Barbadian immigrants, immigrants who filled the kitchen with their "talk of politics" and Garveyism when she was growing up. Marshall saw herself as a product of the political consciousness of her Barbadian immigrant community. Because of her upbringing, she felt that her activism was "something that I came to in a very *natural way*" in the 1950s and 1960s.[45] To this woman who remembered going through a "whole period of rejecting [the West Indian] part of [her]self,"[46] Marcus Garvey was a source of ethnic pride. His idealization of "Negro peoples of the world" paved the way for her to reconcile her multiple heritages as a Caribbean and an African American. As a cultural icon for Marshall, he embodied the duality of her West Indianness and Americanness, in one sense, and what was developing as Marshall's literary vision of creating a diasporic black community in yet another.[47]

As evidenced by the tension between white liberals and the black left on June 15, 1964, at Town Hall, Marshall's movement toward a black nationalist stance reflected new developments and changes in black political culture in the 1960s as well. The panelists' concentration on the emerging discourses of separatism, militancy, and even violence revealed the changing tactics of black organizing, especially among new and younger black leaders. As the NAACP and SCLC continued to espouse nonviolent tactics and integration in their civil right struggles, younger organizations emerged and articulated a much more militant platform. The Student Nonviolent Coordinating Committee (SNCC), which was started with the help of integrationist groups such as SCLC, revoked whites' membership by 1966 and, like the Congress of Racial Equality (CORE), was dominated by Black Power ideologues between roughly

1966 and 1969. The Black Muslims, too, were gaining ground in the 1960s, when Malcolm X, whose parents were also Garveyites, advocated black rights "by any means necessary"—suggesting that the use of violence was well within the rights of African Americans. The Black Panther Party, in the urban ghettoes of Oakland and of Harlem and other areas of New York, was by far the most militant group in the eyes of the American public. Their bouts with the local police and guerrilla warfare tactics sought to challenge the status quo in northern cities. This political organizing was coupled with urban riots in black centers in the late 1960s, as well as with the attempts of blacks from various political backgrounds to create political and social ties with African independence movements.[48]

SNCC, for example, had become disillusioned with white liberals and their exercise of power in the South. Despite recognizing that assaults against white student organizers would alert white northerners to the brutality of southern racism, black SNCC organizers were still uncomfortable with the increasing number of whites whom they felt were dominating the planning and direction of the Freedom Rides for voter registration, to the detriment of local, less-educated blacks who were often intimidated by whites' self-assuredness. SNCC's growing distrust of white liberals came to a head in 1964 with the Democratic Party Convention in Atlantic City, New Jersey. SNCC had painstakingly organized the Mississippi Freedom Democratic Party (MFDP), seen by SNCC as a bottoms-up challenge to the white Mississippi political machine, only to be denied a high-profile, publicly supported platform by the convention's credentials committee. President Johnson, the vice-presidential hopeful Hubert Humphrey, and others connected to the White House worked behind the scenes to offer the MFDP some level of recognition but not full participation in the convention. SNCC supporters of MFDP staged a televised sit-in at the convention in protest but left Atlantic City with a sense of defeat and betrayal at the hands of whites supposedly sympathetic to the freedom struggle.

There was growing tension between SNCC and traditional black leaders like the Reverend Dr. Martin Luther King, Jr., as well. According to William Chafe, Humphrey in fact recruited King and others to endorse the compromise at the Atlantic City convention in 1964. Most black leaders of the older generation cautioned SNCC not to alienate its white liberal allies, including labor benefactors who provided financial support. In 1965, King further alienated SNCC organizers when he agreed, in a last-minute deal with federal officials, not to cross the Edmund Pettus Bridge, in Selma, during a major protest in Alabama against the maltreatment of marchers who were supporting voter registration drives. King and the protesters turned back from the bridge singing "Ain't Gonna Let Nobody Turn Me Around."[49] To black young activists from organizations like SNCC, King's compromise was indicative of African American leaders' lack of true power to effect change in the United States, especially those who depended on the support of white liberals, public officials, and other allies. Thus, when Stokely Carmichael and others asserted the importance of "black power," in 1966, much to King's chagrin, it was no surprise that the freedom movement shifted from a nonviolent ideology to a new era of militancy.

The Black Muslims (the Nation of Islam) and the Black Panther Party became increasingly attractive to young African American men and women. The Black Muslims were led by the Honorable Elijah Muhammad but found particular currency in the young Malcolm X, an ex-convict turned black militant leader who appealed to young blacks tired of waiting for white America to help them secure their civil liberties. Malcolm X, before his separation from the Nation of Islam, was a vocal opponent of nonviolence, arguing that it forced blacks to endure bullets, beatings, and murders at the hands of white racists. He believed in armed defense when necessary to combat the brutality that faced African Americans in their struggles. He also felt that blacks had to become self-sufficient and rely on their own nation building before they could build alliances with sympathetic whites.

With their paramilitary dress style and open display of guns, members of the Black Panther Party were often seen as the poster children for a new and urban black militancy. The Party, started in Oakland, California, in 1966, had a ten-point platform that included programs to monitor police brutality, inform blacks of their rights, and provide services such as free breakfasts to children in urban areas. The platform also included raising consciousness about the need for blacks to control their own neighborhoods and communities. When the party's leader, Huey Newton, was jailed for allegedly killing a white police officer, Black Panther chapters sprang up in northern cities across the nation as a telling sign of support. The Black Panthers were heavily scrutinized by police and federal agents. Many of the Party's members were harassed, jailed, or killed by government officials, who deemed them subversive and who wanted to shut down the organization.

The escalating violence associated with the black masses in urban ghettoes, however, revealed the frustration and restlessness of black youth in the 1960s. The worst riots actually happened after the Town Hall debate: Watts in 1965, Newark and Detroit in 1967. According to Allen Matusow, in his study on the 1960s, "43 racial disorders occurred in 1966 and 164 during the first nine months of 1967."[50] They were often sparked by blacks reacting to white police brutality against blacks. Seemingly incomprehensible, particularly to whites, the riots gave voice to an overwhelming feeling among blacks in northern cities that whites bore a disproportionate responsibility for black poverty and disempowerment. With Newark as an exception, black rioters often avoided black-owned businesses and targeted white-owned businesses and white passers-by. Rioting became a form of lashing out and fighting back against racial injustices. At the news of King's death, in 1968, urban black centers once again went up in flames. In cities like Baltimore and Chicago, blacks mourned their leader for peace, while warning—through fires, looting, and violence—that they increasingly saw nonviolence as futile.

Amiri Baraka (the former LeRoi Jones) emerged as the leader of the Black Arts Movement, which he and other black artists saw as the creative complement to the growing militancy of black people and political organizing. Although the goals of the Black Arts Movement were not easily and clearly defined by all of its proponents, a few key characteristics linked the works produced under the auspices of the movement during that era. The Black Arts writers celebrated an aesthetic that accentuated a connection to the black masses and thus a disconnection from white and African American bourgeois cultures. Hoyt Fuller, editor of *Negro Digest,* the journal often heralded as the most influential vehicle of the Black Arts Movement, remarked that "[t]he Negro revolt is as palpable in letters as it is in the streets."[51] In *The Black Aesthetic,* the cultural critic Addison Gayle added, "The serious black artist of today is at war with the American society as few have been throughout American history."[52]

Black Arts writers emphasized the political function of art, recalling Du Bois's "art for propaganda" in the 1920s, and consequently paid less attention to the literary forms of art thought to be a by-product of Western hegemony. The focus, instead, turned to Africa as a means of dismantling the power that Western culture had over black culture and cultural practices in the United States. The Black Arts ideology was deeply influenced by the emergence of successful African liberation movements throughout the British, French, and Belgian colonies on the continent, beginning in the 1950s. Black Arts writers and intellectuals, as well as most African Americans, drew inspiration from the successful independence movements in Ghana, in 1957, and Guinea, in 1958, followed by similar movements in nations such as Nigeria, in 1960, Sierra Leone, in 1961, Kenya, in 1963, and Zambia, in 1964.

Several black militant leaders of the time felt especially empowered by the pan-Africanism inspired by these new African nations as a means to build black political leadership, help secure the independences of other nations, and deny the power of white-minority rule.[53] A series of poems, plays, critical essays, and manifestos appeared in the 1960s in black journals such as *Negro Digest/Black World, Soulbook,* and the *Journal of Black Poetry,* which were published to support and develop the new militant works of black writers. Often with an eye toward Africa, these journals, featuring the essays and creative works of African Americans such as Amiri Baraka, Sonia Sanchez, Larry Neal, and Don Lee, created a political and literary discourse that helped foster an oppositional relationship to America for many younger blacks of the era.

Marshall was not considered part of the emerging Black Arts Movement, and her work was seldom featured in any of the leading black literary journals of the period. African American artists and intellectuals of the Black Arts Movement sometimes questioned Marshall's emphases on both West Indian *and* African American communities and challenged where she stood culturally as a second generationer who claimed allegiances to both cultures. In the *Crisis of the Negro Intellectual,* written in 1967, Cruse pejoratively remarked that Marshall represented the "West Indian of traditionally 'divided' loyalties."[54] Marshall tried to explain the tenor of the times in an interview with Daryl Cumber Dance: "I've been at times loudly claimed by the African American literary community as well as the West Indian, and occasionally as loudly disclaimed by both.

It used to hurt and exasperate me years ago—the disclaiming part of it
—and it still does to some degree."[55] Other second generationers such as
Malcolm X and Stokely Carmichael were part of the black militant era,
but they seldom insisted upon exploring in detail the links between
West Indians and African Americans.[56] Marshall, conversely, insisted
that she would bring her West Indian and African American backgrounds to her discussions of civil rights for blacks. For people like Larry
Neal, one of the Black Arts Movement's most vocal leaders, her commitment to explore West Indian themes was exacerbated by the fact that her
1969 novel, *The Chosen Place, The Timeless People,* featured an interracial
love affair.[57]

Despite questions surrounding her "loyalty," Marshall was very re-
sponsive to black literature's new direction in the 1960s, especially its
emphasis on African imagery and the development of an ethno-specific
ethos of blackness. She observed:

> I think it's [the Black Arts Movement] all to the good. Because we are
> attempting to reconstruct our personality in our own terms. I see writ-
> ers as image makers, and one of the ways that we can begin offering
> images of ourself [*sic*] which truly reflect us, which begin to throw off
> the negative images that the West has imposed on us is to begin hav-
> ing our literature offer to the Black reader the image of himself that is
> positive and creative. I don't think a people can really progress until
> they think positively of themselves. Cultural revolution is about how
> you see yourself. What you think of yourself, part and parcel of other
> aspects of the Revolution, the political revolution.[58]

The change in her work after *Brown Girl, Brownstones* reflected the influence of both the Black Arts and the emerging cultural nationalism of
African Americans on her political awareness.

At the time of the Town Hall debate, Marshall was already working on
her second novel, *The Chosen Place, The Timeless People* (1969), which
she had determined would have a larger political vision than *Brown Girl,
Brownstones.*[59] She felt that the personal struggle for freedom explored
through her second-generation heroine, Selina, in *Brown Girl, Brownstones* was not enough for the "political revolution" and that her writing, like the philosophy of the Black Arts Movement, had to create a vi-

sion for the empowerment of black people. She sensed that she needed to make a statement that included and supported the struggles of blacks in the two communities she claimed as her own, the West Indian and the African American. Marshall also concluded that she "had to bring about a synthesis of the two cultures and in addition, to connect them up with the African experience."[60] Situated in a fictional Caribbean island, *The Chosen Place, The Timeless People,* then, presented "a kind of place," "a sort of focal point"[61] through which Marshall could critique the black diaspora's relationship to the West, using the contemporary prism of the civil rights struggles and the West Indian and African independence movements of the late 1950s and 1960s.

Although the anticapitalist and leftist influences in both *Brown Girl, Brownstones* and *The Chosen Place, The Timeless People* are similar, the differences between the two novels are striking on several levels. Indeed, both books are critiques of the devastating effects materialism and capitalism can have on blacks. In *Brown Girl, Brownstones,* Marshall suggests that Barbadian immigrants mistakenly let their desire to "buy house" and achieve financial success destroy their relationships to each other. In *The Chosen Place, The Timeless People,* West Indian laborers are misused by American and British capitalists and by the island's petit bourgeoisie.

Yet, Marshall's flirtation with black and white alliances in *Brown Girl, Brownstones* undergoes a radical transition in her second novel. In *Brown Girl, Brownstones,* Marshall contemplates a black female heroine's personal struggles with a parent culture and the white American mainstream. Selina's conflicts with the black community, both African American and Caribbean, are finally resolved by her recognition that her burgeoning sense of selfhood is dependent on the strength and guidance of other blacks. Marshall, however, does not quite resolve the tensions between blacks and white Americans that are apparent in *Brown Girl, Brownstones.* White racists such as Mrs. Benton, who denies Selina's access to American culture, are easily excluded from the confraternity evidenced at the novel's conclusion. Yet, white characters such as Rachel Fine, who finally helps Selina realize her trip to the Caribbean, continue to play a role in the black person's search for freedom.

In *The Chosen Place, The Timeless People,* Marshall again deals with the question of white and black alliances through the personal friendship of the main characters, Saul and Merle, but with very different results. Saul is a Jewish liberal and quasi-Marxist who has come to the fictional Caribbean island of Bournehills to help the local blacks build their community. He is well respected by the Bournehills folk, especially Merle Kimbona, who is very vocal about her disregard for white interference in Bournehills's local life. However, although Marshall offers a sympathetic reading of Saul, she finally resists his centrality to the salvation of Bournehills, which the local dignitaries describe as "like someplace out of the Dark Ages."[62] She extracts him from Bournehills's history, which, she intimates, ultimately belongs to the Bournehills people and what they decide to do for themselves. Merle and Saul, the interracial and politically allied lovers, are forced to separate at the end of *The Chosen Place, The Timeless People*. Merle must leave to find her self in Africa and with her African husband and African-Caribbean child. Marshall's conclusion demands that Saul must also leave Bournehills, and the Bournehills people must challenge Western influences and claim their futures on their own terms.

Even though Marshall's work was not published in the leading Black Arts journals, pieces were featured in *Freedomways*, the journal Harold Cruse once called the "special province of John O. Killens' Harlem Writers [sic] Guild."[63] In fact, an excerpt from *The Chosen Place, The Timeless People* appeared in the journal as early as 1964, five years before the novel was published by Harcourt, Brace & World. From its inception, the journal was subtitled "Quarterly Review of the Negro Freedom Movement," and the aims of the journal were laid out by the editors in the first issue. They included an attempt to "strengthen . . . the relationship among peoples of African descent in this country, in Latin America, and wherever there are communities of such people in the world"; an attempt to "provide a public forum for the review, examination, and debate of all problems confronting Negroes in the United States"; and the determination to avoid "special interests to serve save those already clearly stated —no political, organizational or institutional ties."[64]

The journal's ties to the American left—despite its promise to have "no political, organizational or institutional ties"—were clear, evidenced by the editorial board's outside affiliations with the Communist Party and the overwhelming contributions by people from left-wing organizations such as the Harlem Writers' Guild. Although it was not quite an organ of the Communist Party and the Harlem Writers' Guild, as Cruse suggests in *The Crisis of the Negro Intellectual,* it did have a leftist slant and was supported by white and black Communists and left-wingers.[65] Marshall's presence in the journal suggests her continued relationship with the left movement, but her relative absence from the quarterly, with only two works published between 1961 and 1970, also intimates larger, simmering issues between left-wing politics and black nationalism both inside and outside the journal's editorial circles.

Marshall's 1964 excerpt for *The Chosen Place, The Timeless People* was part of a special *Freedomways* issue on the Caribbean islands. She contributed the excerpt entitled "Return to the Native" and also served on a "special committee of volunteers"[66] used as consultants for this summer issue on the Caribbean. A few things stand out about Marshall's contribution to the issue. First, "Return to the Native" features Leesy and her grandson Bull, who later becomes Vere in *The Chosen Place, The Timeless People.* It does not feature the major characters Merle and Saul, who have more dominant roles in the novel and, perhaps, may have been considered too linked to the petit bourgeoisie by the editors. The chapter excerpt, instead, features the life of the lumpen proletariat, the working class in Bournehills of which the novel's Merle and Saul are not a part. "Return to the Native" revolves around the work experiences of the migrant worker Bull in Florida and New Jersey and the elderly woman Leesy in Bournehills. Bull tells Leesy about his life in the cane fields of the United States and the way he was treated as worker in a frightening capitalist system. Leesy tells Bull of her concerns about the closing of the European-controlled "Cane Vale," on which the Bournehills folk are dependent for the sale of their cane crops. The chapter ends with Leesy's hope that she will be able to cut "a few canes" for herself to survive the season.

The tone of the excerpt chosen for the Caribbean edition of *Freedomways* raises the question of why Marshall chose not to include something more representative of her evolving black nationalist stance. In part, the question can be answered by what Ronald and Abby Johnson argue was *Freedomways*'s attempt to "steer . . . clear of the new nationalistic literature and discussions of the black aesthetic."[67] Although writers such as Don Lee and Audre Lorde were featured in *Freedomways* in 1967 and 1970, respectively, the journal seldom published the works of writers involved in the Black Arts Movement. In an appraisal of the work published over five years in *Freedomways,* in 1966, even Ernest Kaiser, who was a regular contributor to the journal, conceded that "[t]hree possible criticisms are that not enough young, unknown Negro writers have found their way into the magzine [*sic*]; [and] that the language of the magazine is too sanitary, not earthy enough as a fighting people's organ."[68] Marshall's and others' advocacy of a black cultural nationalism was perhaps too powerful for the editorial staff, which seemed to consistently distrust the new black militancy and its separatist ideology.

Other black leftists who had nationalist leanings like Marshall's often published in *Freedomways'* competitor, the *Negro Digest,* which became *Black World* in May 1970. The *Negro Digest* was re-established in 1961 by the publisher John Johnson, after being out of print for ten years. Integrationist in the first half of the 1960s, it became more militant in the mid-1960s under the leadership of Hoyt Fuller and through the influence of Black Arts leaders such as Larry Neal and Amiri Baraka. Several writers and artists thought of the journal as the voice of the Black Arts Movement. Contributors from its most militant days in the mid- to late 1960s include several members of the black left, some of whom advocated a new type of Negro revolution in the 1964 debate: John O. Killens, Ossie Davis, and Ruby Dee.[69] Ossie Davis and Ruby Dee both contributed articles on black theater to the April 1966 issue. They also contributed articles to *Freedomways.*[70] John O. Killens, who did not contribute often to *Freedomways,* was perhaps the most prolific of the Town Hall debaters, contributing several articles and commentaries to *Negro Digest/Black World* between 1966 and 1975.[71]

Not fond of writing nonfiction, Marshall wrote only a few cultural essays during the 1960s, one of which appeared in *Freedomways.*[72] The essay "The Negro Woman in Literature" was not an essay per se but a transcript of a talk in spring 1965 at a conference sponsored by the Harlem Writers' Guild. This essay marked the last time she contributed to the journal, although her fiction was regularly reviewed in *Freedomways.* Marshall shared the platform at the conference with Sarah E. Wright, Abbey Lincoln, and Alice Childress. Reprinted in the journal in the winter of 1966, the women's speeches were of the general conference variety and were similar in their themes. Sarah E. Wright discussed what it was to be a woman, "a mother, a responsible-minded citizen," arguing that the realities of black womanhood were different from negative portrayals of black women in American culture.[73] The lyricist Abbey Lincoln discussed music and talked about the black woman's "glorious and enduring love" for black men as represented in songs by Billie Holiday, Bessie Smith, and Mahalia Jackson.[74] Alice Childress focused on contemporary understandings of the dominant black matriarch and on unfair portrayals of black women who were forced to be strong in light of their "struggle against racism."[75]

Although Marshall's talk was very similar in theme to those of Lincoln and Childress, her response was different in at least two ways. First, she criticized white America and white authors in particular for historically perpetuating negative characterizations of black women in literature, referencing the canonized names of Gertrude Stein, Thomas Nelson Page, and William Faulkner. This use of white America in her discussion of black women was very different from Lincoln's talk on black women "singer-artists"; her talk carefully specified the ways in which black women challenged images given by "hostile, racist-oriented" white poets.[76] It was also different from Childress's talk, which presented a general and historical framework of black women's struggles in the United States. By contrast, Marshall's last words at the Harlem Writers' Guild conference were a challenge to blacks to avoid the decadence that she believed afflicted whites:

> I have always felt that one of the reasons the white man in this country has been so hard on us is that he suspects we have something going for us that *he* doesn't have any more, that he has lost. How shall I define it—an expressive quality, a strength that comes from suffering, a feel for life that hasn't been leached out of us by a fat, complacent, meaningless existence; a basic health in the midst of the sickness around us, and that once we are given the opportunity for this to come to flower, we would be a formidable people.[77]

Marshall felt that the image of blacks was dependent on "Negro writers" like herself who had to "prove this right" and recapture the black image in literature.

Marshall's "Negro Woman in American Literature" became a site for carving, demanding, and anticipating a place for herself within a tradition of black women's writing in the United States. Thus, she avoided what she perhaps saw as the pitfalls of leftist alliances *and* the pitfalls of the growing male domination of African American cultural aesthetics, especially as a vehicle of black protest in the 1960s. In the essay, Marshall identifies the encouraging images of black womanhood offered for and by black women, citing Dorothy West, Gwendolyn Brooks, and Alice Childress. She includes herself and her book *Brown Girl, Brownstones* in her discussion of trail-blazing black heroines and black women writers. According to Marshall, these trailblazers created black heroines who were not one dimensional; they were not written only as foils for white or African American male characters but were "fully realized" and an encouraging response to racism and black male chauvinism in literature. She observed:

> In considering authors like Gwendolyn Brooks, Dorothy West, and others, we move in the whole area of the Negro woman writer. It seems to me that she has two main problems, a dual cross to bear, if you will: one, that of being a woman in a society which, despite its protestations, does not take women seriously, which does not really accept the fact that a woman has a need to fulfill herself quite apart from her role as a wife and mother. The second problem is the one I have been talking about all along: the attempt on the part of American society to condemn us to categories, and thus rob us of our humanity.[78]

Her speech echoed the emerging voice of black women within civil rights, leftist, and other freedom struggles in the United States, women who were beginning to share their concerns publicly not only about white American racism and imperialism but about the gender struggles in liberation movements, as well. Her keen insights in 1965 anticipated the literary interdialogues scholars would observe between Marshall and writers such as Toni Morrison, Maya Angelou, Audre Lorde, and Alice Walker, who were acclaimed in the next decade for creatively challenging white and black male literary and cultural solipsisms with their focus on black women in black cultural spaces.

Marshall's most important essay of the period, however, appeared in 1973 in the journal *New Letters*. Entitled "Shaping the World of My Art," the essay served as a manifesto that detailed the ways in which Marshall linked black women, West Indian and American cultures, the African diaspora, and her political awarenesses of leftist and nationalist politics. Black literature, according to Marshall, had a "central role to play" in the development of a "base upon which they [blacks] must build," "an ideological underpinning for the political, social and economic battles they must wage."[79] Marshall saw her literature as contributing to the "knowledge of one's culture, one's history,"[80] especially as it reconstituted the historical links between African Americans and West Indians, who she envisioned as "the two great wings of the black diaspora in this part of the world."[81]

The goal of her literature, she wrote, was specific to her political vision for the black diasporic community: "the rise through revolutionary struggle of the darker peoples of the world and, as a necessary corollary, the decline and eclipse of America and the West."[82] She observed that her literature formed a continuum that both resisted Westernization, especially as informed by capitalism and materialism, and used "archetypal African memory" as a means of preserving a black communal sphere and values outside the Western nation-state.[83] She saw her literature as using the past to help (re-)create a future for blacks, dependent on their connection to the African diaspora, and, more important, their ability to use the collective pasts to unite and "revers[e] the present order" of their oppressions in Western cultures.[84]

Marshall added that the development of her literature was dependent on the voices of black women who were "at once Afro-American, Afro-Caribbean," because through these women she could "bring together all the various strands (the word is synthesis) and thus make of that diverse heritage a whole."[85] She observed that her use of women was based on a response to the absence of black female voices in literature of the past, as she had noted in her talk "Negro Woman in Literature." She wrote that her emphasis on black women was also based on the political consciousness she had learned from black women while growing up. It was a political consciousness that seemed to inform their lives, which provided a telling example, as she once stated to Daryl Dance, of the African proverb "It's woman's power on which a society ultimately depends."[86] Women thus became the focal point as she identified the means by which she could envision a union among blacks in the diaspora.

"Shaping the World of My Art" provided an opportunity for Marshall to openly articulate the pedagogic function of her literature, especially as it served as a guidepost for envisioning a connection between African American and West Indian cultures. Other self-reflexive analyses and commentaries of her work appeared only after this initial synthesis of her literature in the essay. In 1973, when the essay was published, Marshall still participated in the leftist circles of the Harlem Writers' Guild and the Association of Artists for Freedom. She also continued her relationship with Black Arts intellectuals, staying involved in the national and international conferences sponsored by various organizations in Black Arts groups. Marshall saw both movements as part of a larger political framework through which she could heighten both her black readers' awareness of their unequal relationship with white cultural and economic hegemony and their understanding of the ways in which their particular struggles for liberation were connected to other struggles of "darker peoples" in Africa, America, and the West Indies. Resisting the orthodoxies of both leftist and black nationalist movements, "Shaping the World of My Art" anticipated the creative space Marshall carved for herself and her literature as a vehicle for imagining a suggestively utopian union among class-based struggles, black cultural traditions, and the threat of black revolution, acting in concert against the dominance of Western societies.

## Diasporic Identity and Praisesong for the Widow

It is in the 1983 novel *Praisesong for the Widow* that the pedagogic function of Marshall's work as amplified in "Shaping the World of My Art" was finally realized. Considering the importance of this novel to the fruition of Marshall's political vision as a second-generation immigrant writer, I analyze *Praisesong for the Widow* in the remainder of this chapter. *Praisesong for the Widow* appeared ten years after "Shaping the World of My Art," in which Marshall predicted that this "yet to be written novel" would complete a "trilogy" with the other novels *Brown Girl, Brownstones* and *The Chosen Place, The Timeless People*.[87] Marshall promised that *Praisesong for the Widow* would "in some way be concerned with Africa." She also wrote that her use of Africa became "the metaphor for the psychological and spiritual return back over history, which . . . Black people in this part of the world must undertake if we are to have a sense of our total experience and to mold for ourselves a more truthful identity."[88] In 1983, *Praisesong for the Widow* stood as the creative work that provided the fictional script for Marshall's goals of placing blacks outside Western culture, geographically, psychologically, and culturally, and within the realm of "Africa," where blacks could realize the importance of living in relation to one another and moving beyond the limitations of Western imperialism.

*Praisesong for the Widow* represents a significant step in Marshall's creative development because it evidences the movement toward reconciling leftist and black nationalist consciousnesses in Marshall's work. Marshall continued to disavow the economies of materialist and capitalist-driven societies. But, she flatly denied the potential efficacies of white and black political alliances by the time she wrote *Praisesong for the Widow*. Marshall replaced the leftist orthodoxy of class struggles regardless of race with a discourse of class in relation to race. With *Praisesong for the Widow,* she established a powerful critique of bourgeois and Western culture by interrogating the possibilities of African diasporic existences for blacks.

Whereas *Brown Girl, Brownstones* and *The Chosen Place, The Timeless People* can be thought of as exemplars of the classic leftist texts produced by black artists and intellectuals of what Michael Denning terms the "cultural front," *Praisesong for the Widow* demands a disconnection from white cultural politics—even in its most radical and sympathetic forms. In *Praisesong for the Widow,* Marshall enacts the discourse of the American left, while embracing a black nationalist ideology that denies that whites can play a role in the creation of an independent black cultural sphere. Marshall begins *Praisesong for the Widow* with class struggles that are located in black cultural wars for self-preservation. The main heroine, Avey, loses her sense of racial identity because, in her attempt to participate in mainstream America, she abandons the black working class and thus abandons the pulse of black culture. She can assert her selfhood only by undergoing a radical independence from mainstream America and by engaging a diasporic identity through her ties with African American and Caribbean communities.

Marshall first portends these cultural wars by introducing the self-reflexive negotiation of Avey's name. Avey is short for Avatara, which in

the Hindu language of Sanskrit means "reincarnation of a deity."[89] Avey
was named after her great-great-grandmother by her Great-Aunt Cuney,
from the South Carolina Sea Islands. Yet, over the years, Avey learns to
think of herself as Avey Johnson, the more palatable, Westernized version of her adult persona. Even the intimacy of Avey, the name she affec-
tionately embraced before her middle years, is subsumed by the homog-
enization of her last name, Johnson, which imparts a life marred by the
impact of African slavery in the Americas. As Avey experiences social
and economic mobility in American society, moving from the streets of
Harlem to the suburbs of New York, she can think of herself only in a distant, self-alienating way. With her movement from Halsey Street, in
Brooklyn, to suburban North White Plains, she assumes the identity of
Avey Johnson and thus relinquishes the affirming power of her cultural
legacy for the (dis)comfort of middle-class American life.

The fragmentation evidenced by Avey's negotiation of her name underscores a fragmentation of cultural and racial selves employed by Marshall in her criticism of bourgeois cultures in all three novels of the trilogy. The narrative voice introduces Avey Johnson as she is taking a
cruise on the *Bianca Pride* to the Caribbean islands. The name of the
cruise line itself signifies on the premium Avey often affords American
imperialism. "White Pride" intimates Avey's willful acceptance of white
America's preoccupation with luxury, materialism, and financial wealth.
Marshall illuminates the vastness of the *Bianca Pride* to insist upon the
inherent decadence of mainstream American culture in which Avey tries
to locate herself. The cruise reminds the reader of Avey's distance from
African Americans of the laboring classes, who must settle for "the annual boatride up the Hudson to Bear Mountain,"[90] and her distance from
the people of the Caribbean islands, whom Avey registers only as part of
the sights and sounds of her vacation. Additionally, the cruise emphasizes Avey's participation in the dominance of American wealth and
power. As a tourist, Avey not only proves disconnected from the black
folk but validates and perpetuates American capitalism and its often debilitating effects on the economies of the Caribbean.

In her response to the decadence of Western culture, however, Marshall is careful to destabilize her heroine's participation in the American
mainstream. Avey's third trip to the Caribbean islands on the *Bianca
Pride* does not reaffirm the comfort of her middle-class existence but, in

contrast, mocks a black female self that takes great esteem in her Americanization. As the cruise gets under way, Marshall's heroine feels disoriented from herself and from the North American excess of the *Bianca
Pride* that she had so admired before. Avey attempts to find solitude on
the ship, hoping to rid herself of the "peculiar sensation"[91] in her stomach caused by the surreal dream of Great-Aunt Cuney's beckoning call
back to Tatem, where she vacationed every summer of childhood. Yet,
the *Bianca Pride* does not lend a respite from the excess of leisure activities, elaborate dining, and American passengers; instead, it becomes the
encroaching, white hegemonic space that she must escape to command a
sense of normalcy.

The dream of Great-Aunt Cuney's beckoning call launches the irreconcilable dichotomy between Western and African-derived cultures that
Marshall creates in *Praisesong for the Widow*. Great-Aunt Cuney, the matriarch of the family, insists upon Avey's return to Tatem, which symbol-
ically represents a return to her black cultural roots. To will Avey back
to Tatem with her "Come/Won't you come"[92] and pleading eyes, Great-
Aunt Cuney invades Avey's new environs in the suburbs of North White
Plains, and the fight that ensues in the dream announces Avey's desire to
be accepted as part of American middle-class life. Determined to assert
her "hard won life of the past thirty years," Avey ignores Great-Aunt
Cuney and, with a "renewed fury," "hammer[s] away" at her. Avey refuses to distance herself from a bourgeois existence in American society.

Although Avey attempts to ignore the dream and find solitude on the
ship, the encroaching power of the American mainstream manifests itself
in the confines of the *Bianca Pride,* where Avey cannot escape white
American passengers although she tries to avoid contact with them for a
short while. Revealing Avey's overwhelming sense of disorientation,
Marshall employs the *Bianca Pride* for its narrative confinement. The
overpowering presence of Western dominance on the cruise hinders
Avey's attempts at momentary solitude:

[W]hen she did find one of her favorite spots deserted, she wouldn't
have it to herself for long. Some group fresh from breakfast, or one of
the many snacks served throughout the morning, would make its appearance only minutes after she had settled into a deck chair, drawn
the light cardigan she had brought with her around her shoulders and

closed her eyes. Their voices crashing into the dusky orange silence behind her lids. Their faces looming abnormally large and white for a second as her eyes opened.[93]

Avey moves from place to place on the cruise to avoid the mob of white American passengers, passengers who follow her with their "sun-baked bodies" and "idle chatter" of food, shopping, and small talk.[94] As symbols of white American dominance, they invade and usurp her space, making the cruise ship a virtual prison. Marshall suggests that to truly escape the intrusive power of white America, Avey must relinquish her desire to be a part of the decadence of the American mainstream.

Avey's implication in her own oppression provides a fictional platform for Marshall's larger commentary on middle-class-led and civil rights institutions echoed in the 1964 Town Hall debate. Avey's attempts at solitude are hindered by her desire to re-insert herself into the cruise's symbols of luxury after she has had some time "come right again" and enjoy the privileges of her class status.[95] Marshall's implicit critique of Avey, who is unaware of the part she plays in her own cultural demise, mirrors Marshall's lingering invectives against leading black middle-class leaders. As an activist, Marshall suggests that the fascination with integration and acceptance by a white population in postwar America has blinded the black bourgeois class to the needs of the black working class. At the Town Hall debate, she noted, "One of the most insidious features of this society is that it has made for economic and social separation between the Negro community—the old colonial tactic of divide and rule still obtains."[96] She also suggested that a fascination with white American culture only perpetuates blacks' oppressions as racial minorities, leaving them ill prepared to fight for their liberation as blacks in American society.

Avey brings what Marshall determines as the problems arising from black participation in bourgeois lifestyles to the fore, especially in its post–civil rights articulation. Almost two decades after the Town Hall debate, Marshall uses Avey to creatively indict the ways in which blacks often play a role in the powerlessness they experience as they willingly accept the social values of Western cultures. Avey feels psychological distress because her tentative attempt to escape white passengers and their bourgeois activities on the *Bianca Pride* is not an unequivocal contemplation of her participation in the American mainstream, nor is it an exercise in reconnecting with the black folk community of her dream. Despite her aunt's beckoning call back to Tatem, Avey's eventual rush to get away from the *Bianca Pride* is a rush toward North White Plains, her understanding of home, and not the places conjured in her dreams.

Indeed, when Avey finally decides to leave the cruise, she is prepared only to return to her comfortable life in the suburbs, dressed in her "muted beige and navy print . . . dress" with summer gloves and matching purse. She has visions of returning to the life that she knows and understands in the most bourgeois of American ways: relaxation at home in the suburbs. The ultimate symbol of her affluence—her dining room—is what grounds her as she thinks of home:

> Everything was as she had left it: her special crystal in the china closet, her silverplate—all eighty pieces—in its felt-lined case. Later, she would make herself a cup of tea and drink it here at the table in the half-light.[97]

Her fantasies of leaving the ship and going home to North White Plains are filled with signs of her bourgeois existence. In North White Plains, she feels she can gain the composure that she could not summon amid the confusion of the *Bianca Pride.*

Marshall triggers the metaphysical drama of Avey's dislocation and thus enacts, in radical fashion, what she suggests is the disorientation blacks feel when they do not challenge their allegiance to Western culture. Avey's experiences of dizziness, nervousness, and stomach illnesses embody the severe consequences of not severing ties with the West and of not reconnecting, as readers learn as the novel progresses, to other blacks in the diaspora. Avey thinks that she is leaving the cruise to return to North White Plains. However, Marshall forces her heroine to face the psychological trauma of her cultural loss as a black woman in mainstream America. In *Praisesong for the Widow,* Avey pays the price for thinking of home as North White Plains, and she finds herself caught in a vortex of black Caribbean encounters during a plane layover in Grenada en route to the United States.

As an outgrowth of Marshall's interactions with black nationalist and American leftist communities, Avey represents Marshall's ultimate posi-

tion that *radical* steps must be taken to secure personal and collective independence from white dominance in any form. Avey's overwhelming
disorientation amplifies the dislocations that Selina expresses in mainstream America in *Brown Girl, Brownstones* and that Merle undergoes as
a postcolonial woman in an interracial love affair in *The Chosen Place, The
Timeless People*. In 1964, Marshall made gestures toward this ideological position against Western cultures and interracial alliances in the Town
Hall debate, where she began to distance herself and her politics from
Euro-American and European influences. With *Praisesong for the Widow*,
Marshall finally illustrates the ways in which cultural and political independences for blacks are most effective when exercised apart from white
political and social rule.

Radical whites such as Rachel in *Brown Girl, Brownstones* and more
important characters such as Saul in *The Chosen Place, The Timeless People* are exorcised from the black communal experience in *Praisesong for
the Widow*. In this third novel, the white passengers, hotel clerks, and
neighbors remain nameless. White characters, instead, become symbolic
of American culture and the debilitating effects it has on Third World
communities. Marshall's emphasis shifts to the bonds blacks like Avey
can make with other blacks in the diaspora—her Great-Aunt Cuney, in
Tatem; the Caribbean folk; and her African American daughter, after her
experience in the Caribbean islands.

Moreover, *Praisesong for the Widow* advances Marshall's questioning
of black-white political alliances first posed on a serious level in *The Chosen Place, The Timeless People,* in 1969. Marshall paints Saul, the white
radical from *The Chosen Place, The Timeless People,* as a sympathetic
character, one who serves as a creative foil to the suffering that Merle and
the other people of Bournehills experience. Yet, he stands within the narrative as the symbol of Western wealth and, thus, Caribbean poverty. His
ability to help the Bournehills folk with his foundation grant serves to
remind readers of the exploitation blacks have experienced as laborers
for the First World. His presence confirms the Third World's position of
dependency in a postcolonial context.

Further, Saul's presence in the narrative invokes the seductive
prospects of allegiances with white radicals within a Western cultural
framework. Here, Marshall's own challenges to the American left are
front and center. Saul, with "his old, instinctive 1930's Marxist antipa-

thy toward all bosses,"[98] no doubt is sincere, even in his voyeurism. Sex, however, complicates Merle's understanding of her larger purpose: to reclaim the island and her culture for the people of Bournehills. Marshall intimates that the problem lies not in Merle's affection for Saul but in her subsequent inability to demand that distance from U.S. imperialism that her affair with Saul hinders and her ultimate journey toward a diasporic identity demands. Merle's fear of confronting the next step—making that reconciliation with her daughter who lives in Africa—is enabled by the affair she has with Saul. Only by severing her ties with Saul can she begin "to go back before [she] can go forward, really forward"[99] and enact that radical independence from the West.

I discuss Merle and Saul at length because the questions regarding black-white alliances explored in some detail in *The Chosen Place, The Timeless People* are finally answered in the most vocal ways in the dramatic and surreal experiences of Avey in *Praisesong for the Widow*. The questions are answered, of course, through absences—the unwillingness to afford whiteness any subjectivity. Marshall seeks to focus on the consequences of cultural identification with whiteness. Although economically stable, Marshall's heroine in *Praisesong for the Widow* is culturally lost. She has yet to feel truly comfortable in the American mainstream; she can no longer find the courage to re-establish a relationship with the black community in which she was raised. Her involvement in Western culture is more blatant than Selina's and Merle's in *Brown Girl, Brownstones* and in *The Chosen Place, The Timeless People,* respectively; Avey is older than Marshall's previous heroines and has experienced a longer life marred by Western dominance that has informed, shaped, and thus limited her identity. Because of this, Marshall writes a sequence of events that work through the spiritual and supernatural realms to actively push Avey further and further away from the American mainstream and toward black topographies from her past and present.

In the 1964 Town Hall debate, as she was writing *The Chosen Place, The Timeless People,* Marshall insisted with frustration:

At this point, our full energies in this struggle have to be directed toward bringing together the mass of the Negro people, because there is no point in looking for support and help from the white liberal or from the white man. Period.[100]

In 1969, *The Chosen Place, The Timeless People* seemed to echo this frustration, although Marshall, no doubt because of her leftist ties, could not resist the possibilities of alliances with whites, even as she finally denied the value that such allegiances offered to blacks. By contrast, when writing *Praisesong for the Widow,* she took more radical steps to embrace an exorcism of white influences, building on her growing concern in the 1960s and 1970s with creating black-led, black-supported social and political structures. In 1977, as she was writing *Praisesong for the Widow,* she was more forthright in articulating her goals for blacks in the diaspora:

> I don't think the political thrust can be really effective until there is a new thinking on the part of the black man. The cultural [and] the political revolution have to go hand in hand and that's why the example of China is so important. China closed its doors to the insidious influence of the West. They said: "Keep out your televisions, keep out your materialistic values, we are involved in the serious business of not only transforming our society materially, but also making for a new man in China.[101]

By 1983, *Praisesong for the Widow* employed a similar construct of closing one's mind, if not one's doors, to European and white American influences. In an interview with Lisa Sisco and Melody Graulich, in 1992, Marshall stated that she had based *Praisesong for the Widow* on an African American tale of the Ibos, who, when brought to the Americas as slaves, were similarly able to turn away from the West with surprising power. She commented:

> *Praisesong for the Widow* started with a place. I came across this place called Ibo Landing in a book entitled *Drums and Shadows,* which was a series of interviews with some very old people who lived on the Sea Islands, off the coast of Georgia and South Carolina. Nearly everyone spoke of a place on one of the islands called Ibo Landing. According to a story handed down over the years, a group of Ibo slaves decided they didn't like the looks of America as soon as they were brought ashore and turned around and walked back home across the Atlantic Ocean. That's how *Praisesong* began, with that folktale.[102]

The source for *Praisesong for the Widow* is deliberately grounded in black folk culture. Intertextually, it provides a history of rebellion and a process of revolt against mainstream American culture for Avey, who is the descendant of the Ibo people in the Sea Islands. Ibo Landing becomes one of her black cultural treasures; it is the site in Tatem to which she is beckoned by Great-Aunt Cuney on the *Bianca Pride*. Extratextually, the use of the folktale offers yet another way for Marshall to rely on black culture and cultural traditions as a means of empowering the personal and collective struggles of blacks in the diaspora.

Merle's and Selina's unfinished battles against the West in *Brown Girl, Brownstones* and in *The Chosen Place, The Timeless People* manifest themselves in the battle that Avey, by novel's end, is able to engage more fully. Readers can only imagine Selina's soul-searching trip to the Caribbean and Merle's search for her daughter in Africa at the end of Marshall's first two novels. However, Marshall enacts Avey's battle in *Praisesong for the Widow* with a long and painstaking process, hinting at the seriousness of the work that must be done. Marshall truly actuates Avey's fight in the liminal space of Grenada, where, after disembarking from the cruise ship, Avey experiences a bizarre night of dreams and visions that defy the laws of time with nonlinear sequences of the past and the present. Waiting for her plane to the States on an overnight stay, Avey dares to remember the forbidden—the ways in which her family's home in Harlem used to be a sacred place of self-renewal, a respite from an outer self displayed to American society. Avey is able to recall Halsey Street, which in Grenada becomes life-sustaining for Marshall's disoriented heroine.

"What the devil's gotten into you, woman?"[103] her husband Jerome's apparition asks on the hotel balcony, prefiguring Avey's psychological return to her past life and thus warning her against returning to the poverty of their earlier life in New York City. The memory of Halsey Street becomes traumatic for Jerome even at his death and in the afterlife but becomes life-sustaining for Avey as she first experiences that radical turn from mainstream American culture. Part of Avey's burgeoning awareness on the hotel balcony is the return to the place where she felt she knew her self, a self that once possessed an inner strength lost in the upward climb with her husband to the American mainstream. With the time and space to reflect, Avey no longer feels that she commits the ultimate act of betrayal by going "back where [they] started"[104] and reclaiming her personal and cultural history.

Marshall's evocation of Avey's ability to overcome her fear marks a step toward power. When Avey gives up her fear of confronting the poverty of her life within African America, and even of confronting her dead husband, who refused to let her honor their past lives in the communal space of New York City, she begins to reorient her political and cultural consciousness outside middle-class American life. In turn, she is able to express the pain that she had denied for all of those years:

> And Avey Johnson mourned Jay [Jerome], sobbing wildly now, the tears raining down on her gloved hands gripping the pocketbook on her lap. This was a much larger grief, a far greater loss, and as if in recognition of this the plaintive voice of the sea in the darkness eight stories below rose up to mourn with her.[105]

Marshall situates the signifiers of Avey's middle-class existence, namely the "gloved hands" and "pocket book," alongside the image of a grief-stricken self "bent over almost double on the side of the recliner."[106] This juxtaposition provocatively reveals the change that has taken place as Avey is finally able to express what she has lost culturally in her bourgeois existence. The image of her crying on the balcony articulates movement toward a release from her cultural bondage. In the quiet of the Caribbean night, Avey is able to release her middle-class reserve, the "rock of her calm,"[107] to form questions that she feared asking before: "Couldn't they have done differently? Would it have been possible to have done both?"—namely "Rescue themselves from Halsey Street" and preserve the "most valuable part of themselves"?[108]

Her answers come in "disconnected words and images," mirroring her disoriented state but nonetheless asserting the necessity of gaining a keen awareness of the power rendered in having the courage to reclaim one's cultural past. The free indirect discourse of the text superimposes Avey's emergent awareness on the omnipresence of Marshall's political didacticism through the narrative voice. Avey's thoughts coalesce with the narrator's to establish the importance of this moment of recognition, the movement from unconsciousness to a focused avowal of the black (female) self and, by inference, the black diasporic sphere. The blending of the first and third persons at this critical point in the text offers a moment of self-awareness for Avey but, tellingly, for Marshall's black readers, as well. The message garnered from Avey's "sleeper's wake" is charged with Marshall's affirmation of black heritage as a tool of empowerment against the West. The answers to what is needed are exhorted in lengthy and a nonidentifiable voice:

> Awareness. It would have called for an awareness of the worth of what they possessed. Vigilance. The vigilance needed to safeguard it. To hold it like a jewel high out of the envious reach of those who would either destroy it or claim it as their own. And strength. It would have taken strength on their part, and the will and even cunning necessary to withstand the glitter and the excess. To take only what was needed and to run. And distance. Above all, a certain distance of the mind and heart had been absolutely essential.[109]

Here Marshall suggests the narrative importance of the Ibo motif that threads its way throughout Avey's journey. The voice of Avey's great great-grandmother is conjured: "Her body she always usta say might be in Tatem, but her mind, her mind was long gone with the Ibos[.]" Further, Marshall provides awareness, vigilance, strength, and distance as the apparatuses that can and should be used by diasporic blacks to resist the temptations of Western culture. Although Avey is in the West, she, like her great-grandmother before her, must actively learn not to embrace Western culture as her own.

This juncture in *Praisesong for the Widow* establishes the relationship Marshall imbues between a radical independence from the West on one hand and a subsequent journey toward the African diaspora and diasporic identities on the other. With diaspora, Marshall imagines the alternative to integration into American and European cultures; it stands as the source on which blacks in the West Indies and the United States can rely for liberation and cultural affirmation. Yet, too, Marshall's use of diaspora affords a creative space to reconstruct, work through, and evidence past struggles and past triumphs of blacks displaced by the Atlantic slave trade. The African diaspora, especially as presented to readers in *Praisesong for the Widow*, allows Marshall to "us[e] the past," as she once reflected, "as existing us in the present and in the future."[110]

Marshall hones the symbiosis between personal journeys and the collective experiences of blacks in multiple locales in all of her novels, but in *Praisesong for the Widow* especially. It is not until Avey makes those movements toward the knowledge of the diaspora that she experiences a spiritual journey that can be fully activated. She awakens from her night in Grenada to embrace a self free of the cultural baggage of her middle years and is prepared to embrace the search for meaning in her life:

> It was as if a saving numbness had filtered down over her mind while she slept to spare her the aftershock of the ordeal she had undergone last evening. Or that her mind, like her pocketbook outside, had been emptied of the contents of the past thirty years during the night, so that she had awakened with it like a slate that had been wiped clean, a *tabula rasa* upon which a whole new history could be written.[111]

With her "tabula rasa," Avey leaves the plush hotel and walks a deserted beach unmarred by the tourism and excess of the island. The image Marshall creates of the deserted beach suggests the cleansing of Avey that has taken place the night before in the hotel room. Not only is the section of the beach deserted, but it is characterized by its purity: "Down from where she was walking on the tree-shaded upper level of the beach, lay the wide, flawless apron of sand. Not a footprint was to be seen. At the bottom of the slight incline the low-breaking waves foamed up and withdrew with scarcely a sound."[112] Avey gravitates toward this section of the beach "without being conscious of it"[113] and has a natural, even primordial, desire to follow its path.

During her journey on the beach, Avey encounters Lebert Joseph, who ultimately serves as her guide to finding herself and other blacks in the Caribbean landscape. In the third book of the novel, "Lavé Tête," Lebert is the mortal incarnation of the African and diasporic deity Legba, the god who, according to Henry Louis Gates, Jr., "alone can set an action in motion and interconnect the parts."[114] The inscription of the book imparts Lebert/Legba's narrative importance for Avey's psychological journey. It reads "Papa Legba, ouvri barrière pou' mwe [Papa Legba, open the gates for me]," and is followed by Randall Jarell's words: "Oh, Bars of my . . . body, open, open!"[115]

With the call to Papa Legba in the Haitian Vodun Introit, Marshall illustrates both the importance of Avey's agency in freeing herself of personal bondages and the absolute necessity of the (re)quest for assistance from a black diasporic source. The Vodun Introit initiates Avey's desire to remove the shackles of her past, simultaneously asserting the role blacks in the African diaspora must play to bring her across the threshold. As the incarnation of the ancestral African and diasporic god Legba, Lebert has been chosen as the figure who must transport the wayward Avey back to reclaim her diasporic identity.

The importance of the diaspora motif cannot be underestimated in *Praisesong for the Widow*. The motif engages tropes of Africa in Black Arts literature, while it enunciates Marshall's goals of linking "the two great wings of the black diaspora," which she first suggested in "Shaping the World of My Art," in 1973. It is no coincidence that the ancestral figure chosen to guide Avey is a deity worshipped by people not only in Haiti, as the Vodun Introit suggests, but also in West Africa, parts of South America, and southern portions of the United States. The connections Marshall demands between African American and West Indian cultural and historical experiences are no longer extratextual, dependent on the relationships readers can make between her novels in the trilogy, but are located within the novel proper as Avey experiences life in the United States and Grenada. African American memories and Caribbean experiences coalesce to remind her, and the reader, of cultural practices that link diasporic blacks as descendants of African slaves in the Western hemisphere.

Central to Marshall's exploration of diasporic existences for African Americans and Caribbeans in *Praisesong for the Widow* is a positioning of Africa as homeland, as a site for imagining the common heritage of multiple black cultures. Speaking of *Praisesong for the Widow* in an interview before the novel's release, in 1983, Marshall stated,

> In the book that I am working on presently, I have gone back to some of the legends that are an important feature of early Black American life and try to hook them up with the legends in the West Indies. One of the things that is striking about them is that those legends reflect a tremendous nostalgia for Africa.[116]

Marshall incorporates and relies on this nostalgia to situate Africa as the originator of black culture for the African diaspora. She had traveled to the African continent in 1977, with Black Arts groups, and in 1980, while writing *Praisesong for the Widow*, she spoke of the experience in the same nostalgic manner as the "spiritual, emotional and affective facet" of a "return."[117] Like the legends, Africa in *Praisesong for the Widow* is an ideal, a constructed site through which blacks can engage an "authentically" black experience that disregards national and ethnic boundaries. For Marshall, Africa can be found in most black cultural landscapes in *Praisesong for the Widow*: Harlem, Brooklyn, Grenada, South Carolina's out-islands, and Carriacou.

The rum shop owner Lebert actuates an "Africa," a black topos of origin that Avey's great-aunt Cuney first sowed with Avey's dream on the Bianca Pride. Lebert helps manifest what Great-Aunt Cuney and the deity Legba can only attempt to do in supernatural form: bring Avey back to a black consciousness. With his talk of his ensuing excursion to Carriacou and its importance to the psychological and spiritual well-being of Grenadian out-islanders, Lebert pushes the windows of Avey's mind. His talk prods her to recall the events that further impel her movements toward the site of cultural blackness:

> "It was this dream I had!" The small part that was still her old self heard her declare, and was astonished. Could this be Avey Johnson talking so freely? It was the place: the special light that filled it and the silence, as well as the bowed figure across the table who didn't appear to be listening. They were drawing the words from her, forcing them out one by one.[118]

It is in this space of the rum shop, with its "special light[,] silence"[119] and spiritual libation, that Avey's cultural past meets up with her present. Her aunt's "Come . . . won't you come" in the dream gains new meaning because it is superimposed on Lebert's account of the excursion. Carriacou and Tatem's Ibo Landing resonate culturally, although one is set off the coast of Grenada and the other off the coast of South Carolina, in the United States. Less culturally fragmented, Tatem and Carriacou are symbolic representations of what diasporic blacks secure from the journeying process back to an African heritage. Carriacou and Ibo Landing, as

the most "African" of points in both geographical locations, allow diasporic blacks to do what Avey's forebear had learned to do when she was
alive: maintain the distance from the West that became a key to survival.

The importance of Africa as a cultural ideal resounds in Lebert's question "What is your Nation?" posed to Avey in the rum shop. Indeed,
Lebert's question is Marshall's own. His question gives voice to Marshall's provocation of a diasporic identity that recognizes difference as it
celebrates unity in all three books of her trilogy. Lebert, for instance, attempts to assert the necessity of a black community that defies African
displacement and brings dispersed blacks together to celebrate their
African lineages. However, Avey's response is a sign of her cultural infancy, or, rather, her inability to envision what it means to form connections with other blacks: "I'm afraid you've mistaken me for someone
from around here, or from one of the other islands. . . . I'm from the
States. New York [.]"[120]

Avey does not yet realize that Lebert's questioning of her nationhood
is a challenge to Western constructions of the nation-state, of cultural
particularities, and is an open acknowledgment of the tribal affiliations
of Africa before the devastating effects of the Atlantic slave trade.
Lebert's calling of African nations—Cromanti, Moko, Banda, Temne—in
all their forms does not separate the black diasporic community but, in
fact, strengthens it through the collective power of its diversity. Lebert
knows the power of knowing one's nation, and he has seen the pain of
not knowing: "You's not the only one, oui. . . . It have quite a few like
you. People who can't call their nation. . . . Is a hard thing. I don' even
like to think about it."[121] As Avey's cultural guide in her yet to be fully
understood fight against Americanization, he suggests that in knowing
her nation, she can draw upon the strength of her cultural inheritances
and the cultural inheritances of other blacks in the diaspora.

Lebert convinces Avey to join him on the excursion and to travel by
boat to the small island of Carriacou. Although she experiences initial
misgivings about following Lebert to an unknown place, she feels as if
she is finally surfacing from her disoriented state and finding a sense of
well-being: "She was feeling more dazed and confused than ever, yet
there now seemed to be a small clear space in her mind: looking out from
it she found the scene on the wharf less overwhelming today, less
strange."[122] The boat ride becomes Marshall's inversion of the African

Middle Passage from the continent to the Americas, a symbol of both Avey's return to her cultural homeland and a radical revolt against the West. It offers a new self, one connected to her living past through memory but mature enough to understand the importance of the cultural legacy that must shape her identity. That she travels over water, recalling the Middle Passage *and* the walk that the Ibos made over the Atlantic Ocean, reverses the power that slavery in the Americas and its systemic vestiges have exercised over her life.

As Avey steps onto the wharf in anticipation of her trip to Carriacou, she is reminded of her childhood trips to Bear Mountain, in New York. The memory of these trips establishes her reconnection to other diasporic blacks. The sights and sounds of the wharf remind her of a time in her life when she felt a bond to other African Americans from New York who went to Bear Mountain not to just "eat fried chicken and potato salad" and to relax but to "lay claim" to their collective heritage. The child Avey experienced ties to these people that manifested themselves in the silk threads that seemed to spring from her small body:

> As more people arrived to throng the area beside the river and the cool morning air warmed to the greetings and talk, she would feel what seemed to be hundreds of slender threads streaming out from her navel and from the place where her heart was to enter those around her. And her threads went out not only to people she recognized from the neighborhood but to those she didn't know as well. . . . While the impression lasted she would cease being herself, a mere girl in a playsuit . . . , someone small, insignificant, outnumbered . . . ; instead, for those moments, she became part of, indeed the center of, a huge wide confraternity.[123]

With this image, Marshall sets the stage for the adult Avey's introduction to the elderly West Indian women who are her fellow passengers on the boat ride to Carriacou. The memory of her silk threads are in her consciousness as she is placed between these black women, who become a part of the "huge wide confraternity" she has just recalled from her childhood. The text's temporal juxtaposition of the past and the present situates these women, in Avey's mind, as the West Indian incarnation of the African American women from her Harlem community: they are the pillars and protectors of the diasporic legacy and the people who bring wayward members, like Avey, back into the fold of communal life. Just as Lebert serves as her guide to a diasporic sphere, these women serve as her stewards as she purges the last remnants of her old, bourgeois self and embraces a diasporic identity. They quiet her with "maternal solicitude" as she divests herself of her final "troubling thoughts," and they offer her the support and strength she needs as she experiences the final purging, the excretion of her body's bondages, which take place before she reaches the excursion site.[124]

*Brown Girl, Brownstones* and *The Chosen Place, The Timeless People* end before the reader actually experiences Selina's and Merle's radical resistance to Western culture. Marshall suggests the rewards of their revolts against bourgeois existences at the conclusion of *Praisesong for the Widow.* That Avey finally finds a diasporic identity is articulated by her ability to dance the creole dance in the "Beg Pardon" ritual of Carriacou. Although she is not able to dance the dance of her nation, she does find promise in the creole dance, the dance of the diaspora, where "anybody that feels to can dance now" and make a spiritual and psychological return to an African homeland.[125]

Encouraged by Lebert and the West Indian women, Avey dances the dance of her journey, the dance that tells of her independence from the West and her embrace of an African diasporic culture. The dance she chooses is an old dance but a new dance for Avey, who has never dared to join in the Beg Pardon before: it is the Ring Shout of her childhood Tatem, enlivened with the "stylishness and sass" of her young adult self, now imbued with the understanding of her connection to the African diaspora in its "bare bones and . . . burnt-out ends."[126] In the black cultural space of Carriacou, she finally re-forms ties with other blacks in the United States and in the Caribbean: "Now, suddenly, as if she were that girl again, with her entire life yet to live, she felt the threads streaming out from the old people around her in Lebert Joseph's yard."[127] Claiming the African diaspora, Avey is able to claim her self. When asked her name by an elder from Carriacou as the novel concludes, she responds, "Avey, short for Avatara."[128]

"As the history of people of African descent in the U.S. and the diaspora is fragmented and interrupted," Marshall confided to Maryse Condé in 1984, "I consider it my task as a writer to initiate readers to the challenges the journey entails."[129] With her use of diaspora, Marshall recuperates these "fragmented and interrupted" histories in her literature to provide a discursive critique of Western cultural supremacy. Through her heroines, she demands journeys that West Indians, African Americans, and other African people must make to enact their own political and cultural independence. As a second-generation Caribbean immigrant, Marshall employs diaspora as a home space for herself but also as a home space for her black readers—West Indian and African American —who dare to consider blackness, in its multiplicity, as the site of power for diasporic people in the Western hemisphere.

# CHAPTER 3

# Sister-Outsider

African God(desse)s,
Black Feminist Politics,
and Audre Lordre's Liberation

"Over and over again in the 60s I was asked to justify my existence and my work, because I was a woman, because I was [l]esbian, because I was not a separatist, because some part of me was not acceptable," Audre Lorde recalled in a speech given at Harvard University in 1982. "Not because of my work but because of my identity. I had to learn to hold on to all the parts of me that served me, in spite of the pressure to express only one to the exclusion of all others."[1] Although Paule Marshall reconciles Caribbean and African American heritages through a romanticization of an African diaspora, Lorde employs tropes of Africa with different goals in mind. Like Marshall, Lorde enacts Africa as the site for discovering racial awareness. However, she also enacts Africa as the site that validates her ties to multiple racial, cultural, and sexual communities. In this chapter, I examine the ways in which Audre Lorde—a second-generation immigrant of Grenadian and Barbadian heritage—uses imaginings of Africa to maintain and contain "all of the parts of me that served me" in her poetry, autobiography, and political essays. Lorde's Africa politicizes her Caribbean and African American identities, while it suggestively legitimates a lesbian consciousness that destabilizes racial and sexual boundaries.

This chapter focuses on an analysis of African god(dess) figures in the poetry of *The Black Unicorn* (1978) and in *Zami* (1982), Lorde's "bio-mythography."[2] I suggest that Lorde's employment of Africa works on several levels in her writings. First, Lorde's imaginings of Africa attempt to resolve her fraught relationships with Black Arts intellectuals and white feminists in the 1970s and early 1980s.[3] Through representations of African god(desse)s, Lorde engages Black Arts and mainstream feminist ideologies even as she provides new visions for understanding black womanhood. Second, Lorde's Africa functions as a discursive site of difference that Lorde invokes to empower herself as well as others. Lorde uses black god(dess) figures in both *The Black Unicorn* and *Zami* to establish the uniqueness of black and lesbian-feminist consciousnesses. Yet, Lorde also manipulates these and other tropes of Africa to create bridges between American, African, and Caribbean communities that are not closed off to those outside the African diaspora. Lorde presents Africa and its cultural formations in the black diaspora as alternatives to Western and patriarchal traditions for the multiple communities in which she participates.

I also assert in this chapter that Lorde uses tropes of Africa to challenge the limitations of a Caribbean identity as it is passed on to her by her West Indian parents. First-generation immigrants, Lorde's parents had always planned to return to the islands, until their hopes were dampened by the Great Depression. As Ira Reid notes of most early immigrants who never considered the United States home, they were unable to fully comprehend and support their daughter's subject-position as an active participant in (African) American culture. They often presented Lorde's Caribbean heritage as a means to escape white American domination, without understanding the profound impact growing up in the United States had on her identity construction.

In my reading of *Zami* in particular, I offer an examination of the ways in which Lorde's use of Africa in *The Black Unicorn* ultimately matures to incorporate a Caribbean heritage by the time that she reflects on her life in the early 1980s. The Caribbean cultural identity that seemed to limit her participation in multiple communities is resituated in her bio-mythography as part of that black diasporic consciousness that allows Lorde to engage difference and to challenge white and patriarchical hegemonies in the most empowering ways. *Zami* finally grapples with the partial silence Lorde has placed on her Caribbean heritage in both her writings and her public identity as a black lesbian in the 1960s and 1970s and embraces that heritage as part of Lorde's liberation as a vocal black lesbian committed to the value of difference.

This chapter is divided into three sections. I begin my analysis with a discussion of Lorde's commitments to the struggles of U.S. black and mainstream feminist liberation movements in the 1970s. In this first section, I suggest the ways in which Lorde's problematic relationships with leaders in both movements underscored her imaginative focus on African god(desse)s in her work.[4] This section is followed by close readings of African god(dess) figures in *The Black Unicorn*, first published in 1978. Here, I draw connections between Lorde's poetic form and the political and artistic debates she had with white feminists and Black Arts intellectuals at the moment of writing *The Black Unicorn*. Finally, I turn to her biomythography, *Zami*, which extends and moves beyond tropes of Africa first employed in *The Black Unicorn*. In this final section, I maintain that with the biomythographic style of *Zami*, Lorde identifies Africa and the Caribbean as spaces where she can construct the particularities of black lesbian identity, while simultaneously working through a discourse of difference to build coalitions and communities with others.

## "Who Said It Was Simple?": Audre Lorde and Her Liberations

> But I who am bound by my mirror
> as well as my bed
> see causes in color
> as well as sex
> and sit here wondering
> which me will survive
> all these liberations.[5]

In the summer of 1979, the May–June issue of *The Black Scholar* carried "The Black Sexism Debate" as part of its readers' forum. The debate featured responses from intellectuals, feminists, and artists to the controversial essay "The Myth of the Black Macho: A Response to Angry Black Feminists," published by the sociologist Robert Staples in the journal's previous issue. In his essay, Staples argued against black women's involvement in the mainstream Feminist Movement, suggesting that racism and classism alone were the key oppressors of black men and women. He was particularly critical of the feminist and women-identified language of Ntozake Shange's play *For colored girls who have considered suicide/when the rainbow is enuf* (1976) and Michelle Wallace's *Black Macho and the Myth of the Superwoman* (1979). Using Shange and Wallace as examples, he maintained that the emergent and "angry" black feminists sought only to blame and denigrate black men for sexism in African America while not recognizing the ways in which black men, more than their female counterparts, were marginalized in the larger society.[6]

In a letter to readers, the editors of *The Black Scholar* prefaced the journal's black sexism debate with what they saw as the goals for publishing responses to Staples's essay. "We believe," the editors explained, "that the effort to clarify the nature of black male/female relationships is an important step in the process of re-uniting our people and revitalizing the struggle against oppression."[7] They suggested that the onus of shedding light on tensions between black women and men was on the black media, and not the white media, which, according to the editors, could not "be expected to permit any constructive change." In an attempt to spark "stimulating and enlightening dialogue," the editors took it upon themselves to solicit comments from leading artists and intellectuals of the era, as well as from the larger reading audience. With its black sexism debate, *The Black Scholar* attempted an in-depth exploration of interactions between black men and women but, in reality, exposed the simmering issues between black feminists and black men and women at the height of the Black Arts and Feminist Movements.[8]

*The Black Scholar* initiated the sexism debate with Audre Lorde's response to Staples's essay. Hers preceded those of other black artists and intellectuals, including M. Ron Karenga, Kalamu Ya Salaam, and the feminists June Jordan and Ntozake Shange. Lorde challenged Robert Staples on several accounts, exposing the limitations of his criticisms of black feminists in the mainstream Feminist Movement. She observed that black women had the right to speak as women, just as black men had the right to speak as men. She also suggested that the call to female coalition building was not a denial of black manhood but, instead, an affirmation of black womanhood. Although she recognized the plight of black men in America, Lorde noted that this recognition did not preclude the reality that black women suffered from abuse by black men because they were women. She contended that black women could not and would not remain silent even when understanding "structural underpinnings of sexism" perpetuated by black men.[9] "One oppression does not justify another," she concluded, as she challenged Robert Staples and others to critically consider the ways in which women's fights against oppression worked toward the common goal of creating a livable future for all marginalized peoples.[10]

*The Black Scholar*'s debate on sexism in the summer of 1979 was only one of many in which Audre Lorde participated throughout her career. However, the years between 1978 and 1983 were particularly challenging, as she wrestled with the promises and limitations of the Black Arts and Feminist Movements that dominated the liberation struggles of the 1970s. Audre Lorde was a second-generation Caribbean immigrant, born in New York in 1934. Her parents emigrated from Grenada and Barbados, and they, unlike their youngest daughter, seldom participated in the cultural and political formations of their host society. Lorde observed that her West Indian heritage often served as both "an asset and a liability" when she was growing up.[11] Her parents used it to protect Lorde from white American racism but also to deny their daughter's racial identity as it emerged in African America. Lorde resisted her parents' attempts to distance themselves and their children from American blacks. In *Zami,* she notes that she first became political when she was denied ice cream because of her race in the nation's capital, Washington, D.C.[12] It was a political identity that her immigrant parents never claimed for themselves, but one that ultimately informed Lorde's response to her life experiences as a black and lesbian woman in the United States.

By the age of eighteen, Lorde had grown accustomed to transgressing racial and sexual boundaries while participating in the feminist and black consciousness groups emerging in places like Greenwich Village and Harlem in New York City. Coming of age in postwar America, she left her parents' home to form alternative communities in the black leftist circles of Harlem and in the bohemian and "gay-girl" cultural spaces of Greenwich Village, where she, her friends, and her lovers forged bonds that supported their political views, lesbian identities, and women's issues. Although she felt that her participation in groups like the Harlem Writers' Guild was useful to her growing racial awareness, she believed that lesbian and women-identified women were the only people in the United States who crossed racial lines and made "any real attempt to communicate with each other" in the 1950s.[13] Lorde's involvement in lesbian and feminist communities reinforced a commitment to building bridges across racial lines as she became more involved in the black consciousness movements of the next two decades.

Feminists were organizing themselves politically as a marginalized group by the 1960s, building on the racial protests and radical politicization of college students of the era.[14] Young women's involvement in various organizations—from SNCC to the Student Democratic Society (SDS)—provided a space for them to build an indigenous leadership, even as they often were subjected to the chauvinism of their male counterparts. Several women active in the civil rights struggles and in the leftist movements became eager to deconstruct the inequality and exploitation they experienced both in organizations designed to challenge discriminatory practices and in American society as a whole. First as part of entities made up of both men and women and later as part of women-centered groups, they began to agitate for changes in the status quo and for opportunities equal to those of men.

This agitation among younger women was coupled with the concerns of maturing women in the professional sector. Annoyed by the Equal Employment Opportunity Commission's lack of true power to address the complaints of women and by the lack of support for the Equal Rights Amendment, various activists began working together to form the National Association of Women (NOW), in October 1966. Although this organization had several structural problems, including a limited capacity to build bridges between state chapters and the national office, NOW worked through several legal channels to accuse airlines and large corporations of sex discrimination and to lobby for the passing of several reforms to protect women's rights. One of NOW's most significant accomplishments was its members' tireless efforts to build a constituency that led to the passage in Congress of the Equal Rights Amendment in 1972.[15]

The Feminist Movement that Lorde participated in represented an uneasy mix of women's concerns ranging from sex roles in the public sphere to women's relationships to the impact of patriarchal systems on their personal lives. Radical feminism, with its emphasis on what the cultural critic Stewart Burns calls "alternative forms of intimacy," was often at odds with a feminism that promoted women's connections to the men in their lives and their families.[16] Lesbian feminism—although a source of power for Lorde and more than a few others—often became a point of contention in mainstream organizations that were not quite able to accept lesbian feminist politics as part of a universal platform for the liberation of all women. Further, mainstream feminism often glossed over the unique needs of women of color. The one thing that seemed to identify these various strands of feminism as a movement is that several had an undergirding interest in women's rights to empowerment and equal opportunity—although most advocates for women's rights had different understandings of what that meant.

Lorde's attempts to reconcile her racial, gender, and sexual identities within the Black Arts and Feminist Movements did not come without a cost. She became increasingly disappointed with the separatist ethos of the Black Power and Black Arts Movements, as well as with the unwillingness of black male leaders to openly deal with gender and sexual politics. Lorde also felt uncomfortable with white feminists who were reluctant to identify racial discrimination as part of the platform of the mainstream Feminist Movement. Lorde and an increasing number of women of color grew leery of the inability of white women to acknowledge the ways in which minority women's concerns were different from those of white women. Lorde explained in an interview with the black feminist Claudia Tate in 1983:

> When people of a group share an oppression, there are also certain strengths that they build together. But there are also certain vulnerabilities. For instance, talking about racism to the women's movement results in "Huh, don't bother us with that. Look, we're all sisters, please don't rock the boat." Talking to the black community about sexism results in pretty much the same thing. You get a "Wait, wait . . . wait a minute: we're all black together. Don't rock the boat."[17]

The political activities and fervor of the Black Arts and Feminist Movements became avenues for exploring the power of Lorde's black, feminist, and lesbian identities. But, they also became the vehicles through which Lorde challenged the silencing and othering of voices like hers that did not easily conform to the agenda of either movement.

By 1977, Lorde openly vocalized her concerns with the solipsisms of white feminists and masculinist Black Arts leaders. The black sexism debate in *The Black Scholar* in 1979 was part of a series of public debates and discussions in the late 1970s and early 1980s among black artists and white feminists in political coalitions and on conference circuits. Lorde turned to poetry, prose, and public speaking engagements as means of arguing for the changes she felt were necessary in liberation struggles. Although she saw herself primarily as a poet, she used her essays and speeches to help develop a political vision of how oppressed people were to overturn the hegemonies of Western and patriarchal cultures.

"For the master's tools will never dismantle the master's house," she warned a group of feminist women at the Second Sex conference held at New York University in 1979. She explained: "They may allow us temporarily to beat him at his own game, but they will never enable us to bring about genuine change. And this fact is only threatening to those women who still identify their master's house as their only source of support."[18] Lorde participated as a commentator on the "Personal and Political" panel at the Second Sex conference but found herself disappointed by conference planning that systematically excluded the voices of black women and black lesbians from panels on subjects ranging from feminist theory to existentialism. Lorde argued that the absence of black women at the conference revealed the glaring reality that white women were unwilling to confront their own racism, and thus they still relied on "the tools of a racist patriarchy . . . to examine the fruits of that same patriarchy."[19] In their celebration of feminism, white, middle-class women failed to consider the ways in which they denied the legitimacy of women who were different in racial, economic, and political ways. Lorde asserted that white women must not just tolerate difference but must make use of it to fight for the "joint survival" of white women and women of color.

Lorde responded to mainstream feminism in a similar fashion at the National Women's Studies Association conference held three years later, in 1982. In her keynote speech, she was candid about her frustration at the racism that permeated American society, but specifically the mainstream Feminist Movement. She told her audience:

> My response to racism is anger. I have lived with that anger, ignoring it, feeding upon it, learning to use it before it laid my visions to waste, for most of my life. Once I did it in silence, afraid of the weight. My fear of anger taught me nothing. Your fear of that anger will teach you nothing, also.[20]

Lorde then recalled the anger she had experienced as part of the Feminist Movement when white women ignored racial issues and failed to address the similar, yet unique concerns of black women. She suggested that part of white women's reluctance to engage in dialogue with black women grew out of fear—their inability to openly and honestly address internal racisms. Moreover, white women often felt unable to challenge racism, Lorde asserted, because they were afraid to do so in a public sphere. She argued that anger could be used as an "arsenal . . . against those oppressions, personal and institutional, which brought that anger into being."[21] She called upon white women to listen to the anger of black feminists but also to use their own anger to alter the ways in which they fought against oppressions of all kind.

Lorde's talks and discussions with white feminist groups suggested that white women's fear of black feminism echoed the fear expressed by black masculinist intellectuals such as Robert Staples in *The Black Scholar* in 1979. But if Lorde felt that white women ignored racial issues in the search for their own feminist power, she felt that black consciousness leaders often denied the voices of black women altogether. While mainstream feminists obfuscated the ways in which they silenced black women and other women of color, Black Arts intellectuals were often adamant about the subordinate and supportive role women should play in the black revolution in the United States. Audre Lorde may have battled white feminists in the 1970s, but it was a battle between friends and comrades attempting to resist the limitations of American society. Lorde's battles with Black Arts intellectuals, in contrast, were battles for her survival as a black woman, and specifically her survival as a woman who loved women.

Most mainstream feminists accepted Lorde's sexual identity as a component of her feminist politics. The Feminist Movement included many lesbians who often felt oppressed because of their gender and sexual orientation. Although battles in the early 1970s within groups such as NOW created fissures between heterosexual and lesbian feminists, by the late 1970s lesbians were more easily embraced as sisters and leaders in the Feminist Movement.[22] Some straight women experimented with lesbian sexuality, while others embraced a lesbian-feminist ideology as an alternative to engaging in sexual relations with men. As Lillian Faderman observes in *Odd Girls and Twilight Lovers,* lesbianism for some women was often seen as the ultimate form of resistance in the face of sexism and patriarchy.[23]

By contrast, leaders of the various black consciousness groups openly criticized black feminism and were even more critical of black lesbian feminists such as June Jordan, Barbara Smith, and Audre Lorde in the Black Arts Movement. In 1973, Stephen Henderson included Audre Lorde's work in *Understanding the New Black Poetry: Black Speech and Black Music as Poetic Reference,* a book that was part anthology and part theoretical manifesto for the black poetry emerging in the 1960s and early 1970s. His book engaged several other writings by artists and critics such as Larry Neal, Amiri Baraka, and Clarence Major, all of whom were trying to define a racialized voice for the Black Arts Movement.[24] Henderson anthologized Lorde's early poems "Naturally," "Coal," and "Father Son and Holy Ghost" in the third section of his book, entitled "The New Black Consciousness, The Same Difference." He observed that, as "a meticulous, skillful poet, her work should be better known."[25] Henderson's acceptance and endorsement of Lorde as part of the rank and file of new Black Arts poets predated the fury that her open affirmation of lesbianism caused among black writers, artists, and intellectuals.

In a 1979 interview with the white feminist Adrienne Rich, Lorde suggested that she had "come out" publicly as early as 1971 with her "Love Poem," published in *Ms.* magazine that year.[26] It was supposed to appear in the poetry volume *From a Land Where Other People Live,* published by Broadside Press in 1973, but a black male editor had rejected it. However, Sonia Sanchez, a poet of the Black Arts Movement, recalls that Lorde came out in black artistic circles around 1974.[27] Black women writers and activists like Sanchez were aware of Lorde's sexual orientation, but they wondered why she decided to claim it as a platform against oppression, especially since she was aware of the backlash it would cause within Black Arts political and social organizations.

Two issues were at hand in her interactions with Black Arts intellectuals, and they proved much more volatile than any of Lorde's critical dialogues in the Feminist Movement. First, Lorde was politically allied with a white community during the separatist era of black political consciousness. Leaders in the Black Arts Movement such as Ishmael Reed and Amiri Baraka saw black women's political alliances with white women as bourgeois and antithetical to the struggles of people of African descent. This particularly rang true for black men who considered black consciousness struggles, as Robert Staples observed in 1979, to be inextricably linked to fighting the oppression of blacks by white, classist societies.

The real problem lay in Lorde's lesbian identity, however. Some Black Arts intellectuals viewed her lesbianism, and the lesbian identities of other high-profile black women such as Gloria Hull, Barbara Smith, and June Jordan, as destructive to the cohesiveness of the alliances between black men and women needed for the success of racial liberation. Lorde's friend Sonia Sanchez noted, "The climate against her was a very real climate" by 1978.[28] As Lorde and others voiced their concerns over the sexism prevalent in African America and in the movement in particular, they were shunned by black men who felt that gay black women were traitors to the race. Barbara Smith and Audre Lorde collaborated with straight and lesbian women of color under the disdainful eye of black masculinist intellectuals to create Kitchen Table: Women of Color Press, which provided publishing opportunities for minority women.[29] Barbara Smith and Lorraine Bethel served as special editors for the Black Women's issue of *Conditions: Five* in the fall of 1979. That issue of the journal marked a milestone in the emergence of black feminist and lesbian criticism. With key developments in black lesbian publishing and self-organizing, Lorde's and others' lesbian-feminist politics became synonymous with a supposed attempt by black feminists to destroy the unity that the Black Arts Movement publicly espoused.

In May 1978, the battles between Lorde and black masculinist thinkers in the Black Arts Movement reached a climax. Lorde participated in the Fourth National Conference of Afro-American Writers, at Howard University, a conference characterized by its antifeminist tone. The *Washington Post* carried an article on the tensions between black feminists and black consciousness leaders at the conference in its Monday, May 8, edition. The journalist Hollie West noted that, although the theme of the conference was "The Impact of the '60s through the Prism of the Present," the focus seemed more on "sexual politics and the Afro-American writer."[30] Nathan Hare, a clinical psychologist, gave the keynote address, stating that "the bourgeois white women's movement was threatening unity between the black male and female."[31] Hare's was not the lone antifeminist voice at the conference. Despite the attempt by Barbara Smith to help others recognize the experiences of black lesbians and feminists, several conference attendees voiced their reservations about committing to a lesbian-feminist perspective. The psychiatrist Frances Welsing even dared to suggest, in response to Smith's talk, that "an endorsement of homosexuality mean[t] the death of the race."[32]

Lorde's reply to the conference came by way of an essay published in *The Black Scholar* in its seventh issue of 1978. She was not invited to speak at the Fourth National Conference of Afro-American writers but came to the conference flanked by a group of supportive women friends.[33] The essay, "Scratching the Surface: Some Notes on Barriers to Women and Loving," was explicit in its reference to the May event. Lorde did not mention her opponents by name in the essay, but she challenged the ideologies of the Black Arts Movement, which often denigrated women's attempts to "explore the possibilities of a feminist connection with non-Black women."[34] She began the article by defining the forms of "human blindness"—"racism," "sexism," "heterosexism," and "homophobia"—that had often marginalized her life. She insisted that these forms of human blindness sought only to deny the value of difference in people's lives.

One of Lorde's primary goals in the essay was to challenge the black literary and political communities' fears of women-identified politics as expressed at Howard University earlier that year. Women-identified politics, she argued, were necessary for black liberation. She suggested that black men could be liberated only when black women were, as well. She continued, making specific reference to the fear of lesbianism in the black artistic and intellectual community:

Today, the red herring of lesbian-baiting is being used in the Black community to obscure the true face of racism/sexism. Black women sharing close ties with each other, politically or emotionally, are not the enemies of Black men. Too frequently, however, some Black men attempt to rule by fear those Black women who are more ally than enemy.[35]

Although the essay engaged in conversation mostly with black men who were critical of her lesbian-feminist politics, Lorde did not leave any stone unturned. She also found time to directly challenge black heterosexual women who were fearful and critical of homosexuality and what it meant to the racial struggle. Specifically, she made reference to Welsing's comments at Howard:

At a recent Black literary conference, a heterosexual Black woman stated that to endorse lesbianism was to endorse the death of our race. This position reflects acute fright or a faulty reasoning, for once again it ascribes false power to difference. To the racist, Black people are so powerful that the presence of one can contaminate a whole lineage; to the heterosexist, lesbians are so powerful that the presence of one can contaminate the whole sex. This position supposes that if we do not eradicate lesbianism in the Black community, all Black women will become lesbians. It also supposes that lesbians do not have children. Both suppositions are patently false. As Black women, we must deal with all the realities of our lives which place us at risk as Black women—homosexual or heterosexual.[36]

The essay ended on a note similar to Barbara Smith's plea for sisterhood at the Fourth National Conference of Afro-American Writers. Lorde concluded with an appeal to black women, homosexual and heterosexual, that they not be divided by the schisms that masculinist leaders of the Black Arts Movement often created between them.

"Scratching the Surface" illuminated a key development in Lorde's political voice in the late 1970s. Although the essay was written primarily for a black and heterosexual audience in 1978, it illustrated an emergent theme of black lesbian consciousness obvious in most of Lorde's speeches and writings between 1977 and 1983. Not only was she more vocal about her lesbianism as a political identity after 1974, but she began to develop creative and political means to strategically use her black and lesbian identities to contest the boundaries of the mainstream Feminist and Black Arts Movements. Beginning with essays such as "Poetry Is Not a Luxury," published in *Chrysalis* magazine in 1977, Lorde emphasized the ways in which her supposedly marginalized subject-positions as black, woman, and lesbian proved to be sources of strength in her enunciation of the struggles of oppressed people in the United States and around the world. She posited, in speeches and essays such as "The Transformation of Silence into Language and Action" (1977), "An Open Letter to Mary Daly" (1979), and "Scratching the Surface," that her non-Western, nonheterosexist, and nonpatriarchal identities provided means of exploring alternatives to Western political and social hegemonies.[37]

Central to Lorde's emergent voice was a new emphasis on African women and religious god(desse)s, influenced by a visit she made with her children to West African countries, including Dahomey, in 1974. In "Scratching the Surface," within her critique of the antifeminist backlash in the Black Arts community, Lorde carefully pointed out that black women in Africa had historically built coalitions around female and women-identified issues. She observed, "Black women have always bonded together in support of each other, however uneasily and in the face of whatever allegiances which militated against that bonding. We have banded together with each other for wisdom and strength and support, even when it was only in relation to one man."[38] To convince her readers, she referred to the Amazons of ancient Dahomey, the documented co-wife marriages in the west coast of Africa, and the West African Market Women Association in contemporary African societies. She also made a particular reference to the traditional acceptance of same-sex relationships between women in African countries, where "routinely, the women involved are accepted members of the communities, evaluated not by their sexuality but by their respective places in the community."[39]

Lorde employed a similar strategy in *Essence* magazine in 1983, although this time her audience was made up primarily of black women. In the essay "Eye to Eye: Black Women, Hatred, and Anger," Lorde argued that black women must not let anger at oppression stop them from realizing the connections they must make with each other. Lorde lamented the fact that black women often "unleashed" their anger at other women, instead of channeling the anger in the right direction and working together to challenge oppressive structures in American society. Lorde reminded black women that they were "African women together" and thus linked to African women from the past and present who worked together to "care for each other."[40] Again, she pointed to the traditions of black women's nurturing in the African cultures of Dahomean, Benin, and Ashanti women. However, in this essay, she also created a continuum between historical African female figures and black women in the diaspora, such as Harriet Tubman in the United States and the maroon women of Brazil. She suggested that together these African and diasporic women illustrated the strength of black women and the possibilities of what could be accomplished if black women worked together as women.

The diligence with which Lorde employed figures of African women and African cultural traditions in essays such as "Scratching the Surface" and "Eye for an Eye" created ostensibly divergent, yet carefully linked conversations with the Black Arts and feminist communities. In Lorde's dialogues with black artists and intellectuals, tropes of Africa often responded to the heightened emphasis on Africa in the imaginative literature, art, and cultural politics of African Americans in the late 1960s and 1970s. As early as 1964, Malcolm X, the former leader of the Nation of Islam, after his historic trip to Ghana, was discussing the role that Africa played in the lives of African Americans.[41] Stokely Carmichael had by 1970 established a platform that identified connections African Americans should make to contemporary African struggles.[42] The Black Scholar, one of the leading journals for black intellectuals at the time, featured a series on pan-Africanism beginning in February 1971.[43] In fact, the journal published an article about apartheid and black women the same year that it featured the black sexism debate that included Staples, Lorde, and others.[44] The following year, in April, the entire journal was dedicated to the "new societies" of Africa. By the late 1970s, most African Americans in intellectual circles were attempting to embrace the struggles of black Africans through a pan-African ideology, especially as apartheid became the dominant form of oppression in the southern region of the continent.

During this time, the emphasis on pan-Africanism had gained growing currency among blacks in newly decolonized African countries, in the United States, and in parts of the Caribbean. The successful move of Ghana toward independence in 1958, followed by the granting of independence to several other African countries, provided inspiration to blacks in the Western Hemisphere who understood that the success of their civil rights struggles was linked to black Africans' attempts at nation building. As black nation-states emerged, African leaders themselves made impressive, although often thwarted, efforts to build strategic alliances with each other. Ghana hosted the first Conference on Independent States in 1958, which was followed by a second conference, in Addis Adaba, in 1960. The goal was to provide support to the liberation movements of African societies still under white-minority colonial rule. Those convened also aimed to create common policies across independent states to strengthen the individual social, political, and economic stabilities of the decolonized countries.[45]

The African bloc at the United Nations in the years between roughly 1958 and 1960 represented another potential force for the creation of well-coordinated alliances between black African leaders on the world stage. African leaders were part of regular meetings at the United Nations and often tried to work through key issues that would impact the collective future development of independent African states. The Organization of African Unity (OAU), established in 1963, was another platform for concerted efforts to build and promote pan-Africanism. The OAU, first under the tutelage of Ghana's president, Kwame Nkrumah, attempted to strengthen solidarity between the independent member states, while taking positions in the international community on colonialism, civil rights, and South African apartheid.[46]

Pan-Africanism was traditionally considered a construct of West Indians and African Americans such as W. E. B. Du Bois, Marcus Garvey, and "back to Africa" activists in the early years of the twentieth century, but it began to take on a new meaning when enlivened by the post–World War II liberation struggles and unifying efforts of Africans on the continent. In the United States especially, African Americans urged black African leaders to engage in dialogue about their common struggles, and many formed structured and informal alliances with African liberation organizations. Several blacks from the United States, including Bob Moses, James Foreman, Malcolm X, and James Garrett, traveled to Africa for OAU meetings and various international conferences and encouraged African leaders to attend U.S. forums and discussions on pan-Africanism and black self-sufficiency. Notably, African leaders took the support of blacks in the United States seriously. Not only did they travel to converse with their African American comrades in the struggle, but also they solicited the support of African Americans to put pressure on an international community to police the injustices that still occurred in parts of Africa, particularly those under white-minority rule.[47] As apartheid became an ever-pressing issue in South Africa, African Americans became even more emphatic about their understandings of Africa's liberation as part of their own.

Lorde's reflections on Africa attempted to engage the Afrocentricity of African America, while locating and affirming lesbian and women-centered consciousnesses through the historicity of African cultural practices and formations. According to Sonia Sanchez, most of the controversy of Lorde's homosexuality in the 1970s had to do with "what this meant in our movement toward Africa,"[48] since leaders in the Black Arts Movement often considered homosexuality a bourgeois proclivity and a "corruption of the western world."[49] By highlighting strong, feminist figures in Africa, as well as the existence of "sexual contact between members of the same sex"[50] in African communities, Lorde took the opportunity not only to affirm her black and lesbian identities but also to provide a historical and non-Western precedent for homosexuality. Lorde strategically maintained that she was preserving vital aspects of African culture in the Americas by embracing the women-identified politics of African women whom she used as sources of empowerment.

The "movement toward Africa" in the Black Arts Movement also coincided with a focus on ancient female power and women's spirituality in the Feminist Movement. In her poetry collection *The Black Unicorn* (1978) and in essays such as "Poetry Is Not a Luxury," Lorde began to make specific references to African god(dess) figures as ancient sources of power through which women could distance themselves from Western and patriarchal cultures. White feminists such as Mary Daly and Merlin Stone were making similar moves in their feminist scholarship, with the hope of advocating women's liberation outside the masculinist structures of American society. In *Beyond God the Father* (1973), Mary Daly challenged the patriarchal base of the Christian church. The feminist Merlin Stone, in *When God Was a Woman* (1976), examined the development of the female goddess in Neolithic and Paleolithic times. In its sixth issue in 1978, *Chrysalis: A Magazine of Women's Culture,* a leading feminist journal, featured "The Politics of Women's Spirituality" and a twenty-four-page catalog of women's writings on the subject.[51]

Lorde's use of African women and god(dess) figures in her essays, speeches, and poetry provided personal affirmation as a second-generation immigrant and black lesbian, as well as a way to underscore the importance of alternative visions to sexist, racist, and patriarchal societies. In response to the homophobia of the Black Arts Movement and the racism of the Feminist Movement, Lorde constructed African, female, and lesbian spaces to affirm her black lesbian identity. This construct further allowed Lorde to reclaim a racial self seemingly denied by the limits of her parents' understandings of Caribbean heritage. African and women-identified women provided the means through which she legitimated the specificity of her struggles and confirmed her right to have a voice as a black woman and a lesbian. Yet, Lorde's imaginings of Africa as she spoke to feminist and Black Arts audiences also conveyed the ways in which she put forth new tools to "dismantle the master's house," as she suggested at the Second Sex conference in 1979. If the "master's tools" could not be used, Lorde proposed that tropes of both Africa and black feminist poetics provided new paradigms that opposed the oppressions of sexist, racist, Western, and patriarchal frameworks.

## The Black Unicorn: Introducing the African God(dess)

"The woman's place of power within each of us," Lorde explained in "Poetry Is Not a Luxury," "is neither white nor surface; it is dark, it is ancient, and it is deep."[52] Writing in *Chrysalis* in 1977, Lorde emphasized the importance of poetry in the lives of women, arguing that poetry was not a "luxury" but rather a "vital necessity of our existence." She observed:

[Poetry] forms the quality of the light within which we predicate our hopes and dreams toward survival and change, first made into language, then into idea, then into more tangible action. Poetry is the way we help give name to the nameless so it can be thought. The farthest horizons of our hopes and fears are cobbled by our poems, carved from the rock experiences of our daily lives.[53]

According to Lorde, poems were ways of demanding self-exploration and actuation. They both "formulate[d] the implications of ourselves" and "what we dare[d] to make real."[54] In "Poetry Is Not a Luxury," Lorde located the poetic voice—the "revelatory distillation of experience,"[55] as she termed it—within a woman's ability to "come more into touch with our own ancient, non-[E]uropean consciousness of living."[56] Challenging the precepts of the "white fathers" who have historically told women "I think, therefore I am," Lorde posited that women's power comes from "[t]he Black mother within each of us—the poet—[who] whispers in our dreams: I feel, therefore I can be free."[57]

In "Poetry Is Not a Luxury," Lorde linked the act of writing poetry to the equally important act of tapping into a non-Western and uniquely female power. Lorde identified poetry as the primary vehicle through which she and other women could radically change Western society. At the moment of writing "Poetry Is Not a Luxury," Lorde was finishing *The Black Unicorn,* a collection she had started as early as 1974. Lorde's poems in *The Black Unicorn* impart the ways in which poems, for Lorde, afford a language to challenge and then transform oppressions faced by women and other marginalized people. In this section, I offer a close reading of *The Black Unicorn* to highlight the ways in which Lorde employed imaginative poetic forms and tropes of Africa to politically engage the Black Arts and Feminist Movements. Poetry, in a non-European and strategically feminist framework, offered a lifeline through which Lorde sought to establish personal and collective voices.

The 1977 essay "Poetry Is Not a Luxury" staged the site for *The Black Unicorn,* in which Lorde engages the ancestral and spiritual powers of poetry with a focus on her African and feminist heritages. "The Black mother within each of us" and the woman's poetic voice coalesce to enact a journey toward self-discovery for Lorde and for her readers who dare to seek a "chaos which is Black[,] which is creative[,] which is female[,] which is dark."[58] Explaining her emphasis on the "black mother poet," in a 1979 interview, she further commented, "I'm not saying that women don't think or analyze. Or that white does not feel. I'm saying that we must never close our eyes to the terror."[59] Unifying poetry and voice, darkness and creativity, Lorde envisioned the black mother poet as the tap root that launched her emerging gender, racial, and political awarenesses.

In *The Black Unicorn,* the black mother poet appears as both the African god(dess) and the autobiographical first person. Providing alternatives to Western, heterosexual, and patriarchal social formations, the African god(dess) connects the poet's experiences to an ancient source of power, establishing a voice through which Lorde, as the poet, evolves to demand a language of her own. Black women warriors and Orisha figures are conjured and called upon in *The Black Unicorn* to help Lorde assert her own liberation. The mythological and African arcs of the volume create a fluid relationship that links poetic voice, Lorde's autobiographical "I," and black women, past and present, real and immortal.

The first section of the volume, featuring poems such as "Dahomey," "125th Street and Abomey," "From the House of Yemanjá," and "Coniagui Women," discloses the matrilineal grounds on which Lorde discovers and envisions her poetic self. In the poem "Dahomey," the poetic persona first describes her connection to an African past and then assumes the voice of African foremothers:

> It was in Abomey that I felt
> the full blood of my fathers' wars
> and where I found my mother
> Seboulisa[60]

Africa here is both the present-day Africa of Dahomey, as the poem's title suggests, and the ancestral Africa of Abomey, the ancient African kingdom where arts and culture flourished. The juxtaposition of Dahomey and Abomey creates a continuum between past and present in the poem that later serves Lorde's desire to discover a new voice by recuperating an ancestral black lineage. A spiritual return to an African mythicism becomes possible mostly through the welcoming arms of Seboulisa, the god(dess) of Abomey, who is "standing with outstretched / palms hip high / one breast eaten away by worms of sorrow / magic stones resting upon her fingers / dry as a cough."[61] Seboulisa, seemingly marred by her one-breasted body, exudes black female strength. Although one-breasted, she is not resigned but, instead, offers her power with her "magic stones" to those in need of spiritual renewal.

In "Dahomey," Seboulisa becomes one with the everyday women of Abomey, who are living incarnations of her power to resist oppression:

> In the dooryard of the brass workers
> four women joined together dying cloth
> mock Eshu's iron quiver
> standing erect and flamingly familiar
> in their dooryard[62]

The poetic persona gains strength from the god(dess) Seboulisa but also from the real-life female manifestations of Seboulisa found in the "dooryard" of the African topography. Lorde manipulates language through a poetic form that positions these women as "erect," phallic, and deceptively masculine symbols. Thus, she creatively locates the politics of women bonding in opposition to those who challenge their collective force. By the third stanza of the poem, the black mother poet is no longer an observer of the strength of Seboulisa and the other African women; instead, she, too, takes on their power: "bearing two drums on my head I speak / whatever language is needed / to sharpen the knives of my tongue."[63] Lorde suggests that the African mythology and foremothers offer a poetic voice—"whatever language is needed"—so that female power can emerge.

In "125th Street and Abomey," Lorde transports Seboulisa's "magic stones" to African America, linking black women from ancient Abomey and Harlem. Seboulisa is the black female spirit who can recall "old victories" that prove useful to the black mother poet in contemporary times:

> I surrender to you as libation
> mother, illuminate my offering
> of old victories
> over men over women over my selves
> who has never before dared
> to whistle into the night[64]

Seboulisa recalls past struggles with the poet's enemies and provides a historical memory for overcoming new trepidations. Seboulisa possesses the power to remind the poet of her past strength, affording courage in the face of new challenges:

> Take my fear of being alone
> like my warrior sisters
> who rode in defense of your queendom
> disguised and apart
> give me the woman strength
> of tongue in this cold season[65]

The poet identifies herself as one with the ancient warriors of Abomey, who, because of Seboulisa, relinquished their fears to assert their strength. Lorde suggests that in the "cold season," where the enemies of "men," "women," and "selves" abound, Seboulisa gives the "most precious"[66] gift of voice. The poet finally establishes her connection to Seboulisa, revealing to Seboulisa that she is her "severed daughter."[67] But, she is the daughter that "all the world shall remember"[68] because she speaks out, resists fears of voicelessness, and demands to be heard.

Appearing at the height of Lorde's conversations with white feminists and Black Arts intellectuals, the poetry of The Black Unicorn explores Lorde's particular feminist concerns with the discourses of U.S. liberation struggles. Lorde's decision to use African god(desse)s maintained her feminist voice, as it imparted the uniqueness of her experiences as a searching second-generation immigrant and person of African descent in the United States. Yet, too, her focus on African god(desse)s attempted to counter the invisibility of black women in both the Feminist and the Black Arts Movements by demanding their centrality in the poetic realm of The Black Unicorn. Lorde sought to reclaim affirming spaces for black diasporic women through the ancient resources of African women, who, in the first section of The Black Unicorn, anticipate the poetic voice's movement toward racial, cultural, and sexual freedoms in a diasporic context.

The androgynous configuration of Lorde's African god(desse)s, such as Seboulisa and Eshu in "Dahomey" and "125th Street and Abomey," raised the stakes of Lorde's discursive enterprise in her poetry collection.

In *The Black Unicorn,* Lorde asserts the significance of women-bonding, without denying the voices of ancestral women and men in her search for power. The trajectory of the collection progresses to establish Lorde's personal strength, while the gender ambiguity of African figures within the structure of the poems work through and against the limitations of hierarchical social formations. In *The Black Unicorn,* Lorde describes the one-breasted Seboulisa as a "local representation of Mawulisa," who is the "Dahomean female-male, sky-goddess-god principle."[69] Eshu is the "mischievous messenger" whose part in religious rituals is "danced by a woman with an attached phallus."[70] Lorde employs these and other warrior figures to situate alternative means of viewing the world within a non-European and nonpatriarchal framework.

As a supporter of the mainstream Feminist Movement, Lorde criticized the "either/or"[71] paradigm that dominated the language of white feminist politics. She felt that the pervasiveness of "patriarchal thinkers" within the movement undermined any true attempts to challenge the social stratifications of American society. In essays and speeches such as "Poetry Is Not a Luxury"(1977), "Age, Race, Class, and Sex: Women Defining Difference" (1980), and "The Uses of Anger: Women Responding to Racism" (1981), she dealt with racism especially, arguing that racism was a misguided engagement of difference through which white women perpetuated Western patriarchy and thus, in an attempt to access their female power, denied Lorde her own.[72]

In a talk given at Amherst College, in 1980, she explained:

> White women face the pitfall of being seduced into joining the oppressor under the pretense of sharing power. This possibility does not exist in the same way for women of [c]olor. The tokenism that is sometimes extended to us is not an invitation to join power; our racial "otherness" is a visible reality that makes this quite clear. For white women there is a wider range of pretended choices and rewards for identifying with patriarchal power and its tools.[73]

It was in the previous year, at the Second Sex conference, that she had warned that "the master's tools will never dismantle the master's house."[74] *The Black Unicorn* underscored the importance of using new tools, namely imaginings of Africa, to "dismantle the master's house" of

Western cultures. The collection's ambiguously gendered African women served as metaphors for a non-European and nonmisogynist duality that Lorde called upon throughout her poems to deny the existing cultural, racial, and sexual hegemonies. As a theoretical manifesto, *The Black Unicorn* established a means of attaining female power, while protecting and celebrating the multiplicity of the reader's own experiences as Other—even to Audre Lorde. Within the poems, black god(desse)s stage the struggles and tribulations of Lorde as black woman, as they provide a new frame of reference—the black mother poet—through which she and others can locate themselves outside essentialist constructions of race and gender. African mythology conduces a more egalitarian and open search for cultural, spiritual, and personal affirmation.

Lorde's attempts at positioning Africa as a site of duality parallel the use of Africa as a homoerotic utopia. This engagement of Africa had particular implications for her involvement in the Black Arts Movement. As the black mother poet of *The Black Unicorn,* Lorde learns the secrets of homosexual desire through Africa, where, in "Walking Our Boundaries," "our voices / seem too loud for this small yard / too tentative for women / so in love."[75] The sexual ambiguity of Orisha helps Lorde maintain and establish a lesbian-centered politics, one denied by the emergent resistance to homosexuality in the black cultural nationalism of the 1970s.

In *The Black Unicorn,* Lorde stages her battles with black cultural nationalism front and center not only by locating empowered women—the Coniagui foremothers, the Fon of Dahomey, Amazons, and other warriors —in Africa but by locating homosexuality in an African past and present. Lorde combines the ambiguity of African mythology with historical references to women-bonding in order to position lesbianism in West African cultural practices. Thus, Lorde maintains that lesbianism is not antithetical to Africa—a "corruption of the Western world" or the "death of the race," as many in the Black Arts Movement believed—but is central to the development of African religious and social traditions.

Lorde includes a "Glossary of African Names Used in the Poems," which heightens the connections she makes between historical women-bonding in Africa and her black lesbian and feminist politics. The glossary narrativizes Lorde's fascination with African god(desse)s and warriors who are women-oriented, angry, and divine. It also provides a guide to African religious figures that she attempted to document in her conversations with white feminists and black artists and intellectuals. Thus, Seboulisa is not just the "mother" with "one breast eaten away by worms of sorrow," as she is in "Dahomey" and later in "125th Street and Abomey." Rather, as the glossary informs the reader, she also becomes one with Mawulisa, who is featured in "Meet." The poem "Meet" proposes that Mawulisa, as a male-female god(dess), paves the way for the black lesbian feminist poet to enjoy the "solstice" of homoerotic love:

> Woman when we met on the solstice
> high over halfway between your world and mine
> rimmed with full moon and no more excuses
> your red hair burned my fingers as I spread you
> tasting your rough down to sweetness[76]

The glossary situates Mawulisa's historic presence in Dahomean and Yoruban culture. It also affords Lorde's strategic and poetic use of Mawulisa's power to celebrate her love for women. In "Meet," the poetic voice attests to the strength she gains from Mawulisa's presence: "Mawulisa foretells our bodies / as our hands touch and learn / from each others hurts."[77] However, now, Mawulisa sits in the shadows of the poetic frame, as Lorde's own agency through women-loving gains momentum.

Poems such as "Meet" echo the shift in tone that the collection *The Black Unicorn* eventually undergoes. Lorde once remarked, "The poems in *The Black Unicorn* have always felt to me like a conversation between myself and an ancestor Audre. The sequence began in Dahomey when I visited the country with my children in 1974, and continued for the next three years."[78] Lorde's conversation commenced with a recovering of ancestral figures but then continued by identifying the role these figures played in her life. Indeed, the sequence of poems maps the power Lorde commands, if even through a symbiotic relationship with African god(desse)s, in the "conversation between [her]self and an ancestor Audre" that is taking place. By the second part of the volume, the ancestors to whom she pays homage give way to the emergence of Lorde as prophetic voice.

With "Harriet," which begins the second section, *The Black Unicorn* migrates textually from a focus on ancient and present-day African communities to the ways in which African warrior women are reincarnated in the New World spaces Lorde occupies. The gender(ed) slipperiness of the black ancestral figures in part one provides the ground on which Lorde's own linguistic authority as women-oriented woman evolves. "Harriet," for instance, reflects on the pains of the journey toward black womanhood:

> Harriet there was always somebody calling us crazy
> or mean or stuck-up or evil or black
> or black
> and we were
> nappy girls quick as cuttlefish
> scurrying for cover
> trying to speak trying to speak
> trying to speak
> the pain in each others' mouths[79]

The ambiguity of the self-referential "I" that permeates poems such as "A Woman Speaks" and "From the House of Yemanjá" in the first section is dismantled here in "Harriet."[80] The authorial voice does not play on the relationship between the black poet Lorde and the African god(dess). The pain is real and particular to the mortality of the contemporary black woman. The poem's authorial voice emerges as distinct, even separate from the voice of Seboulisa, the dominant African god(dess) figure in the first section.

"Harriet" introduces the presence of Lorde as the poetic "I," as the black lesbian warrior voice taking center stage: "I remember you Harriet / before we were broken apart / we dreamed the crossed swords / of warrior queens."[81] What was left unspoken by "keeping our distance / in silence / averting our eyes" in the days of youth is now given agency through the act of writing itself. The poetic "I" asks her sister-friend Harriet: "Harriet Harriet / what name shall we call our selves now / our mother is gone?"[82] Yet, the last three lines frame both a question and a proposition for self-naming. The disappearance of the black mother poet —Seboulisa, Mawulisa, and the Coniagui women—reveals a symbolic transfer of power. The metaphoric loss of a mother allows for the daughter's voice to speak and articulate an empowered self.

It is not surprising that "Harriet" and poems such as "Sequelae" and "The Litany for Survival" were first written as journal entries, which hold Lorde's "feelings that sometimes have no place, no beginning, no end."[83] As part of Lorde's "conversation" with an ancestral self, these poems reflect the black mother's desire for women to "feel [and] therefore . . . be free," as Lorde contended in "Poetry Is Not a Luxury." Lorde confided to Claudia Tate:

> I went through a period once when I felt like I was dying. I wasn't writing any poetry, and I felt that if I couldn't write I would split. I was recording in my journal, but no poems came. I know now that this period was a transition in my life. The next year, I went back to my journal, and here were these incredible poems that I could almost lift out of it.[84]

As journal entries, the poems reflect the intensity of her growing engagement with Africa, an idealized site of empowerment that she experienced during her visit to West African countries. The transitional period in which the poems were conceived was fraught with the tensions of her dialogues with white feminists and black artists and intellectuals. The urgency of the poems, then, suggests the discursive space of freedom that Lorde sought through employing tropes of Africa. Representations of Africa became sources for working through her feelings, and even through pain, so that poetry initiated a new platform for radical change. By merging a black feminist poetics with her politics as a black and lesbian woman, Lorde pushed and even contested the boundaries of the Feminist and Black Arts Movements.

Ultimately, in poems such as "Litany for Survival," Lorde locates the ways in which her imaginings of Africa can be used in the lives of others, as well. In this way, Lorde's Africa is very different from Marshall's Africa in *Praisesong for the Widow*. Tropes of Africa from *The Black Unicorn* map Lorde's own self-creation, but also the existence of alternative cultural and social formations to which all marginalized people in Western and Western-influenced cultures can turn. In "Litany for Survival," Lorde finally becomes the empowered descendant of African god(desse)s, a descendant who hopes to offer her wisdom to others:

For those of us
who were imprinted with fear
like a faint line in the center of our foreheads
learning to be afraid with our mother's milk
for by this weapon
this illusion of some safety to be found
the heavy-footed hoped to silence us
For all of us
the instant and this triumph
We were never meant to survive[85]

As a poet, Lorde claims that survival comes from voice. Silence is the enemy that denies self-actuation. Language through poetry enacts the "litany" for self-transformation. In "Transformation of Silence into Language and Action," a speech written the same year as "Litany for Survival," Lorde added:

My silences had not protected me. Your silence will not protect you. But for every real word spoken, for every attempt I had ever made to speak those truths for which I am still seeking, I had made contact with other women while we examined the words to fit a world in which we all believed, bridging our differences.[86]

In this speech, given at the Modern Language Association conference in 1977, Lorde observed that survival was dependent on the courage to claim a language and a poetic voice that renders one visible. Through the milk of the "black mother poet," Lorde and others who were "imprinted with fear" and unable to act could utilize imaginings of Africa to demand their own survivals.

However, I want to distance myself from literary critics such as Claudine Raynaud and AnaLouise Keating, who too hastily celebrate Lorde's use of the black god(dess) and warrior figures as illustrative of the ways in which she dismantled Western hierarchical structures and asserted her agency as a black lesbian.[87] Although Lorde introduced the necessity of nonpatriarchal and nonsexist paradigms by infusing her poetry with black female power, she also ran the risk of privileging one hierarchical voice over the other. This problematic practice can be evidenced by her efforts to capitalize "black" in her essays, arguably beginning around 1977, as she simultaneously began to decapitalize "america," "white," and "european."[88] This inversion suggests that her representations of black and female identities were dependent on her negation, if even through language, of European and male social systems.

Further, her use of particular African figures failed to engage the problematic relationship that some of these figures had in struggles against oppression in Africa. This case could be made for Marshall's use of Africa, as well. Lorde's examples of black female power often came from historically powerful nations in Africa, nations well known for their participation in what some consider the most horrible event in African continental history: the Atlantic slave trade.[89] No doubt, her use of Africa was an American imaginative construction, one fueled by the identity politics of Lorde, Marshall, and other blacks in the Americas at the height of the black consciousness movements in the Western hemisphere. As a product of the Black Arts and Feminist Movements in the United States, the structural paradigm of *The Black Unicorn* deconstructed the existing paradigms that gave value to whiteness and maleness; however, it replaced those by privileging a black female power that proved detrimental to oppressed peoples in African societies. Lorde gained her voice from cultures—if even in non-Western articulations—that were grounded in some of the same hierarchical structures that she attempted to dismantle in her work.[90]

Yet, contemporary feminist, black, and gay communities find Lorde's work useful because Lorde imagined tropes of Africa that used black and female specificity to make Africa a spiritual and psychological tap root available to all. In 1977, for example, Lorde wrote that Africa was the site where white women could find their "ancient" and thus alternative source of power in the contemporary moment.[91] In *The Black Scholar,* in 1978, she maintained that Africa stood as the place where African Americans learned to resist the temptation of replacing Western patriarchy with a new kind of patriarchy invented in the colonial and postcolonial world.[92] Five years later, in *Essence* magazine, Lorde presented Africa as the land to which black women turned to remember the ways in which they had historically nurtured and supported one another.[93]

Perhaps the best example of the ways in which Lorde used Africa as a liberating site for diverse communities can be found in "An Open Letter to Mary Daly," published by Lorde in *Top Ranking: A Collection of Articles on Racism & Classism in the Lesbian Community* (1980).[94] The letter was a response to Mary Daly's *Gyn/Ecology: The Metaethics of Radical Feminism,* which Daly had sent to Lorde in the spring of 1979. Written on May 6, 1979, Lorde's letter to Daly voiced her displeasure with the absence of black god(dess) figures in Daly's book, while questioning Daly's celebration of European goddesses at the expense of black spiritual figures. Lorde initially wrote the letter to Daly, but, without receiving a reply, she opened it to the feminist community.[95]

By opening her letter to a feminist audience, Lorde announced the racism in the Feminist Movement and pointed to the importance of African female power in women's attempts to reclaim, in Daly's words, "the mystery of her own history, and [to] find how it is interwoven with the lives of other women."[96] Daly's *Gyn/Ecology* attempted to trace women's power through an analysis of myth and ritual. The study spanned the ancient cultures of European mythic women and the rituals of the Third World, as well as the religions of American women before the twentieth century. Although Lorde applauded Daly for the timeliness of her study, she criticized Daly for obscuring the strength of black women, and only "dealing with noneuropean [*sic*] women . . . as victims and preyers-upon each other."[97] Lorde was particularly critical of Daly's decision to focus on African genital mutilation to the exclusion of other, empowering cultural practices by African and other non-European women.

The absence of African god(dess) and warrior figures in Daly's study of spiritual power cut to the heart of the unspoken racisms in white feminist culture. Lorde reminded Daly and her feminist audience that white racism must be dealt with through an open dialogue among women:

> I began to feel my history and my mythic background distorted by the absence of any images of my foremothers in power. . . . To dismiss our Black foremothers may well be to dismiss where [E]uropean women learned to love. As an African-[A]merican woman in white patriarchy, I am used to having my archetypal experience distorted and trivialized, but it is terribly painful to feel it being done by a woman whose knowledge so touches my own. . . . What you excluded from *Gyn/Ecology* dismissed my heritage and the heritage of all other noneuropean [*sic*] women, and denied the real connections that exist between all of us.[98]

Lorde strategically employed African goddess figures in the letter to solidify the importance of "the real connections that exist between all of us" in her open conversation with a feminist community. She called upon African figures from *The Black Unicorn*—Oyo, Mawulisa, and the Dahomean Amazons—to construct a language through which she and other women could learn to avoid the silent racisms that she felt informed Daly's study. Lorde contrasted African genital mutilation with the existence of strong and supportive networks of African women and the nonsexist framework suggested by the androgynous African god(dess) figures. By referencing historical and mythical black women, she thus suggested the transformative power all women gained from learning about ancestral women of European *and* non-European cultures. As with *The Black Unicorn,* tropes of Africa provided a particular site of liberation, standing as signposts for the necessity of working through racisms and sexisms to ultimately build bridges across racial and sexual boundaries.

The recognition of African female power was liberating for Lorde, and also for others who read her letter to Daly. The letter forced a dialogue in feminist circles, and many feminists responded to the letter in various journals across the country.[99] The feminist community's response to Lorde's open letter helped realize what Lorde had earlier surmised as "The Transformation of Silence into Language and Action" at the Modern Language Association conference in 1977. Lorde first met Daly at that conference, and she saw her letter to Daly in 1979 as an attempt to "break a silence which I had imposed upon myself shortly before that date."[100] Lorde had previously made the decision to avoid talking to white women about racism. However, she soon became "aware of [her] mortality"[101] after one of many cancer scares, and she felt self-conscious about the many silences she had never taken the time to break. At the 1977 conference, she decided that she could no longer keep silent but had to speak and act on the knowledges that she knew "beyond understanding."[102] Her letter to Mary Daly was an act of breaking her silence in the Feminist Movement.

Lorde signed her open letter to Mary Daly "in the hands of Afrekete," again foregrounding the power she placed in recovering a black mythic source for all women. That feminists such as Merlin Stone, author of *When God Was a Woman* (1976), and Judy Grahn, author of *Another*

*Mother Tongue* (1984), later asked Lorde about Afrekete and the other goddesses she mentioned in her letter to Daly suggests the social and political influence that Lorde's revisionist enterprise had in the feminist community.[103] Bringing Afrekete and other god(desse)s to a mainstream white feminist audience transformed Lorde's earlier "silences" into a "language" and, therefore, an "action" that opened dialogue across racial boundaries and helped women further recognize one another. According to Angela Bowen, Lorde responded to Merlin Stone's request for more information by referring her to the glossary of *The Black Unicorn*. She also responded with an affirmation of Afrekete, who, as Lorde told Stone, "is wise and wilful [*sic*] and not to be messed with. . . . Check her out. I am her daughter."[104]

## Africa and the Caribbean in Zami

Absent from the matrix of black god(desse)s in *The Black Unicorn*, Afrekete figures prominently in Lorde's "biomythography," *Zami: A New Spelling of My Name*. *Zami*, Lorde noted, made use of a new literary form, crossing the borders of "the elements of biography and history of myth."[105] First published in 1982, *Zami* was Lorde's attempt at auto-writing—her poetic way of re-creating and envisioning herself through a retrospective look at the past. As "fiction . . . built from many sources,"[106] *Zami* disrupts linear constructs of time, carefully engaging episodic moments with women to craft a feminist community through which Lorde experiences her power.

Who is Afrekete? In *Zami*, Lorde describes her as "her [Mawulisa's] youngest daughter, the mischievous linguist, trickster, best-beloved, whom we must all become."[107] Afrekete replaces Mawulisa's son Eshu/Legba of *The Black Unicorn* in Lorde's poetic consciousness and becomes the preeminent figure that explains, embodies, and finally transforms Lorde's black lesbian identity. In *The Black Unicorn*, Eshu is thought of as the sexually ambiguous figure, yet simultaneously as one who is "identified with the masculine principle."[108] By contrast, Afrekete asserts the particularities of a feminist power gained through women. As a female deity, yet also an ambiguously gendered figure,

Afrekete further constructs the strength found in women-oriented communities and the role women play as nurturers to each other.

In *The Signifying Monkey,* the literary critic Henry Louis Gates, Jr., describes the role of Es(h)u, the masculine counterpart of Afrekete. As one of the gods who survived the Middle Passage to find a home in the Caribbean, South America, and parts of the United States, Es(h)u remains the god of "unreconciled opposites, living in harmony." He is also the god of discourse, who becomes the interpreter and mediator of life. Gates observes:

> Esu is the sum of the parts, as well as that which connects to parts. He is invoked and sacrificed to first, before any other deity, because of this: "He alone can set an action in motion and interconnect the parts." This aspect of Esu cannot be emphasized too much. The most fundamental absolute of the Yoruba is that there exist, simultaneously, three stages of existence: the past, the present, and the unborn. Esu represents these stages, and makes their simultaneous existence possible, "without any contradiction," precisely because he is the principle of discourse both as messenger and as the god of communication.[109]

Gates's consideration of Es(h)u provides a map for understanding Lorde's emphasis on Afrekete in her biomythography. The primacy Lorde affords Afrekete in *Zami* seeks to re-imagine Lorde's past, reveal her present, and demand a possibility for her future as a woman who encourages bonds between women. Lorde's focus on Afrekete pivots around Afrekete's devices as "interlocutor," one who lives, breathes, explores, and defines multiplicities "without any contradiction." Lorde enacts Afrekete to imagine a self that is the living version of the god(dess): the black woman who connects and empowers multiple and seemingly irreconcilable communities.

In the remainder of this chapter, I address the ways in which Afrekete's presence in *Zami* works in relation to the appearances of African god(dess) and warrior figures in *The Black Unicorn*. As the aboriginal symbol of Yoruban religious traditions, Afrekete is the ancient black mother poet who legitimates Lorde's homoerotic desires for other women. By challenging the boundaries of the real and the mythical, her presence as both god(dess) and lover exposes and celebrates Lorde's sexual intimacy with women, legitimating the strength and sustenance Lorde gains from her erotic and homosexual utterances.

However, Afrekete also plays the role of the African mythical figure who is able to help Lorde make connections to and to build coalitions with racial, gender, sexual, and class Others. Most literary and feminist critics such as Claudine Raynaud (1988), Chinosole (1990), Jeanne Perrault (1995), and AnaLouise Keating (1996) identify *Zami* solely as a feminist and women-centered text.[110] I posit that the specificity of Lorde's feminist enterprise in *Zami* does not preclude the political goal of engaging multiple audiences through a dialogue of difference, which undergirds the use of Afrekete as the imaginative character who, in Henry Louis Gates, Jr.'s words, can "interconnect the parts." Further, Afrekete, as a literary device in particular, is strategically situated to reconcile Lorde's relationship with a Caribbean (mother) culture. In *Zami,* Lorde works through African diasporic and feminist spaces of West Africa and the Caribbean—that is, non-European and nonpatriarchal paradigms—to represent alternative modes of self and community, while creating a language through which she can still maintain dialogues with the overlapping and ostensibly divergent artistic, political, intellectual, and deeply personal groups in which she participates.

Afrekete frames Lorde's biomythography, demanding the circularity of women-bonding threaded throughout the narrative. As bookends, she underscores what Henry Louis Gates, Jr., observes as the defining characteristic of Es(h)u: "the ultimate copula, connecting truth with understanding, the sacred with the profane, text with interpretation."[111] In the epigraph, Lorde offers her self-naming act as a libation to Afrekete—a symbol of her self-interpretive quest. She then stages *Zami*'s community of women by first locating the ways in which she, her lovers, friends, foremothers, and Afrekete form a covenant of women-bonding: "To the journeywoman pieces of myself. / Becoming. / Afrekete."[112] As she concludes her biomythography, she similarly calls upon the interpretive qualities of the ancient African god(dess). Lorde revises Afrekete as a lover named Kitty who connects "text with interpretation." Playing on the ambiguity of Kitty/Afrekete, Lorde imagines the eroticism of sexual intercourse that validates her women-identified politics.

The last episodic frame, where Afrekete is mortalized as Kitty, explores the fluidity of spiritual and physical existences. At once, Afrekete is Kitty, the African American lover with a "broad-lipped beautiful face"[113] who repairs Lorde's fractured spirit, and the African god(dess) who helps Lorde explore the spiritually regenerative spaces of sexual intimacy. Encouraged by Kitty/Afrekete, Lorde experiences "loving as a manifestation." She finds that sex with Kitty/Afrekete evokes personal authority:

> Something about Kitty made me feel like a rollercoaster, rocketing from idiot to goddess. By the time we had collected her mail from the broken mailbox and then climbed six flights of stairs up to her front door, I felt that there had never been anything else my body had intended to do more, than to reach inside of her coat and take Afrekete into my arms, fitting her body into the curves of mine tightly, her beige camel's-hair billowing around us both, and her gloved hand still holding the door key.[114]

The intensity of their lovemaking enacts an eroticism that helps Lorde tap into her deepest "roots, new definitions of our women's bodies"[115] before unknown. Kitty/Afrekete, through the act of lovemaking, offers Lorde the spiritual gifts that Afrekete, the god(dess), provides. The meshing of the flesh brings not only sexual ecstasy but gifts from a black female past, "bring[ing] live things from the bush"[116] through their sexual encounters. As one who is spiritually and culturally omnipotent, Kitty/Afrekete engenders the essence, the core, of Lorde's female consciousness.

The best way to consider the importance of Afrekete in Lorde's lesbian-centered biomythography is to address Lorde's understanding of eroticism as a powerful tool for self-liberation. Speaking to a feminist audience at Mount Holyoke College in 1978, she argued: "The erotic is a resource within each of us that lies in a deeply female and spiritual plane, firmly rooted in the power of our unexpressed or unrecognized feeling."[117] She observed that the erotic was experienced on multiple levels, but none that surpass the "sharing of joy, whether physical, emotional, psychic, or intellectual" between women that allowed them to understand how the erotic could serve as a life force.[118] Lorde's relationship with Kitty/Afrekete builds on the erotic and the ways in which it can operate in women's lives.

In Kitty/Afrekete and Lorde's short-lived affair, the erotic functions on a physical and psychological level. Sex with Afrekete/Kitty engenders spiritual and sexual freedom for Lorde:

> Afrekete Afrekete ride me to the crossroads where we shall sleep, coated in the woman's power. The sound of our bodies meeting is the prayer of all strangers and sisters, that the discarded evils, abandoned at all crossroads, will not follow us upon our journeys.[119]

Her relationship with Kitty/Afrekete initiates an attempt to create new "journeys" unimpaired by the fissures between women. Lorde utilizes the sacred knowledges women can create for each other. The eroticism explored in the sexual encounters between Kitty/Afrekete and Lorde symbolizes the moment beyond the "crossroads" when women recognize the power in each other, acknowledging the intuitive, spiritual resources in their lives. The sensations of homoerotic sex between Kitty/Afrekete and Lorde foregrounds the erotic urge as one that is sacred and valuable.

Lorde refuses to verify Kitty as real lover or fictional construction in *Zami*'s matrix of narrative forms, and thus she positions her own authority as black lesbian. Kitty/Afrekete mysteriously disappears from town and the text, and only later does Lorde realize that Kitty had "gotten a gig in Atlanta for September, and was splitting to visit her mama and daughter for a while."[120] Kitty's textual absence presents several opportunities for the biomythographic longings of *Zami*. If *Zami* is simply read as autobiography, Kitty's sudden disappearance proves the loss of an intense, ephemeral, yet life-affirming love affair. If *Zami* is read for its mythological utterances, however, Kitty's disappearance demands that Lorde, the new black goddess, usurp her place.

Kitty leaves for Atlanta in search of her other/biological daughter, but she gives Lorde the freedom to live her life as a black, lesbian, feminist poet without fear. In talking about her dreams for her daughter, Kitty/Afrekete shares her dreams for Lorde:

> "She's going to be able to love anybody she wants to love," Afrekete said, fiercely, lighting a Lucky Strike. "Same way she's going to be able to work any place she damn well pleases. Her mama's going to see to that."[121]

Kitty later observes that she and Lorde are alike, virtually the same: "And that's what I like about you; you're like me. We're both going to make it because we're both too tough and crazy not to!"[122] She leaves Lorde with the confidence that "what [sh]e had to pay for that toughness" of being a black woman who loves women is worth the pleasures, both spiritual and sensual, her loving enables. The explicitness of their sexual encounters puts Lorde at the threshold of self-actuation and changes her from "an idiot to a goddess" so that she can, in fact, become Afrekete. Kitty's subsequent departure from the central focus of the last frame of the biomythography mirrors that of the god(dess) figures in the second, third, and fourth parts of The Black Unicorn: she fades into the background—disappears in some respects—as Lorde emerges.

At the beginning of Zami, Lorde writes that she is becoming Afrekete, but if this is turned on its head, the power she yields as both narrator and actor throughout Zami positions Lorde as Afrekete from the beginning. Her embodiment of Afrekete does not simply occur at the end of Zami's events in the late 1950s. Rather, Zami, as a revisionist exercise in the form of autobiographical writing, enacts Lorde's role as Afrekete from the narrative opening. Usurping the role of Afrekete at the moment of writing the autobiographical self provides the opportunity for locating a community of women to whom Lorde owes "the power behind [her] voice."[123]

Lorde imagines herself as Afrekete when revising her relationships with women who have helped shape her feminist consciousness: Genevieve, Ginger, Eudora, Muriel, and even her Caribbean mother. Acting as Afrekete, the interlocutor, Lorde the autobiographer can script and manipulate the ways in which all of the women in her life—"kind and cruel"[124]—are necessary to the voice she finds as a black and lesbian woman. Her lovers come from diverse backgrounds. Genevieve, with whom she never consummates a relationship, is a sexually abused adolescent who ultimately commits suicide. Ginger is an African American woman from Connecticut who thinks that Lorde is the "accomplished lover from the big city."[125] Eudora is an older white American expatriate who lives in Mexico, and Muriel is a young white woman who leaves Lorde devastated by the dissolution of their love affair.

However, in re-experiencing her relationship with these women through the interpretive powers gained as Afrekete, Lorde understands the ways in which these women have empowered her. Women like Eudora teach Lorde pain but also teach her that she is "a woman connecting with other women in an intricate, complex, and ever-widening network of exchanging strengths."[126] As she imagines and constructs the blueprint for a community of women in *Zami,* Lorde fits diverse women on a continuum, creating a complex web through which she establishes the power in loving women. She also provides a language of working through silence and difference to build communities across seemingly disparate experiences.

Yet, Lorde ultimately works through silence and difference to form communities not made up solely of her female friends, foremothers, and lovers. Like *The Black Unicorn, Zami* engages in dialogue with the Black Arts and mainstream Feminist Movements and thus stages the conversation of difference within the specificity of Lorde's relationship with women. Lorde is careful at the moment of writing *Zami* to discuss the ways in which her writings and political activities are committed to recognizing difference, while exploring the possibilities of the liberation struggles of feminists, blacks, and other marginalized peoples. In 1983, a year after *Zami* was published, she argued:

> In our work and in our living, we must recognize that difference is a reason for celebrating and growth, rather than a reason for destruction. We should see difference as a dialogue, the same way we deal with symbol and image, in literary study. "Imaging" is the process of developing a dialectic, a tension between opposites that illuminates the differences and similarities between things in apparent opposition. It is the same way with people. We need to use these differences in constructive ways, creative ways, rather than in ways to justify our destroying each other.[127]

In *Zami,* Lorde maps this difference through women and sees herself as someone who speaks from and for an inclusive feminist perspective. Yet, the articulation of difference in the biomythography provides a "dialogue" that attempts community-building with various populations despite perceived dissimilarities in the human experience.

The importance of this engagement of difference in *Zami* becomes most salient as Lorde reconstructs her relationship with her Caribbean mother. The literary critic Claudine Raynaud sees Lorde's mother, Linda Belmar Lorde, as a metaphoric extension of the African god(dess) motif in *Zami*. She observes, "While Kitty is Afrekete, she is also an incarnation of Lorde's mother. . . . By means of this evocation, Afrekete and Lorde's mother are brought together and blended into one woman."[128] According to Raynaud, the attention paid to Lorde's mother illuminates Lorde's revisionist exercise of working from non-Western and nonpatriarchal frameworks to further reveal the importance of black and feminist frames of reference. That Lorde utilizes her mother's native home of Carriacou to affirm her racial and sexual identities confirms the ties she makes between her mother and her mythical and historical forebears in the African diaspora.

My reading provides an alternative understanding of Lorde's mother in *Zami,* although it recognizes the continuum finally created between Lorde's mother and the maternal legacy Lorde envisions with African diasporic women and god(dess) figures. Within the narrative, the character of Lorde's mother works in relation *to* Afrekete, but also *against* the lesbian, feminist, and politically black yearnings of the African god(dess). In Lorde's attempt to utilize difference, she strategically manipulates what she understands as the dissonances created by her mother and by her Caribbean heritage. She fits both the character of her mother and her own Caribbean background within the liberating feminist and black paradigms explored throughout *Zami* and *The Black Unicorn.*

In *Zami,* Lorde describes a fraught and tense relationship with her mother, Linda Belmar Lorde. Linda resists Americanization, resists participation in political culture, and sees life through the prism of her past experiences in Grenada. As a Grenadian immigrant, Linda was distrustful of whites, recognizing America's racialist society and where she fit in its hierarchy; she was equally disdainful of African Americans, who seemingly did not share her class aspirations, were supposedly less educated, and perhaps were a clear reminder of the limitations imposed on her in the United States. Further, she referred to Lorde's lovers as her "friends," aware of but never approving of Lorde's homosexuality. In *Zami,* Lorde writes that her mother is a strong woman, but also one who limited Lorde's ability to politically engage her lesbian, American, feminist, and black selves. If Afrekete is positioned as the nurturing "mother" who helps Lorde tap into her "deepest roots" of black and female consciousnesses, Lorde's biological mother is the distant, foreign mother who restricts Lorde's mobility.

Linda's presence in *Zami* anchors Lorde's emphasis on African and lesbian cultures, because, although she is Lorde's mother, she stands as the dissonant voice with which Lorde must contend. Linda covertly symbolizes the masculinist and patriarchal frameworks Lorde has to work through, acknowledge, and engage in order to maintain dialogues across racial, sexual, and gender boundaries. *Zami* grapples with Linda's presence in Lorde's childhood years and her absences in the years of Lorde's sexual, feminist, and racial discoveries. Linda inculcates a Caribbean culture, a "truly private paradise of bluego and breadfruit handing from the trees,"[129] to which her daughter turns to escape the realities of U.S. racism. Yet, too, Linda uses memories and patois to generate a "home" from which Lorde is ultimately cut off. Lorde redefines "home" as she discovers her political and sexual identities in the United States, with her multiple ties to the "gay-girl" Village circles and to African American and white radicals during the postwar era. Home shifts from the Caribbean to an American political landscape that allows Lorde to "copy . . . from her mother what was left unfulfilled"[130] and to resist her mother's unwillingness to accept the multiple identities of her second-generation immigrant daughter.

After the childhood and teenage episodes in *Zami,* Linda is virtually absent from the text. However, Lorde, who imagines herself as Afrekete, uses Linda's absence to inform her own search for home in multiple locales where women build bridges despite diverse female knowledges. The mother's absences anticipate the effort to reach out to Linda in an exploration of a self-sustained community of women. Nonetheless, Lorde evokes her mother on her own terms, making Linda useful to black and lesbian politics. Lorde hearkens the mother's birthplace of Carriacou and uses the mother strategically to construct new possibilities of African diasporic cultures as sites of liberation for herself and others.

Lorde initiates this rediscovery of African diasporic culture in the Caribbean with the refrain: "Island women make good wives; whatever happens they've seen worse."[131] It is a refrain passed down to her by her mother.[132] The refrain suggests that the mother's understanding of womanhood positions Lorde outside constructions of her black and racialized identities: Lorde is not a black woman, as she seeks to claim, but an *Island* woman. Caribbeanness, not blackness, is from whence she gains her female power. Similarly, it identifies the patriarchal and masculinist society in which Lorde is expected to participate. "Island women make good wives" not simply because they are strong women but because they can be strong for their men. Lorde's mother insinuates that Lorde can gain her much-desired strength from her commitment to male cultural yearnings within Caribbean culture. She has the potential to make a good wife, and in essence woman, because she can sustain life and family within a patriarchal system.

The attention paid to Caribbean heritage in *Zami* suggests the links Lorde attempts to make between her mother and the mainstream feminist and Black Arts intellectuals whom Lorde challenged. The heterosexual, patriarchal, and deracinated language of the mother's refrain converges with the discourses of white feminists and masculinist Black Arts intellectuals who refused to acknowledge the importance of separating themselves from the homogeneity of experiences demanded in Western societies. The mother's conventional understanding of Lorde's identity echoes the voices of patriarchal and racist thinkers in the Feminist Movement, as well as those of the heterosexists of the Black Arts Movement. Lorde's mother, like white feminists, demanded that Lorde obscure a racial identity for a female one. Similarly, she suggested that Lorde's female identity could be determined only by her relationship to men, underscoring the chauvinistic ideologies of male leaders in the Black Arts Movement.

Lorde's mother gives voice to an oppressive language that must be challenged, deconstructed, and made useful in a non-Western and non-patriarchal sphere. Lorde reinterprets her mother's ideals of Caribbean womanhood by imagining alternative connections to West Indian women through tropes of Africa, which emerges again as the site of personal and collective liberation from oppression. "Island women make good wives; whatever happens, they've seen worse"[133] is rescripted in *Zami* to punctuate Lorde's second-generation Caribbean immigrant, American, black, and lesbian identities in new ways. The women are no longer just "Island women"; they are *black* women. Even more so, they are black women who enunciate an African past:

> When I visited Grenada I saw the root of my mother's power walking
> through the streets. I thought, this is the country of my foremothers,
> my forbearing mothers, those Black island women who defined them-
> selves by what they did. "Island women make good wives: whatever
> happens, they've seen worse." There is a softer edge of African sharp-
> ness upon these women, and they swing through the rain-warm streets
> with an arrogant gentleness that I remember in strength and vulnera-
> bility.[134]

Lorde complicates the apparent dominant social order of her mother's
Caribbean by distinguishing why these women make good wives,
namely because of the women-nurturing communities they built away
from a male domination. Lorde re(dis)covers the legendary out-island
Carriacou women of her mother's matrilineage. As women who "survived the absence of the sea-faring men easily" by loving each other,
these foremothers constitute a community of women who historically,
culturally, and politically resonate with Lorde's attempt to use tropes of
Africa and diasporic cultures to legitimate her experiences as a black lesbian. The Carriacou women creatively frame Lorde's construction of
women-centeredness, becoming the historical and cultural referents for
claiming a feminist power.

Lorde's strategic use of these women in her revisionist project once
again establishes the source of black female power within black and lesbian cultural domains. She "outs" a homosexual Caribbean community
and thus enacts a process of continuous placing and displacing in the
text. Lorde displaces her mother's heterocentric idea of Caribbean culture and places Caribbeanness within the locus of black lesbian-femi-
nism. She also identifies the Carriacou lesbians as kin. Although the ties
are ambiguous at best—for example, her Aunt Anni lived with these
women but was not necessarily a part of their community—she envisions herself as their progeny: she is the one who lives their legacy of
women nurturing women. Their presences within the text and within
her cultural past provide the background for her attempt at constructing
her life in relation to women.

Aware of the dissonances her use of Carriacou creates with her
mother, Lorde then imagines Linda as part of the homosexual community
through which she feels empowered. Lorde does not deny her mother a

place within the community of women; rather, she re-centers her mother as part of the matrilineage of women-nurturing. Not only does Lorde sense that she and her mother share the same legacy—that is, her mother was born in the loving hands of Anni—but also she posits that her mother shares the same formidable strength as the forebears of Carriacou. She cites her mother's strength as indicative that black "dykes" have been around for a long time.

Lorde observes that her mother's strength mirrors that of the Carriacou women who "tend" to each other when their men are absent:

> As a child, I always knew my mother was different from the other women I knew, Black or white. . . . Different how? I never knew. But that is why to this day I believe that there have always been Black dykes around—in the sense of powerful and women-oriented women —who would rather have died than use that name for themselves. And that includes my momma.[135]

Recognizing and acknowledging her mother's homophobia, Lorde uses "black dyke" to re-narrativize the fissure between mother and daughter that dominates the biomythography proper. Lorde intimates that, although the mother is absent from the rest of the narrative structure, her presence can be found in the spiritual and cultural connections that place both Lorde and her mother within the same sphere of liberated female consciousness. Through the black diasporic lesbian women from whom they both descend, Lorde is able to attempt a reconciliation with her mother that is made possible in biomythographic form.

Ultimately, Lorde's attempt to work through the dissonance with her mother represents a goal, on a much larger scale, of engaging the differences that often separated Lorde from other communities. As she completed *Zami,* Lorde supported gay and lesbian organizations, engaged in dialogue with black intellectuals in leading journals and magazines, continued conferencing with white feminist groups, and reached out to feminist communities in Germany, Grenada, Australia, St. Croix, and other locales across the globe.[136] Indeed, *Zami* supports an engagement of difference that Lorde often posited was the fount of her political and social vision. "[I]t is not those differences between us that are separating us," Lorde said, in 1980. "It is rather our refusal to recognize those differences, and to examine the distortions which result from our misnaming them and their effects upon human behavior and expectation."[137] In an interview almost ten years later, Lorde added, "Liberation is not the private property of one group."[138] *Zami* thus enacts tropes of Africa to celebrate black and lesbian identities, while still emphasizing the importance of working in concert with others.

In *Zami,* Lorde suggests that her identity as a "black lesbian feminist poet" relies of "images of women"—black and white, old and young, real and mythical—who led her "home."[139] Although Lorde's home was finally gained through Africa and its diaspora, it was not exclusive to an African or black diasporic identity. Lorde's home developed in the more fluid and metaphysical spaces that bridged her ties to multiple racial, cultural, and sexual communities. A year before her death from cancer, in 1992, Lorde told Charles Rowell:

> I am now part of the U.S. colonial community, as well as part of the international community of people of color. I am also part of the Black women's community, I am part of many communities. Poetry is a way of articulating and bringing together the energies of difference within those communities, so those energies can be used by me and others to better do what must be done.[140]

From 1987, Lorde lived on the Caribbean island of St. Croix, where she felt the pulls and joys of her diverse heritages and political allegiances. St. Croix's position as both Caribbean island and U.S. territory covertly mirrored the paradox of Lorde's journey in and through various racial, sexual, national, and gender homes. Lorde's political identities were eminently anchored in her U.S. experience as a black lesbian woman and a Caribbean immigrant of the second generation, while she employed the multiplicities of racial and sexual selves to imagine Africa as a liberating site for all. Yet, the black feminist poetics and politics of *The Black Unicorn* and *Zami* ultimately enabled Lorde to move beyond tropes of Africa and toward those diverse homes in St. Croix, Germany, and elsewhere that celebrated liberation through communities of difference.

# CHAPTER 4

# "How to Be a Negro without Really Trying"

Piri Thomas and
the Politics of
Nuyorican Identity

It is ironic that Paule Marshall and
Audre Lorde recalled their tenures in black radical groups with some
fondness, while the Nuyorican writer Piri Thomas remembered a very
different experience. Marshall once reflected, "I don't know how much
I got out of [the Harlem Writers' Guild] in terms of real solid help for
my own work, but just the kind of support from being with people
who were attempting the same thing was at that point in my development very important."[1] In contrast, Thomas, in a 1980 interview, commented:

> In the Guild others were reading and others would talk about it, and I
> waited patiently and no one asked me. So finally I said, "I would like
> to read too." And one man said, "You're not a member." But John
> Oliver Killens looked at me and said, "You read, Piri." . . . I thought

that arrogance came only from the whites. There was arrogance there
too, and of course I was very forward in wanting to read also. I didn't
feel the need to be with the group.[2]

This difference in the memories of the Harlem Writers' Guild elucidates
the contested meanings of black identity for second-generation artists
and intellectuals. Blackness becomes the initial site of belonging for the
West Indian Americans Audre Lorde and Paule Marshall. It is the place
in which they can imagine and participate in an African diasporic community on their own terms. However, blackness becomes the site of ambiguity for the Spanish Caribbean author Piri Thomas. It is the site where
he must negotiate his ambiguous and often fraught relationship with
white and African America. It is also the site that disrupts his connection
to his native Hispanic culture.

Thomas discusses his sense of dislocation in African America in his
1967 autobiography, *Down These Mean Streets,* which tells of his life as a
Nuyorican youth growing up in Spanish Harlem. The autobiography
chronicles his life in the 1940s through his release from prison in 1957,
while raising questions about the subject-positions of Afro-Latinos in
the postwar period. In a 1963 letter, Thomas revealed the importance of
his autobiography as an enunciation of his past life *and* the cultural moment of 1960s.[3] At once, the letter connected his memories of childhood
to his contemporary inquiry about racial and cultural selves. Reflecting
on a recent discussion with the editor of *Down These Mean Streets,* he
noted the anger he felt as the darkest child in a Puerto Rican immigrant
household, the subject that permeates a major portion of the autobiography.[4] Yet, he tellingly ended the correspondence by pondering the historical and volatile era of the 1960s that impelled the writing of his book:
"Today, because of this fantastic Negro social revolution that is explod-
ing throughout the world and . . . throughout the United States, many
Negro writers are finding an open market for their inner sensitivity and
escense [sic] of personal involvment [sic]. What about the Puerto Rican
Negro, whose tongue speaks Spanish and skin shouts Negro?"

The central narrative of *Down These Mean Streets* poses just this question as Piri fights to exist in a world where his humanity as a dark-
skinned Puerto Rican male is often denied. It is a narrative reminiscent
of the black male autobiographical works such as the *Autobiography of*

*Malcolm X* (1965), Claude Brown's *Manchild in the Promised Land* (1965), and Eldridge Cleaver's *Soul on Ice* (1968).[5] All of these autobiographers, Thomas included, protested the dehumanization experienced by men of color, who were often denied access to jobs, quality educations, and the social fabric of American life because of racial and gender discrimination. As part of the burgeoning black protest genre of the 1960s, their first-person accounts of the black urban experience provided a new, revolutionary articulation of black manhood that would not be denied.

However, *Down These Mean Streets,* in contrast to the autobiographies written by African American men, evokes Thomas's battles with *multiple* communities. It reveals battles with African America, as his comments on the Harlem Writers' Guild attest. Yet, most important to the writing of his lived experience, *Down These Mean Streets* documents his battles with a white American society that sees Piri only as black, thus denying his multicultural heritage, and with the Puerto Rican community, which refuses to engage the ways in which his racial self has been reconstructed in an American cultural landscape. The autobiography also enunciates battles with the self. Piri makes a journey toward embracing an African heritage, seeking to reverse the internal self-hatred he feels because of his mixed-racial status.[6] Piri's battles, then, are those that express his tenuous relationships with black, white American, and Puerto Rican communities, and also his struggles with his self-image as a second-generation Caribbean immigrant.

In this chapter, I offer a close reading of *Down These Mean Streets,* building on previous discussions of the racial and cultural wars of the postwar moment. Specifically, I examine the ways in which *Down These Mean Streets* is not just the autobiography of a black Puerto Rican male, as several critics received it in 1967. Most major newspapers and journals —African American and white—reviewed the autobiography for its contribution to the emerging black protest and nationalist genre.[7] In the *New York Times Book Review,* for example, Daniel Stern heralded it for "claim[ing] our attention" because of "the honesty and pain of a life led in outlaw, fringe status, where the dream is always to escape."[8] William Hogan, of the *San Francisco Chronicle,* called *Down These Mean Streets* "a document of our time—a tough, stomach-turning lyrical one by a black Puerto Rican who has been trying for a long time to figure out what goes in this society."[9] The African American writer and radical John O. Killens, in *Negro Digest*, reviewed *Down These Mean Streets* as "one man's lonely journey to his blackness[,] to his selfhood, his identity."[10]

Against these definitions, I argue that *Down These Mean Streets* should be read as a story of the *negotiation of blackness* as Piri tries to find community amid the binary racialization politics of the United States. Thomas's autobiography complicates Belafonte's, Marshall's, and Lorde's understandings of black identity for Caribbean immigrants because it voices the complex reality this identity places on Thomas's Spanish Caribbean and masculine self. With the publication of his autobiography, in 1967, Thomas set the stage for the cultural and racial discourses of Spanish Caribbean immigrants that emerged later in the 1970s, if only because Thomas located his inability to wholly accept the limitations of his black subject-position. Thomas's readings of blackness in *Down These Mean Streets* are ambiguous at best, enunciating the cultural conundrum of other dark-skinned Puerto Rican immigrants of the era. Could he— could they—in fact, be black and Latino at the same time?

The 1960s, of course, were a volatile time for many Americans, but the decade had a special impact on the social formation of blacks and Puerto Ricans in urban ghettoes. As mentioned in previous chapters, the integrationist politics of organizations such as the NAACP and SCLC gave way to the radicalized movements of young adults who were no longer willing to accept a strategy that was seemingly unable to secure the civil rights of ethnic, racial, and language minorities.[11] Urban unrest left an indelible mark on the 1960s, when mostly black and Latino urban dwellers rebelled against many of the injustices featured in Thomas's autobiography: inadequate housing, lack of resources, and the racial and language biases within American social life and policy.

New political organizations led by young black and Latino cultural nationalists began to emerge. Alongside the Black Panther Party and the Nation of Islam, discussed in earlier chapters, the Young Lords Party developed its own thirteen-point platform to fight for the liberation of Puerto Ricans both on the island and on the mainland. As a militant U.S. Puerto Rican organization, made up primarily of second generationers, the Party was founded in Chicago, in 1967, before being organized in New York, in 1969.[12] The group was known for its attempts at prison reform, for protests against the inadequate health-care system at Lincoln Hospital in *el barrio,* and for its breakfast program that, like that of the

Black Panthers, fed several inner-city youth and homeless people nutritional meals each morning. Like most militant groups of the era, the Young Lords Party engaged in several disputes with the police and with government officials as it worked toward its goal of liberating all Puerto Ricans from what it understood as the capitalist machine. Because of the imprisonment of several of its members and internal problems within the organization, the group was defunct by the early 1970s. Nevertheless, while active, it was considered an important voice of second-generation Puerto Ricans.

Almost as part of the protest and the radicalization of blacks and Latinos in urban ghettoes, Thomas's *Down These Mean Streets* appeared in 1967—the same year that there were more than one hundred rebellions in American cities, including the mass revolts mentioned before in the urban centers of Newark, New Jersey, and Detroit, Michigan.[13] Thomas's work was one of the first to launch the Nuyorican literary movement, in which artists and intellectuals such as Tato Laviera, Sandra María Esteves, and Felipe Luciano employed Puerto Rican music and folk culture and their African and Taino heritages to challenge America's white cultural hegemony. As Thomas's letter to his editor revealed, Thomas wrote his autobiography as he reflected on and participated in these various social and cultural movements after his release from prison in 1957. While writing his autobiography, Thomas marched for civil rights in the South with black activists such as John O. Killens, and he worked with urban and marginalized teenagers during the urban-riot era in places like New York.[14] The frustrations created by the disadvantages of his youth in the 1940s and 1950s, documented in *Down These Mean Streets,* provocatively mirrored those he experienced as a working-class man during the civil rights struggle and as part of the black and Puerto Rican consciousness movements.

Thomas's questioning of the possibilities of black and Latino identities in *Down These Mean Streets* emerged not only against the backdrop of the racial and cultural wars with mainstream America but also within the U.S. Puerto Rican community. Puerto Ricans had been migrating to the United States since the early 1900s, a movement facilitated by the U.S. government's decision to grant citizenship to all residents of its commonwealth in the Jones Act in 1917. Thomas's parents were part of the first migration wave, 1900–1945, when many Puerto Ricans left the island because of the stagnancy of the sugar cane industry. By 1930, according to Lawrence Chenault's 1938 study, 52,774 first-generation Puerto Ricans resided in the United States.[15] Between 1910 and 1945, Puerto Ricans were leaving the island at a rate of approximately 2,600 a year.[16]

The greatest growth in migration from the island actually did not occur until after World War II, when the recruitment program of mainland companies, the economic shifts caused by Operation Bootstrap, and more affordable transportation between Puerto Rico and the United States propelled the increase in immigration, especially to various neighborhoods in New York. Between 1944 and 1945, 14,794 people emigrated from Puerto Rico to the mainland in search of economic opportunities. The following year, as an example of the sharp increase, the number reached 34,405. By the time Thomas wrote *Down These Mean Streets,* the out-migration from Puerto Rico between 1960 and 1970 was at approximately 214,000.[17]

Thomas's parents, like other immigrants from Puerto Rico, entered an American racial economy very different from the one they had experienced on the island. The boundaries between races in Puerto Rico had historically been destabilized by widespread intermarriage and interracial sexual liaisons among the European, African, and indigenous populations, and hence the boundaries had also been destabilized by the development of a creole society.[18] Racial discrimination existed, but the discourses on race and racial identities fell outside the racial binaries of black and white identity in the United States. Even though Puerto Rico was economically and socially tied to the United States because of its commonwealth status, the various categories for racial selves in Puerto Rico provided an alternative to the black and white racializations most Puerto Ricans encountered after they migrated to the ghettoes of large American cities.

Attempting to assimilate into American social and political culture, Puerto Ricans had to confront the discrimination they experienced as an immigrant population that was often unable, because of its racial ambiguity, to fit easily into American racial categorizations. As the early studies of Puerto Rican immigrants by U.S. social scientists and cultural historians such as C. Wright Mills et al. (1950), Elena Padilla (1958), and Joseph Fitzpatrick (1959) reveal, racial tensions in the United States fueled racial prejudices within the Puerto Rican community, prejudices arguably not as pronounced on the island proper. Or, perhaps better stated, settlement in the United States brought Puerto Ricans' often ignored racial prejudices to the fore.

In their 1950 book on Puerto Ricans in New York, C. Wright Mills et al., for example, noted the problem race caused for Puerto Ricans who were not accepted as part of white American society but who were reluctant to become a part of African America.[19] In 1958, Elena Padilla further argued that the often tense relationships between African Americans and white Americans were the most difficult aspect of American culture for Puerto Ricans to understand.[20] She also noted that "intermediate" and black Puerto Ricans often preferred to be considered Puerto Rican by the "outgroup"—white Americans—because Puerto Rican identity was perceived to carry a "better status" than (American) "Negro."[21] In 1959, Joseph Fitzpatrick observed that white Puerto Ricans' public postures toward nonwhite Puerto Ricans were often fraught with the desire that Americans not perceive Puerto Ricans as black. He concluded in his article "Attitudes of Puerto Ricans toward Color" that Puerto Ricans were increasingly "sensitive to the social and economic advantages of being white."[22]

American understandings of racialized identities—within African American, white, and U.S. Puerto Rican communities—bring to bear Thomas's negotiation of blackness in *Down These Mean Streets*. Thomas may finally identify himself as black in his autobiography; however, black identity, especially as performed by Piri in the text, becomes a political and public identity and not necessarily a private or personal frame of reference. Piri's acceptance of a black self is at once a moment of racial awareness and cultural loss: it provides the disruptive movement in the text/his life that threatens his ties to family and to his Puerto Rican self. *Down These Mean Streets* differs drastically from the autobiographies of African American men such as Malcolm X, Brown, and Cleaver because, while the articulation of blackness marks a moment of freedom for African American men, the articulation of blackness causes confusion and further self-destruction for Piri. Piri is not liberated by his black consciousness, as are Malcolm X, Brown, Cleaver; thus, that consciousness of a black self undergirds a suspended tension in the autobiography, a tension that is never quite resolved.

"I don't think I opted for it," Thomas once observed when asked about his identification with the African American tradition. "I think the whole world believed me to be a *negrito*."[23] Giving voice to the lack of agency in the process of American racialization, Thomas's comments situate the development of a racial self that complicates Piri's understanding of his Caribbean one in *Down These Mean Streets*. Unlike the black experience explored in the previously examined works of Belafonte, Marshall, and Lorde, the use of blackness is articulated in *Down These Mean Streets* in very different ways. With Thomas, blackness is not written as a goal, a movement toward empowerment, as with Belafonte, Marshall, and Lorde. It is conceived as a burden that must be accepted, dealt with, and overcome. The role Thomas assigns blackness is evidenced not only in the documentation of a lived experience but, perhaps more tellingly, also in the literary and strategic use of blackness and its negotiation in the written autobiography.

In the following analysis of *Down These Mean Streets*, I locate Thomas's negotiation of blackness as threefold. I argue that the negotiation of blackness is enunciated first by its absence in Piri's idyllic and homosocial world of Puerto Rican street culture, where selfhood is defined in ethnic and gendered terms.[24] Puerto Rican male subjectivity defies race, if not culture. Instead, it is based on the politics of the street, where masculine strength—having *corazón*—establishes a sense of belonging and humanity for urban youth often ignored by mainstream America. For Piri, his fellow gang members, and even the poor Italian kids with whom they fight, the street becomes the battleground for warding off the dislocation they feel as second-generation immigrants, a place for demanding new terms on which their humanity can be defined.

Second, the absence of blackness on the streets proves most telling because of its central presence in the worlds in which Piri is not able to assert his citizenship on his terms, namely in school, in the workplace, and in his Puerto Rican home. School and the American social economy are the sites where Piri is reminded of his subhumanity, not as a Puerto Rican but as a black male in the United States. In school and in the job market, he experiences the disruption of his black identity in his American life and the insecurity of being both black and Puerto Rican. Home, too, offers the most painful and psychologically damaging of experiences: it is where the internal racisms of his father and siblings, who themselves are dealing with the racial binarisms of America, exacerbate the racisms of the larger society. His family's unwillingness to acknowledge his African heritage leaves Piri unable to emotionally survive his second-class citizenship as a black person in the United States.

Third, Thomas's use of blackness in *Down These Mean Streets* creates a particular literary syllogism that maps its negotiation in the protagonist's (and autobiographer's) life. Thomas suggests that Puerto Rican identity provides cultural capital, although contested, that black identity does not afford. In Piri's estimation, to be Puerto Rican is to be a man. The homosocial environs of his Puerto Rican gang provide a sense of manhood—Latino manhood—that negates the emasculation he experiences outside Spanish Harlem. By extension, Piri sees manhood as a sign of his humanity. His understanding of manhood makes him feel as though he belongs as a youth, and it is the thing that gives him a sense of his personhood as he travels down South and especially when he is incarcerated in the Comstock prison.

Blackness, on the other hand, provides much bleaker options for the narrator-protagonist. Piri does not envision the possibility of a masculine identity within a black one. Thus, he does not envision a means of articulating his humanity within a racist world that does not acknowledge the humanity of persons of African descent. Bluntly stated, to be black is to have no cultural capital whatsoever. Hence, blackness—its negotiation—is articulated as the moment of crisis in the text. It is the moment of self-destruction because it is the moment, in Piri's mind, of utter dehumanization. The shifts in movements between Puerto Rican and black identities assert the important role of blackness—as proscribed, embraced, denied—in Piri's utterance of his self-worth and humanity as an ethnic minority in the United States.

## "Mean Streets," Public Identity, and the Negotiation of Blackness

Thomas's autobiography begins where most do: with his childhood experiences in his family and urban enclave. The first section, "Harlem," immediately introduces young Piri's cultural loss as a second-generation immigrant and his attempt to create a substitutive Puerto Rican culture within Spanish Harlem. "Cutting Out" and "Puerto Rican Paradise" in particular assert the problematics of Piri's search for a sense of self that impels his embrace of a life on the streets, where he can escape the limitations of his immigrant parents' lives and the critical, hegemonic gaze of mainstream America. Home houses a disengaged father struggling with his role as provider in the U.S. economy. It also houses a mother whose memories of her paradise island cannot protect her children—or her husband—from the harsh realities of the urban ghetto.

The young Piri probes his mother about Puerto Rico but soon learns that her memories provide no solace against the encroaching presence of American culture. "Moms . . . did everybody love each other—I mean like if everybody was worth something?" he asks in his attempt to define his own self-worth, hoping to use his mother's memories of a homeland as a spiritual tap root.[25] His mother responds in the affirmative: "those around you share *la pobreza* with you and they love you"; yet her answer is displaced by the coldness of New York that seems to demand control over their lives:

> The door opened and put an end to the kitchen yak. It was Poppa coming home from work. He came into the kitchen and brought all the cold with him. Poor Poppa, he looked so lost in all of the clothes he had on. A jacket and coat, sweaters on top of sweaters, two pairs of long johns, two pairs of pants, two pairs of socks, and a woolen cap.[26]

His mother's "greenlands and golden color of the morning sky" are no match for the more powerful symbolism of his father's lost figure in the United States. The home of the tenement apartment is not a respite from the family's marginalization in American society, as the mother intends. Instead, it becomes a testament to Piri's displacement at the fringes of Puerto Rican and mainstream American cultures. The small tenement apartment is the site of Piri's alienation from his parent's home and the America that supposedly is his birthright.

It is no wonder, then, that Thomas relives the street as Piri's alternative homespace, where he can escape the dehumanization of his parents, who are not able to confront the hegemonic powers of the Works Progress Administration (WPA), white employers, and home relief to se-

cure a more than marginal existence for their family. The street is a locus
for Puerto Rican youth and their "paddy boy" nemeses, who learn to develop their own articulations of selfhood based, in part, on the manhood
not allowed their fathers at home:

> It was all part of becoming *hombre,* of wanting to have a beard to
> shave, a driver's license, a draft card, a "stoneness" which enabled you
> to go into a bar like a man. Nobody really digs a kid. But a man—cool.
> Nobody can tell you what to do—and nobody better.[27]

Piri negotiates understandings of "becoming *hombre*" by challenging
what he perceives as the ways in which he is denied recognition as a man
in American society: the policing of his body by New York officers; the
humiliation he feels as he serves as cultural broker for his immigrant
mother as she deals with welfare institutions; and even the emasculation
he experiences as he watches his father's inability to keep a steady job.
The negotiation of manhood and its articulation take place in the reputation Piri attempts to build on the streets. On the streets, Piri can both
redefine and dismantle the power structure of an American hierarchical
system. Street rules demand a "becoming *hombre*" that positions societal
vendettas within personal struggles over turf with paddy boys, which,
in Spanish Harlem, translates into fights with Italian immigrant youth.
The street is the place where he can build his reputation through his sexual prowess with young women and the ability to fight with his gang. In
short, in the street, he becomes the man that he is not allowed to become
outside, in mainstream society.

   Thomas's idyllic remembering of his childhood, ironically, was not
originally a part of *Down These Mean Streets.* In fact, when Thomas
added the chapters on his childhood, he thought that he was close to
finishing his autobiography and was working on a second novel, featuring the fictional character Monz. *Down These Mean Streets,* then entitled
*Home Sweet Harlem,* was about Piri's immediate past. It told of Piri's
seven years in prison, his pain at being marginalized in the United States,
even his reflections on walking the color line in his teenage years.
Thomas's childhood Piri was saved for the fictional character Monz,
whose antics were a source of sadness but also evoked the often unspoken beauty of life in Harlem. However, in 1963, Thomas was convinced

by his editor to add the Monz character, namely the young Piri, to the
autobiography proper. Thomas recalled:

> Mr. Camerons' [sic] smile was almost unbearable and sitting across the
> table in the resturant [sic] I almost felt impulsed to tell him to go screw
> himself, and I think I did, again he smiled and said[,] "You think you're
> writing a second book, well you're not, it's only what's missing from
> the first one."[28]

Monz's character was then rewritten to incorporate the autobiographical
"I," and the rewriting of Monz's experiences to those of the younger Piri
makes up the first chapters of the autobiography.

Most readings of Thomas's childhood narrative question his problematic rendering of a street culture that, although harsh, made Piri feel alive
and energetic and gave him an awareness of self. Both Thomas (the autobiographer) and Piri (the narrator-protagonist) assert Piri's manhood, not
contemplating the ways in which his "becoming *hombre*" is homophobic, misogynistic, and even pathological. Latina feminist scholars such as
Marta Sánchez (1998) and queer theorists such as Robert Reid-Pharr
(1997) argue that, as an autobiographer, Thomas is guilty of endorsing
his narrator-protagonist's street life.[29] He does not offer a critical, self-
reflexive analysis that articulates a cognizance of his early path toward
self-destruction and incarceration and the role he played in it. Unlike autobiographers such as Claude Brown in *Manchild in the Promised Land*,[30]
Thomas, in the retelling of his childhood experiences, does not condemn
his childhood antics but instead presents them in a chimerical style that
positions childhood, particularly as it is re-imagined, as the most life-
affirming moment in Piri's cultural past.

These readings preclude an understanding of the structural impor-
tance of Thomas's childhood sequence to the autobiographical whole.
This is not to argue that the readings are wrong. It is an attempt to show
the inherent truth in the critique most post-1960s scholars such as
Sánchez and Reid-Pharr offer of Thomas's 1967 autobiography. However,
I would add to these readings that Thomas's first "Harlem" section provides, in rhetorical fashion, a means of situating the devastating role
Thomas, the author, and Piri, the protagonist, see blackness as playing in
his/their life, especially when the transition is made from childhood to

teenager years in a larger American society. That "Harlem" does this on the most problematic of terms and in the most chauvinistic language further undergirds Thomas's understanding of Piri's childhood moments with his gang as the moments before the crisis: they are the moments before his insular Puerto Rican life is severely affected by the racially gendered politics of American culture. Thomas's narrativizing of his childhood selectively conjures a Puerto Rican child self, if even through its New York street articulation, that is able to override any power white American racism has over him. "Harlem" suggests a world of a much distant past, so much so that it is written as a fictional world before it can be articulated as a world that was actually lived. The literal transition from a fictional Monz to an autobiographical "I" enunciates the subconscious way of understanding and re-imagining a childhood past very different from Thomas's present while he was writing *Down These Mean Streets*.

What is most problematic about Thomas's recounting of his childhood is what seems to give value to the autobiography as a literary production.[31] Thomas's chapters on Piri's childhood provide a preface for the dismal turn his life takes after he leaves the security of his gang culture for a new life in the suburbs of New York. The textual movements from childhood to life as a young adult register as two separate and antithetical lived moments. Thomas's change in voice surreptitiously emphasizes the painful schism that took place in Piri's life as he no longer participated in his Puerto Rican gang culture and was forced to participate in the white world of Long Island, where he first experienced the limitations of a black self.

Thomas announces the shift from childhood to teenager years, from Puerto Rican to black, by his family's move to Babylon, a town on Long Island. Babylon, more so than the "alien turf" of the Italian youth on 114th Street, is the place where he is most aware of his racial otherness, both inside his family and in the larger suburban community. In Babylon, the childhood memories of gang fights, stealing, roller skates, and his inventive entrepreneurship are replaced with memories of resentment toward his father, brother, and white America. Piri becomes more conscious of his black identity—is made more conscious of his black identity—and thus recognizes that his painfully obvious, yet still unacknowledged black self hinders his acceptance in the American mainstream.

School, as the bastion of mainstream identity politics, is the place that situates Piri's blackness at center stage. It is in the school district of Babylon that Piri begins the negotiation of blackness that ruptures the initial voice in the text and thus changes the enunciation of his life as a Puerto Rican male. What Thomas previously suggests is young Piri's self-consciousness about his dark skin, wiry hair, and flat nose is now juxtaposed with the limitations that his physical make-up places on his participation in the all-white world of Long Island. Having been less evident in the more accepting and multicultural world of Harlem, his level of self-consciousness is now increased by the actions of white school children, who understand American citizenship in very provincial terms.

Even Piri's most potentially dangerous encounter with Italian youth in Harlem does not prepare him for the racial discrimination he experiences in Babylon. The marginalized Italian youth of the Harlem streets are able to at least acknowledge the multiplicity of his Puerto Rican heritage, even if they are determined to denigrate him as both a "spic" and a "nigger." However, in the more economically stable area of Long Island, where the lines between white and black, middle class and poor are drawn, white students, for the most part, have phallocentric fears about Piri's racial status:

> "Christ, first that Jerry bastard and now him. We're getting invaded by niggers," said a thin voice. "You said it," said another guy. "They got some nerve. My dad says that you give them an inch them apes want to take a yard."[32]

It comes as no surprise that Piri is rejected by his classmates because of interracial sex. Piri feels tolerated, even feels that he is finding his place in the suburban environment, until he dares to approach the symbol of white supremacy: the girl next door. He knows that a friendship with Marcia, the "pretty, well-stacked girl, with black hair and white softness," is a potential social death; yet, he is confused by what he perceives as her mixed messages—the politeness on one hand, the subtle rebuff on the other:

> She smiled again, and I walked away not liking what I was feeling, and thinking that Crutch was right. I fought against it. I told myself I was

still feeling out of place here in the middle of all these strangers, that paddies weren't as bad as we made them out to be. I looked over my shoulder and saw Marcia looking at me funny-like. When she saw me looking, her face changed real fast. She smiled again. I smiled back. I felt like I was plucking a mental daisy:
You're right, Crutch.
You're wrong, Crutch.
You're right, Crutch.
You're wrong, Crutch.[33]

Crutch, his African American friend from the Harlem streets, had warned him about Long Island and about the racial prejudices of Babylon. However, Piri is not sure that he cannot find a home outside the urban enclave and in Long Island, where perhaps "paddies weren't as bad as we made them out to be." Yet, his ambiguous racial status is deemed unacceptable, finally, by his white classmates. He becomes one with the "colored kid" Jerry, who made the mistake of not knowing his tenuous place—much like Piri—and got "some girl in trouble."[34] Although Puerto Rican identity again is afforded a particular cultural capital, as his fairer brothers will later attest, Thomas is accused of passing for Puerto Rican "because he can't make it for white."[35] He is ultimately deemed black, even if he is possibly Puerto Rican, and thus is not able to have equitable relationships with white Americans.

With "Babylon," Thomas provocatively introduces a passing trope that advances the central tension in the autobiography: the conflicting realities of Piri's black and Puerto Rican selves. No longer armed with an affirmed identity gained from his homosocial world of the Puerto Rican youth gang, the maturing Piri has to find his place within an American cultural economy, which tellingly demands his second-class citizenship in racist terms. White America will not acknowledge that Piri is Puerto Rican; they accuse him of "passing" for white. Piri cannot yet come to terms with the stigma of being black. He leaves Babylon to return to Harlem, but he cannot escape the power that white cultural hegemony demands of his life. Engaging the adult world means engaging white American culture and thus participating in the duplicitous games that seek to create a color line between those who belong to the national community and those who do not.

Babylon occasions an initiation into a contested relationship with white America in which Piri's Puerto Rican identity is consistently called into question. In Babylon, Marcia accuses Piri of sounding, thus being, like the African American Jerry. Upon his return to Harlem, Mr. Christian, a white employer, poses the same question about Piri's authentic self:

> ". . . Where do you live?"
> "109 East 104th Street."
> "Isn't that, um, Harlem?"
> "It's called the *Barrio.*"
> "The Bar-ree-o?"
> I smiled. "Yes, sir, it's Spanish for 'the place'—er—like a commu-
> nity."
> "Oh, I see. But you're not Puerto Rican, are you?"
> "My parents are Puerto Ricans."
> "Is Thomas a Puerto Rican name?"
> "Er—well, my mother's family name is Montañez," I said, wonder-
> ing if that would help prove I was a Puerto Rican.[36]

Mr. Christian, with Thomas's apropos use of the pseudonym, is the more mature version of Marcia and Piri's Babylonian classmates. Piri has not escaped Babylon but instead has found it in the midst of America's social and supposedly moral community.

I point to the aforementioned passage at length because it reveals the following about Piri's burgeoning understanding of his life: Puerto Ricanness affords a cultural currency; blackness carries the weight only of discrimination in American proper. Mr. Christian's actions seem to confirm Piri's suspicions. The employer dismisses Piri, although in a friendly manner, as a potential door-to-door salesman, whereas Louis, his white Puerto Rican friend, is hired immediately. If Puerto Ricanness does not hold as much cultural value as white Americanness, at least it is not as socially debilitating as being of African descent. As the hiring of his friend Louie attests, his Puerto Rican immigrant status does not place him at the fringes of the job market, but his black status does. Mr. Christian's friendly and phony persona is no compensation for locking Piri out of the job opportunity for "young men, 17–30" because of his and America's racial prejudices.

Piri, too, is guilty of playing the racial politics established by white American society. Of course, Piri cannot pass for what he is. However, he does make sure that he "proves" himself Puerto Rican by offering the sacrificial cultural signs to his prospective employer: *el barrio,* his mother's maiden name, the history of his surname. In fact, he does pass as Catholic, which becomes the religious symbol of Latino cultural iden- tity—although his family is really Protestant. He even goes so far as to construct an American identity from the island, where, as he tells Mr. Christian, "a lot of . . . Americans . . . got married to Puerto Rican girls."[37] This structuring of his Puerto Rican identity displaces the potential African Americanization of his name to insist upon its origin in a white American forebear; he is not of black American but, in fact, of white American descent.

Piri means to establish his cultural identity not solely as a sign of cul- tural solidarity with Puerto Ricans but as a means of separating himself from African Americans. In recounting what happened at the interview, Piri is reminded by an African American friend that "a Negro faces that all the time," to which Piri responds: "I know that . . . but I wasn't a Negro then. I was still only a Puerto Rican."[38] Better stated, Piri was *prepared* to be only Puerto Rican. For Puerto Ricans like Louis, English language ac- quisition can afford white status. Yet, for Piri, who no longer sounds Puerto Rican with his urban-inflected English and "picturesque" slang, it seems to afford an African American self. Arguably, for Piri, the hard- est part of experiencing Christian's racial prejudices is the realization that that he, too, will have to suffer the injustices of the American Negro.

Piri's response is to fight back in the only way he knows: "swinging in Harlem, my Harlem, next to which Babylon was like cotton candy— white and sticky, and tasteless in the mouth."[39] "My Harlem," of course, means Spanish Harlem, where Piri sells and takes drugs and re-estab- lishes ties with members of his old Puerto Rican gang. His "boys," with their special articulation of *puertorriquenidad,* offer a particular cultural haven for Piri. They allow him to be *un hombre,* at least as he understands manhood, in ways that white America disavows. As participant in the homosocial world of Latino machismo, Piri is able to feel comfortable in a cultural and gendered location not limited by the problematics of his racial one. Indulging in the social ills often associated with urban exis- tence, Piri returns to the life of the streets to reclaim his manhood:

I'd meet my boys, and all the other hearing and seeing suddenly became unimportant. Only my boys were the important kick, and for good reasons—if I had boys, I had respect and no other clique would make me open game. Besides, they gave me a feeling of belonging, of prestige, of accomplishment; I felt *grande* and bad.[40]

Unable to demand respect outside the urban underground, Piri uses the power available to him through his relations with his Puerto Rican male friends as a means of denying his marginalized status and, in essence, demanding his humanity.

The strength Piri gains from his camaraderie with young Puerto Rican men in particular presents the complex relationship between the codes Piri himself attaches to his cultural and racial selves. The sense of self he feels in the presence of his Latino male friends contrasts with the weakness he feels when his group identity does not and cannot overshadow a racial one. His return to Harlem and to his childhood gang is marked by fights that engender feelings of manhood and community: "What a world! Whether you're right or wrong, as long as you're strong, you're right."[41] Piri goes back to the hip life of Harlem, and he feels indestructible with "his hands," the security of his Puerto Rican gang.[42] In contrast, when put in a white cultural milieu again, especially without his gang, Piri is left vulnerable to situations that heighten his own awareness of a racial self. Offering an immediate textual transition from fights with the Puerto Rican gang to an experience with a group of white teenagers on 86th Street in the next chapter, Thomas writes:

Finally I got out and started putting down shoe leather. But the paddies were hot on doing me up real nice. One of them got so close to me I saw his face over my shoulder. I stopped short and he ran right into a slap with all my weight behind it. I told him cool-like, "Motherfucker, I punch men and slap punks." . . . I heard him scream out from between his slit lips: "You dirt, fucking shine! I'll get one of you black bastards."

I screamed back, "Your mammy got fucked by one of us black bastards." *One of us black bastards. Was that me?* I wondered.[43]

Piri's verbal slippage enunciates both white society's response to his racial otherness and his internalization of that response. He identifies as black and yet is repelled by the subconscious identification. In a self-reflexive mode, he admits that he is offended by the racial identity assigned to him by white Americans: "It really bugged me when paddies called us Puerto Ricans the same names they called our colored aces,"[44] although he realizes that his other Puerto Rican male peers do not feel so threatened.

The unabridged version of this passage truly locates the codes Piri has for racial and cultural selves more than the version readers actually experience in the edition of *Down These Mean Streets* published in 1967. In the original manuscript, Piri's musings on his subconscious acceptance of the derogative "black bastard" are tellingly followed by another passage:

> I thought," [sic] about that way out feeling [of] . . . having my hand slap that Blanco dead in his boca (mouth) and that for a time when ever he looked at that fat lip, he'd know I had put it on him. "Me." A Porto Rican.[45]

"'Me.' A Porto Rican [sic]" rescripts "black bastard." As a means of renaming the self, even in hindsight, it re-establishes the personhood Piri rediscovers with his Puerto Rican gang. His fists become a way of asserting his manhood, which is tellingly imagined here in a Puerto Rican and not a black identity. For Piri, the racial identity becomes disempowering, even dehumanizing: he becomes a "black bastard" and thus is unable to be a man in American society. "Porto Rican," however, gives him the power to challenge white society—if only with his fists. Thus, he can restore the dignity he has gained from his life on the streets.

Yet, Piri's ephemeral self-identification as black is not so easily resolved; Thomas's narrative voice negotiates the movement toward blackness that his autobiographical self begins to experience. The passage in the manuscript that includes "Me. A Porto Rican" is replaced in the published version by a passage that makes a textual transition to Piri's relationships with two of his best African American friends, Brew and Crutch, and the conversations he begins to have with them about being black in the United States. Prior to this conversation, these friends had been absent or at least peripheral to the autobiographical narrative, even though it was clear that they had been part of Piri's childhood years in Harlem. Crutch, especially, had been mentioned as a friend from the street but was never given the primacy in the narrative that Louis, Crip, and other members of Piri's gang had.

Piri's contemplation of his blackness, if even in its denial, is dependent on these relationships with his African American male friends. Brew, for example, becomes the main source of support and the sounding board for Piri's racial angst. For the first time, Piri tries on a black identity in the presence of Brew, who, with his street smarts, can identify the conflict that Piri and other Puerto Ricans, as racial and ethnic minorities, feel. In turn, Piri is able to find an opening to discuss the negation of his personhood in racial and cultural terms. With a maturing clarity, he finally learns to articulate the pain of claiming both a black and a Puerto Rican identity:

> "Brew," I said, "I hate the paddy who's trying to keep the black man down. But I'm beginning to hate the black man, too, 'cause I can feel his pain and I don't know that it ought to be mine. Shit, man, Puerto Ricans got social problems, too. Why the fuck we gotta take on Negroes' . . . ?"[46]

Piri fails to admit his own color complex against persons of African descent, even though Brew is cognizant of his friend's racial prejudices. Piri's angst is not just a question of American citizenship, as he would like Brew to believe, but also one that disavows African heritage for more personal reasons. As in the scene with Mr. Christian, Piri still believes in the aesthetic and cultural value given whiteness, particularly within American society:

> I felt my hair—thick, black, and wiry. Mentally I compared my hair with my brothers' hair. . . . I felt my nose. "Shit, it ain't so flat," I said aloud. But mentally I measured it against my brothers'. . . . *Why did this have to happen to me? Why couldn't I be born like them?* I asked myself.[47]

For Piri, Puerto Rican identification is manageable and even acceptable as long as the racial ambiguity of Puerto Ricanness does not have to take on the cultural ostracism that blackness seems to demand. Piri begins to hate his brothers for what they are and what he is not. He realizes that whiteness may not offer economic wealth ("Puerto Ricans have their own social problems"), but it does offer a level of social being that seemingly cannot be claimed by identifying with other blacks in the United States.

His realization of the limitations of blackness is tellingly a lesson learned from his Latino (Cuban) father, who, although of African descent, claims he is simply of Indian/Taino ancestry. Piri's father is carefully crafted in the autobiography to embody the racial tensions within the Hispanic Caribbean community of the era highlighted by social scientists such as Mills and others: he has learned the racial binarisms and the values placed on them in the United States, and he has obviously imparted these lessons to most of his family members, including Piri, who struggles with racial diversity even within the family proper. Piri decides to go "down South" with Brew to learn what it is like to be a Negro in the United States, locating himself in the hotbed of America's racial crisis between blacks and whites after World War II. However, his family warns him that he is looking for the wrong source to claim an identity: "So whatta you got to find out, eh?" [his brother] said. "You're crazy, stone *loco*. We're Puerto Ricans, and that's different from being *moyetos*."[48] Piri sees his trip down South as the only way he can ease the confusion caused by his ambiguous racialization. The South becomes the source of real racial politics, where a man with one drop of Negro blood is black and thus is always-already a part of the African American community. At his most candid, Piri admits that he does not know the answers he will find, but he knows that to "find out what's happenin'"[49] with white American society and with even himself, he needs to make a pilgrimage to a place that he has never visited.

Thomas writes Piri's sojourn down South in the dialectical framework of what the literary critic Robert Stepto would call narratives of immersion and ascent.[50] Piri "ascends" the Puerto Rican folk/family to assert his individual black self. Yet, he travels to the South to immerse himself in the "tribal literacy"[51] of a substitute African American folk culture. With his section "Down South," Thomas suggests that Piri's travels may initiate the claiming of a Negro ancestry but also the death of a Puerto Rican one. He insinuates that in the postwar era, to find what it means to be black in the United States is to give up a Puerto Rican self. At his most strategic, Thomas locates a metaphoric death in "Funeral for a Prodigal Son," which just by its mere title foreshadows the end of Piri's close-knit relationship with his family and community. The chapter, positioned before the trip to the southern states, locates the trials Piri will undergo as the "prodigal son" who chooses to shun his community for a life outside its ethnic structure. Departing, Piri tells his father, "You protect your lying dream with a heavy strain for a white status that's worthless to a black man. You gonna have to wake up to the fact that you ain't white, but that's all right. . . . There's pride galore in being a Negro."[52] With these comments, he deepens the divide between himself and his Puerto Rican family.

Once down South, Piri and Brew meet Gerald, a mulatto, who, as the literary critic Eugene Mohr smartly surmises, is able to articulate Piri's racial conundrum with a clarity that is beyond Piri's seventeen years.[53] As a "one-eighth colored"[54] man who appears more phenotypically European than Piri, Gerald serves as Piri's alter ego in the "barroom sociology" of his black immersion experience. Gerald, a writer, faces the same problem that Thomas faces in his writing of the voyeurism of his narrator-protagonist in the South. Both Piri and Gerald have gone to southern states to claim a black past that they are not quite sure is theirs. Part of their struggles down South are embedded in a decision that ultimately has to be made. Will they be a part of the black community, and thus able to create narratives—in Thomas's case an autobiography, in Gerald's case, a historical account—that chronicle the I/we eth(n)os of their sojourns? Or, will they decide to distance themselves from the African American communal voice, empathizing with its racial struggle but reserving a space that their whiteness can afford, if only in a marginal way?

These questions introduce Piri's trip down South in the most interesting ways. The chapter "Barroom Sociology" sets up the sociological implications, as it were, of his attempt to "find me," as he tells his mother, below the Mason-Dixon Line. Even in the midst of Brew's disparaging comments and the invasive questioning of Gerald's racial allegiances, Piri feels that the bartender is a kindred soul, "except," as Piri observes, "that he was a Negro trying to make Puerto Rican and I was a Puerto

Rican trying to make Negro."[55] Although Brew has decided that Gerald is like the previously confused Piri—another "self-chosen white man"[56] —Piri cannot help being drawn emotionally to a man who finally utters a racial self that Piri has, as yet, been unable to voice with conviction:

> "*Adiós*, Gerald, take it smooth." I waved a hand and wasn't sure I meant it. But I found it hard to hate a guy that was hung up on the two sticks that were so much like mine.[57]

Gerald's conversation with Piri and Brew maps a psychological odyssey that Piri himself has undergone up to this point. Tightly structured in the chapter, the conversation, which, in actuality, is a series of conversations on the same subject, offers a narrative movement dependent on Gerald's growing self-definition of his racialization. In the conversation, Gerald migrates and develops from a racially mixed man to a Negro to a Puerto Rican and ultimately to a white man in a way that mirrors—if even in its antithesis—the racialization Piri has straddled. Of course, the difference is that Piri decides that he is Negro. Gerald, in a similar vein as Piri's relatives, feels that he is Puerto Rican, the next step to being white. Gerald, in short, assumes the cultural status that the darker Piri has not. Gerald concludes:

> I found out tonight that I am out of place. Not as a human being, but as a member of your race. I will say that you hit it on the head when you insinuated that I was trying to be a Puerto Rican so I could make the next step to white. You're right! I feel white, Mr. Johnson; I look white; I think white; therefore I am white. And I'm going back to Pennsylvania and be white.[58]

Gerald leaves the company of Brew and Piri with a new sense of himself: he is a white man. Piri, on the other hand, remains with Brew, cements his racial allegiances, and perhaps does the only thing he knows to do to assert both his blackness and his manhood: he looks for a woman at the jukebox, musing that "pussy's the same in every color."[59]

However, Thomas later suggests that, as Piri experiences the racism of whites in southern states, "pussy," in fact, is not "the same in every color." The only way for Piri to reclaim his manhood—his personhood—

is to challenge the white patriarchal system: "I wanted to break out against this two-tone South; I wanted to fuck a white woman in Texas."[60] Here, his misogynistic utterances, which have undergirded most of the autobiography's discussion of his sexual liaisons with women, come to the fore. The role he assigns women is one of property. Women, both white American and Puerto Rican, become the sites on which Piri asserts his subject-position but also his sense of dislocation. "Copping girls drawers" and his relationship with women in Spanish Harlem give him a feeling of Puerto Ricanness, and, in turn, a sense of self-value within a social formation. In contrast, his sexual and romantic liaisons with white American women reflect, if not heighten, his awareness of white American racism. Marcia, his girlfriend from the hospital, the woman on the train, and even the prostitute in Texas all begin to enunciate his impotence in the face of white American supremacy.

It is not just the prostitute's whiteness that is important to Piri's sexual escapade but the fact that she is white American *and in the South*. The two loves of Piri's life are indeed white women. Yet, they are white Puerto Rican women and thus part of his proprietary understanding of a Caribbean and masculine ethos. In fact, Brew questions Piri's relationship with white Puerto Rican women. Piri's response negotiates the differences, especially as he experiences them, between white Americans and whites within his Puerto Rican community:

> "Piri, your girl, Trina, she's white, ain't she?"
> "Yeah. So?"
> "Ah mean, ain't you-all so down on paddies?"
> "Trina's Puerto Rican, Brew."
> "But still white, man. Jus' like a Porty Rican spade is still a spade."
> "Shit, Brew," I said, "you getting things all fucked up. Trina ain't like the other kind of *blancos*. She's different."[61]

Piri's burgeoning hatred for things white seems to be a cultural one and not one predicated simply on race. Trina and Piri's mother are Puerto Rican and thus fall outside the problematics he identifies with living within white American culture. In addition, white Puerto Rican women are given a cultural currency in Thomas's autobiography that is not afforded even to white Puerto Rican men, who seek to use their white and male statuses to gain access to white America. White Puerto Rican women such as Trina, his mother, and his aunt provide and sustain an *isla* heritage that protects his sexual and personal freedoms as a Puerto Rican male of African, Spanish, and Taino descent. Through his love for and obsession with the purity and goodness of these women, he attempts to reclaim racial and Caribbean selves often denied him in the United States.

Piri's actions in the Texas brothel, then, announce a strength that he can muster only through a sex act that degrades what white America values. Paradoxically, to perform his manhood through the misuse of white American women, he has to pass as Puerto Rican and relinquish the identity he has assumed in his travels southward. In short, he cannot claim the black identity that makes him want to strike out at the symbol of white domination in the belt of white American racism. Piri must use a Mexican man to authenticate his Puerto Ricanness. He can gain access to the object of his hate only by relying on the *latinidad* of his Mexican friend to help him gain entry into the site of prostitution:

> "We would like a room and a couple of girls," [his Mexican friend] replied in a soft Texas drawl.
> The clerk said, "What does this boy here want?" He just looked at me.
> "What's your name?" he asked.
> I looked blank. Then, playing my role to perfection, I looked at my Mexican friend and said in Spanish, "What did he say?"
> "You don't understand English?" the clerk said. "Where you from? *Dónde tú eres?*"
> I lit up my face like I had just come off a banana boat.
> "Puerto Rico," I said, smiling.
> The clerk sidled over to my Mexican friend and whispered to him, "He ain't a nigger, is he?"
> My friend assured him that I wasn't.[62]

This cultural masquerade is one that Piri eagerly performs to demand the validity of his black manhood in the South. It does not matter that he pays ten dollars for sleeping with a white woman and that his friend pays only five. Piri wants to "prove something" through the intimate, ex-

ploitive, and authoritative language of sex that often conflates sexual intercourse with the exercise of power in the most heinous of terms. The
prostitute thinks that she is exploiting Piri because of the high price her
body and his color demand. Piri thinks that he is exploiting the prostitute because he has hidden behind his Puerto Ricanness to force her to
have sex with a black man.

Most interesting are the scene's textual absences that are not available
in the published version of the autobiography. Too graphic for publication in 1967 and perhaps even today, the original, unedited version
points to the psychological crisis of the self that undergirds Piri's desire
to use a white prostitute as the vehicle for denying the authority white
Americans have over his body. The sexual intercourse between Piri and
the prostitute is much more explosive in the original manuscript. It is one
of violence and hurt, desire and catharsis, almost mirroring Eldridge
Cleaver's account of his rape of white women in *Soul on Ice*. In the original scene, the narrator-protagonist adds, "I climb up on top of her, and I
force myself to kiss her. And then I fuck her; I screw her, I have intercourse with her, I wail, I push, I shove, I rip, I scream. . . . And, though
I cannot really help myself, she feels good."[63] The white woman, of
course, is oblivious to her customer's inner turmoil and thus is not in
tune with Piri's sexual performance as both an act of agony and a means
of redeeming a lost agency. Lingering on the bed, she asks, in broken
Texas Spanish, if he wants more, not knowing that he is about to unveil
his real identity as an English speaker and, consequently, an American
Negro: "'I just want you to know,' I repeated, 'that you got fucked by a
nigger, *by a black man.*'"[64]

Of course, the ontological reference to black man is circumscribed by
the politics of the American nation-state. The white Texan woman sus-
pects that Piri is black; hence, he is charged more than his Mexican
friend. Even the proprietor of the house of prostitution is worried not
that Piri is of African ancestry per se but that he is American Negro.
Again, the original manuscript of *Down These Mean Streets* proves helpful here. The first remembrance of the proprietor's words in the unedited
version of *Down These Mean Streets* gives utterance to the differences, especially for white Americans, between foreign blacks and blacks native
to the United States. The published text reads: "Well, you know, we got
all kinds of people coming in, all kinds of foreigners, and Spanish peo-

ple who come from Argentina and Colombia and Peru and Cuba, and that's all right, but we got to keep these damn niggers down."[65] In the original version, the proprietor adds: *"and some of them come over and they are so black that we don't know, you know?"*[66] The irony, of course, is that Piri again passes for something that he is: that black "Spanish" person who comes from a foreign land. Yet, as he travels down South, he does not feel that he can be Puerto Rican as that is constructed in an American context. As a bilingual speaker who is American-born, he must face a new reality that allows him to be black, and accepted as black, even as he is Puerto Rican. Without the two affirmations of a Puerto Rican and a black self, he is still disempowered.

Language is the tool by which he mediates the enunciation of a black Caribbean self. Spanish and English are both used in the brothel as dismantling tools: Spanish is used as the point of entry, English as the means of deconstructing the sexual, racial, and cultural politics of his stay in the South. In the original, unedited version of the brothel scene, symbolic images of his mother and Brew come through his mind at the moment before he switches from Spanish to English, from foreign-born to native black. These two prominent figures in his life are anchors for the enunciation of Puerto Rican and American black selves, even at their most problematical, giving him the strength to give voice to his black manhood through the power of an English tongue. His words to the prostitute in English are like weapons.[67] They are a means of lashing out at the white world, if only through words, in a way that momentarily lets him feel his strength and regain his power.

Couched in the most odious and abusive of sexual acts, however, Piri's display of his black manhood at best illustrates the anxiety and fear he feels as he is forced to embrace a black racialized self. His experiences down South confirm and undergird the hatred for whites that he first experienced in New York. They also demand a new articulation of manhood, at least in his mind, that goes beyond the sexual abuse of white women and the miscreant behavior of his days on the street: "I'm going to kill, I'm going to kill somebody. If I don't kill, I'm going to hurt one of these paddies."[68] His feelings of dehumanization as a black male make him want to lash out in the most dehumanizing of ways. He realizes that he is capable of taking the life of those who will not allow him personal freedoms.

Piri's heightened sense of his fear is exacerbated by the unexplained departure of Brew, his "ace" and "one brother,"[69] and by the death of his Puerto Rican mother upon his return to New York. Their absences in Piri's life and in the autobiographical text remove the last vestiges of a means to channel his hatred and thus to guard a part of his own humanity, even as other people seek to take it away. Brew had tried to teach Piri the ABC's of dealing with white America as they sojourned down South.[70] However, without Brew there as a reminder, Piri forgets the last and most important lesson: to care.

Similarly, his mother's death takes away the comfort and love of a Caribbean world where he is valued for his racial ambiguity, where he's not "black" but "brown, a nice color, a pretty color."[71] His mother's death covertly marks the beginning of Piri's downward spiral into the depths of dehumanization, partly caused by the life choices he soon makes for himself. The original version of the autobiography again amplifies the importance of his mother's presence and the devastating impact of her death. It highlights the voice of compassion and reason that he loses when she is no longer there as the symbol of his humanity. Contemplating his hatred for whites, his ability to kill a "paddy," his subconscious meanderings often include the voice of the mother:

> "[O]h, shit, Mom, I can't be good today, man, I got to be good tomorrow, because today I've got to be a man. And it looks like every day is going to be today for me; and there ain't going to be any tomorrows for me to be good. I know, Momma, I know, Momma."[72]

In some ways, Piri silences his mother through his diatribe and denies the power of her goodness to contain his hatred for white Americans. Yet, her presence, if only in subconscious form, offers a moment of reflection for Piri before he enters the abyss. In contrast, he is at a loss for words at her burial site, wanting to "say something so last and special to Momma" but being able to say only, "*Bendito,* Momma, I'm sorry."[73] The next time he reaches out to his mother comes when he actually injures a white policeman and is also in danger of dying: "I felt my mouth forming words, 'Mommie . . . I don't . . . Mommie, no *quiero morir.*'"[74]

In a recent interview with *Motion* magazine, Thomas revealed that Doña Lola, his mother, once said to him that "death is not dying, son, death is a state of *lo malo* (the bad)."[75] He added, explaining her words: "Death is the state of . . . all the horrors and all the hungers and all the pain, and all the promises that never come to be." Piri's cry to his mother, then, is about more than just his literal death. It vocalizes his near-certain social death, caused by his life of crime and drugs after his return from the South. This is not just the death of his Puerto Ricanness, as explored earlier in "Funeral of a Prodigal Son." At least that death had the potential to offer spiritual renewal, an ability to create a creolization of his black and Puerto Rican selves. The impending death caused by the shootout is much more devastating. It is a death where the possibility of tomorrow seems remote, where Piri, the robber, assaulter, and drug addict, has reached a point of no return.

The liberating hatred of whites by black autobiographers such as Malcolm X becomes a self-destructive one for the twenty-year-old Piri, who is afraid of living as a black man in American society: "[A]ny language you talk, if you're black, you're black. My hate grew with me. I was scared of the whole fucking world."[76] Malcolm X's hatred is channeled into a black cultural nationalism; Piri's, by contrast, is channeled into a street life in which he debases himself almost as much as the racist and classist society with which he fights. Not only does Piri undergo the agonizing life of mainstreaming and drug addiction, but he sinks into a hard-core life of crime: theft, armed robbery, and, most threatening to himself and to society, battery and assaults on his victims. Prison, ironically, becomes the moment that saves him from himself (I might also add, from his blackness), as well as ridding society of a menace: "Jesus, I thought, I finally shot some Mr. Charlies. I shot 'em in my mind often enough."[77] For Piri, the limitations of his black identity, both its psychological and social limitations, enforce a path to prison that seems inevitable. His thoughts of physically harming Mr. Charlie—the symbol of white cultural supremacy—meet reality when he is sentenced to "not less than five, no more than fifteen years"[78] in prison for attempted armed robbery and felonious assault.

In his work on black autobiographers, Kenneth Mostern observes, "Blackness is metaphorized as being imprisoned to begin with; being in jail is ground zero of the experience of blackness."[79] Although he is specifically talking about the political autobiography of Angela Davis, his comments point to Thomas's enunciation of his seven-year incarceration. I would add, however, that Piri's language of containment, fear, and anger is no longer simply embedded in a psychological crisis over accepting a black identity. The black prison experience in *Down These Mean Streets* is written as ground zero, as Mostern contends, but not as ground zero for the experience of blackness itself. The autobiographical text of *Down These Mean Streets* strategically positions the ways in which imprisonment demands a movement from identity crisis and self-destruction toward self- and group awareness. Blackness is less of a personal strain for Piri in prison.[80] His experience of blackness is more of a means of understanding, and thus having the tools to undermine, the racist and dehumanizing penal system in the United States.

As Eugene Mohr suggests in his work on Piri Thomas, Piri's earlier professions of "I'm black, I'm black" in the previous section of "Down South" give way to an articulation of an imprisoned sense of community that includes "blacks and browns," with whom he identifies. Piri is not forced to pronounce himself as black or Puerto Rican, but he can be both or neither, depending upon the situation. His friendships in prison, especially as explored in his later autobiography, *Seven Long Times* (1974), reveal a cultural openness (or closure, depending on how you read it) in which African Americans and Puerto Ricans create community as non-whites by choice or circumstance. Thus, his fight against white American society in prison is much more a fight against what he understands as institutionalization—the thing that disproportionately makes black and Puerto Rican convicts believe that they are third-class citizens in America.

What Eugene Mohr fails to mention in his reading of Piri's prison experience, but a point that I would like to closely examine, is that in prison Piri actually regains a sense of his Puerto Ricanness and suggestively is able to initiate steps toward reclaiming his humanity. This metaphoric tool used by Thomas is a very important aspect of the narrative, especially as it identifies the ongoing shifts between Piri's Puerto Rican and black identities. Mirroring the best narratives by black ex-convicts, and perhaps turning them on their heads, Thomas's text illustrates the ways in which Piri has to lose a former (read: African American) self to gain a primordial (read: Puerto Rican) self again in prison, where he has the time and space to reflect: "For the first time I was aware that I didn't know myself. . . . I wanted something better for my stick of living."[81] Bluntly said, Piri must reach ground zero, namely U.S. blackness, before he can build himself back up to assert his personhood. And, as I have argued earlier, his personhood appears available in Piri's eyes only through a Puerto Rican self. It is not coincidental that Piri finds his humanity in an atmosphere where he can once again be Puerto Rican and not simply African American.

Prison provides an interdependent community of "blacks and browns," as Thomas himself observes, but it more tellingly provides a kin base of Puerto Ricans with various racialized identities who recreate the homosocial environs of Piri's previous years in Spanish Harlem. Thomas himself glosses over the reconstruction of this environment in his eight short chapters on prison in *Down These Mean Streets,* but readers see its preeminence in Piri's prison community as relived in Thomas's 1974 prison narrative, *Seven Long Times.*[82] His friends, indeed, are a mixed group: Johnny Lee is white; L'il Henry is African American; but the rest of the crew—Bayamón, Pancho, Gordo, Bimbo, Zorro, Santurce, and Piri—are all Puerto Rican.

I am not suggesting that Thomas's recounting of his time in prison in *Down These Mean Streets* is disingenuous, but only that it is recalled, scripted, and narrativized with particular goals in mind. One of those goals seems to be the creation of a public identity for Thomas as black at the time he was writing *Down These Mean Streets* in the 1960s, using the global rendering of blacks and Puerto Ricans to displace the initial utterance of the crisis of black identity that informs the majority of his first autobiography. In *Down These Mean Streets,* Piri's focus on the challenge of being institutionalized, especially in the context of the larger fight against discrimination against ethnic minorities, allows Thomas to talk about the prison experience without fully addressing the shift in his identification from an American Negro in "Down South" to a Puerto Rican in the prison culture.

I do suggest, however, that Thomas's attempt to maintain a semblance of a black American identity in *Down These Mean Streets* is informed by the racialized, nationalist identity politics of the 1960s, which were very different from the multicultural, pluralist politics that began to shape the cultural landscape of the 1970s. *Seven Long Times,* in rewriting Thomas's prison experience as related in *Down These Mean Streets,* covertly echoes the ways in which the increase in America's immigrant population after

1965 demanded more nuanced understandings of ethnicity and ethnic allegiances and the role they played in nation building. By the 1970s, cultural pundits, the popular press, and leading scholars such as Novak (1973) and Gans (1979) had begun to seriously contemplate the persistence of ethnic identities and communities, despite century-long efforts to Americanize immigrants and their children. Americans in turn were making concerted and much celebrated efforts to retain their ethnic identities through various real and symbolic cultural practices.

Although black cultural nationalism had not disappeared by 1973, the decade's discourses on cultural pluralism and multiculturalism at once articulated and expanded the dynamics of assimilation possibilities for ethnic minorities and children of immigrants. Particularly for immigrant second generationers of color, like Piri Thomas and other Puerto Ricans, a paradigmatic shift toward the validation of ethnicity in American culture created the space for an exploration of black and Latino selves as not necessarily oppositional. Assimilation into the racial binarisms of the United States was no longer the goal, as educators, theorists, social scientists, and cultural critics contended.[83] Instead, the goal was to "recognize the uniqueness and value of every culture" and thus to change the relationship of ethnic minorities to dominant culture(s).[84] In short, by the 1970s, Thomas, like Audre Lorde, was provided the intellectual, cultural, and perhaps even deracinated space to consider the possibilities of multiple identity constructions.

In *Down These Mean Streets*, Piri's fight to join the "human race" is often written as a self-motivated, individualized experience.[85] It is only in *Seven Long Times* that readers experience Piri's movement toward self-improvement as more than an individual act, as one nurtured by a Puerto Rican communal voice. The most poignant and suggestively "human" moments of his prison experience are usually those when Piri is surrounded by the comradeship of his Puerto Rican friends:

> Bayamón had a guitar that had been sent to him and was strumming some home music from Puerto Rico. Pancho and Santurce were rapping out a bongo and conga beat. Zorro was using his comb on the side of a tin can and the rest were clapping hands and stomping feet in perfect Latin rhythm, like Afro-Latin. Gordo was singing a chant, "Wa-wan-

co, wa-wan-co." Not to be left out, I made clucking sounds, trying to do a passable impression of *los palitos,* "the little sticks" that are struck together and give an on or off beat.[86]

Prison allows Piri to re-enter a communal experience of Puerto Rican expressiveness that is lost in his trip down South and in his Skid Row existence once he returns to Harlem. Notably, Piri does not *want* to be left out. He finds it imperative that he assert his Puerto Ricanness, that he, too, enunciate a "passable" *puertorriquenidad* even amid the supposedly undifferentiated "black and brown" community of the prison system. Also, Thomas's writing of his prison days in *Seven Long Times* incorporates a black Puerto Rican identity that supersedes, even moves beyond, the paradigmatic shift between African American and Puerto Rican that *Down These Mean Streets* articulates. Piri is not African American, nor is he simply Puerto Rican. His participation in the making of Afro-Latin beats suggests a Puerto Rican communion that is able to both acknowledge and incorporate his black Hispanic presence.

An African American self, although donned, is not presented to be as self-actuating as a Puerto Rican one. Piri *does* join a mostly African American clique of the Black Muslims while in Comstock. He joins it in his search for dignity and self-respect, but he does not remain in the religious group. Although he appreciates the Muslim's style of living, and even changes his name to Hussein Afmit Ben Hassen for a while, Piri is not able to gain the spiritual and cultural renewal he experiences privately with his Puerto Rican male friends. His Puerto Rican friends give him a cultural tap root, namely Puerto Rico, that the Muslims with their cultural nationalism cannot provide:

> "Caramba," Pancho studied his drawing. "Just looking at this scene— wow." . . . And looking at the scene of El Morro in my hands, he said, "you ought to go there when you get a chance, Piri. It's like *nada* else."
>
> "Yeah," I nodded my head thoughtfully in agreement, "I ain't never been there, all right. Kinda like *mi madre* used to talk up storm about the island. You know, stuff about how beautiful it was, with all them *chevere* beaches and mountains, all different *frutas,* and all the sunshine one could stand. Yeah, Pancho, Puerto Rico is on my agenda."[87]

This scene in *Seven Long Times* amplifies and even negates the amorphous cultural location of "blacks and browns" used in *Down These Mean Streets.*[88] It gives the Black Muslims a peripheral presence in the day-to-day existence of Piri's private prison life and thus unearths a Puerto Rican community that literally and figuratively gives Piri Puerto Rico through drawings, songs, and shared memories. In *Down These Mean Streets,* no doubt because of the publishing moment and because of their popularity/notoriety in American media, Black Muslims are given an entire chapter. In *Seven Long Times,* published seven years after *Down These Mean Streets,* the Nation of Islam is afforded three paragraphs, which simply discuss the ways in which the Muslims "walked in dignity" and "put forth their thoughts . . . in quiet, soft-spoken voices, with courtesy and self-respect."[89]

The passages on the Black Muslims in *Seven Long Times* are tellingly preceded by the narrator-protagonist's discussion of hearing "Afro-Latin music on congas, bongos, timbals, guitars" in the east wall—beats that again help Piri imagine the freedom engendered through the recuperation of a Puerto Rican self: "My mind threw me back to the outside where I saw myself with a *chevere* woman doing some together *alma* steps in a dancehall."[90] The contrasting images of the Black Muslims, whom he purports to respect, and the imagining of himself in the salsa dancehall, something forbidden for single men within the Nation of Islam, provide a stark example of the ways in which Thomas frames Piri's personal and cultural power within a Puerto Rican identity.

In the extended account of Piri's prison experience in *Seven Long Times,* the African American cultural nationalism symbolized by the Black Muslims is replaced by Piri's ongoing homosocial interactions with his Puerto Rican friends, who are able to support his individual as well as cultural growth by sharing the day-to-day life cycles of prison: lunches, free time, and even birthdays. The uneasiness of his experiences with Black Muslims as related in *Down These Mean Streets*—he mistakenly offers brothers cigarettes, improperly addresses the imam, and has difficulty interpreting the language of the nationalist religion—gives way to what Thomas, at his most candid, in *Seven Long Times,* identifies as Piri's sense of "coming from a family" when in a Puerto Rican social environment.[91] Shared experiences, music, and the re-creation of Puerto Rican cultural spaces in the company of Latino men afford a sense of community for Piri. The tone of Thomas's recollection of his experience in the Nation of Islam never suggests that the Muslims do—or, for that matter, can—offer Piri a cultural self. Instead, although presented in a favorable light, Black Muslims are written as Other to his private, Puerto Rican identity in prison.

My argument that Piri attempts to regain his humanity through a rearticulation of his Puerto Rican identity is supported by the ways in which he fights institutionalization with both rhetoric and actions that attempt to maintain his Puerto Rican manhood. In the company of his Puerto Rican prison clique, Piri feels that his manhood is no longer threatened by a black self, but it does seem threatened by what Thomas suggests is its corollary of containment: (homo)sex in prison. Piri's anxiety over a black identity wanes, but he becomes anxious about the "sex in the can," the alternative means of loving and living in an all-male environment.

It is not so much that Piri's homophobic language renders a Puerto Rican voice, although it arguably gives utterance to Latino machismo. The enunciation of masculinity, instead, is embedded in a language of a free, "authentic" self that is positioned outside prison and inside a Puerto Rican cultural milieu. Homosexuality becomes the moment of crisis, as did African Americanness in the earlier moments of the text, because it precludes Piri's participation within a heterosexually biased society upon release. Piri wants to return to a Puerto Rican self outside prison, where he can visit Puerto Rico, see Tía Angelita, and marry his girlfriend, Trina. Piri's anthem "They Ain't Gonna Break Me" is a fight against what he understands as his two nemeses: the racist penal system that forces men to live out sexual lives that bar them from a "normal" identity outside of prison and the prison men who succumb to the institutionalization of sex as they search for means of sexual expression.

In "Tearing the Goat's Flesh: Homosexuality, Abjection, and the Production of a Late-Twentieth-Century Black Masculinity," the queer theorist Robert Reid-Pharr provides perhaps the best analysis of Thomas's use of homosexuality in his prison sequence. He writes:

> To strike the homosexual, the scapegoat, the sign of chaos and crisis, is to return the community to normalcy, to create boundaries around blackness, rights that indeed white men are obliged to recognize.[92]

Reid-Pharr reads Thomas's *Down These Mean Streets* alongside the auto-biography of Eldridge Cleaver and the novel *Giovanni's Room* by James Baldwin. He argues that Thomas in particular "deploys the figure of the homosexual at precisely those moments when the complex ambiguity of his 'standing' within his various communities is most apparent."[93] I agree with Reid-Pharr's analysis of Thomas's use of homosexuality but would push his argument one step further, acknowledging the shift in Thomas's formal use of blackness and Puerto Ricanness within Piri's prison environs. The chaos that homosexuality brings to Piri's blackness does not necessarily initiate another moment of crisis. In fact, blackness, particularly if read as African Americanness, no longer becomes the ever-present, overriding identity issue for Piri. However, (homo)sex in prison initiates a moment of crisis for Piri's understanding of his Puerto Rican-ness recovered within prison walls. In some ways, Piri's articulation of the chaos homosexuality presents to his identity is on a very simple, na-tivistic level: "I came in here my father's son. . . . I'll be damned if I go out my mother's daughter."[94] Piri makes the psychological return to the kinship of his Latino father, whom he had culturally left before. More telling, Piri sees homosexual advances and even his own latent desires as that articulation again of institutionalization that will ultimately hinder him from having a "normal" relationship on the "free side" with the quintessential ideal of Puerto Ricanness: namely the Puerto Rican woman.

Two examples advance my point. The first, from *Down These Mean Streets,* is the occasion when Piri is confronted by Claude, an effeminate gay man and not one of what Piri describes as the "asshole artists," who participate in (homo)sex for violent aggression or sexual release. Claude wants to establish a romantic liaison with Piri and asks Piri to be his "daddy-o." Piri is almost receptive to Claude's offer, almost seeing Claude as a "real" woman across the green bars on his prison cell. But, he later retracts, reminding himself that "outside is real" and "inside is a lie":

> "Claude," I said, "if I gotta break your fuckin' jaw, I will. They've put a wall around me for fifteen years, but I've got something real outside, and it makes no difference when I get out, married or not, she's mine, and there'll be no past for the two of us, just a stone present and a cool future.[95]

The second example is a drug-induced dream in prison, taken from *Seven Long Times*. The dream, quoted at length, renders an "outside" reality imagined as the antithesis to homosexualization, that is, institutionalization, in prison:

> Oh, holy mackerel, gee whiz, diggit!! I'm home. I can't believe it. I'm really back. Oh, man, is Trina gonna be surprised. . . . Oh, Trina, I ain't ever gonna fuck up again. . . . You and me . . . we're gonna check out of *El Barrio* and find some place in Puerto Rico and raise lambs and make *mucho* babies. . . . Shit, baby we'll get us a *finca* way up in the mountains of Borinquen with all kinds of mango trees, *aguacates,* and all the other goodie trees. We'll make mucho beautiful love by the light of multi-colored sunsets and wake up to the sunrise with more of the same. Baby, *chica,* like no more I'm *un numero* called "18193." I'm Piri like always, and I'm free. Caramba, hon-ee, splitting to Puerto Rico will mean we can cover ourselves with blankets of warm Puerto Rico breeze and dig all kinds of music from singing *pajaritos* and chirping *coquís.*[96]

I juxtapose these two passages because, when they are read together, Piri's "something real outside" is translated into his relationship with Trina, who is able to sustain Puerto Rico for him. Trina's ethnic identity and her gender allow Piri to participate in a "normative" creation of "*mucho* babies," which he represents as the essence of the Puerto Rican family, and thus as a symbol of belonging in a Puerto Rican communal structure. Piri, ironically, does not envision a normal life outside in *el barrio* of Spanish Harlem. In Harlem, (homo)sex, as his childhood experience in the gay men's apartment attests,[97] and African Americanness remain threats to his Puerto Rican male self. It is only when he imagines a life with Trina *in* Puerto Rico, a place where he has never been but that he is determined to visit, that he is able to truly relinquish his feeling of nothingness—his 18193 status as a number and not a human being. Tellingly, he rejects Claude, who is male and African American, for Trina, who is Puerto Rican and a woman. Claude is attractive to him, perhaps in the same way that African Americanness becomes an attractive option to Piri as a black Puerto Rican in the United States. However, Trina becomes the prize that helps him maintain his Puerto Rican manhood and selfhood. Piri needs Trina, whom he can have only through heterosexism, to consummate his reconnection to a Puerto Rican cultural heritage.

Of course, Piri eventually loses Trina, who marries another man while he is in prison and later has a child. He is paroled after a seven-year prison stay and returns to the place that has been an ongoing source of great pride and pain, of cultural renewal and personal destruction: "I fought to keep from being swallowed up again by Harlem's hustles and rackets."[98] If not a losing one, Piri's battle as a parolee seems to challenge his hard-earned understanding of his humanity within the prison walls. His cries of "I want . . . to be somebody" and "I am an *hombre* that wants to be better"[99] often fall on deaf ears as he tries to assert his humanity in both Harlem's streets and the American cultural economy.

*Down These Mean Streets* ends not as a testament to Piri's triumphs as a racial, sexual, and human being but, rather, in a similar way as its beginning: the story of a Latino second generationer still trying to find and articulate his place in American society. The sense of knowing regained in prison—that sense that he is ultimately a black Puerto Rican—gives way to an uncertainty about what Harlem will ultimately choose for him. The last professed thoughts of the book conjure Trina and Brew—his yesterdays—in a way that still leaves him confused about a racial self: "I was a kid yesterday and my whole world was yesterday. I ain't got nothing but today and a whole lot of tomorrows."[100] As the autobiography concludes, his Puerto Rican buddy asks Piri if he's "making it" outside prison, to which Piri responds, "Yeah." However, his affirmative answer is a long way from being convincing, even to Piri, as the "sad-assed" bolero has the ultimate and prophetic last words.[101]

So, what about the Puerto Rican Negro, whose tongue speaks Spanish and whose skin shouts Negro? At the moment of writing *Down These Mean Streets* in the 1960s, Thomas himself seemed unable to answer the question he posed throughout his first autobiography. He confided to Wolfgang Binder in their 1980 interview that he was still experiencing an identity crisis as he wrote his first book:

> I felt both Puerto Rican and Black, you understand? During the sixties
> I was so strongly into the Black movement that almost all my friends
> were Black, Black. And I was talking Black, and I was feeling Black.
> There was a Puerto Rican woman who was married to a Black doctor,

> Dr. Barrows, and sitting one day in her house she looked at me and said, "*Ay bendito, Piri, te vamos a perder.*" She meant that culturally, and it shook me. I was shaking! . . . She had said that with such pain; I was ready to become an American Black, and yet I knew that I was not fully accepted by Blacks! I sensed that also when I was a member of the Harlem Writers' Guild.[102]

The tension of racial and cultural identities in *Down These Mean Streets* is ultimately left unresolved. Piri may become black at various moments, but he never seems to give up his need to be Puerto Rican. Readers do not experience the easing of this tension around racial and gender binaries until his later autobiographies, written in the 1970s: *Seven Long Times,* which, in fact, revises his prison experience, and *Savior, Savior, Hold My Hand* (1972), which talks of his work with inner-city youth. Yet, Thomas's negotiation of blackness in *Down These Mean Streets* helps situate the emerging identity politics of Spanish Caribbean immigrants in postwar America. It is one of the first cultural productions by a black Latino in the twentieth century that engaged—if even in the most problematic ways—the racial discourses of American society.[103] In *Down These Mean Streets,* Thomas attempts to work through racial, cultural, and gendered selves in ways that anticipate the cultural productions of second generationers at the turn of the century. *Down These Mean Streets* initiates the use of blackness by ambiguously racialized Caribbean immigrants in particular, who, as I argue in the final chapter, appear to have more success in locating their racial and cultural selves.[104]

# CHAPTER 5

# "Diasporic Intimacy"

Merengue Hip Hop,
*Proyecto Uno*, and
Representin'
Afro-Latino Cultures

The horns blast, illuminating the rhythms of Cheryl Lynn's 1978 disco classic, "To Be Real." The frenetic merengue beat then attempts to take over. Magic Juan of *Proyecto Uno*, a merengue hip-hop quartet, raps first in Spanish and then in English:

| | |
|---|---|
| Fui a la discoteca | [I went to the discotheque |
| A ver si me conseguía | To see if I could get |
| Una fresca | A drink] |
| Got myself some rum | |
| Cause where I come from | |
| Sometimes you need some[1] | |

As the African American beats of "To Be Real" compete with the Dominican rhythms of the tambora and the güira for dominance, the spatial nexus conjured by *"El tiburón"*[2] is deliberately unclear. Magic Juan speaks of the 'hood in his lyrics; yet, neither the chorus nor the listener is certain whether his character's home is *aquí* or *allá*, New York City or Santo Domingo. The double entendre of the song situates *el tiburón*, literally the shark, as the cultural hegemonic power that tries to hinder the character's border crossing. In the character's voyeuristic interplay with women at the club, one that metaphorically represents his leap from one cultural locale to the other, *el tiburón* attempts to assert authority without success:

> Magic Juan:
> Y cuando llegué        [And when I arrived
> Llegó el tiburón       The shark arrived
> Y con él se me fue     And with him, she left me
>
> Chorus:
> Allí está, allí está         There he is, there he is
> Se la llevó el tiburón . . . The shark carried her away
> No pare[s], sigue sigue      Don't stop, keep on going. . . .
> No pare[s], sigue sigue      Don't stop, keep on going. . . .]
>
> Magic Juan:
> Okay, tanto, encontré otra chica que estaba mejor
> [Okay, enough, I found another girl who was better]

With "*no pare[s], sigue sigue,*" Magic Juan's character is encouraged to affirm the reality of his bicultural experience. He can be anywhere in the Dominican diasporic landscape at any time, disclaiming the boundaries of New York City and the Dominican Republic as he claims his right to both worlds:

> She looked good
> So, of course, I lied on my girl
> From the 'hood
> Ella preguntó si tenía novia y yo dije no
> [She asked if I had a girlfriend, and I said no]

The policing of cultural bodies is shunned in "*El tiburón.*" Cultural identity cannot be confined by the link to one novia, one locale. Ethnic particularism is replaced by the transgression of boundaries: the lyrics jump from one female to another, and, finally, the musical rhythm settles on an equivocal African American/Dominican beat during the most politically powerful lines. For the hip hoppers of *Proyecto Uno,* the transgression is just the beginning.

The emergence of *Proyecto Uno's* merengue hip-hop sound in the 1990s epitomizes what George Lipsitz understands as the benefits of "crossroads" in his analysis of popular music: "Collisions occur at the crossroads; decisions must be made there. But the crossroads can also provide a unique perspective, a vantage point where one can see in more than one direction."[3] Merengue hip hop fuses merengue and hip-hop styles and instrumentations to produce disruptions and layers, creating new sounds through the blending of island and African American musical formations. In songs like *"El Tiburón,"* Proyecto Uno uses the multi-directionality of merengue hip hop to unveil and imagine a cultural engagement with African American *and* Spanish Caribbean cultures. Post-1965 migration waves from places like the Dominican Republic and Puerto Rico to urban American centers have linked Latino second generationers, either by similar economic circumstances or racial backgrounds, to African Americans and black Caribbean immigrants from Barbados, Jamaica, and other countries. The donning of an American identity has been significantly undergirded by the acquiring of a *black* American self. For the Latino second generationers of *Proyecto Uno,* who attempt to participate in multiple cultural locations, a new identity as black in an American cultural sphere puts them at the crossroads—a place where, as George Lipsitz asserts, "decisions must be made."

In this chapter, I offer an analysis of the merengue hip-hop music of *Proyecto Uno,* a group started by two Dominican Americans in New York City. My goal is to establish a framework for engaging the cultural performances of second-generation artists at the close of the twentieth century. Although this chapter serves as a conclusion to my earlier chapters, it seeks to open rather than close intellectual debates on the representations of Caribbean American and second-generation identities in music, literature, and other expressive forms. I create a discursive space for examining the cultural productions of "new" second generationers—made up of post-1965 immigrant youth like "Herbie" from the book's introduction—who illuminate issues of race, ethnicity, and gender through the language of hip hop to offer their own spin on the Caribbean migration narrative.

This chapter's focus on music is influenced by the scholarly examinations of African American and Latino musical genres by cultural theorists such as Hazel Carby (1990), Farah Jasmine Griffin (1995), and Frances Aparicio (1998).[4] Their various readings on music as sites in which racial, sexual, and cultural identities are negotiated provide a lens through which I offer my close readings of selected songs written and produced by *Proyecto Uno*'s members. Although the works by these scholars differ in tone and direction, their analytical readings of music— which include examinations of lyrics, vocals, and instrumentations— suggest the importance of music to the ways in which identity is socially and culturally produced.

*Proyecto Uno* was started by its member Nelson Zapata and its producer, Pavel de Jesús. The group has had modest success on the charts in the United States and was once the poster child of "Jelly Bean" Benitez's record label, Home of Latino Artists (HOLA) Recordings, which sought to introduce Latino and urban black musical fusions to a larger American market. The group has been most successful, however, in Latin America, where its award-winning songs such as *"Brinca"* and "Another Night" have been number one hits.[5] *Proyecto Uno* has inspired and often helped create the other merengue hip-hop acts such as *Los Ilegales* and *Sandy y Papo* in the Dominican Republic and *Fulanito* in the United States.

Given the contemporary debates over hip-hop culture, the study of the cultural expressions of *Proyecto Uno* and other second-generation immigrants seems long overdue.[6] Debates over hip-hop music have permeated popular culture and media with special attention given to rap's lyrical contents, glorification of the "gangsta" lifestyle, and embrace of male chauvinism and misogyny.[7] Hip-hop culture has been a particular issue for parents of Caribbean second generationers and scholars of migration studies. Latino listeners and practitioners of hip hop whom I interviewed for this chapter often asserted that their parents thought that a love for hip hop and participation in African American cultural practices were signs that they were neglecting their cultural roots.[8] The migration scholars Min Zhou, Alejandro Portes, and Mary C. Waters seem to agree. In their work on second-generation immigrants, Zhou and Portes observe that hip hop can be seen as a "cloaking" of a Caribbean identity in "black

American cultural forms."[9] Similarly, Mary Waters notes that "American-identified" second generationers who "speak black English with their peers, . . . listen to rap music, and . . . accept the peer culture of their black American friends" seem to give up their Caribbean ethnicities to participate in African America.[10]

I disagree with these conclusions and in their place ask: What eludes contemporary discourses on hip hop in America when people simply focus on its misogyny or, as it relates to both African American and Caribbean youth, the loss of an "authentic" cultural self? As Tricia Rose and Robin Kelley suggest in their studies of hip-hop culture, when scholars, social critics, and American citizens focus solely on the "anti-societal" aspects of hip hop, they fail to grasp the covert motifs *behind* the cultural discourses of youth that are taking place in urban dwellings.[11] Especially as it pertains to Latino hip hoppers in the United States, the most recent focus on hip-hop culture as an "adversarial culture," or one representative of the "values and norms of the inner city," unnecessarily limits an understanding of the exploration of black identity constructions evidenced in the cultural imaginings of second generationers like the members of *Proyecto Uno*.[12]

For example, what can scholars learn from songs like *"El tiburón,"* which are neither cloaked in African Americanness nor politically or culturally distanced from it? *"El tiburón,"* along with other merengue hip-hop songs by *Proyecto Uno,* creates a musical crossroads that proffers a multicultural, diasporic lens. The use of samples from a bona fide African American jam like "To Be Real" is not arbitrary. Beats of "To Be Real" in *"El tiburón"* situate the poetics of place: the inner city, basement parties, black Chicago, black New York, the black Caribbean. The merengue hip hop of *Proyecto Uno* suggests a means by which its members flow and ebb within the place deemed African America as they simultaneously explore the complexities of their Spanish Caribbean identities. *Proyecto Uno* covertly implies that the borrowing of sounds is *very* political. "To Be Real" undergirds the narrative of *"El tiburón."* "You've got to be real, you've got to be real" the instrumentation implores, mimicking the actual lyrics of Cheryl Lynn. The second generationers of *Proyecto Uno* position African America as speaking to its Afro-Latino brethren: "You've got to be real." The sounds of *Proyecto Uno* encourage the legitimization of

Latino culture. "You've got to be real" insinuates that "you've got to be real" to your black and Hispanic identities.

In this chapter, I do not make any attempts to glorify hip-hop culture or persuade readers to ignore the misogyny embedded in the lyrics of *Proyecto Uno*'s performative songs. In fact, I plan to place these particular elements of the group's music within a larger discussion that explores what Paul Gilroy terms "diasporic intimacy." In his essay "Cultural Studies and Ethnic Absolutism," Gilroy's use of diasporic intimacy advances that black musical genres such as hip hop can serve as sites for expressing immigrants' particular ethnospecific struggles for power and agency in the United States. They also provide a means of discussing the dialectic at play when the black diaspora reconvenes—through commercialized media, proximity, or both—to build on similar cultural practices and to create black Atlantic dialogues that undermine boundaries once instituted by the sovereignty of nation-states.[13] At once, the merengue hip hop of *Proyecto Uno* can suggest a means of resistance to domination —societal, parental, cultural—and a means of engaging, interacting, and thus changing the multiple cultures of African descendants who, perhaps not so ironically, find themselves in the postcolonial predicament of living side by side in U.S. urban landscapes.

The changing sound of musical genres such as merengue, for instance, articulates the ways in which the music made by *Proyecto Uno* elucidates the "self-identity, political culture and grounded aesthetics" of a diasporic intimacy in the making.[14] Merengue has often been called *la voz dominicana.*[15] The merengue hip hop of *Proyecto Uno,* then, can be seen as this voice in transition, or, as Paul Gilroy would term it, the voice "invented in the jaws of modern experience."[16] Modern experience both determines and reveals the phenomenal music-making process of merengue hip hop. The lyrics written by *Proyecto Uno*'s members, the sampling of old and new hip-hop beats, and the inversion of merengue from the Dominican Republic reveal that the music-making process—or, as the ethnomusicologist Christopher Smalls suggests, the "musicking"—entails much more than the making of music itself.[17] Modern experience—that is, the deconstruction of nation-states and the popularity of hip hop— impels artists to envision a transfertilization of postcolonial black musical genres in the production of their merengue hip hop. However, the modern experience of American xenophobia and its proximity to other African-derived cultures also encourages a merengue hip-hop musicking that documents and solidifies a postmodern interconnectedness between multiple sites of blackness in the United States.

This chapter's analysis of *Proyecto Uno*'s music is organized into three sections. First, to contextualize the discussion of the group's fusion of merengue and hip hop, the first section gives a historical background of merengue and its importance to the construction of cultural nationalism in its birthplace, the Dominican Republic. It pays special attention to the employment of merengue in the racial politics of nation-building on the island. The next section turns to Dominican migration to the United States, identifying the social formations of Dominican communities in places such as Washington Heights in New York City. This section sets the stage for the subsequent discussion of hip hop and the ways in which it develops as both a response to the urban crises of second-generation youth and a genre that reveals dialogues between African Americans and Caribbean immigrants in the United States. Finally, the last section gives a close reading of several songs by *Proyecto Uno*, examining the group's performance of black and Latino identities. This final section explores the racial, gender, and sexual identities represented through the imaginative terrain of hip-hop culture in *Proyecto Uno*'s music.

## Negrophobia: Race, Merengue, and the Dominican Nation

On the jacket cover for Angel Viloria's *Merengues Vol. 2,* recorded in April 1953, the liner notes read, "Probably one of the greatest events in the history of recorded music was the transplant of the merengue, *of Spanish origin,* brought to the colonies of the New World."[18] In 1975, Luis Alberti, a well-known composer during Rafael Trujillo Molina's dictatorship in the Dominican Republic (1930–1961), remarked that he did not think that merengue "had anything to do with African or Negroid rhythms."[19] Instead, he observed, merengue was "a mix of Spanish [influences] and our peasant songs from the interior[.]"[20] Conversely, contemporary scholars, particularly ethnomusicologists living outside the

Dominican Republic, often resist the Hispanization of merengue.[21] In his study of merengue, Paul Austerlitz concludes that the Dominican Republic's "myriad musics include a wealth of African-derived styles . . . ; and many styles, such as merengue and mangulina, that fuse African and European elements."[22]

It is difficult to talk about merengue, even in its hip-hop form, without considering its importance to the development of a cultural identity for the Dominican diaspora. Since the dictatorship of Rafael Trujillo Molina, discussions of merengue have often been connected with discussions of race, class, and the communal struggle of Dominican identity against "outside"—usually Haitian and American—cultural forces. Knowing the power of music, Rafael Trujillo Molina used merengue to establish a sense of Dominican nationality. As Deborah Pacini Hernández observes in *Bachata: A Social History of Dominican Popular Music,*

> Under [Trujillo's] tutelage Dominican popular music responded to a very specific agenda: propaganda. He first used merengue in his 1930 political campaign; but even after he seized power and up until his death, he continued to use music, particularly merengue, to indoctrinate and control the populace.[23]

Trujillo's use of music to gain and maintain power reverberated in the number of pro-Trujillo songs that were commissioned or created "voluntarily" during his dictatorship. Paul Austerlitz notes that *Antología musical de la era Trujillo,* a collection of music published in the Dominican Republic, contains "three hundred merengues" dedicated to Trujillo.[24] Trujillo's use of music as propaganda was significant to the formation of national identity. Not only did he use music to quell possible insurrections from both the elite and the Dominican proletariat; he also used music in the production of what Etienne Balibar terms a "fictive ethnicity," an imagined sense of Dominicanness.[25] The success of Trujillo's propaganda is obvious: by the 1950s, most Dominicans from different strata of society had taken a regional folk music—*merengue cibaeño*—and claimed it as their own, often discarding their previous musical allegiances.[26]

Trujillo's attempt to create a national identity for the Dominican Republic often centered around the de-Africanization of the national community and its newly claimed national music. The production of fictive ethnicity supported by Trujillo's negrophobic regime insisted that the Dominican Republic was not a black nation; black was a designation reserved for its neighboring country, Haiti. In 1937, at the onset of his dictatorship, Trujillo called for a one-time execution of all "blacks," meaning Haitians, in the Dominican Republic. This state-sponsored annihilation of many Haitians—and even many dark-skinned Dominicans—was one of many steps in the attempt to reclaim a Hispanic and white genealogy for Dominican society. The massacre had lingering effects on the racial climate and national narratives of Dominican culture.

Linked to the antiblack sentiment during Trujillo's dictatorship was the regime's negation of black influences on merengue itself. The national merengue was a form derived from a white(r)-populated area of the Dominican Republic, the Cibao region, and thus was not typically associated with African cultural expressions, although it arguably included African-derived elements in its percussive rhythms. Even though bands such as Luis Alberti's *Orquesta Presidente Trujillo* experimented with Afro-Cuban drumming and African American jazz, Trujillo's regime invented a national narrative for merengue that located it as a commercialized product of Iberian culture. Working with Alberti and other *merengueros,* the regime "gentrified" merengue in an attempt to distance it from an association with black and working-class roots. The Trujillo-influenced folklorist Flérida de Nolasco once noted, "Dominican folk music cannot be but a derivation of Spanish music, adjusted to the environment, corrupted when it has fallen into inexpert hands, and sometimes contaminated black music [*sic*], of savage stupidity."[27] The cultural legacy of Trujillo's dictatorship thus was the establishment of music as a symbol of Dominican culture and as the essence of a Dominican identity strategically and systematically stripped of the country's black heritage.

State repression under Trujillo led to at least two aspects of Dominican cultural formation: the marginalization of black ancestry on the island and the parallel political and economic turmoil that increased levels of out-migration after Trujillo's assassination in May 1961. The assassination brought further political unrest and uncertainty to a country that had historically suffered from poverty and political instability. This unrest continued under the next president, Joaquín Balaguer, who, although promising economic expansion, instituted national programs that supported industrialization and adversely affected agricultural economies and the masses of Dominican laborers who resided in rural areas.[28]

The post-Trujillo era has been characterized by a mass exodus of Dominicans first among the middle class and increasingly among those of working-class and rural origins. As dictator, Trujillo severely restricted out-migration. By contrast, Balaguer, in order to defuse the political unrest invoked by fighting between political factions, eased emigration restrictions with the support of U.S. officials, who feared the repercussions of trouble in the Caribbean basin. The United States began to grant more visas in the early 1960s, especially between 1961 and 1963.[29] Moreover, in 1965, out-migration was supported by changes in U.S. immigration policy brought about by the Hart-Celler Immigration Reform Act of 1965.[30] Political activists and radicals were the first to migrate to the United States in the early 1960s. They were followed by urban, middle-class Dominicans who had benefited under Balaguer's presidency from increased opportunities in the industrial sectors of the city but who could not receive adequate compensation for their labor in the failing economy. Soon, Dominicans from rural backgrounds who had first been forced to migrate to cities such as Santo Domingo to search (unsuccessfully) for work joined the mass exodus to American cities like New York.[31]

Trujillo set the stage for the migration of Dominicans to communities of African-derived cultures in the United States. The United States had had a long and often contentious history with its Caribbean neighbor; as Silvio Torres-Saillant and Ramona Hernández reveal, its interest in the Dominican Republic dates back to the early years of the twentieth century. It had occupied/invaded the Dominican Republic in both 1916 and 1965, ostensibly to secure democratic forms of governance, but, perhaps more realistically, to safeguard its own economic interests and national security. The Dominican Republic thus became a strategic site from which to challenge the power and autonomy of the black nation Haiti, the threat of European imperialism, and communism in America's backyard.[32]

By 1990, there were 332,713 Dominicans in New York alone.[33] According to the migration scholars Patricia Pessar, Sherri Grasmuck, and Eugenia Georges, Dominicans migrated to the United States in search of

better economic opportunities and to escape political repression.[34] The
United States was seen as an attractive site because of its historical and
powerful presence in the cultural and social economies on the island. Yet,
upon arrival, Dominican immigrants often found a shrinking labor market, deindustrialization, housing discrimination, and racial and class
prejudices in American society. They settled in ethnic enclaves where interaction with other minority groups, those also shut out of the labor
market and social economy, became the norm. Urban Dominican ghettoes, such as Washington Heights, in upper Manhattan, or Corona,
Queens, became cultural satellites alongside the older communities of
African Americans, Puerto Ricans, and black immigrants from other
Caribbean islands.


## Urban Crisis, Roots, and Rap: Second-Generation Youth in Post-1965 African America

The development of hip-hop culture paralleled the influx of Dominican
immigrants to the United States. Created in the Bronx in the 1970s, hip-
hop culture responded to the limitations of the postindustrial city, where
urban youth experienced a decline in educational opportunities, economic support services, and affordable and safe housing. In her seminal
study of rap music, Tricia Rose notes that hip hop emerged as a youth
movement that explored the crisis of urban existence, as it simultaneously became a site for pleasure and fun.[35] African American, West Indian, and Latino youth attempted to comment on and critique their marginalized statuses in urban ghettoes while establishing a regenerative
space that offered communal support from "posses," "crews," and other
b-boys and girls. Urban youth created a culture where agency was
gained through alternative paradigms of power legitimated by themselves. Break-dancing, graffiti writing, disc jockeying, and the lyrical
play of the spoken word positioned urban youth as a constituency in
New York that would be heard.

  As hip hop developed in the 1970s, it was a negotiation of urban crises
for African American, West Indian, and Latino hip hoppers, but it was
also a negotiation of racial and ethnic identities and allegiances for

Caribbean second generationers. Although Rose challenges us to resist the temptation to racialize hip hop, the interaction and confluent experiences of youth from African American and Caribbean cultures supported a transculturation that announced and legitimized the shared lifestyles of various black ethnic populations in the United States. In his discussion of diasporic intimacy, Paul Gilroy points out that black musical genres such as hip hop "enact the ties of affiliation and affect" that become key components of "black Atlantic creativity."[36] West Indian youth in particular, despite the commonly held belief that African America is the singular origin of the genre, helped shape the development of hip hop's cultural practices. One of hip hop's first identifiable elements, disk jockeying, was influenced by the toasting style found in the dance scene of urban dwellers in Kingston, Jamaica. DJ Kool Herc (né Clive Campbell) came to the United States from Jamaica in 1967, and he used toasting and the Jamaican sound system to establish his own style of slicing, layering, and voice-overs at dance parties in the 1970s. Grandmaster Flash (né Joseph Saddler), a second-generation Barbadian immigrant, also helped establish the hip-hop sound with the use of breaks and percussive beats while disc jockeying. Another Barbadian second generationer, Afrika Bambaataa, of "Planet Rock" fame, brought black, Latino, and white youth together in his "Zulu Nation," establishing a sense of community through the common language of hip-hop music and culture.[37]

Latino youth, primarily of Puerto Rican heritage, were essential to the development of hip-hop culture, as well. Latino and black youth danced to the same beats, partied together, and often formed alliances in local performance groups that featured rapping, freestyling, and break-dancing. As Juan Flores is careful to point out, Puerto Rican and black cultural fusions in the emergent days of hip hop relied heavily on shared experiences in New York's urban ghettoes and the recognition of the racial oppressions urban youth experienced as minorities in the face of white supremacy. He observes, "In everyday street life and in the heat of rap practice, black and Puerto Rican B-boys were virtually interchangeable: whether you were one or the other was for practical purposes a matter of relative indifference."[38] Although Puerto Rican youth did not highlight Puerto Rican cultural expressions in hip-hop musicking at its genesis, artists such as Charlie Chase of the Cold Crush Brothers and the Puerto

Rican b-boys of the Rock Steady Crew played major roles in the evolving discourses of hip hop as an urban social movement.

In the late 1970s and 1980s, Dominican youth were an increasing presence in New York hip-hop culture. The Latino scholar Mandalite del Barco, for example, remembers that Puerto Rican *and* Dominican hip hoppers were part of Afrika Bambaataa's "Zulu Nation" from the beginning.[39] Migration and settlement in New York ghettoes put Dominican youth in contact with other communities of African descent, and this produced particular anxieties for a Spanish Caribbean population that had long had a problematic relationship with its African heritage. The youth population of this community was often forced to live in the cultural milieus of two worlds: American society, which insisted that the majority of Dominicans were black, pointing to their African ancestry, phenotypes, and Caribbean otherness, and the Dominican diaspora in both New York and the Dominican Republic, which insisted upon the richness of their European heritage and their separation from the class and racial subject-position of African America. Post-Trujillo migration by Dominicans to the United States generated a Dominican American community that had to fight for economic and cultural survival in New York and, more telling, had to learn ways to contextualize Dominican identity in an American environment.

First-generation immigrants, more often than not, attempted to recreate the island culture in the landscape of the United States by the mid-1980s. This re-creation of island culture was a way of lessening the pains of homesickness, cultural disorientation, and the lack of sustainable job opportunities in postindustrial New York. First-generation Dominicans in New York forged a community that created or, as Benedict Anderson would suggest, "imagined" a sense of group identity and belonging.[40] The Cuban-born scholar Gustavo Pérez Firmat calls the re-creation of home "substitutive," arguing that "it consists of an effort to create substitutes or copies of the home culture."[41] The Dominican substitutive community was ever-present in locales such as Washington Heights, where merengue music blasted, Spanish bodegas abounded, and even the underground racket of the numbers game was part of everyday life. As one islander noted of her mainland counterparts, "Dominicans in New York want to be more Dominican than the Dominicans themselves."[42] Patricia Pessar, in her study of Dominicans in New York, observes:

> In their private lives, Dominicans, like other recent immigrants, remain committed to a variety of cultural practices brought from home. For example, a recent study of Dominican households in Washington Heights found that 95 percent cooked mostly Dominican food, 88 percent spoke mostly Spanish at home, and well over half listened mostly to Dominican music and watched mostly Spanish television. Similarly, when Dominicans have some free time, they are most apt to socialize with family and Dominican friends.[43]

In re-creating Dominican culture in New York City, Dominican immigrants, especially of a parent generation, found a means to affirm an inculcated sense of a Dominican self. In turn, they limited the ways in which they had to engage the racial politics and xenophobia of the larger U.S. society.

In their studies of identity constructions for Dominicans in the diaspora, Silvio Torres-Saillant and Jorge Duany examine and map the anxieties over race, specifically over blackness, experienced by immigrants. Silvio Torres-Saillant observes that Dominican culture often presents and displays "greater indeterminacy" in response to African heritage than any other Caribbean culture in the Western hemisphere. As it pertains to first-generation immigrants especially, he notes, "In the United States, countless Dominicans, particularly dark-skinned ones, find themselves having to choose among options that their historical experience has not prepared them to recognize."[44] Similarly, Jorge Duany explains, "The persistence of a Dominican identity in the United States may be interpreted in part as resistance to the prevailing racial order."[45] His comparative study of migrant experiences in Puerto Rico and on the mainland reveals that racial categories become a tense, if not fictive, discourse for Dominican migrants in host communities.

The studies by Torres-Saillant and Duany, along with the cultural representations of Dominicans of the second generation in New York, suggest that the substitutive Dominican enclave proved rather problematic. How could Dominican New Yorkers coming of age in the 1980s, who were

often forced to act as cultural brokers for their parents, forced to acquire
an English tongue, and forced to take on a (black) American identity,
embrace a substitutive culture that did not mirror the complexities of
their Latino and American lives? Nelson Zapata, the founder of *Proyecto
Uno,* was born in the Dominican Republic. He moved to New York as a
child and became an avid participant in hip-hop culture with his friends.
His story, as Gustavo Pérez Firmat suggests of the Cuban American experience, reveals that "[n]o matter how great the effort, substitution is always partial."[46] The substitution of Dominican culture, although important, did not reflect what had become an important aspect of defining
Latino identity in the multiethnic site of New York: a connection, although often contested, to African America through music, language,
and proximity to native-born blacks and Caribbean immigrants in urban
areas. The merengue blasting through Dominican locales and the
plethora of island-based cultural formations evident in New York City
reaffirmed an island identity. But, too, as Firmat reveals, they "rest[ed] on
a particular kind of historical elision that overlook[ed] personal, historical, and geographical discontinuities."[47]

For some Dominican Americans of the hip-hop generation, merengue,
as the nationalist symbol of Dominicanness, became the contested terrain
for asserting their bicultural existences. In the 1990s especially,
merengue hip hop emerged as a genre that attempted to reconcile and
celebrate the multiple subject-positions of Dominican second generationers in the United States. Johnny Salgado, of *Proyecto Uno,* discussing
the group's 1996 album, explains, "The music of *New Era* is the music we
listen to, Merengue, R&B, and hip hop. It's our lives . . . it's New York
City."[48] By the 1990s, New York City was much more than the substitutive culture of the Dominican enclave. Instead, it had become the site
through which Dominican second generationers could engage and try on
multiple enunciations of black, Caribbean, and Latino identities.

The emergence of merengue hip hop revealed the negotiations of new
cultural formations taking place in the lives of Latino youth. *Proyecto
Uno* was the first to commercialize the merengue hip-hop sound from the
underground scene with its *"Todo el mundo"* single, released in 1990.
*Proyecto Uno* was followed by Two in a Room, a group of Dominican hip
hoppers and friends from Washington Heights, who recorded *"El trago"*
in 1994 and *"Ahora!"* [Now] in 1995. *Fulanito,* made up of former mem-

bers from Two in a Room, released its merengue hip-hop cut "*El hombre más famoso de la tierra*" in 1997, building on the success of *Proyecto Uno* with its release of subsequent albums on the labels J & N Records and H.O.L.A. Recordings. Even Dominican hip hoppers from the islands, such as *Sandy y Papo* and *Los Ilegales,* attempted to profit from the popularity of the merengue hip-hop fusion started by Latinos in New York.[49]

The 1990s are often characterized by the dominance of West Coast gangsta rap; however, merengue hip hop and other hybridizations of Caribbean and hip-hop musicking paralleled the emergence of hard-core rap in African America. *Proyecto Uno*'s members were four of many second generationers attempting to stake their claim to African American and Caribbean discourses. As the American public began to insist that hip hop was an African American cultural practice in magazines, the record industry, and even video programs, Latino and West Indian youth argued that hip hop was more about the sharing and borrowing of diasporic cultures taking place on the stage of urban America. In the 1990s, even as gangsta rap dominated the urban music charts, rap had a new vocabulary that included the voices and styles of its Caribbean American practitioners.

Spanish rap broke through the language barrier of hip-hop culture to produce the first bilingual jams by Latin Empire, Mellow Man Ace, and El General. Born Jamericans, a hip hop/reggae duo of two Jamaican Americans from Washington, D.C., released *Kids from Foreign* in 1994. Dark Latin Groove (DLG), a West Indian and Puerto Rican act from New York, made its self-titled album in 1996, featuring rap, salsa, and reggae. Perhaps the most successful group was The Fugees, which included two Haitian Americans, Wyclef Jean and Pras, and the African American songstress Lauryn Hill. The Fugees, and the individual projects of the group's members, illustrated the possibilities of cultural ties between African American and Caribbean musics, places, and people with blends of hip-hop, reggae, and Haitian and Spanish rhythms and lyrics. The Fugees' success opened the door to other artists such as Big Punisher, Jennifer Lopez, and even *Proyecto Uno*—artists who were then able to establish, through the language of Caribbean hip hop, that "We are what we do"; as *Proyecto Uno*'s Magic Juan asserts, "It's all 100 percent real with us."[50]

## Rappin' Merengue, Keepin' It Real

In this section, I examine the ways in which *Proyecto Uno*'s imaginings of cultural situatedness in New York evidence the formations of social blackness, as they simultaneously narrate the particularities of Latino identities. *Proyecto Uno*'s songs, but, more important, its members' relationships to black and Hispanic communities, reveal the celebrations and the contradictions of working through and in between Hispanic, black Caribbean, and African American cultures. Produced and written by the group's four members, the songs attempt to conceive the ultimate hip-hop jams of the New York party scene with drinks, dancing, and sexual freedom, while also illuminating the other side of the urban experience for second-generation youth: dislocation, marginalization, alienation, and, ultimately, an attempt to belong.

My theoretical frame for reading the music of *Proyecto Uno* relies heavily on the work of Juan Flores in his essay "'Qué assimilated, brother, yo soy asimilao': The Structuring of Puerto Rican Identity in the U.S."[51] In this essay, Flores suggests that assimilation for Caribbean immigrants does not have to mean the surrender of a Caribbean culture in exchange for participation in an (African) American one. He questions: "How is it [assimilation] to be defined in terms other than loss of the old and acquisition of the new, or as the fateful confrontation between two unequal and mutually exclusive cultural monoliths?"[52] In his essay, he seeks to answer the question by mapping "definitive moments" for "this alternative dynamic" of assimilation processes that attempt to reconcile Caribbean and American cultures. These "definitive moments" are defined by Flores as the "state of abandon," "rediscovery of the island," "return and re-entry," and "branching out." Flores's conceptual mapping is most helpful because he reveals that his moments are not "stages in a chronological sense" but "more of a range of constantly intersecting possibilities and responses arising simultaneously at the individual and collective levels."[53]

In the first "definitive moment," the "state of abandon," Flores outlines the struggles of immigrant youth who are concerned with articulating bicultural identities amid the parochialism of an island-tinged neighborhood and the racism of American society. This "state of abandon" is characterized by poverty, the inequalities of white supremacy, and the exclusion that Latinos often experience after migration to the United States. Flores's second moment, "rediscovery of the island," then illuminates the ways in which Latino youth embark upon psychological odysseys back to the island homeland. Flores notes that the return to an island heritage impels the re-envisioning of culture and thus the revising of national icons, including musical genres such as merengue, which have been used historically to explore cultural identity. The third stage, "return and re-entry," according to Flores, employs a spatial mobility that "heighten[s] the sense of the duality of cultural life and expression" intrinsic to Spanish Caribbean society.[54] Understanding the possibilities of transnational, bicultural existences, Flores suggests that Latinos can now "return and re-enter" the cultural space of New York, creating diasporic and multicultural ties that validate their identities. Finally, the "branching out" stage implies an affirmed sense of a cultural self: confident of their hyphenated Americanness, young Latinos can "branch out" and relate to other ethnics in the New York youth subculture.

Several music critics identify *Proyecto Uno*'s merengue hip-hop sound by the most popular and commercial dance grooves, but this focus neglects other songs that help provide a more inclusive and provocative narrative of the ways in which music is used to explore Latino and black heritages in the United States.[55] *Proyecto Uno* often locates New York as the quintessential party heaven, but also as the stage on which Latino male desire for community, home, and selfhood are played out. Analyzing *Proyecto Uno*'s songs, I posit that the multiplicity of meanings contained in the group's songs on "love" actually reveal yearnings of "belonging" for second-generation Latino youth. In an interview with *Variedades,* a member of *Proyecto Uno* reflected that *Proyecto Uno*'s songs were meant to "forget the rules and things that give stress," but, too, they were about "things that happen to us everyday, if not to us, to our friends."[56] His statement suggests that the "state of abandon" in Flores's framework is not too far removed from the attempt to claim a right to New York life through music, dance, and pleasure. Nelson Zapata, the founder of the group, admits that he developed the merengue hip-hop sound after feeling "homesick" in the United States. Existing between the two worlds of the Dominican ethnic enclave and hip-hop culture, Nelson tried to mix merengue, which he really did not like until high school, with the hip-hop and house sounds of the New York streets.[57]

One of *Proyecto Uno*'s earliest songs, "Another Night" (1994), written by Nelson Zapata, suggests Flores's "state of abandon," as it evokes the cultural dislocation of second-generation youth. The lyrics of the song in particular reveal a sense of isolation. "Another Night" details both repetition and darkness: the night—which metaphorically contains all the evils of inner-city life—is experienced over and over again by the singer.[58] This night in New York, unfortunately, is no different from any other:

| | |
|---|---|
| Aver, ¿qué hora es? | [Let's see, what time is it? |
| 3 de la mañana | Three in the morning |
| Todavía no me llama | She hasn't called me yet |
| Hay que olvidarse de eso | One must forget about that][59] |

The questioning of the hour conjures both anticipation and the despair that anticipation can provoke. Waiting on the woman insinuates the dreaming of deliverance from the "state of abandon." Yet, the singer determines that there is no hope. He must forget the possibilities of salvation and deal with the reality of *barrio* life. The waiting, in short, is a dream deferred:

| | |
|---|---|
| Quiero llamarte, | [I want to call you, |
| pero no estás | But you are not there] |
| I wonder, wonder, wonder | |
| Who is loving you tonight | |
| Another night | |
| Otra noche | [Another night |
| Sin tenerte | Without having you.] |

The singer seems to know that the woman/love exists, although he cannot find her. He believes that there is a way out of the darkness: "I wonder, wonder, wonder who is loving you tonight." Yet, he questions whether he will ever have the strength to seek out that type of love:

| No puedo más | [I cannot go on anymore |
| Ya no sé que hacer | I no longer know what to do |
| No soy el mismo | I'm not the same |
| Desde el día aquel | Since that day] |

The English verbalization of "Another Night" situates the problematics of an American identity in the "state of abandon." "Another Night" circumscribes the Spanish, early on suggesting that the Spanish verses better articulate a lost self:

| Another Night | |
| Otra noche | [Another night |
| sin tenerte | Without having you] |
| Another Night | |
| Otra noche | [Another night |
| sin tu amor | Without your love] |
| Another Night | |

Yet, the cry in English finally illumines the American identity that is also very much a part of a Latino one: "Since you've been gone, you got me calling, calling your name." The lamenting in English finally mirrors the pain asserted in the Spanish lyrics. The circular motion of the song, which details an overlapping of Spanish and English, suggests the circular, unbreakable reality of nights in *el barrio*. It is "another night" in the "state of abandon": there is no love, no hope. The singer in "Another Night" is always looking (*"Chicas aquí, chicas allá / Pero ninguna que me llené de felicidad"* [Girls here, girls there / But none who filled me with joy]), but never finding happiness.

The symbolism of woman as subject of the song and object of the singer's desire evokes the "state of abandon" as a destabilization of masculine power. As Frances Aparicio observes in *Listening to Salsa,* the loss of the woman in Latin American music echoes a loss of self, especially as understandings of self and identity are often embedded in the phallocentric languages of men. Aparicio argues,

This metaphorical malaise . . . should be explained beyond the individual realm and recontextualized within the conditions of modernization in which the absence and abandonment of women of the domestic sphere distances and diminishes men's patriarchal power and control.[60]

Aparicio is specifically speaking of the relationship between migration, urbanization, and boleros. However, her discussion proves helpful here in exploring the metonymic relationship I have suggested between women and the American terrain in my reading of *Proyecto Uno*'s "Another Night." The use of the woman in this song engages historical and rhetorical feminizations of countries in patriarchal discourses of exploration, annexation, and conquest.[61] The absence of the woman's body mimics the absence—the seemingly unattainable claiming—of the *American* body. She—his love/America—cannot be conquered in the migration process. The singer feels disoriented because he cannot claim his selfhood *through* the woman, nor *in* American environs.

Additionally, this lack of citizenship imagined in the song works through a reality of migration that indeed impels the immigrant male's insecurities: the changing role of Latina women. The male's disorientation is configured by both the harshness of New York City and, as Deborah Pacini Hernández observes, the growing independence and liberation of women in the new urban landscape. In her study of bachata, a rural style of Dominican music, Hernández notes that the tenor of bachata music changed between the 1960s and the late 1970s and 1980s to expose the increasing conflicts between men and women spawned by migration to urban areas and women's participation in the labor market.[62] Her observations on bachata resonate with the social scientific research by Sherri Grasmuck and Patricia Pessar on Dominicans' internal and external migrations. Grasmuck and Pessar observe that women experience a particular freedom as urban migrations and entrance into the labor market put them in the public sphere.[63] This freedom of Dominican women in the United States is often a source of tension between Dominican men and women.

As a corollary, *Proyecto Uno*'s "Another Night" metaphorically gives voice to the inversion of Caribbean social and cultural values, exploring male-female relationships. The man is at home, waiting in the darkness of urban existence. The woman, conversely, is outside the house. In fact, she is in those streets that seem to be a source of fear and longing for him.

In the United States, she gains a freedom that he has not yet gained. He fears that she might not come back: *"No sé que hacer, baby, si no estás / Lo lindo es que yo sé que tú no volverás"* [I don't know what to do, baby, if you are not here / The beauty (of it) is that I know that you are not going to return]. And thus, he, in fact, might be lost forever.

The singer of "Another Night" speaks as much to his male friends as he does to the absent woman/American community. The song takes place in the homosocial culture of young Latino men. The singer's friends are there to empathize with his abandoned, disoriented state. They respond to him directly: *"Qué hora es? / 3 de la mañana."* They also participate in a call-and-response format supported by the polyrhythms of the beat. The lead singer mourns his lost love; the other singers' antiphonal response reveals that he is not alone. They, too, experience his cultural loss. As a collective male enterprise, "Another Night" suggests that the attempt to regain control over the woman's body is an attempt to claim agency in an American society that seems to escape Latino men's control. To figure out where the woman is—in a way—is to ease their pains of dislocation and to regain a sense of power and belonging.

In *"No hay nada"* (1994), *Proyecto Uno* employs similar strategies for revealing the crisis of the urban experience. Written by Nelson Zapata, Magic Juan (Wilson), and Pavel de Jesús, *"No hay nada"* adds another layer to this "state of abandon": the heightened awareness of racial identities in American social and political culture. Magic Juan, the Dominican rapper of the group, admitted in *Urban Latino* that Latin Americans have criticized *Proyecto Uno* for "killing the tradition of merengue with a black rapper," namely himself. But, he insisted, "We're Latinos from NYC who speak Spanish and English and many times Spanglish. That's who we are and what we're going to keep projecting as a group."[64] "Who we are" includes a sense of one's marginality, but also a sense of one's relationship to African American, West Indian, and Latino cultures in the United States. It also asserts that second generationers like Magic Juan can be both black and Dominican at the same time.

*"No hay nada"* underscores the language of hip hop as a language that embraces multiple voicings of blackness, even within the U.S. proper. The multifocality of the song moves from the "state of abandon"—that is, *"no hay nada"* [there is nothing]—to the possibilities of social blackness as an empowered subject-position for Latino hip hoppers. The per-

formance of blackness in the song challenges discourses of white supremacy on the island and in the United States. Here, hip hop, as a raw,
urban, and often political culture, becomes the form through which
black Latino identities emerge from and alongside interactions with
other black ethnicities in the United States. Hip-hop musicking suggests
a "new topography of loyalty and identity," as Gilroy writes of diasporic
intimacy, "in which the structures and presuppositions of the nation-
state have been left behind because they are seen as outmoded."[65] "No
hay nada," then, maps the shifting cultural formations of Latino hip hoppers who attempt dialogic relationships with blacks in the United States,
as well as in the black Atlantic world.

"No hay nada" begins with a moaning, sorrowful rap over a slow
dancehall and merengue rhythmic fusion:

| | |
|---|---|
| Hey, hey, hey | |
| Ando buscandola | [I am looking for her[66] |
| Imaginandola | Imagining her |
| Vivo soñando con ella | I live dreaming of her |
| Todos los días | Everyday |
| Por la mañana | In the morning |
| Me despierto | I awake |
| Por sin amor | Without love |
| Me siento muerto | I feel dead |
| No sé qué puedo hacer | I do not know what I can do |
| Si no me conformo | If I don't find |
| Con una mujer | a woman][67] |

As in "Another Night," the metaphor of the desired woman suggests the
desire for one home community that is accepting of the singer for who he
is: he wants to belong; he wants love. The singer intimates in "No hay
nada" that he has been trying to act as if all were fine, despite living the
tension of island and American existences, which is marked in the song
by unfulfilling relationships with other women:

| | |
|---|---|
| Levanto chicas | [I pick up girls |
| Como nada | Like nothing |
| Pero no sé | But I do not know |

| Si es por mi | If it is because of me |
| O si son interesadas | Or if they are interested[68] |
| Al principio, no pregunto | At first, I don't ask |
| Si nos sentimos bien | If we get along well, |
| Nos quedamos juntos | We remain together |
| Y yo digo, | And I say, |
| ¡Qué satisfación! | What satisfaction! |
| Las chicas quieren | The girls want |
| Un pedazo de la acción | A little piece of the action] |

And you know I ain't a punk that will front
If they want to hump
I'll give them what they want

La unica cosa que quiero es una vida,
[The only thing that I want is a life]

Llena de fame, dinero y atrevidas
[Filled with fame, money, and adventurous women]

It could be argued that the singer's plaintive cry articulates only a search for romance, but I want to suggest an alternative and more complex way of reading his lament for love. "If they want to hump, I'll give them what they want" speaks specifically to those women with whom he explores his sexuality and masculine power. Suggestively, the verse provides a metaphoric lens into the forced masking of bicultural—black and Latino —identity encouraged by a "they"—the women with whom he interacts —but also the unspoken, yet ever-present "they" of the parent generation. The singer verbalizes the contradictions he experiences. He wants to suggest that he is able to withstand the pressure of parents' cultural desires, but, in reality, it *is* a front: "*No / Es una mentira / Deseo amor*" [No / It's a lie / I desire love]. Ultimately, he wants that one woman, that singularity of consciousness that reconciles black, Caribbean, and Latino heritages.

At this juncture in the song, the lyrics and the instrumentation create dissonant dialogues with each other. This dissonance codifies the tensions embedded in challenging island cultural formations to attempt black diasporic intimacies. The singer admits that he does not know what to do; however, he speaks to a "*tú*," using the Spanish second person, who seems to constantly answer back with the supportive bass line of a dancehall beat. Yet, the singer is not quite ready to reach out to blackness without reservation. He continues to rhyme:

| | |
|---|---|
| A veces me da calor | [At times it makes me hot |
| Pero también me da dolor | But too it pains me |
| Por falta de amor | Being without love |
| Por lo que yo veo | From what I see |
| Dicen que bien por el tiempo | They say that it is good for the time |
| Pero eso no lo creo | But that I do not believe] |

Here, "they" become most explicit: it is first generationers who tell the second-generation youth that life is unproblematic, especially as they seek to maintain essentialist and deracinated understandings of Hispanic cultures. However, this singer proclaims that he needs more: "They say it is good for the times, but that I do not see." He needs love, and he has to find it somewhere else, perhaps through black cultural evocations.

"But anyway, let's get it on girl / take a trip into the private, one world" he raps, and the introductions into "the private, one world" are marked by a drastic change in the Latino voice, which echoes the dancehall beat that undergirds the song's lyrics. The singer's voice shifts, taking on a Jamaican dialect, to explore his search for cultural reconciliation:

> One gal me love, one girl me need
> She's the only girl who make me succeed
> One gal me love, one girl me need
> She's the only girl who make me succeed
> Right now I'm looking for a special girl
> Treat her right, make her queen of my world
> Give her diamond, give her pearl
> One who can rule my universe

The switch to a black West Indian voice situates the poetics of place: the singer can be imagined as a Caribbean immigrant in urban America, try-

ing to affirm himself amidst the racism of the United States and prejudices of an immigrant community. The dancehall beat then explodes, letting the singer fully express his dilemma in a global context:

> Inna Puerto Rico, you know they wan' love
> Inna Ecuador, you know they wan' love
> Inna Panama, you know they wan' love
> Inna Santo Domingo, you know they wan' love

The "inna" prefacing the countries' names elucidates the inner, bicultural self looking for a place to express a multiplicity of identities, both
old and new world. "Inna" also suggests the struggle within a person,
not simply a country. Panama, Cuba, and Puerto Rico are conjured for
the purpose of identifying with Panamanian, Cuban, and Puerto Rican
Americans who are trying to construct havens for their emerging existences. The Jamaican dialect sequence ends with "Inna New York, you
know they wan' love." This ending positions Latino youth with other
marginalized and racialized groups together in one community, namely
hip hop, as they undergo the same struggles.

The obvious vacillations between lament and joy in "*No hay nada*"
work through the "state of abandon" even as they gesture toward the
ability to use merengue, African American, and West Indian musical
genres to identify connections to other black and Latin American communities. Musical purists and even second-generation migration scholars
often show concern over what this identification with black cultural
practices means for a second-generation population already threatened
by racism and class immobility in postwar America. Millie Quezada, a
performer in the New York–based merengue group *Millie, Jocelyn, y los
Vecinos,* fears that Dominican youth in New York, through their embrace
of other American cultures, will be like "Third- and fourth-generation
Puerto Ricans [who] have lost, are losing, their language, [and] are losing
their heritage." She explains, "They're going through some kind of turmoil about who they really are, they are Americans or they are Puerto Ricans. That's going to happen with the Dominicans."[69]

Social scientists such as Alejandro Portes, Min Zhou, M. Patricia Fernández Kelly, and Richard Schauffler posit arguments against intercul-
tural interaction in more classist and racist terms. Portes and Zhou note

that the immigrant youth's connection to the native poor "exposes [him] to the adversarial subculture developed by marginalized native youths to cope with their own difficult situation."[70] M. Patricia Fernández Kelly and Richard Schauffler conclude that maintaining one's immigrant identity often affords a "hopeful" self-image that is "bolstered by [the immigrant's] negative definitions of groups that have experienced arrested mobility."[71] In their studies, the scholars use segmented-assimilation models that argue that exposure to native co-ethnics—for Dominicans, mostly blacks and other Latinos—leads to the destruction of an authentically ethnic culture and impels the downward economic mobility of immigrant families that have come to the United States with middle-class aspirations.

However, *Proyecto Uno*'s musicking in songs like "Another Night" and "*No hay nada*" suggests that the interdialogues with other black and Latino populations in the United States do not hinder a sense of ethnicity but, instead, support it. Thinking beyond the unfortunate emphasis given to economic mobility in social scientists' discussions of immigrant youth, I want to suggest the ways in which immersion in hip-hop culture generates not only a knowledge of a black diasporic community but also a knowledge of one's ethnic self. Paul Gilroy, in his discussion of Caribbean immigrant hip hop from Britain, observes that diasporic intimacy preserves "vernacular culture" that is "no longer either dependant upon or simply imitative of the cultures" of African America. Gilroy's understanding of this diasporic intimacy enunciates the ways in which hip-hop musicking for Dominican second generationers can both engage and challenge "ethnic absolutisms" of black and Latino identities in the United States, while simultaneously grounding its participants in the specificity of Dominican American youth experiences.[72]

Within *Proyecto Uno*'s music, this dialectical impulse of hip-hop culture takes place. Started by two Dominican Americans, *Proyecto Uno* later added another Dominican American rapper, Magic Juan. However, the group's Dominican members finally decided to develop their merengue hip-hop sound with the help of two Nuyoricans, Erik Morales and Johnny Salgado. *Proyecto Uno* is promoted as a Dominican New York group, and most people consider it as such, but the influence of the Puerto Rican singers is clear in songs such as "Latinos" (1996) and the salsa-tinged "*Empujando al cielo*" (1999).[73] The influence and interchange are also clear in *Proyecto Uno*'s urban "lingo" featured in the "P1 Dictionary" of its *New Era* (1996) album, where terms like "*dominiqueño*," defined by its members as a "*mezcla de un Dominicano* [sic] *y un Puertoriqueño* [sic]" [mix of a Dominican and a Puerto Rican] become one means of self-conceptualizing.[74]

In *Dangerous Crossroads*, George Lipsitz writes that Nuyoricans identify with African Americans to "affirm the African aspects of their own culture and distance themselves from the prestige of hierarchies of white supremacy."[75] The Dominican hip hoppers of *Proyecto Uno* work through these same negotiations of race and class in their identifications with Puerto Rican, West Indian, and African American cultural practices and peoples. Still, merengue music provides the language through which these cultural interactions are translated. Despite concerns over Dominican hip hoppers' affinity for the cultural styles, forms, and expressions of native "co-ethnics," the interaction with other black and Latino populations in New York often drives what Juan Flores terms a recapturing of an "isla heritage." Flores writes, "If the first moment is the state of abandon, the second is the state of enchantment, an almost dream-like trance at the striking contrast between the cultural barrenness of New York and the imagined luxuriance of the Island culture."[76] He concludes that this return to the island is predicated not only on a wish to distance one's self from the white supremacy of the Americas but also on the negrophobic world of the island itself. The psychological odyssey that immigrant hip hoppers make to the Dominican Republic often entails an embrace and legitimation of black and working-class roots. Since merengue has been historically situated as the national icon of Dominican identity, it is employed and often inverted by groups such as *Proyecto Uno* to ensure a return to the "isla heritage" that affirms the multiplicity of Dominican experiences in the United States.

*Proyecto Uno*'s founder, Nelson Zapata, relied on a particular type of merengue to re-imagine and claim his island roots in what Flores identifies as the second definitive moment in the "rediscovery of the island." First playing the güira and trying out a stint in a merengue band at Seward Park High School, he brought merengues from *fusilamiento* artists to his hip-hop style:

> I asked [Pavel de Jesús] if what he was doing with house music he
> could do with merengue. . . . I was like, well, if you sample this beat
> like this and that beat like that, probably you could sample the tamb-
> ora; and he said bring your ideas and let's see what we can do. So I
> brought a whole bunch of records from my house, Johnny Ventura,
> Ramón Orlando, and we tried to come up with a beat. We did a whole
> tape with a beat, like a merengue beat, sampled.[77]

Paul Austerlitz defines *fusilamiento* as "basing merengues on foreign
hits," but he also identifies the emergence of this merengue style in the
1970s with *merengueros* who attempted to socially and culturally imagine Dominicanness outside the legacy of Trujillo in the Dominican Republic.[78] Zapata's choice of musicians—Johnny Ventura and Ramón Orlando, who were leaders of *fusalimiento* in the post-Trujillo moment—
suggests his own attempts to reflect upon and resist the racial and class
prejudices of Dominican cultural formations. Zapata's notion of
merengue was influenced not by the Trujillo merengues of the 1930
through the 1960s, which suppressed African influences and working-
class geneses, but instead by the post-Trujillo experimental merengues
of Ventura and Orlando, which relied heavily on percussive, fast-paced
rhythms, sexually risqué lyrics, and representations of the lived experiences of working-class populations.

In songs like *"Merengue con letra"* (1997), *Proyecto Uno* makes use of
the discourses of post-Trujillo merengues by Orlando and Ventura to introduce new musical media that demand recuperations of black and
working-class Latino cultures. *"Merengue con letra"* begins with a driving merengue beat, reinforced by a techno bass line. The saxophone
and the guitar proffer a repetitive pulsation to suggestively recapture the
percussive sound once suppressed in the national merengue sanctioned
under Trujillo's regime. The primacy historically given to the melodic
structure in Trujillo-style merengues is usurped by the booming,
effervescent rhythm and by Magic Juan's verbal dexterity:

> Magic Juan
> El tiburón del año          [The "shark" of the year
> El negrito del swing        The "brother" of swing

| Que te hace daño | Who can do harm to you |
| Y ahora con la artillería | And now with the artillery |
| | |
| Y la letras son mias | And my lyrics |
| Todavía brincando (hey) | Still getting excited |
| Todavía bailando (hey) | Still dancing |
| Todavía tomando (hey) | Still drinking |
| Y todavía pegando (hey) | And still jamming][79] |

The braggadocio of the lyrics in the "rediscovery of the island" moment reinterprets the disorientation experienced by the singer in songs such as *"No hay nada"* and "Another Night." In *"Merengue con letra,"* where Magic Juan's words and the kinetic music become "artillery," the "state of abandon" has now shifted to an understanding of the value and power of first embracing, then inverting, and finally using an island heritage as "armor" against American-induced identity crises. Magic Juan's flamboyant rap style asserts the awareness of place, although he identifies merengue in the dialectic framework of island and American situatedness: *"Magic Juan con la artilleria / Bergen County y Santo Domingo / Para toda mi gente latina /* We ain't no joke" [Magic Juan with the artillery / Bergen County and Santo Domingo / For all of my Latino people / We ain't no joke]. The inversion of merengue—literally "(w)rapped" in Magic Juan's lyrical play—establishes that *Proyecto Uno*'s use of merengue is a serious enterprise.

The seriousness of the endeavor, however, relies on the seriousness of letting loose, dancing, and having fun. Rescued from the salon-style and gentrified merengue of Trujillo's era and its legacy, *Proyecto Uno*'s *"Merengue con letra"* becomes the "phattest" dance groove. The frenetic pace of both the rapping and the instrumentation makes the lyrics almost unintelligible, and the beats reveal the authoritative voice: the song is about dancing, movement, and a carefree lifestyle dependent on the urban Latino male's utmost fantasy:

| Aquí viene el moreno | [Here comes the black Rapper |
| Rastrero, soltero | Player, single (rapper) |
| Sin esposa | Without a wife |

| | |
|---|---|
| ¿Qué me importa | What do I care (if) |
| La vida es corta? | Life is short? |
| No hay tiempo pa' romance | There's no time for romance |
| No quiero novia | I do not want a girlfriend |
| No quiero chance | I do not want a chance |
| Quiero romo y mujeres | I want rum and women |
| Understand, entiendes | Understand, understand] |

Despite the emphasis on lyrics in the title of the song, the *body* becomes the site of pleasure, both for Magic Juan's persona and for the listening/dancing audience. Robin Kelley's work on Malcolm (Little) X and the zootsuiters of the 1940s, discussed in chapter 1, proves useful here because it identifies the ways in which urban youth of color, as he argues in *Race Rebels,* recuperate their bodies through leisure to resist the lack of agency they experience outside youth culture.[80] The cultural fusions of rapping in Spanish and mixing techno/hip-hop beats with merengue highlight an attempt to engage the multiple sites and pleasures of the ghetto dance floor. The New York hip-hop party, the Santo Domingo *discoteca,* and even the rural, working-class *colmados* of island *barrios* all serve as cultural spaces for enacting social blackness: "*Yo soy el unico negrito del swing,*" Magic Juan raps, "*por todos los barrios* / Boyzz so y'all besta recognize" [I'm the only "brother" of swing for all of the neighborhoods / Boyzz so y'all besta recognize]. Magic Juan's rap persona, echoing the fusions of the music, claims his right to multiple enunciations of Afro-Latinoness.

Juan Flores observes that the "rediscovery of the island" is followed by Latinos' "return and re-entry" into the American urban ghetto. He writes, "The third moment is located back in New York, but the passage there, the return and reentry, is infused with those new perspectives gathered in the course of cultural recovery."[81] As Flores asserts, the "return and re-entry" into the New York urban culture has two important consequences, one of which informs the cultural productions of second-generation artists and intellectuals. First, the "return and re-entry" allows Latino youth to see the substitutive community differently. They can finally recognize the cultural and spiritual taproot of the island that a parent generation cherishes. Flores contends that the previous need to escape the parochial world of their parents is now replaced with a need to embrace their parents' substitutive community in New York, which enables vital connections to the island. Although the substitutive culture in the United States is flawed, the Latinos of the second generation begin to realize that they have the power to change understandings of Latino culture in the United States. The "return and re-entry" details immigrants' ability to re-educate others about their racial and ethnic selves.

I would add to Flores's framework that "return and re-entry," especially in the case of *Proyecto Uno,* are characterized by the development of merengue hip hop as a musical genre. Flores makes this observation in his discussion of "Spanglish" transculturations in Nuyorican poetry, but this moment in the "return and re-entry" also describes *Proyecto Uno*'s use of music to explore Hispanic and American cultural hybridities. Merengue hip hop, observes a member of *Proyecto Uno, "es un reflejo de la realidad, de nuestras experiencias. [S]omos eso, la mezcla de dos culturas"* [it is a reflection of reality, of our experiences. (W)e are that, the mix of two cultures].[82] He adds, giving a detailed analysis of the genre:

> Nosotros en cambio cogimos el merengue y lo alteramos poniéndole música house y hip hop en la base, un poco de rap, de rhythm & blues y de todo lo que escuchábamos en la calle. . . . No es una cosa planeada de hacer esto o lo otro porque puede pegar o está de moda. Lo que pasa es que cada uno de nosotros (los miembros del grupo) venía de haber escuchado todo tipo de música americana en la calle. Pero por nuestras raíces escuchábamos salsa y merengue. Y como las dos cosas nos gustan, pues nos salió natural el mezclarlas.[83]
>
> [In turn, we picked merengue and altered it, putting hip hop and house music in the bass, a bit of rap, of R&B, and all that we used to listen to in the street. It is not a planned thing to do this or the other, because it is catchy or in style. What happens is that each of us (the members of the group) came from having to listen to all types of American music in the streets. But because of our roots, we listened to salsa and merengue. And like the two things we like, well, it came natural to us to mix them.]

The "natural" feeling of musicking for *Proyecto Uno* demands the affirming possibilities of embracing native and island cultures, and doing so through the multicultural dialogue of hip hop. The members of *Proyecto Uno* employ merengue to situate Hispanic hip hop as culturally both black and Latino, allowing merengue hip hop to flow and ebb among African American, Latin American, and Caribbean cultural sites. Hip hop and merengue are "mixed" in the "return and re-entry" to reveal the *"realidad,"* to use the term of *Proyecto Uno,* of emergent Afro-Latino consciousnesses. Dominican and Puerto Rican New Yorkers can look *aquí* and *allá.* Recovering island heritages is central to the celebration of diasporic ties with blacks in the Americas.

In *"¿Qué sabes tú?"* (1996), the second-to-last cut on the *New Era* album, the rapper announces how to make the merengue hip-hop sound:

> Okay, todo el mundo           [Okay, everybody
> Con los manos                 With their hands]
> Lesson one on how to make
> A *Proyecto Uno* record
> First you gotta buy yourself
> A kick
>
> [bass beat "kicks" in]
>
> And after that what you need . . .
> Wait, hold up, Nelson
>
> Buscame                       [Find me
> Una tambora "heavy" allí     A "phat" tambora there]
>
> [tambora sound]
>
> All right, sí                 [All right, yes
> Y despúes de eso              And after that
> Llega un sample               Comes a sample
> Y despúes de eso              And after that]
> You need to find
> A hot old school beat
>
> ["Good Times" by Chic can be heard][84]

As the old school beat from Chic's "Good Times" kicks in, *Proyecto Uno*'s evocation of its trademark sound is mostly about the polyrhythms produced. Noticeably, the lyrics of "*¿Qué sabes tú?*" are rap lite, as are most of the lyrics on *Proyecto Uno* songs with driving bass lines. The lyrics are fun, simple—characteristically merengue hip hop. Merengue hip hop in the "return and re-entry" moment suggests the use of *sound* as the true bearer of political resistance for Latino youth in hip-hop culture. As with other songs such as "*Merengue con letra*," the instrumentation of "*¿Qué sabes tú?*" gains dominance over the actual words. The emphasis on instrumental rather than lyrical ascendance imagines both hip hop and merengue in new, Latino New York terms.

Music critics such as Philip Brasor often respond to the lyrics of *Proyecto Uno* as "cookie-cutting songwriting," contrasting them to the more political and substantive lyrics of the Beatnuts and groups such as Juan Luis Guerra's *Grupo 4:40*.[85] At their best, *Proyecto Uno*'s lyrics are witty and rhetorical. At their worst, they are trite and misogynist. Their focus on women—sometimes romantic, as in "Another Night" and "*No hay nada*," other times rather crass, such as in "*El grillero*" (1996) and "*El tiburón*"—engenders and sustains sexist and patriarchal discourses within island, black diasporic, and Latin musical genres.[86]

Notwithstanding debates over *Proyecto Uno*'s lyrics, the emphasis given to sound in the group's recordings articulates the battles over culture waged through instrumental explorations. George Lipsitz argues the importance of understanding the "politics of sound" in hip-hop music making. Suggesting the hip hop is "grounded in the philosophies and techniques of African music," he maintains that the rhythms and samples of hip hop provoke dialogues with each other, and "hearing one enables the others to make sense."[87] African historical memories appear not simply to legitimate ties to African cultures but to use African-derived and African diasporic styles in the musicking practices of the Americas. *Proyecto Uno*'s employment of rhythms in merengue hip-hop sound demonstrates the workings of this dialogic response to interactions with African diasporic communities in the United States. The antiphonal sound, as George Lipsitz responds, "enables the others to make sense": it provides a space for the combination of sounds to offer new cultural meanings. But, sound is also used to position new social and cultural locations for *Proyecto Uno*'s members. Sampling, inversions, and even alternating bass lines stake the group's claim to congruities between Hispanic and black cultural formations.

Paul Gilroy observes that sound often "encapsulates the diasporic intimacy" through a "formal use of diverse cultural elements" in black musical genres.[88] This intimacy of sound underscores what Flores understands as the last definitive moment in the contours of Latino identity construction, "branching out." "Branching out" is different from the latent response to the "state of abandon," where the immigrant youth experiences a cultural loss. "Branching out," as the moment of cultural awareness, is the moment of interrelating with other co-ethnics on one's own terms. Juan Flores defines "branching out" as the "selective connection to and interaction with the surrounding North American society."[89] It happens after "rediscovery of the island" and "return and re-entry" because it builds on an awareness of the ripe potential of connections with native heritages and adoptive communities.

To Flores's understanding of "branching out," I want to offer another layer—one more receptive to the cultural process taking place. First, "branching out," as Flores's theoretical framework suggests, establishes a more empowered relationship to African America for Latino and Caribbean hip hoppers. The diasporic language of merengue hip hop demands a dialogue at this moment: African America is no longer just speaking to the members of *Proyecto Uno,* but *Proyecto Uno*'s members are assertively answering back. This dialogue through music situates the members of *Proyecto Uno* as black and Latino, African American and Caribbean. In the final branching-out process, one cultural identification is not antithetical to the other.

Yet, in *Proyecto Uno*'s case, "branching out" locates a movement in the direction of island culture, as well. *Proyecto Uno*'s members are careful to legitimate their connections to Latin America as they celebrate their New York experiences, and the social and cultural blackness imagined in their songs sends a powerful message against the valorization of whiteness at the expense of marginalized peoples of color in the Spanish Caribbean. With the transnational flow of ideas, people, and even productions of culture, *Proyecto Uno*'s merengue hip hop both constructs and deconstructs geopolitical spaces and boundaries. The particularity of lives lived outside the island and within Latino enclaves in New York parallels a commitment to *"los raices,"* as *Proyecto Uno* describes it, in island cultures. *Proyecto Uno* reaches out to African America, but its members do not forget the changes their experiences in the United States can forge in their parent communities.

A fine example of this "branching out" process is evidenced by *Proyecto Uno*'s song *"Ven y te enseñaré"* (1994), from the *In Da House* album. Sung primarily in Spanish, *"Ven y te enseñaré"* speaks to an island and parent audience in particular. It begins with a strong house beat. Synthesized drums permeate the underlying rhythm, suggestively supporting the political undercurrents of the message:

| | |
|---|---|
| Ven y te enseñaré | [Come and I will teach you |
| A vivir, | To live |
| No digas nada | Do not say anything |
| Y acompáñame | And accompany me |
| Ven y te enseñaré | Come and I will teach you |
| Hasta el fin | Until the end |
| A tu lado, | At your side |
| Siempre estaré | I will always be][90] |

"Come and I will teach you until the end," the singer croons, positioning himself as both mentor and wise one. The song metaphorically conjures the beckoning of a parent culture to a U.S. Latino space and suggests an inversion of traditional transmissions of culture. Culture is passed not from elder to child but from child to elder. The singer intimates that he has much to teach the parent generation, not just American society, about Latino culture.

*"Ven y te enseñaré"* is most evocative when read against the transformation of Spanish Caribbean identity constructions in the United States as experienced by second generationers. Spanish lyrics sung in ballad style over a sampled hip-hop beat suggest that the Americanizing of island culture practices may, in actuality, be a celebratory prospect for Latino culture. In the song, the singer invokes a sense of cultural loss experienced by a parent culture, inverting and revising a sense of cultural loss first explored by the youth himself in the "state of abandon" of songs such as "Another Night" and *"No hay nada."* The absence of the

"tú" to whom he speaks hints at the daunting, if not quite spoken, presence of the parent generation's fears. Yet, he insinuates that Latino and Latin American cultures can be re-envisioned in a more perfect way:

| | |
|---|---|
| Yo sé que a veces piensas, | [I know that at times you think |
| Que todo está perdido | That all is lost |
| Y no encuentras solución | And that you cannot find a solution |
| Pase lo que pase, | Whatever happens |
| Nunca te des por vencido | Never give in to defeat |
| Y escucha mi canción | And listen to my song |
| No te dejes caer, | Don't fall |
| Pues hay una mañana | Since there is a tomorrow |
| Un día tú pierdes, | One day you lose |
| Pero otro ganas | But another you win |
| Lo puedes hacer | You can do it |
| Si es con buena fe | If it is with good faith |
| Stay positivo, | Stay positive |
| Cuenta conmigo | Count on me |
| Positivo hasta el final, | Positive until the end |
| Es la clave de triunfar, | It is the key to triumph |
| No te duermas, | Do not sleep |
| Llega a la meta | Get the goal] |

The singer sees himself as the source of cultural awareness, begging the parent population to accompany him: "*Soy tu hermano, dame tu mano*" [I'm your brother, give me your hand]. His authoritative voice suggestively identifies a proprietary right to island and American cultures. He can guide, in short, because he can imagine the possibilities of both worlds.

The lyrics that end the song, "Let me show you / Let me show you," are interestingly supported by the call-and-response chorus of "love life, take the chance." *This* life—not a past life—emerges as "la meta," the goal. The limitations of the parent cultural formations give way, and the new way of constructing *latinidad* by Latino youth of African descent in the United States can give African *and* Hispanic diasporas fresh beginnings. "Tak[ing] the chance" suggests taking a chance to explore new understandings of black and Latino selves. "*Ven y te enseñaré*," as a collaborative effort of Pavel de Jesús, Nelson Zapata, and Johnny Salgado, reveals that the Latino of the hip-hop generation is more than willing to share his knowledge of black and Hispanic identities with his parent culture and, in turn, the rest of the world.

The future of *Proyecto Uno* and the merengue hip-hop fusion is yet to be determined. Most recently, *Proyecto Uno* was still recording, but its lead rapper, Magic Juan, had left the group for a solo career. Questions about the future of this musical genre, of course, are the same as those for the cultural representations of most new second-generation immigrants who find themselves at the crossroads of American and Caribbean cultural terrains. In *Nations Unbound*, Basch et al. discuss a "transnational social field" that will allow the next generation of Caribbeans on the island and in the United States to maintain ties to both societies, as first generation Caribbean immigrants have begun to do in the 1980s and 1990s.[91] Jones-Correa notes the impact of the availability of dual citizenship for immigrants from the at least twenty Caribbean and Latin American countries that provide legal recognition to those residing outside the nation-state.[92] In some ways, *Proyecto Uno*'s merengue hip-hop sound speaks to the possibilities of having these two worlds, of challenging the attempts, at multiple levels, to police one's cultural domain. The group's popularity in Latin America and in the United States suggests a cultural duality that situates the crossroads as a rather empowering site for youth who have the opportunity to embrace both ethnic and racial identities.

Still, *Proyecto Uno*'s musicking reminds us that the Latino identities of its members have been deeply influenced by African American culture. Merengue hip hop, although transnational in scope, reflects an ongoing participation in dialogues in and with African America. Nelson Zapata notes, "We brought that New York style and we wanted to show South America how Latin culture is in the U.S."[93] He insinuates that the group's *latinidad* is informed by a "New York style" that incorporates the diasporic intimacy of multiple black communities (re)convening in urban sites. In their songs, the group's members remind listeners that it is not just about their Spanish Caribbean "realness" but also about their black "realness." What is evident in the sound and samplings of the first albums is fully articulated in the *New Era* album of 1996. *Proyecto Uno* was not just about mixing African American, West Indian, and Hispanic musical genres. It was about bridging black and Caribbean cultural selves. Magic Juan and Nelson Zapata, the Dominican American members, became "*los hermanos chocolate*" [the chocolate brothers] in the album's liner notes but also within the lyrical play of the songs themselves. In the "P1 dictionary," from the 1996 album, which incorporates "definitions of our lingo," the Dominican hip hoppers especially reconceptualized themselves as the "Brothers of the crew."[94]

Whether this announcement of a racial identity ultimately reshapes Dominican and other Spanish Caribbean cultures in the substitutive worlds of American cities or on the islands is a tale for the future. Often, a parent generation is less than receptive to outside forces, especially from the mouths of babes. This reality has often been the case in perceptions of *los retornados,* migrants who return to the Dominican Republic, particularly those of the U.S. second generation, who often change the fabric of island life.[95] But perhaps music is afforded a cultural space that eludes, even as it participates in, the ideological battles over race, ethnicity, class, and culture. In that case, the late-twentieth-century musicking of *Proyecto Uno* works in concert with the cultural texts of earlier second-generation artists and intellectuals like Belafonte, Thomas, Marshall, and Lorde in this study. Merengue hip hop may not promise the future, but, even in its infancy, it points toward the prospects of a cultural response that may create a diasporic intimacy for future generations, if not the second generation at the start of the twenty-first century.

# Postscript

In "Cultural Identity and Diaspora," Stuart Hall observes:

> Perhaps instead of thinking of identity as an already accomplished fact, which the new cultural practices then represent, we should think, instead, of identity as a "production," which is never complete, always in process, and always constituted within, not outside, representation.[1]

The works of the artists and intellectuals examined in *Constructing Black Selves* suggest that identity is, in fact, ever-changing, "in process," as Stuart Hall argues, a never-ending negotiation of multiple social and cultural formations. Harry Belafonte, Paule Marshall, Audre Lorde, Piri Thomas, and *Proyecto Uno* utilize the culture industry to identify the ways in which identity for second-generation immigrants can be socially and culturally imagined. Through their cultural narratives, they also imply that Caribbean, African American, and even American identities do not need to be exclusive.

Contemporary migration scholars often ask the question: To which America do second-generation black immigrants assimilate? Unfortunately, "assimilation," as most Americans understand it, often negates the dynamics of engaging American and Caribbean cultural politics. This study argues that African America becomes a powerful site of assimilation for Caribbean second generationers and that the racialization of Caribbean immigrants in the United States plays a dominant role in the acculturation process. But, this in itself is not the whole story. Assimilation is far more complicated than simply giving up one culture for another. If identity is truly a "production," as Stuart Hall suggests, then assimilation for black immigrants is perpetually an enunciation of relationships to multiple racial, sexual, gender, and ethnic communities in the United Sates and the Caribbean, if not beyond.

Indeed, the artists and intellectuals in this study reveal that African American culture affords the discovery of Caribbean American identities. African America, however, is employed by second-generation artists and intellectuals to articulate the multiple constructions of identity taking place, even outside African American social, intellectual, political, and cultural spheres. When asked about her connection to African America, Paule Marshall once observed, "I don't make any distinction between African American and West Indian. All o' we is one as far as I'm concerned. And I, myself, am both."[2] Piri Thomas, by contrast, responded, "My people come from Puerto Rico, and my father comes from Cuba. I have different bloods in me: African blood; Taino blood; blood of the *conquistadores*. But, I am a human being. Period."[3] Marshall's and Thomas's comments elucidate the diverse and often conflicting responses of second-generation immigrants to questions of assimilation.

Thus, I have replaced the question of migration scholars with my own: *How* do second generationers construct black selves that engage Caribbean and African American cultures? With analyses of selected cultural texts by second-generation immigrants, this study has shown the diversity of answers: Harry Belafonte asserts a Caribbean identity to demand citizenship as a black man in the United States. Paule Marshall and Audre Lorde use the imaginings of Africa to suggest ties among blacks in the diaspora. Piri Thomas flirts with an African American identity but ultimately feels uncomfortable with its limitations. Finally, *Proyecto Uno* resists the boundaries of African America and the Spanish Caribbean to create new enunciations of black identity for U.S. Latinos at the turn of the twentieth century.

Although this book focuses on Caribbean immigrants of the second generation, it ultimately illuminates the often unspoken, yet shifting nature of African American identity in the postwar moment, as well. If black immigrants' identities change and evolve in African America, to be sure the identities of native-born blacks undergo the same cultural processes. This truth pushes the boundaries of what we conventionally consider African America but also, more important, what we conventionally perceive as African American identity. As persons of African descent (re)convene in the United States to create new cultural practices, African America includes more than just the descendants of U.S. slavery and the systemic challenges faced by these native-born blacks who encounter and grapple with slavery's legacy every day. African America also embraces the memories of slavery for other blacks from the diaspora, who have decided to make their homes in the United States. African American identity, then, echoes the diverse cultural experiences, discourses, and languages of blacks—native-born and immigrant—who work through allegiances and conflicts to forge communities in the twentieth century.

Because African American identity changes in response to interactions between native-born blacks and immigrants in the United States, this process should shape the formation of African American Studies. In writing about children of black immigrants from Caribbean islands in postwar America, I challenge the monolithic and canonical interpretations of the African American experience in academia. This study demonstrates the necessity of shifting paradigms in African American Studies, of deconstructing the hegemony of African American culture in our scholarship, to incorporate the voices of black immigrants and their children who use their cultural productions to reveal the multiplicity of experiences for blacks in the United States. Harry Belafonte, Paule Marshall, Piri Thomas, Audre Lorde, and *Proyecto Uno* show us that the diversity of black American cultures has been evident throughout twentieth-century American history. Collectively, their voices pose a challenge to the future direction of scholarship in African American Studies.

# NOTES

## NOTES TO THE INTRODUCTION

1. Alejandro Portes and Min Zhou, "The New Second Generation: Segmented Assimilation and Its Variants," *Annals of the American Academy of Political and Social Sciences* 530 (November 1993): 75.

2. Ibid., 82.

3. Ibid., 81.

4. See Herbert J. Gans, "Second-Generation Decline: Scenarios for the Economic and Ethnic Futures of the Post-1965 American Immigrants," *Journal of Ethnic and Racial Studies* 15, no. 2 (April 1992): 173–192; Portes and Zhou, "The New Second Generation"; Mary C. Waters, "Ethnic and Racial Identities of Second-Generation Black Immigrants in New York City," in *The New Second Generation,* ed. Alejandro Portes (New York: Russell Sage Foundation, 1996), 171–196; and Mary C. Waters, *Black Identities: West Indian Immigrant Dreams and American Realities* (Cambridge, MA: Harvard University Press, 1999). Also see Alejandro Portes and Rubén Rumbaut, *Legacies: The Story of the Immigrant Second Generation* (Berkeley: University of California Press, 2001).

5. See Marcus Lee Hansen, *The Problem of the Third Generation Immigrant* (Rock Island, IL: Augustana Historical Society, 1938); William Lloyd Warner and Leo Srole, *The Social Systems of American Ethnic Groups* (New Haven, CT: Yale University Press, 1945); and Oscar Handlin, ed., "Introduction," *Children of the Uprooted* (New York: Braziller, 1966).

6. Portes and Zhou, 81.

7. See examples in Georges Fouron, "The Black Immigrant Dilemma in the United States: The Haitian Experience," *Journal of Caribbean Studies* 3, no. 3 (1985): 242–265; Philip Kasinitz, *Caribbean New York: Black Immigrants and the Politics of Race* (Ithaca: Cornell University Press, 1992); and Linda Basch, Cristina Blanc Szanton, and Nina Glick Schiller, *Nations Unbound: Transnational Projects, Post-Colonial Predicaments, and De-Territorialized Nation-States* (Langhorne, PA: Gordon and Breach Science Publishers, 1994), among others.

8. Evelio Grillo, *Black Cuban, Black American: A Memoir* (Houston: Arte Público Press, 2000), 12.

9. See U.S. Department of Justice and U.S. Department of Immigration Service, *1998 Statistical Yearbook of the Immigration and Naturalization Service* (Washington, DC: U.S. Department of Justice and U.S. Department of Immigration Service, 1998), Tables 1, 2. Other statistics can be found in E. Willard Miller

and Ruby M. Miller, *United States Immigration: A Reference Handbook* (Santa Barbara: ABC-CLIO, 1996), 14; and in Kasinitz, 25.

10. See Ellwood Cubberley, *Changing Conceptions of Education* (Boston: Houghton Mifflin, 1909); Madison Grant, *The Passing of the Great Race; or, The Racial Basis of European History* (New York: Charles Scribner's Sons, 1916); and Harry H. Laughlin, *Analysis of America's Modern Melting Pot: Hearings before the Committee on Immigration and Naturalization, House of Representatives, November 21, 1922* (Washington, DC: Government Printing Office, 1923). See also Horace M. Kallen, "Democracy Versus the Melting-Pot: A Study of American Nationality," *The Nation* 100, no. 2590 (February 18, 1951): 190–194 and vol. 100, no. 2591 (February 25, 1915): 212–220; and Randolph S. Bourne, "Trans-national America," *Atlantic Monthly* 118 (July 1916): 86–87. For interesting analyses of this period, see Matthew Jacobson, *Whiteness of a Different Color: European Immigrants and the Alchemy of Race* (Cambridge, MA: Harvard University Press, 1998), 68–69; Jeffrey Mirel, "Civic Education and Changing Definitions of American Identity, 1900–1950," *Educational Review* 54, no. 2 (2002): 143–152; and David Tyack, "Preserving the Republic by Educating Republicans," in *Diversity and Its Discontents: Cultural Conflict and Common Ground in Contemporary American Society,* ed. Neil Smelser and Jeffrey Alexander (Princeton: Princeton University Press, 1999), 63–84.

11. See Marcus Hansen, "The Problem of the Third Generation Immigrant," in *Theories of Ethnicity: A Classical Reader,* ed. Werner Sollors (New York: New York University Press, 1996), 202–215.

12. The November 1926 edition of *Opportunity: A Journey of Negro Life* is an early example of a concentrated effort to understand the experiences of black Caribbean immigrants in the United States. As the literary arm of the National Urban League, *Opportunity* featured this special edition on Caribbean immigrants to acquaint its primarily African American readership with blacks from the West Indies.

13. See C. Wright Mills, Clarence Senior, and Rose Kohn Goldsen, *The Puerto Rican Journey: New York's Newest Migrants* (New York: Harper and Row, 1950); see Elena Padilla, *Up from Puerto Rico* (New York: Columbia University Press, 1958); and see Joseph Fitzpatrick, "Attitudes of Puerto Ricans towards Color," *American Catholic Sociological Review* 20, no. 3 (1959): 219–233.

14. I should note that World War II created an economic boom in the United States, and Caribbean immigrant workers were sometimes called upon to supply labor for a variety of industries in urban centers. Migration from English-speaking islands such as Jamaica lagged during the Great Depression, for example, but picked up *slightly* due to the labor shortage of World War II. See Kasinitz, 26.

15. Cited in Philip Q. Yang, *Post-1965 Immigration to the United States* (Westport, CT: Praeger, 1995), 24.

16. Cited in Yang, 24; Kasinitz, 25–31.

17. For more information, see Alejandro Portes and Alex Stepick, *City on the Edge: The Transformation of Miami* (Berkeley: University of California Press, 1993); Frank Moya Pons, *The Dominican Republic: A National History* (Princeton: First Markus Wiener, 1998); and Robert Heinl, Nancy Heinl, and Michael Heinl, *Written in Blood: The Story of the Haitian People, 1492–1995* (Lanham, MD: University Press of America, 1996). For more information about changes in U.S. immigration policy, see Kasinitz, 26–27; Yang, 1–48.

18. Mary Waters, *Ethnic Options: Choosing Identities in America* (Berkeley: University of California Press, 190), 6.

19. Nathan Glazer and Daniel Patrick Moynihan make a passing reference to black West Indians in *Beyond the Melting Pot: The Negroes, Puerto Ricans, Jews, and Italians of New York City* (Cambridge, MA: MIT Press, 1963). Ulf Hannerz makes a fleeting reference to ethnographers' understanding the diversity of black ethnicities in "Some Comments on the Anthropology of Ethnicity in the United States," in *Ethnicity in the Americas,* World Anthropology Series, ed. Frances Henry (The Hague and Paris: Mouton, 1976), 429–438.

20. Joshua Fishman and Vladimir Nahirny and Herbert Gans had their own concerns about Hansen's law, as they articulated in their research from the 1960s and 1970s. See reprint of Vladimir C. Nahirny and Joshua A. Fishman, "American Immigrant Groups: Ethnic Identification and the Problem of Generation," in *Theories of Ethnicity: A Classical Reader,* ed. Werner Sollors (New York: New York University Press, 1996), 266–281. Also see reprint of Herbert Gans, "Symbolic Ethnicity: The Future of Ethnic Groups and Cultures in America," in *Theories of Ethnicity: A Classical Reader,* ed. Werner Sollors (New York: New York University Press, 1996), 425–459. In their 1965 study on American immigrant groups, Joshua Fishman and Vladimir Nahirny challenged Hansen's assertion that "third generation interest" is anything "more than a somewhat appreciative or even indifferent orientation of the grandsons in comparison to that of the sons" (Nahirny and Fishman, 267). Fishman and Nahirny pointed out that third-generation immigrants often lose the language of their immigrant grandparents, arguing that language is a key indicator of cultural preservation in immigrant communities. Further, they suggested that second generationers fight so strongly to negotiate their relationship with the immigrant parent culture and the American mainstream because of the undeniable impact that both cultures have in shaping their identity constructions. Herbert Gans expressed similar concerns with Hansen's work, as best articulated in his groundbreaking article

on symbolic ethnicity some forty-one years after Hansen's address was first published by the Augustana Historical Society. Gans questioned Hansen's use of data, which relied heavily on the experiences of Swedish American academics who were a part of the Augustana Historical Society. Gans argued that Hansen did not have a good sampling of third-generation laymen of Swedish descent in the Midwest. He also suggested that Hansen's analysis of the ethnic revival of the third generation did not provide a systematic exploration of the processes of that revival and thus did not provide a framework by which to understand how ethnic identification could be sustained for future generations. Gans went on to suggest that ethnic identity for third and subsequent generations might be symbolic at best, a leisure-time activity that did not significantly affect day-to-day lived experience.

21. Basch et al., 45.

22. Sherri Grasmuck and Patricia Pessar, *Between Two Islands: Dominican International Migration* (Berkeley: University of California Press, 1991), 13.

23. Caribbeans of African descent are often racialized as "black" under American racial codes, where the "one-drop" rule of African ancestry dominates constructions of race in the American imagination. American cultural hegemony often narrativizes "black" in opposition to "white," which becomes the standard and ideal for defining national identity.

24. Quoted in Susan Greenbaum, *More Than Black: Afro-Cubans in Tampa* (Gainesville: University Press of Florida, 2002), 11.

25. A number of migration scholars refer to "blackness" in their studies of the racial and ethnic politics of Caribbeans, Caribbean immigrants, African Americans, and others in the African diaspora. They also relate the ways in which blackness is perceived by white Americans, Europeans, and colonials. See Basch et al., pp. 40–45; Milton Vickerman, *Crosscurrents: West Indian Immigrants and Race* (New York: Oxford University Press, 1999), 6–9; Silvio Torres-Saillant, "The Tribulations of Blackness: Stages of Dominican Racial Identity," *Latin American Perspectives* (Issue 100) 25, no. 3 (May 1998): 127–131. Although I recognize that the term "blackness" is problematic, it is helpful to my discussion of the ways in which the study's artists and intellectuals identify themselves as black immigrants. Black identity depends on the constructs of race but also on political and cultural affiliations. I want to suggest that blackness moves beyond racial descent to provide critical discourses on racialized, cultural, and ethnic identities. Additionally, while I cannot escape using the term "race," I resist the validation of race as anything other than a social construct. Race, as I use it in the book to discuss black immigrants, becomes a component of blackness.

26. A LaVonne Brown Ruoff and Jerry W. Ward, Jr., eds., *Redefining Ameri-*

*can Literary History* (New York: Modern Language Association of America, 1990), 2.

27. I am especially referencing the work by Dearborn (1986), Sollors (1986), and Boelhower (1987).

## NOTES TO CHAPTER I

1. Tananarive Due and Allison Samuels, "Where Is the Love?" *Essence* 30, no. 10 (February 2000): 85.

2. Ibid., 146.

3. I am indebted to the scholarship of Hazel Carby in *Race Men* (Cambridge, MA: Harvard University Press, 1998). Her readings of race, sexuality, and masculinity in the twentieth century have been influential to the development of this chapter.

4. By the 1960s, Belafonte's image received some criticism from the increasing number of black activist youth disillusioned by the struggle for an integrated society and more interested in Black Power ideology. His use of calypso music early on received criticism from folk purists. Interestingly, Belafonte's most recent comments in 2002 regarding Colin Powell, U.S. Secretary of State during the Bush administration, encouraged some rather harsh rereadings of his 1950s image, especially given his reference to Powell as a "house slave."

5. William Attaway, liner notes for Harry Belafonte, *Harry Belafonte—Calypso,* RCA Victor, LP, LPM-1248, 1956.

6. Calypso is a music that originated in Trinidad, although there are variations of calypso in many Caribbean countries. For more information on calypso and its history, see Donald Hill, *Calypso Calaloo: Early Carnival Music in Trinidad* (Gainesville: University Press of Florida, 1993).

7. Quoted in Arnold Shaw, *Belafonte: An Unauthorized Biography* (Philadelphia: Chilton, 1960), 229.

8. Craig Rosen, *The Billboard Book of Number One Albums: The Inside Story behind Pop Music's Blockbuster Records* (New York: Watson-Guptill, 1996), 3.

9. "The Belafonte Boom," *Look* 20, no. 17 (August 21, 1956): 38. When articles appear without a byline in journals, newspapers, or magazines, I will use the format as it appears in this endnote. Articles without bylines will appear only in endnote citations.

10. Ibid., 41.

11. Jeanne Van Holmes, "Belafonte Gives It All He's Got," *Saturday Evening Post* 229, no. 42 (April 20, 1957): 75.

12. Robert R. Metz, "Crazy for Calypso," in *Harry Belafonte: His Complete Life Story,* ed. Hy Steirman (New York: Hillman Periodicals, 1957), 37.

13. Ibid., 37.

14. Emily Coleman, "Organization Man Named Belafonte," *New York Times Magazine* (December 13, 1959): 35.

15. Ibid., 35.

16. Ibid., 35.

17. "The Belafonte Boom," 41.

18. Van Holmes, 69.

19. Quoted in Richard M. Dalfiume, "The 'Forgotten Years' of the Negro Revolution," *Journal of American History* 55 (1968): 90, 106.

20. Randall Kennedy, *Interracial Intimacies: Sex, Marriage, Identity, and Adoption* (New York: Pantheon, 2003), 258–259.

21. For example, the Production Code Administration (PCA), which policed the Hollywood film industry, began to alter its codes in the 1950s to accommodate some shifts in American society. According to Gregory D. Black in *The Catholic Crusade against the Movies, 1940–1975,* the PCA experienced a decline in influence in the 1950s, especially when independent film producers began to circumvent its rules with alternative films. See Gregory Black, *The Catholic Crusade against the Movies, 1940–1975* (Cambridge: Cambridge University Press, 1997). For a reprint of the Production Codes, see Leonard Leff and Jerold Simmons, *The Dame in the Kimono: Hollywood, Censorship, and the Production Code from the 1920s to the 1960s* (New York: Grove Weidenfeld, 1990), 283–292.

22. For an excellent reading of masculinity in 1950s films, see Steven Cohan, *Masked Men: Masculinity and the Movies in the Fifties* (Bloomington: Indiana University Press, 1997).

23. See Henry Louis Gates, Jr., *Thirteen Ways of Looking at a Black Man* (New York: Random House, 1997), 155–179.

24. For an analysis of Paul Robeson, see Carby, 45–83. I return to the figure of Paul Robeson in the next section of this chapter.

25. See Eric Lott, *Love and Theft: Blackface Minstrelsy and the American Working Class* (New York: Oxford University Press, 1993).

26. *The Birth of a Nation,* dir. D. W. Griffith, perf. Henry Walthall, Miriam Cooper, and Mae Marsh, Epoch, 1915. The central premise of *The Birth of a Nation* is the necessity of keeping blacks outside the ideals of American nationhood. With its obvious pro-South biases, the film suggests that the South and the North should be protected from blacks during the Reconstruction era. The plot revolves around the sexual indiscretions of two black male characters, Silas Lynch, the mulatto who wants to marry Elsie, a white woman, and Gus, who roams the countryside as he attempts to rape the first white woman he can. In the film, these black men serve as symbols of the dangers to whiteness posed by blacks, with their attempts to challenge the signifier of white male supremacy:

white womanhood. The mulatto is a predator to the chaste Elsie, whom white hooded men must ultimately protect from Silas's advances. The youngest Cameron daughter ultimately kills herself before she has to succumb to the sexual assault of the rapist Gus. The film ends with a fight against blacks and, by implication, black manhood. The whites' victory preserves the union between North and South and engenders the birth of an American nation, from which blacks are ideally excluded.

27. See Daniel J. Leab, *From Sambo to Superspade: The Black Experience in Motion Pictures* (Boston: Houghton Mifflin, 1976).

28. See William H. Chafe, *The Unfinished Journey: America since World War II,* 2nd ed. (New York: Oxford University Press, 1991), 3–30; and John Hope Franklin, *From Slavery to Freedom: A History of Negro Americans,* 5th ed. (New York: Alfred A. Knopf, 1980), 422–462.

29. Franklin, 438.

30. Quoted in James Haskins and Kathleen Benson, *Lena* (New York: Stein and Day, 1984), 123.

31. For a discussion of Louis Jordan, see John Chilton, *Let the Good Times Roll: The Story of Louis Jordan and His Music* (London: Quartet Books, 1992).

32. For example, the Trio's recordings "That Ain't Right" and "Straighten Up and Fly Right" reached number one on the race charts in 1942 and 1944, respectively. The Nat Cole Trio played in clubs and theaters such as the 331 Club, in Los Angeles, and at the Loews Theater and Club Zanzibar, on Broadway, in New York. They were also featured in musical interludes in Hollywood films such as *Here Comes Elmer* (1943), *Pistol Packing Mama* (1943), and *Under Western Skies* (1945). By 1949, according to most biographers, Nat King Cole deemphasized his piano and started emphasizing his singing. Songs like "Mona Lisa," in 1950, and "Unforgettable," in 1951, helped introduce Cole to an even larger American pop audience. For more information on Cole, see Klaus Teubig, *Straighten Up and Fly Right: A Chronology and Discography of Nat "King" Cole* (Westport, CT: Greenwood Press, 1994), and Leslie Gourse, *Unforgettable: The Life and Mystique of Nat King Cole* (New York: St. Martin's Press, 1991), from which this information was compiled.

33. The *Nat King Cole Show* was carried by NBC but went off the air because its producers could not find advertisers willing to sponsor an African American program in the 1950s.

34. Again see Gourse. Her argument develops throughout the book but see especially "An Overview," xvi–xxi.

35. The story behind Belafonte's first performance on the *Ed Sullivan Show* suggests Belafonte's relationship with the American left. Before the calypso craze, Belafonte had been a member of the Communist-affiliated American Negro

Theatre. Belafonte was reportedly blacklisted as a Communist sympathizer until Ed Sullivan had Belafonte's name taken off the blacklist. His career soared after his appearance on the *Ed Sullivan Show*. The discussion of Belafonte's leftist politics is beyond the scope of this chapter. However, for more information, see *Scandalize My Name: Stories from the Blacklist,* dir. Alexandra Isles, perf. Harry Belafonte, Morgan Freeman, and Ossie Davis, BET Movies, 1999.

36. Shaw, 177–178.

37. Jon Whitcomb, "Backstage at the Birth of a Hit," *Cosmopolitan* 136, no. 3 (March 1954): 59.

38. "'3 for Tonight' and 19 Stools," *Life* 38, no. 17 (April 25, 1955): 129.

39. Joel Whitburn, *The Billboard Book of Top 40 Albums,* rev. and enlarged 3rd ed. (New York: Billboard Books, 1995), 31.

40. Ibid., 31.

41. Pat Downey, George Albert, and Frank Hoffmann, *Cash Box: Pop Single Charts, 1950–1993* (Englewood, CO: Libraries Unlimited, 1994), 22.

42. Jack Hamilton, "The Storm over Belafonte," *Look* 21, no. 13 (June 25, 1957): 138.

43. "Headliners: Lead Man Holler," *Time* 73, no. 9 (March 2, 1959): 40.

44. Hy Steirman, "The Girls Are Wild about Harry," in *Harry Belafonte: His Complete Life Story,* ed. Hy Steirman (New York: Hillman Periodicals, 1957), 46–47.

45. Van Holmes, 69.

46. For a discussion of the mulatto figure and McKinney, Horne, and Dandridge, see Donald Bogle, *Toms, Coons, Mulattoes, Mammies, and Bucks: An Interpretive History of Blacks in American Films* (New York: Continuum, 1994) 9, 31–34, 166–175. McKinney actually predated Horne and Dandridge. She made her mark in *Hallelujah,* in 1929. However, she appears in a postwar movie, *Pinky* (1949), discussed later. For a better understanding of Horne's struggles as a light-skinned African American singer and actress, see Lena Horne and Richard Schickel, *Lena* (Garden City, NY: Doubleday, 1965). For an account of Dorothy Dandridge's career, see Donald Bogle, *Dorothy Dandridge: A Biography* (New York: Amistad, 1997).

47. Quoted in Renee Romano, "Crossing the Line: Black-White Interracial Marriage in the United States, 1945–1990, Ph.D. diss., Stanford University, 1996, 24.

48. For more information on white America's reaction to intermarriage and integration from the late 1940s until the early 1960s, see Ibid., 21–64.

49. For more information on the coverage of Belafonte's divorce from his first wife, Marguerite, see Hamilton, 141–142; also see Shaw, 194–225.

50. Kasinitz, 24.

51. Performers such as Sir Lancelot, Wilmoth Houdini, and Roaring Lion were first-generation immigrants or transmigrants who had spent some time performing in Trinidad, Europe, and the United States, as well as in other parts of the world. Their bodies, too, became the sites for the negotiated performances of black men in the United States in the first half of the twentieth century. Sir Lancelot, for example, had an established career in the States with his popular radio jingles, nightclub and stage performances, and work in Hollywood in the 1930s and 1940s. Regularly dressed in a tuxedo suit, and thus maintaining a supper club image, he made one of his first stage appearances at the Village Vanguard and went on to bring calypso to the big screen in films like *Two Yanks in Trinidad* (1942), *Brute Force* (1947), and the cult classic *I Walked with a Zombie* (1943). Donald Hill, in *Calypso Calaloo,* notes that he is considered the West Indian who brought calypso music, even in its pop-lite version, to the consciousness of non–West Indian Americans (Hill, 192). Calypso singers such as Wilmoth Houdini and Roaring Lion had a more comedic, carnivalesque appeal to white audiences. Wilmoth Houdini was the Calypso King in New York in the 1930s. He used a carnival motif to appeal to West Indian populations at local cultural events in New York on one hand and to appeal to the white American bohemian society of the Village on the other. Roaring Lion had an image like Louis Jordan's with the West Indian equivalent of the zootsuiter—namely the saga boy. He sang in some of the same venues where Belafonte would later perform, places like the Village Vanguard and the Blue Angel. Interestingly, Donald Hill further notes that Belafonte replaced Roaring Lion at the Village Vanguard, presumably in 1951 (Hill, 108). For more information on calypsonians and calypso singers, see, in addition to Hill, Errol Hill, *The Trinidad Carnival: Mandate for a National Theatre* (Austin: University of Texas, 1972); and Roaring Lion, *Calypso from France to Trinidad: 800 Years of History* (San Juan: Latin American Press, 1987).

52. Quoted in Gates, 167.

53. See Gates, 160; and Taylor Branch, *Parting the Waters: America in the King Years, 1954–63* (New York: Simon and Schuster, 1988), 88.

54. Branch, 185, 306. See Branch for a more detailed discussion of Belafonte's connection to the Civil Rights Movement.

55. Franklin, 409.

56. Chafe, 130.

57. Franklin, 457; and Chafe, 157–158.

58. Tom P. Brady, *Black Monday* (Winona, MI: Association of Citizens' Councils, 1955), 66–67.

59. See John A. Kirk, *Redefining the Color Line: Black Activism in Little Rock, Arkansas, 1940–1970* (Gainesville: University Press of Florida, 2002), 106–138.

60. "Foreign Travel by Americans More Than Tripled," *U.S. News & World Report* (May 24, 1957): 42–43.

61. "Business Abroad: No Recession in Tourist Trade," *Business Week* (May 10, 1958): 72–79.

62. Robert Luis, *Authentic Calypso: The Song, Music, the Dance* (New York: Latin American Press, 1957), 6 [unpaginated].

63. Advertisement, "Nassau and the Bahamas for the Island Home of Your Dreams," *Vogue* (November 15, 1954), unpaginated.

64. "Caribbean Cruise," *Look* (January 11, 1955): 66–67.

65. See Kasinitz, 1–37. In his study, Kasinitz argues that West Indians in the 1930s were more linked to African American culture than were subsequent West Indian immigrants in postwar America. He also contends that white Americans began to see Caribbean Americans as a distinct ethnic group in the United States only after 1965. Also see Irma Watkins-Owens, *Blood Relations: Caribbean Immigrants and the Harlem Community, 1900–1930* (Bloomington: Indiana University Press). Watkins-Owens outlines the intraethnic alliances and conflicts of multiple black communities in New York.

66. I discuss the West Indies Federation in the second section of this chapter.

67. Mighty Sparrow, "Jean and Delilah," *Sixteen Carnival Hits,* Ice (import), CD, 92090, 1992.

68. Even the most arguably "political" song on the *Calypso* album, "Brown Skin Girl," is defused by the soft melodic structure underscored by the guitar. "Brown Skin Girl" explores the theme of American invasion on the island. The original, according to Donald Hill, was from Grenada. See Hill, 9.

69. Harry Belafonte, "Day-O," *Harry Belafonte-Calypso,* RCA, CD, 07863 53801-2, 1992.

70. Quoted in Gates,169.

71. Shaw, 31.

72. Ibid., 45–46.

73. See Robin Kelley, *Race Rebels: Culture, Politics, and the Black Working Class* (New York: Free Press, 1994), 161–181.

74. See Linda España-Maram, "Brown 'Hordes' in McIntosh Suits: Filipinos, Taxi Dance Halls, and Performing the Immigrant Body in Los Angeles, 1930s–1940s," in *Generations of Youth: Youth Cultures and History in Twentieth Century America,* ed. Joe Austin and Michael Willard (New York: New York University Press, 1998), 118–135.

75. Quoted in interview with Stephen Holden, "The Pop Life," *New York Times* (May 8, 1991), Section C, 18.

76. Rosen, 3.

77. For Belafonte's performances discussed in this section, see Harry Belafonte Television Archives, Television and Radio Library, Museum of Television and Radio, New York; and *An Evening with Harry Belafonte and Friends,* dir. Jim Brown, perf. Harry Belafonte, videocassette, Polygram, 1997. Also, I had the opportunity to see Belafonte in concert: Harry Belafonte, Shubert Theater of Performing Arts, New Haven, CT, 11 October 1998.

78. See bell hooks, *Black Looks: Race and Representation* (Boston: South End Press, 1992), 115.

79. "Headliners: Lead Man Holler," *Time* 73, no. 9 (March 2, 1959): 40.

80. Harry Belafonte, "Man Smart (Woman Smarter)," *Belafonte at Carnegie Hall,* RCA, CD, 6006-2-R, 1989.

81. The last twist to the plot is that Jocelyn is not of African descent. Her mother had an affair outside marriage, and she was the result of the affair.

82. *Island in the Sun* Press Book, Black Films Collection, 1939–1984, SCM87-18, Box 6, Schomburg Center for Research in Black Culture, New York, 12–13.

83. Ibid., 14.

84. For example, coverage was included in *Newsweek* (February 11, 1957; February 25, 1957; November 25, 1957), *U.S. News & World Report* (April 26, 1957); *Business Week* (February 23, 1957); and *Time* (May 20, 1957). Heavier coverage, of course, appeared in these journals and magazines when the Federation was established in 1958.

85. Darryl Zanuck resigned from Twentieth Century Fox in 1956 but returned as its head six years later.

86. Darryl Zanuck, "Controversy Is Box Office," in *International Film Annual,* ed. Campbell Dixon (London: John Calder, 1957), 80.

87. *Gentleman's Agreement,* dir. Elia Kazan, perf. Gregory Peck, Dorothy McGuire, and John Garfield, Twentieth Century Fox, 1947; *Pinky,* dir. Elia Kazan, perf. Jeanne Crain, Ethel Waters, and Ethel Barrymore, Twentieth Century Fox, 1949.

88. See, in addition to Bogle, Thomas Cripps, *Making Movies Black: The Hollywood Message Movie from World War II to the Civil Rights Era* (Oxford: Oxford University Press, 1993).

89. Hamilton, 138.

90. Quoted in ibid., 140.

91. Ibid., 140.

92. Joan Fontaine, *No Bed of Roses* (New York: Morrow, 1978), 245.

93. *No Way Out,* dir. Joseph L. Mankiewicz, perf. Sidney Poitier, Richard Widmark, and Linda Darnell, Twentieth Century Fox, 1950; *The Trial,* dir. Mark Robson, perf. Juano Hernandez, Glenn Ford, and Dorothy McGuire, MGM, 1955.

94. *Island in the Sun,* dir. Robert Rossen, perf. Joan Fontaine, James Mason, Dorothy Dandridge, Joan Collins, and Harry Belafonte, Darryl Zanuck Productions, 1957.

95. *Showboat,* dir. James Whale, perf. Irene Dunne, Allan Jones, Charles Winninger, and Paul Robeson, Universal, 1936.

96. *Island in the Sun,* dir. Robert Rossen, perf. Joan Fontaine, James Mason, Dorothy Dandridge, Joan Collins, and Harry Belafonte, Darryl Zanuck Productions, 1957.

97. Fontaine, 245.

98. Cripps, 251.

99. Harry Belafonte, Black History Month Keynote Address, Quinnipiac University, Hamden, CT, 21 February 2000.

NOTES TO CHAPTER 2

1. The title of this chapter, "All o' We Is One," is a common saying often used by Marshall to assert her subject-position as Caribbean and African American. See Daryl Cumber Dance, "An Interview with Paule Marshall," *Southern Review* 28, no. 1 (January 1992): 7. Reviews and critical analyses of Marshall's literature have been extensive. Several recently published books either include a study of Marshall's work or focus on Marshall's literature specifically. See Heather Hathaway, *Caribbean Waves: Relocating Claude McKay and Paule Marshall* (Bloomington: Indiana University Press, 1999); Stelamaris Coser, *Bridging the Americas: The Literature of Paule Marshall, Toni Morrison, and Gayle Jones* (Philadelphia: Temple University Press, 1995); and Dorothy Hamer Denniston, *The Fiction of Paule Marshall* (Knoxville: University of Tennessee Press, 1995).

2. There were two waves of reviews on *Brown Girl, Brownstones,* one after it was published in 1959, the other after it was published in 1981. Early reviews were included in *Black American Literature Forum* (9.3, Fall 1975); *San Francisco Sunday Chronicle* (January 28, 1962); *Time Literary Supplement* (August 19, 1960); *Saturday Review* (August 29, 1959); and *New York Herald Tribune Book Review* (August 16, 1959). Later reviews appeared in *Nation* (245; December 27, 1987); *Freedomways* (22.2; 1982); the *New York Times* (November 22, 1981); and *The Black Scholar* (12; March 1981). Perhaps most significant are the essays written in literary journals, which are too numerous to cite here. However, some analyses by literary and cultural studies scholars on all of her works were included in journals such as *Callaloo* (10.1; Winter 1987); *SAGE* (2; Spring 1985); *CLA Journal* (24.1; September 1980); *Journal of Black Studies* (1; December 1979); *Women's Studies* (5; 1977); and *Novel* (7; Winter 1974).

3. Reviews for *The Chosen Place, The Timeless People* were included in *The*

*Village Voice* (15.41; October 8, 1970); *Freedomways* (10.1; 1970); and *Publisher's Weekly* (August 11, 1969), among others.

4. Reviews for *Praisesong for the Widow* can be found in *CLA Journal* (27.4; June 1984); *Crisis* (90; August-September 1983); *Los Angeles Times Book Review* (February 27, 1983); and *New York Times* (February 1, 1983), to name a few. Reviews for *Daughters* were included in journals and newspapers such as *New Woman* (November 1991); *The Women's Review of Books* (9.2; November 1991); *USA Today* (October 11, 1991); and *Essence* (22.6, October 1991). Because this chapter focuses on the period between 1959 and 1983, *Daughters* (New York: Atheneum, 1991) and *The Fisher King* (New York: Scribner, 2001) are beyond its scope. I should note that *The Fisher King* includes some of Marshall's signature elements of Caribbean and African American interactions, as well as incorporating cultural exchanges with blacks in Europe. Although Marshall's black female characters play a significant role in *The Fisher King,* however, the story is experienced through the lens of a young boy.

5. Belafonte and Marshall both had ties to the left, although Belafonte's ties were not as apparent during his success in 1956 and 1957. For more information on Belafonte's ties before the calypso craze, see *Scandalize My Name: Stories from the Blacklist,* dir. Alexandra Isles, perf. Harry Belafonte, Morgan Freeman, and Ossie Davis, BET Movies, 1999.

6. Upon completing a final version of this chapter for publication, I was informed by a colleague of James C. Hall's chapter on Marshall in his book *Mercy, Mercy Me: African-American Culture and the American Sixties* (Oxford: Oxford University Press, 2001). Although Hall's work did not inform this chapter, as my chapter on Marshall was already written, I find Hall to be a kindred spirit. He not only does an excellent job of evoking Marshall's political ties but also provides a critical analysis of *The Chosen Place, The Timeless People.* In Hall's book, Marshall's work is read alongside the work of William Demby.

7. Lean'tin L Bracks, *Writings on Black Women of the Diaspora* (New York: Garland, 1998); Stelamaris Coser, *Bridging the Americas: The Literature of Paule Marshall, Toni Morrison, and Gayle Jones* (Philadelphia: Temple University Press, 1994).

8. Sabine Brock, "Transcending the "Loophole of Retreat": Paule Marshall's Placing of Female Generations," *Callaloo* 10, no. 1 (Winter 1987): 80.

9. Melvin Rahming, *The Evolution of the West Indian's Image in the Afro-American Novel* (Millwood, NY: Associated Faculty Press, 1986), 110.

10. For more information on the black left and black nationalism, see Harold Cruse, *Crisis of the Negro Intellectual* (New York: Morrow, 1967). Wald's more contemporary understanding of the black left can be found in Alan Wald, *Writing from the Left: New Essays on Radical Culture and Politics* (London: Verso,

1994); also see (in a two-part series) Alan Wald, "African Americans, Culture and Communism," in *Against the Current* (84 and 86; January/February and May/June 2000, respectively): 23–29 (part 1), 27–34 (part 2). In addition, see Michael Denning, *The Cultural Front: The Laboring of American Culture in the Twentieth Century* (London: Verso, 1996).

11. My discussion of Marshall's work in this chapter is confined to her literary career up to *Praisesong for the Widow* in 1983, and thus it does not include an analysis of any links between her political views and artistic expressions in *Daughters* or the more recent *The Fisher King*. My analysis is meant to situate Marshall within a particular cultural moment and to illustrate the ways in which *Praisesong for the Widow* articulates Marshall's understanding of Caribbean and African American cultures at that phase in her artistic development.

12. James A. Wechsler, "Sound Barrier," *New York Post* (Monday, June 22, 1964): 26.

13. Cruse, 193. Henceforth, I will use "Association" and "Association of Artists for Freedom" interchangeably.

14. Wechsler, "Sound Barrier," 26.

15. Ibid., 26.

16. I use terms like these in quotation marks to reference the ways in which Wechsler describes the black and white participants throughout his column.

17. Wechsler, "Sound Barrier," 26.

18. James A. Wechsler, "Sound Barrier: II," *New York Post* (Tuesday, June 23, 1964): 26.

19. Wechsler, "Sound Barrier: II," 26.

20. Wechsler, "Sound Barrier," 26.

21. Lorraine Hansberry, "Black Revolution and White Backlash," *National Guardian* 16, no. 39 (July 4, 1964): 6. Lorraine Hansberry authored a verbatim transcription of the debate in the *National Guardian*.

22. Ibid., 9.

23. Ibid., 7.

24. Killens quoted in Cruse, 197.

25. Hansberry, 9.

26. Ibid., 9

27. Ibid., 8.

28. Ibid., 8. Interestingly enough, Wechsler duly noted these conciliatory tones of Dee, Davis, and Hansberry; Wechsler, "Sound Barrier II," 26.

29. Several recent works have been written on the relationship between the Communist Party, left-wing organizations, and African Americans. For a more in-depth discussion, which is beyond the scope of this chapter, see James Smethurst, *The New Red Negro: The Literary Left and African American Poetry,*

*1930–1946* (New York: Oxford University Press, 1999); Mark Solomon, *The Cry Was Unity: Communists and African Americans, 1917–36* (Jackson: University Press of Mississippi, 1998); and Earl Ofari Hutchinson, *Blacks and Reds: Race and Class in Conflict, 1919–1990* (East Lansing: Michigan State University Press, 1995).

30. In October 1930, Communist International's Negro Commission (made up of representatives of communist parties worldwide) released a "Resolution on the Negro Question" to the public. It proposed a "Negro Nation," to be created in the American South, to which blacks would not be forced to migrate but where they could have self-governance. For more information, see Hutchinson, 43–58.

31. Hutchinson notes that in 1935, at the Seventh World Congress of the Communist International, communists made a push toward establishing relationships with outside black leaders. He writes, "The Comintern gave American Communists the specific objective of organizing a 'united front' to "fight for the equal status for Negroes.' Communists were told they must embrace black ministers, black editors, black businessmen and professionals. It was now more urgent than ever that Party leaders cement ties with the NAACP." Ibid., 123.

32. Quoted in ibid., 235.

33. Alexis DeVeaux, "Paule Marshall: In Celebration of Our Triumph," *Essence* (May 1979): 133, 135.

34. Cruse, 208.

35. Rosa Guy quoted in Jerrie Norris, *Presenting Rosa Guy* (Boston: Twayne, 1988), 13.

36. Norris, 13.

37. The membership roll comes from several sources including the following: Phillip M. Richards, "Foreword" to Julian Mayfield, *The Hit and The Long Night* (Boston: Northeastern University Press, 1989), vii; Cruse; the Harlem Writers' Guild's Web page, http://members.aol.com/HWG1950; and a review of *Freedomways*'s contributor pages, which often mentioned membership, between 1960 and 1970.

38. Emphasis mine.

39. Paule Marshall, "Reena", *Harper's* 1349 (October 1962): 154–163.

40. Irma Watkins-Owens, *Blood Relations: Caribbean Immigrants and the Harlem Community, 1900–1930* (Bloomington: Indiana University Press, 1996), 13; and Ira De Augustine Reid, *The Negro Immigrant: His Background, Characteristics and Social Adjustment, 1899–1937* (New York: Columbia University Press, 1939), 42–43.

41. Paule Marshall, "Shaping the World of My Art," *New Letters* 40 (Autumn 1973): 103.

42. "Marcus Garvey," in *The Norton Anthology: African American Literature,* ed. Henry Louis Gates, Jr., and Nellie Y. McKay (New York: Norton, 1997), 973.

43. Quoted in Hutchinson, 54.

44. Paule Marshall, "From the Poets in the Kitchen," *Reena and Other Stories* (New York: Feminist Press, 1983), 5.

45. Sabine Brock, "'Talk as a Form of Action': An Interview with Paule Marshall," in *History and Tradition in Afro-American Culture,* ed. Günter H. Lenz (New York: Campus Verlag, 1984), 204; emphasis mine.

46. DeVeaux, 124.

47. Marshall notes the following in her interview with Brock: "Not only did it [the Barbadian women's involvement in UNIA] say that they had a political perspective, but they also saw themselves in terms of the larger world of darker people. . . . [T]heir dedication to Garvey said that they saw themselves not just as Black Afro-Americans or Afro-Caribbeans living in this hemisphere, but they saw themselves as part of that larger world. And this has become, of course, one of the themes of my work"; Brock, "Talk as a Form of Action," 197.

48. For more information, see Allen J. Matusow, *The Unraveling of America: A History of Liberalism in the 1960s* (New York: Harper and Row, 1986), 345–375.

49. Burns, 33, 37.

50. Matusow, 362.

51. Hoyt Fuller quoted in Addison Gayle, *The Black Aesthetic* (New York: Doubleday, 1971), xvii.

52. Addison Gayle, "Introduction," *The Black Aesthetic* (New York: Doubleday, 1971), xvii–xviii.

53. For more information on decolonization and emerging African nations, see Immanuel Wallerstein, *Africa: The Politics of Independence* (New York: Vintage, 1961); and Richard Gibson, *African Liberation Movements: Contemporary Struggles against White Minority Rule* (London: Oxford University Press, 1972).

54. Cruse, 207.

55. Dance, 14.

56. Both Carmichael and Malcolm X were careful to point out the interconnectedness between African Americans and Africans as their political platforms developed in the 1960s, however. For more information on the evolution of their political ideologies, see Stokely Carmichael and Charles V. Hamilton, *Black Power: The Politics of Liberation in America* (New York: Random House, 1967), and Stokely Carmichael, *Stokely Speaks: Black Power Back to Pan-Africanism* (New York: Random House, 1971). Selected Malcolm X speeches are collected in George Breitman, ed., *Malcolm X Speaks: Selected Speeches and Statements* (New York: Pathfinder, 1989). Breitman offers introductory comments, which map Malcolm's shifting political allegiances and platforms.

57. Joyce Pettis, "A MELUS Interview: Paule Marshall." *MELUS* 17, no. 4 (Winter 1991–1992): 126.

58. Omolara Ogundipe-Leslie, "Re-creating Ourselves All over the World: Interview with Paule Marshall," *Matatu* 6 (1989): 30–31.

59. Brock, "Talk as a Form of Action," 204.

60. Ogundipe-Leslie, 34.

61. Ibid., 28.

62. Paule Marshall, *The Chosen Place, The Timeless People* (New York: Harcourt, Brace, and World, 1969), 58.

63. Cruse, 247.

64. Quoted in Cruse, 243.

65. In *The Crisis of the Negro Intellectual,* Cruse contends that *Freedomways* was one of the literary vehicles of the Communist Party. (For more information on his discussion of *Freedomways,* see *The Crisis of the Negro Intellectual,* 240–252) However, Abby and Ronald Johnson, in *Propaganda and Aesthetics,* offer a more nuanced understanding of *Freedomways*'s communist ties. They observe: "While the magazine was not an organ of the Communist Party, its supporters were black and white Marxists, many of whom were members of the party. The editor, Shirley Graham, was a Communist, as was her husband, W. E. B. Du Bois. She and one of her associate editors, W. Alphaeus Hunton, had been on the editorial board of *Freedom*. The managing editor, Esther Jackson, was married to James E. Jackson, described by Cruse as 'The leading Negro theoretician in the Communist Party.' As years went on, the editorial board changed, as did the names of contributors. The Marxist orientation of the magazine continued, however"; Abby Johnson and Ronald Johnson, *Propaganda and Aesthetics: The Literary Politics of African-American Magazines in the Twentieth Century* (Amherst: University of Massachusetts Press, 1979), 228.

66. *Freedomways* 4, no. 3 (Summer 1964): 294.

67. Johnson and Johnson, 228.

68. Ernest Kaiser, "Five Years of FREEDOMWAYS: An Evaluation," *Freedomways* 6, no. 2 (Spring 1966): 117.

69. The appearances of Davis, Dee, and Killens in the *Negro Digest* suggest the ways in which their allegiance vacillated between black leftist politics and black cultural nationalism. I argue that they had ties to both political frameworks, although their flirtations with racial politics were not as separatist as were the politics of Baraka, Neal, and, to some extent, Paule Marshall. Davis's and Dee's contributions to the *Negro Digest* were not representative of the militancy that characterized the journal of the period, although I think it is noteworthy that they were invited to appear in the journal. Killens's work, by contrast, has always been hard to canonize. Between the 1950s and 1960s, Killens

vacillates among leftist politics, protest genres, and black cultural nationalism. At times his work seems contradictory, highlighting the tensions between left-ist politics and racial allegiances for black activists and artists in postwar America.

70. Ossie Davis's article for *Negro Digest* was "The Flight from Broadway," *Negro Digest* (April 1966): 14–19; Ruby Dee's was "The Tattered Queens," *Negro Digest* (April 1966): 32–36. Together, they contributed many more articles to *Freedomways*. Between 1961 and 1970, Davis appeared in a few issues, including those for Summer 1965 and Summer 1968. Ruby Dee contributed to the Winter 1965 issue and was listed as a contributing editor in 1970.

71. Interestingly, Killens does not appear in *Freedomways*, perhaps because of the split between Clarke and Killens that Cruse describes in *The Crisis of the Negro Intellectual*. Some of Killens's contributions to other journals are "Broth-erhood of Blackness," *Negro Digest* (May 1966): 4–10; "Another Time When Black Was Beautiful," *Black World* (November 1970); 20–36; and "The Black Culture Generation Gap," *Black World* (August 1973): 22–33.

72. Only a few scattered essays appeared between 1960 and 1975. They were as follows: "Reena," *Harper's* (October 1962); "Fannie Lou Hamer: Hunger Has No Color Line," *Vogue* (June 1970): 126, 191, 192; "Shaping the World of My Art," *New Letters* 40 (Autumn 1973): 97–112; and "Reading," *Mademoiselle* 79 (June 1974): 82–83.

73. Sarah Wright, "The Negro Woman in American Literature," *Free-domways* 6, no. 1 (Winter 1966): 8.

74. Abbey Lincoln, "The Negro Woman in American Literature," *Free-domways* 6, no. 1 (Winter 1966): 11.

75. Alice Childress, "The Negro Woman in American Literature," *Free-domways* 6, no. 1 (Winter 1966): 19.

76. Lincoln, 13; emphasis mine.

77. Paule Marshall, "The Negro Woman in American Literature," *Free-domways* 6, no. 1 (Winter 1966): 25.

78. Marshall, "The Negro Woman in American Literature," 24.

79. Marshall, "Shaping the World of My Art," 107.

80. Ibid., 107.

81. Dance, 14.

82. Marshall, "Shaping the World of My Art," 108.

83. Ibid., 104.

84. Ibid., 111.

85. Ibid., 106.

86. Dance, 19.

87. Marshall, "Shaping the World of My Art," 106–107.

88. Ibid., 107.

89. Quoted in Coser, 63.

90. Paule Marshall, *Praisesong for the Widow* (New York: Putnam, 1983), 14.

91. Ibid., 51.

92. Ibid., 44.

93. Ibid., 54.

94. Ibid., 54–55.

95. Ibid., 53.

96. Hansberry, 6.

97. Marshall, *Praisesong for the Widow,* 26.

98. Marshall, *The Chosen Place, The Timeless People,* 234.

99. Ibid., 359.

100. Hansberry, 7.

101. Ogundipe-Leslie, 35.

102. Melody Graulich and Lisa Sisco, "Meditations on Language and the Self: A Conversation with Paule Marshall," *NWSA Journal* 4, no. 3 (Fall 1992): 293.

103. Marshall, *Praisesong for the Widow,* 87.

104. Ibid., 88.

105. Ibid., 135.

106. Ibid., 134.

107. Ibid., 14.

108. Ibid., 139.

109. Ibid., 139.

110. Ogundipe-Leslie, 37.

111. Marshall, *Praisesong for the Widow,* 151.

112. Ibid., 153.

113. Ibid., 153.

114. Henry Louis Gates, Jr., *The Signifying Monkey: A Theory of African-American Literary Criticism* (New York: Oxford University Press), 37.

115. Marshall, *Praisesong for the Widow,* 148.

116. Ogundipe-Leslie, 36.

117. Maryse Condé, "Return of a Native Daughter: An Interview with Paule Marshall and Maryse Condé," trans. John Williams, *SAGE* 3, no. 2 (Fall 1986): 52. (Original, nontranslated version was first published in *Politique Africaine* [September 1984, 15]: 79—83.)

118. Marshall, *Praisesong for the Widow,* 170.

119. Ibid., 170.

120. Ibid., 168.

121. Ibid., 175.

122. Ibid., 187.
123. Ibid., 190–191.
124. Ibid., 206.
125. Ibid., 241.
126. Ibid., 249.
127. Ibid., 249.
128. Ibid., 251.
129. Condé, 52.

## NOTES TO CHAPTER 3

"Who Said It Was Simple," copyright © 1973 by Audre Lorde. "Dahomey," copyright © 1978 by Audre Lorde. "125th Street and Abomey," "Harriet," "A Woman Speaks," "A Litany for Survival," copyright © 1978 by Audre Lorde, from *Collected Poems,* by Audre Lorde. Copyright © 1997 by the Estate of Audre Lorde. Used by permission of W. W. Norton & Company.

1. Audre Lorde, "Learning from the 60s," in *Sister Outsider: Essays & Speeches by Audre Lorde,* ed. Audre Lorde (Freedom, CA: Crossing Press, 1984), 143.

2. I use god(dess) with parentheses to underscore the importance of the gender ambiguity of African religious icons used in *The Black Unicorn* (New York: Norton, 1978) and *Zami: A New Spelling of My Name* (Watertown, MA: Persephone Press, 1982).

3. Most literary critics date the Black Arts Movement to the years between 1965 and 1970. In this chapter, I refer to the creative and artistic dialogues of black artists and intellectuals during the 1970s as part of the Black Arts Movement, as well. Although the most militant period waned in the 1960s, most artists who were participants in the Black Arts Movement of the 1960s still engaged Black Arts ideologies in the next decade. By designating the 1970s as part of the Black Arts Movement, I hope to suggest some of the political and artistic issues that lingered from the 1960s.

4. My analysis in this chapter relies on most of Lorde's published materials. Fortunately, several of her dialogues with white feminists and Black Arts intellectuals from speeches and essays are part of collections published by Lorde before her death. Also, they can be found in journals of the era. I attempted without success to access the Audre Lorde Papers at Spelman College. The papers were closed indefinitely because of the research being done by another scholar, who was working on Audre Lorde's biography, due out Spring 2004.

5. Audre Lorde, "Who Said It Was Simple," in *From A Land Where Other*

*People Live,* collected in *The Collected Poems of Audre Lorde* (New York: Norton, 1997), 92, lines 12–18.

6. See Robert Staples, "The Myth of Black Macho: A Response to Angry Black Feminists," *The Black Scholar* 10, nos. 6, 7 (March–April 1979): 24–33.

7. "The Black Sexism Debate," *The Black Scholar* 10, nos. 8, 9 (May–June 1979), inside cover.

8. Throughout this chapter, I capitalize Black Arts Movement and Feminist Movement. The Feminist Movement connotes what some consider the Women's Movement or the second Feminist Movement in the United States. Roughly, I am referencing the Feminist Movement in the mid-1960s, 1970s, and early 1980s.

9. Audre Lorde, "Feminism & Black Liberation: The Great American Disease," *The Black Scholar* 10, nos. 8, 9 (May–June 1979): 19.

10. Lorde, "Feminism & Black Liberation," 19.

11. Charles Rowell, "Above the Wind: An Interview with Audre Lorde," *Callaloo* 14.1 (1991): 83. Basch et al.'s research on early Grenadian immigrant communities in the United States seems to support Lorde's understanding of her parents' unwillingness to participate in American culture. Their work notes, of this early immigrant community, "Although many eventually bought homes, raised children, and joined political movements that challenged U.S. racial barriers, most of these immigrants resisted full incorporation into the socio-racial hierarchy of the United States, which positioned them at the bottom. . . . Many Vincentians and Grenadians retained close connections with kin and communities at home, even if they never returned for a visit, and large numbers, reflecting the migration ideology forged during circum-Caribbean migrations, continued to believe they would return 'home' some day." See Linda Basch, Cristina Blanc Szanton, and Nina Glick Schiller, *Nations Unbound: Transnational Projects, Post-Colonial Predicaments, and De-Territorialized Nation-States* (Langhorne, PA: Gordon and Breach Science Publishers, 1994), 66.

12. Lorde, *Zami,* 87.

13. Ibid., 179.

14. For a comprehensive understanding of the Feminist Movement, see Barbara Sinclair Deckard, *The Women's Movement: Political, Socioeconomic, and Psychological Issues* (New York: Harper and Row, 1983): 317–385. For an understanding of the concerns of women of color in the Feminist Movement, see Chandra Talpade Mohanty, Ann Russo, and Lourdes Torres, eds., *Third World Women and the Politics of Feminism* (Bloomington: Indiana University Press, 1991).

15. Stewart Burns, *Social Movements of the 1960s: Searching for Democracy* (Boston: Twayne, 1990): 116–125; Deckard, 317–385.

16. Burns, 129.

17. Claudia Tate, "Audre Lorde," in *Black Women Writers at Work*, ed. Claudia Tate (New York: Continuum, 1983), 101.

18. Audre Lorde, "The Master's Tools Will Never Dismantle the Master's House," in *Sister Outsider: Essays & Speeches by Audre Lorde*, ed. Audre Lorde (Freedom, CA: Crossing Press, 1984), 112.

19. Lorde, "The Master's Tools Will Never Dismantle the Master's House," 110–111, 113.

20. Audre Lorde, "Uses of Anger: Women Responding to Racism," in *Sister Outsider: Essays & Speeches by Audre Lorde*, ed. Audre Lorde (Freedom, CA: Crossing Press, 1984), 131.

21. Ibid., 127.

22. Problems between heterosexual and homosexual women, according to the feminist scholar Barbara Deckard, proved divisive in key feminist organizations such as NOW. The New York chapter of NOW, for example, was "almost destroyed by internal struggles of lesbian demands" (Deckard, 340). Before the 1970s, lesbian feminists seemed willing to remain silent about their lesbian identities as they pushed for equal rights for women. However, by 1970, there was a shift in lesbian-feminist politics, forcing women's groups to advocate for the equal rights of lesbians as well. By 1971, NOW passed a resolution that was affirming of lesbian rights and the place of lesbians within the struggles for women's liberation. See Deckard, 340–343.

23. Lillian Faderman, *Odd Girls and Twilight Lovers: A History of Lesbian Life in Twentieth-Century America* (New York: Penguin, 1991), 206.

24. See Larry Neal and Amiri Baraka, eds., *Black Fire: An Anthology of Afro-American Writing* (New York: Morrow, 1968); Clarence Major, *The New Black Poetry* (New York: International Publishers, 1969); and Larry Neal, "The Black Arts Movement," in *The Black Aesthetic*, ed. Addison Gayle, Jr. (Garden City, NY: Doubleday, 1971), 272–290.

25. Stephen Henderson, *Understanding the New Black Poetry: Black Speech and Black Music as Poetic References* (New York: Morrow, 1973), 390.

26. Audre Lorde, "An Interview: Audre Lorde and Adrienne Rich," in *Sister Outsider: Essays & Speeches by Audre Lorde*, ed. Audre Lorde (Freedom, CA: Crossing Press, 1984), 98.

27. See Angela Bowen, "'Who Said It Was Simple': Audre Lorde's Complex Connections to Three U.S. Liberation Movements, 1952–1992," Ph.D. diss., Clark University, 1998, 196.

28. Quoted in ibid., 197.

29. Kitchen Table: Women of Color Press was launched officially in 1981, although Barbara Smith notes that she and Lorde had begun having planning session for the press in the fall of 1980. See *A Litany for Survival: The Life and Work*

*of Audre Lorde,* dirs. Ada Gray Griffin and Michelle Parkerson, perf. Barbara Smith, Audre Lorde, Sonia Sanchez, Videocassette, Third World Newsreel, 1996.

30. Hollie West, "Sexual Politics and the Afro-American Writer," *Washington Post* (May 8, 1978): B5.

31. Ibid.

32. Ibid.

33. In an interview with Angela Bowen, Sonia Sanchez remembers that Audre Lorde attended the conference with a group of women who served as her protectors from the backlash surrounding her homosexuality; see Bowen, 197.

34. Audre Lorde, "Scratching the Surface: Some Notes on Barriers to Women and Loving," in *Sister Outsider: Essays & Speeches by Audre Lorde,* ed. Audre Lorde (Freedom, CA: Crossing Press, 1984), 47.

35. Ibid., 47.

36. Ibid., 52.

37. See Audre Lorde, "Poetry Is Not a Luxury," in *Sister Outsider: Essays & Speeches by Audre Lorde,* ed. Audre Lorde (Freedom, CA: Crossing Press, 1984), 36–39; Audre Lorde, "The Transformation of Silence into Language and Action," in *Sister Outsider: Essays & Speeches by Audre Lorde,* ed. Audre Lorde (Freedom, CA: Crossing Press, 1984), 40–44; Audre Lorde, "An Open Letter to Mary Daly," in *Sister Outsider: Essays & Speeches by Audre Lorde,* ed. Audre Lorde (Freedom, CA: Crossing Press, 1984), 66–71; and Lorde, "Scratching the Surface."

38. Lorde, "Scratching the Surface," 49.

39. Ibid., 50.

40. Audre Lorde, "Eye to Eye: Black Women, Hatred, and Anger," in *Sister Outsider: Essays & Speeches by Audre Lorde,* ed. Audre Lorde (Freedom, CA: Crossing Press, 1984), 151.

41. See Malcolm X, "OOAAU Founding Rally" in *By Any Means Necessary* (New York: Pathfinder, 1992), 34–67. For example, in a speech for the Organization of Afro-American Unity Founding Rally in New York in June of 1964, Malcolm X discussed the African states' ability to start an organization in which black leaders from different backgrounds would come together to discuss their futures. In the speech, he argued that this unity among African leaders set an example for African Americans. He added that blacks in Africa and in the diaspora must work together. He observed, "We must unite together in order to go forward together. Africa will not go forward any faster than we will and we will not go forward any faster than Africa will. We have one destiny and we've had one past" (40).

42. See Carmichael, *Stokely Speaks: Back to Pan-Africanism.* A good example of Carmichael's pan-African politics can be found in his anthologized speech

"Pan-Africanism," which was given before students at Morehouse and Federal City Colleges in 1970. In 1970, Carmichael observed, "We must begin to understand Africa, not only culturally, but politically, and we must begin to support those movements of liberation that seek to build truly revolutionary states in Africa that will support us" (Carmichael, 206). He contended that African Americans had to make Africa a priority because power for black Africans meant powers for blacks in the United States.

43. See the following issues in *The Black Scholar*: February 1971, March 1971, January 1972, February 1973, July-August 1973, April 1974, July-August 1974, September 1975, September 1976, and October-November 1976. In fact, the journal packaged these issues for $15 and offered the editions to its consumers in an advertisement in its October 1978 issue.

44. See United Nations Centre against Apartheid, "The Effects of Apartheid on the Status of Women in South Africa," *The Black Scholar* 10, no. 1 (September 1978): 11–19.

45. Immanuel Wallerstein, *Africa: The Politics of Independence* (New York: Vintage Books, 1961), 113–114.

46. Ibid., 114. For more information on the OAU and other pan-Africanist groups, see Richard Gibson, *African Liberation Movements: Contemporary Struggles Against White Minority Rule* (London: Oxford University Press, 1972); also see Ronald W. Waters, *Pan-Africanism in the African Diaspora* (Detroit: Wayne State University Press, 1993).

47. Walters, 54–88.

48. Bowen, 196.

49. Ibid., 196.

50. Lorde, "Scratching the Surface," 50.

51. Charlene Spretnak, ed., *The Politics of Women's Spirituality: Essays on the Rise of Spiritual Power within the Feminist Movement* (Garden City, NY: Anchor Press, 1982), v.

52. Lorde, "Poetry Is Not a Luxury," 37.

53. Ibid., 37.

54. Ibid., 39.

55. Ibid., 37.

56. Ibid., 37.

57. Ibid., 38.

58. Lorde, "An Interview: Audre Lorde and Adrienne Rich," 101.

59. Ibid., 101. The "black mother poet" is actually written as the "Black mother who is the poet"; however, I will refer to her as the "black mother poet" throughout my discussion of Lorde in this chapter.

60. Audre Lorde, "Dahomey," in *The Black Unicorn*, collected in *The Col-*

*lected Poems of Audre Lorde* (New York: Norton, 1997), 239, lines 1–4. Because of this chapter's interdisciplinary focus, I have decided to cite poetry in this format to avoid confusion with page citations.

61. Ibid., lines 5–8.

62. Ibid., lines 9–13.

63. Ibid., lines 27–29.

64. Audre Lorde, "125th Street and Abomey," in *The Black Unicorn,* collected in *The Collected Poems of Audre Lorde* (New York: Norton, 1997), 241, lines 11–16.

65. Ibid., lines 17–22.

66. Ibid., line 8.

67. Ibid., line 35.

68. Ibid., line 37.

69. Audre Lorde, "A Glossary of African Names Used in the Poems," in *The Black Unicorn,* collected in *The Collected Poems of Audre Lorde* (New York: Norton, 1997), 331–332.

70. Ibid., 330.

71. Lorde, "The Master's Tools Will Never Dismantle the Master's House," 111.

72. See Lorde, "Poetry Is Not a Luxury"; Audre Lorde, "Age, Race, Class, and Sex: Women Defining Difference," in *Sister Outsider: Essays & Speeches by Audre Lorde,* ed. Audre Lorde (Freedom, CA: Crossing Press, 1984), 118–119; and Lorde, "Uses of Anger."

73. Lorde, "Age, Race, Class, and Sex: Women Defining Difference," 118–119.

74. Lorde, "The Master's Tools Will Never Dismantle the Master's House," 112.

75. Audre Lorde, "Walking Our Boundaries," in *The Black Unicorn,* collected in *The Collected Poems of Audre Lorde* (New York: Norton, 1997), 262, lines 39–42.

76. Audre Lorde, "Meet," in *The Black Unicorn,* collected in *The Collected Poems of Audre Lorde* (New York: Norton, 1997), 257, lines 1–5.

77. Ibid., lines 35–36.

78. Rowell, 90.

79. Audre Lorde, "Harriet," in *The Black Unicorn,* collected in *The Collected Poems of Audre Lorde* (New York: Norton, 1997), 245, lines 1–9.

80. Lorde plays on the autobiographical "I" with the poetic voice in several of her poems in the first section of *The Black Unicorn.* In "A Woman Speaks," for example, she writes: I have been woman / for a long time / beware my smile / I am treacherous with old magic / and the noon's new fury / with all your wide futures / promised / I am / woman / and not white" (lines 25–34). However, she

never identifies the speaker, intentionally leaving the decision to the reader and the way he or she wishes to interpret the speaker's voice. The same can be observed in the poem "From the House of Yemanjá." Lorde writes, "I bear two women upon my back / one dark and rich and hidden / in the ivory hungers of the other" (lines 11–13); yet, she arguably switches the poetic voice in later lines: "Mother I need / mother I need / mother I need your blackness now / as the august earth needs rain" (lines 27–30). See Audre Lorde, "A Woman Speaks" and "From the House of Yemanjá," in *The Black Unicorn,* collected in *The Collected Poems of Audre Lorde* (New York: Norton, 1997), 234 and 235.

81. Lorde, "Harriet," 245, lines 22–24.

82. Ibid., lines 29–31.

83. Tate, 111.

84. Ibid.

85. Audre Lorde, "A Litany for Survival," in *The Black Unicorn,* collected in *The Collected Poems of Audre Lorde* (New York: Norton, 1997), 255, lines 15–24.

86. Lorde, "The Transformation of Silence into Language and Action," 41.

87. See Claudine Raynaud, "'A Nutmeg Nestled Inside Its Covering of Mace': Audre Lorde's *Zami,*" in *Life/Lines: Theorizing Women's Autobiography,* ed. Bella Brodzki and Celeste Schenck (Ithaca: Cornell University Press, 1988), 221–242. Also see AnaLouise Keating, *Women Reading, Women Writing: Self-Invention in Paula Gunn Allen, Gloria Anzaldúa, and Audre Lorde* (Philadelphia: Temple University Press, 1996), 145–179.

88. For an example, see Lorde, "The Transformation of Silence into Language and Action," 40–44; and Audre Lorde, "An Open Letter to Mary Daly," 66–71. Lorde manipulates language in this way as a strategic and self-empowering device. In *Black Women Writers at Work,* Claudia Tate notes that Lorde wanted Tate to capitalize "black" in their interview, although Tate decided not to capitalize the word; see Tate, 100.

89. Several historians suggest that strong African states such as Dahomey and Benin—two empires esteemed in Lorde's *The Black Unicorn*—gained and maintained political power through the external slave trading of members from other African communities. In short, most West African cultures featured in *The Black Unicorn* built their strength and power through hierarchical structures that undermined other societies with which they co-existed. The Amazon women of Dahomey, for instance, were part of a military force that helped maintain the Dahomey dynasty, often at the expense of Africans who were enslaved. See Paul E. Lovejoy and Jan S. Hogendorn, "Slave Marketing in West Africa," in *The Uncommon Market: Essays in the Economic History of the Atlantic Slave Trade,* ed. Henry A. Gemery and Jan S. Hogendorn (New York: Academic Press, 1979), 213–235; and see Walter Rodney, *West Africa and the Atlantic Slave-*

*Trade,* Historical Association of Tanzania, Paper No. 2 (Dar-es-Salaam: East African Publishing House, 1969). For an account of the Amazon warriors from Dahomey, see Stanley B. Alpern, *Amazons of Black Sparta: The Women Warriors of Dahomey* (London: Hurst, 1998).

90. In light of the fact that Lorde was looking for both strength and unity as she reached for Africa as a spiritual tap root, it would seem that the oppressive regimes that led to the power of certain African nations would prove just as problematic (at least to her political vision) as the oppressive societies in which racial and sexual minorities of the 1960s and 1970s found themselves.

91. Lorde, "Poetry Is Not a Luxury," 37–38.

92. Lorde, "Scratching the Surface," 49–50.

93. Lorde, "Eye for an Eye," 151.

94. See Lorde's "An Open Letter to Mary Daly" and other articles on racism in women's communities in Joan Gibbs and Sara Bennett, eds., *Top Ranking: A Collection of Articles on Racism and Classism in the Lesbian Community* (Brooklyn, NY: February 3rd Press, 1980).

95. According to Angela Bowen, Lorde did finally receive a reply from Daly, albeit after Lorde had sent her open letter to the editors of *Top Ranking.* Daly's reply is part of Lorde's papers at Spelman College. The papers, as I mentioned previously, have been closed while Lorde's biography was completed and sent to press during the writing of this book; Bowen, 172.

96. Mary Daly, *Gyn/Ecology: The Metaethics of Radical Feminism* (London: Women's Press, 1979), xiii.

97. Lorde, "An Open Letter to Mary Daly," 67.

98. Ibid., 67–68.

99. For more information on feminists' responses to Lorde's letter to Daly, see Bowen, 175–181. Also see Catherine Madsen, "The Thin Thread of Conversation: An Interview with Mary Daly," *Cross Currents* 50, no. 3 (Fall 2000): 332–348.

100. Lorde, "An Open Letter to Mary Daly," 70.

101. Lorde, "The Transformation of Silence into Action," 41.

102. Ibid., 43.

103. See Judy Grahn, *Another Mother Tongue: Gay Words, Gay Worlds* (Boston: Beacon Press, 1984), 124–125; see Bowen, 180.

104. Quoted in Bowen, 180.

105. Tate, 115.

106. Ibid.

107. Lorde, *Zami,* 255.

108. Lorde, "A Glossary of African Names Used in the Poems," 330.

109. Henry Louis Gates, Jr., *The Signifying Monkey: A Theory of African-American Literary Criticism* (New York: Oxford University Press), 37.

110. See Claudine Raynaud's and AnaLouise Keating's works cited in note 87. Also see Chinosole, "Audre Lorde and Matrilineal Diaspora: 'Moving History Beyond Nightmare into Structures for the Future," in *Wild Women in the Whirlwind: Afra-American Culture and the Contemporary Literary Renaissance,* ed. Joanne M. Braxton and Andrée Nicola McLaughlin (New Brunswick: Rutgers University Press, 1990), 379–394; and Jeanne Perreault, *Writing Selves: Contemporary Feminist Autography* (Minneapolis: University of Minneapolis Press, 1995), 18–30.

111. Gates, 6.

112. Lorde, *Zami,* 5.

113. Ibid., 247.

114. Ibid., 248.

115. Ibid., 250.

116. Ibid., 249.

117. Lorde, "Uses of the Erotic: The Erotic as Power," in *Sister Outsider: Essays & Speeches by Audre Lorde,* ed. Audre Lorde (Freedom, CA: Crossing Press, 1984), 53.

118. Ibid., 56.

119. Lorde, *Zami,* 252.

120. Ibid., 253.

121. Ibid., 250.

122. Ibid., 250.

123. Ibid., 3.

124. Ibid., 3.

125. Ibid., 104.

126. Ibid., 175.

127. Tate, 101.

128. Raynaud, 238.

129. Lorde, *Zami,* 14.

130. Ibid., 58.

131. Ibid., 9.

132. Tate, 104.

133. Here, Lorde seems to gesture toward the "two steps behind her man" 1960s concept of sexual relations in her revising of island women, as well. For a discussion of her thoughts on black women's relationship to black men see Lorde, "Scratching the Surface," 45.

134. Lorde, *Zami,* 9.

135. Ibid., 15.

136. For an understanding of Lorde's activities after writing *Zami,* see Audre Lorde, *A Burst of Light: Essays by Audre Lorde* (Ithaca: Firebrand Books, 1988).

In the last section, "A Burst of Light: Living with Cancer," Lorde documents her commitments to multiple communities around the world. The section includes journal entries from 1984 to 1986. Also for a discussion of Lorde's coalitions in Grenada, see "Grenada Revisited: An Interim Report," in *Sister Outsider: Essays & Speeches by Audre Lorde,* ed. Audre Lorde (Freedom, CA: Crossing Press, 1984), 176–189. For a discussion of Lorde's activities in St. Croix, see Rowell, 83–84. For more information on her activities in Germany, see Audre Lorde, "Showing Our True Colors," *Callaloo* 14.1 (1991): 67–71.

137. Lorde, "Age, Race, Class, and Sex," 114.

138. See *A Litany for Survival: The Life and Work of Audre Lorde,* dirs. Ada Gray Griffin and Michelle Parkerson, perf. Barbara Smith, Audre Lorde, Sonia Sanchez, Videocassette, Third World Newsreel, 1996.

139. Lorde, *Zami,* 3.

140. Rowell, 86.

## NOTES TO CHAPTER 4

All materials from the Piri Thomas Papers are used by permission of Piri Thomas and the Manuscripts, Archives and Rare Books Division, Schomburg Center for Research in Black Culture, New York Public Library, Astor, Lenox, and Tilden Foundations.

1. Brock, "Talk as a Form of Action," 203; Audre Lorde discusses her experiences with the Harlem Writers' Guild in Lorde, "An Interview: Audre Lorde and Adrienne Rich," 91.

2. Wolfgang Binder, "An Interview with Piri Thomas," *Minority Voices* 4, no. 1 (Spring 1980): 74. The title of this chapter, "How to Be a Negro without Really Trying," is the title of the eleventh chapter in Piri Thomas, *Down These Mean Streets* (New York: Knopf, 1967).

3. Piri Thomas Papers, Schomburg Center for Research in Black Culture, Sc MG 180, Box 1, Folder "Biographical Information." In February 2000, when I first accessed the Piri Thomas Papers, the letter accompanied other correspondence from 1963 with editors at Alfred A. Knopf. Piri Thomas was in Río Piedras, Puerto Rico, in 1963, and the typeface used for this letter is the same as that of the others. Incredibly, the Schomburg Center for Research in Black Culture had not yet organized his papers when I visited in February 2000, and I was told that I was the first to look at them. Since my visit in February 2000, the papers have been catalogued and filed. The letter now appears in a different location and is separate from the others. This new location was cited earlier.

4. Piri Thomas Papers, Schomburg Center for Research in Black Culture, Sc MG 180, Box 1, Folder "Biographical Information." The excerpt from the letter

reads: "Mr. Cameron smiled at me after listening to the anger of one child of a batch of six kids, born different in that all were fair and with good hair and he was not and without the hair that a white mans [sic] oil could tame."

5. See Malcolm X, *The Autobiography of Malcolm X* (New York: Grove Press, 1965); Claude Brown, *Manchild in the Promised Land* (New York: Macmillan, 1965); Eldridge Cleaver, *Soul on Ice* (New York: McGraw-Hill, 1968).

6. I have decided to use terms such as mixed-racial status, even though I resist validating racial categories, especially since I consider race to be a construct. However, "race," "racial," and "mixed-race" as terms prove helpful here as they inform discussions on the struggles of racial(ized) discourses within the United States and, in this case, the Puerto Rican island culture, as well.

7. My survey of the book reviews for *Down These Mean Streets* suggests that the autobiography was reviewed primarily by mainstream and African American journals, magazines, and newspapers when it was first published. Later reviews of Thomas's autobiographies, including *Down These Mean Streets,* were published by Latino presses in the 1970s. For example, *Revista/Review Interamericana* published a review of *Down These Mean Streets* as late as 1972 (1 [Winter 1972]: 156–157). Also, publications such as *Revista Chicano-Riquena* in the 1970s, reviewed Thomas's works regularly for a Latino audience.

8. Daniel Stern, "One Who Got Away," *New York Times Book Review* 72 (May 21, 1967): 1, 44.

9. William Hogan, Review of *Down These Mean Streets, San Francisco Chronicle* (December 31, 1967).

10. John O. Killens, "On *El Barrio* and Piri Thomas," *Negro Digest* 17 (January 1968): 95.

11. For a more in-depth analysis of the shift in the Civil Rights Movement to black consciousness movements, see William Van Deburg, *New Day in Babylon: The Black Power Movement and American Culture, 1965–1975* (Chicago: University of Chicago Press, 1992).

12. For more information on the Young Lords (street gang and then) Party, see Rosa Estades, *Patterns of Political Participation of Puerto Ricans in New York* (San Juan: University of Puerto Rico, 1978), 45–51. She discusses the origins of the Young Lords Party and its community activities.

13. Robert Allen, *Black Awakening in Capitalist America* (Garden City, NY: Doubleday, 1970), 126.

14. Personal interview with author on December 4, 1999. For more information on Thomas's activities after prison, see my interview with him in "A Conversation with Piri Thomas," *The Bilingual Review/La Revista Bilingüe* 25, no. 2 (May–August 2001): 179–184.

15. Lawrence R. Chenault, *The Puerto Rican Migrant in New York City* (New York: Columbia University Press, 1938), 57.

16. Cesar J. Ayala, "The Decline of the Plantation Economy and the Puerto Rican Migration in the 1950s," *Latino Studies Journal* 7, no. 1 (Winter 1996): 61–90.

17. Statistics cited in C. Wright Mills, Clarence Senior, and Rose Kohn Goldsen, *The Puerto Rican Journey: New York's Newest Migrants* (New York: Harper and Row, 1950), 45; and Ayala, 61–90.

18. The discussions of the racial categorizations within Puerto Rican island culture are beyond the scope of this chapter. For a more nuanced understanding, which no doubt will inform the readings of the racialized fictions of Thomas, see Juan Flores, *Divided Borders* (Houston: Arte Público Press, 1993), especially sections 1, 2, and 3. Also, earlier yet still useful analyses can be found in Thomas Matthew, "Color in Puerto Rico," in *Slavery and Race Relations in Latin America*, ed. Robert Toplin (Westport, CT: Greenwood Press, 1974), 299–323; see also Melvin Tumin, "Class and Skin Color," in *Social Class and Social Change in Puerto Rico,* ed. Melvin Tumin (Princeton: Princeton University Press, 1961), 227–246.

19. Mills et al., 133. Although beyond the scope of this chapter as well, it is interesting how the study of the Puerto Rican community has evolved in American academia, in part because of the culture wars of the late 1960s. For example, the idea that Puerto Ricans might have to assimilate into African America or white America, which was suggested in the 1940s and 1950s, had changed by the 1970s, especially as Puerto Ricans in the United States began to discuss the U.S. Puerto Rican community. Mills et al., in *The Puerto Rican Journey,* wrote: "When he comes to New York, the Puerto Rican migrant is either plunged into one of two worlds, or must exist between them. If he is white, he must adjust himself to the white culture of New York; if he is not white, he has no choice but to blend into the Negro community. The white migrant must take on the behavior and values of white America. The colored migrant finds that the world to which he must adapt himself is the Negroes' America" (133). By contrast, in 1974, Frank Bonilla published "Beyond Survival: Porque sequiremos siendo puertorriqueños," in *Puerto Rico and Puerto Ricans,* ed. Adalberto López and James Petras (Cambridge, MA: Schenkman, 1974), 438–451. In the essay, Bonilla identifies and locates Puerto Rican identity and community in the United States. In 1975, Miguel Algarín and Miguel Piñero published *Nuyorican Poetry* (New York: Morrow, 1975), which analyzed the particularized aesthetics of poetry by U.S. Puerto Ricans. Also see Eugene Mohr, *The Nuyorican Experience: Literature of the Puerto Rican Minority* (Westport, CT: Greenwood Press, 1982), which discusses U.S. Puerto Rican productions of culture.

20. See Elena Padilla, *Up from Puerto Rico* (New York: Columbia University Press, 1958), 45–81.

21. Ibid., 78–79.

22. Joseph Fitzpatrick, "Attitudes of Puerto Ricans toward Color," *American Catholic Sociological Review* 20, no. 3 (1959): 227.

23. Piri Thomas, "They Have Forced Us to Be Universal" (interview with Carmen Dolores Hernández), March 5–6, 1995, available at http://www.cheverote .com/reviews/hernandezinterview.html. For an edited paper version, see *Puerto Rican Voices in English: Interviews with Writers* (Westport, CT: Praeger, 1997), 171–185. A glossary of Spanish terms appears in the last endnote of the chapter.

24. Throughout this chapter I distinguish between Thomas (the autobiographer) and Piri (the narrator-protagonist).

25. Thomas, *Down These Mean Streets*, 10.

26. Ibid.

27. Ibid., 15–16.

28. Piri Thomas Papers, Schomburg Center for Research in Black Culture, Sc MG 180, Box 1, Folder "Biographical Information." See note 4 for more information.

29. See Robert Reid-Pharr, "Tearing the Goat's Flesh: Homosexuality, Abjection, and the Production of a Late-Twentieth-Century Black Masculinity," in *Novel Gazing: Queer Readings in Fiction*, ed. Eve Kosofsky Sedgwick (Durham, NC: Duke University Press, 1997), 353–376; also see Marta E. Sánchez, "La Malinche at the Intersection: Race and Gender in *Down These Mean Streets*," *PMLA* 113 (January 1998): 117–128.

30. See Brown, *Manchild in the Promised Land*. Brown's autobiographical style is different from Thomas's because Brown is critical of his childhood experiences and his role in these experiences even as he recounts them for a reading audience.

31. A corollary to Thomas's introduction of his childhood narrative is the additions of "Nightmare" and "Mascot" in Malcolm X, *Autobiography of Malcolm X*. Malcolm X's collaborator Alex Haley observed, "From this stream-of-consciousness reminiscing [about Malcolm X's mother], I finally got out of him the foundation for this book's beginning chapters, 'Nightmare' and 'Mascot.' After that night, he never again hesitated to tell me even the most intimate details of his personal life, over the next two years" (427). I made this connection after reading Paul John Eakin, "Malcolm X and the Limits of Autobiography," in *African-American Autobiography: A Collection of Critical Essays*, ed. William L. Andrews (Englewood Cliff, NJ: Prentice Hall, 1993), 151–161. These chapters by Malcolm X offer a suppressed child self that recalls Thomas's first "Harlem" section of *Down These Mean Streets*. Of course, the autobiographers' retelling

of their childhood experiences occasions very different responses to their respective lives. Malcolm X's childhood experiences are written as painful, Thomas's as ones that were enjoyable within the company of other Puerto Rican youth.

32. Thomas, *Down These Mean Streets,* 85–86.

33. Ibid., 84–85.

34. Ibid., 84.

35. Ibid., 86.

36. Ibid., 100. This dialogue has been abbreviated. For full text, please see cited page.

37. Ibid., 100.

38. Ibid., 104.

39. Ibid., 105.

40. Ibid., 106.

41. Ibid., 118.

42. Ibid., 118.

43. Ibid., 119; emphasis in original.

44. Ibid., 120.

45. Original passage appears in the Piri Thomas Papers, Schomburg Center for Research in Black Culture, Sc MG 180, Box 2, Manuscripts Folder 2 of 2; original manuscript of *Down These Mean Streets,* 121.

46. Thomas, *Down These Mean Streets,* 124.

47. Ibid., 121; emphasis in original.

48. Ibid., 143.

49. Ibid., 148.

50. Stepto discusses the narratives of immersion and ascent in *From Behind the Veil: A Study of Afro-American Narrative,* 2nd ed. (Urbana: University of Illinois Press, 1991). For a succinct definition of these narrative forms, see p. 167.

51. Ibid., 167.

52. Thomas, *Down These Mean Streets,* 151.

53. Mohr, 50.

54. Thomas, *Down These Mean Streets,* 173.

55. Ibid., 177.

56. Ibid., 178.

57. Ibid., 178.

58. Ibid., 177.

59. Ibid., 178.

60. Ibid., 187.

61. Ibid., 165.

62. Ibid., 188.

63. Original passage appears in the Piri Thomas Papers, Schomburg Center for Research in Black Culture, Sc MG 180, Box 2, Manuscripts Folder 1 of 3; original manuscript of *Down These Mean Streets,* 272.

64. Thomas, *Down These Mean Streets,* 189; emphasis in published version.

65. Ibid., 188.

66. Original passage appears in the Piri Thomas Papers, Schomburg Center for Research in Black Culture, Sc MG 180, Box 2, Manuscripts Folder 1 of 3; original manuscript of *Down These Mean Streets,* 271.

67. In the original version, the narrator-protagonist even refers to his words in this way: "and I hit her . . . I say . . . I hit her with my words, 'Baby, I just want you to know,' I repeated, 'that you got fucked by a nigger, by a black man!'"; original passage appears in Piri Thomas Papers, Schomburg Center for Research in Black Culture, Sc MG 180, Box 2, Manuscripts Folder 1 of 3; original manuscript of *Down These Mean Streets,* 274.

68. Thomas, *Down These Mean Streets,* 191.

69. Ibid., 191.

70. Brew's ABCs are learned from his Southern mother: "'Mom was asking us to cop a plea to the white man,' [Brew] continued. 'A—accept. B—behave. C—care.'"; Thomas, *Down These Mean Streets,* 134.

71. Thomas, *Down These Mean Streets,* 135.

72. Original passage appears in the Piri Thomas Papers, Schomburg Center for Research in Black Culture, Sc MG 180, Box 2, Manuscripts Folder 1 of 3; original manuscript of *Down These Mean Streets,* 281.

73. Thomas, *Down These Mean Streets,* 196.

74. Ibid., 238.

75. Piri Thomas, "The Inspiration to Write *Down These Mean Streets*" (interview), *In Motion* magazine (April 2, 2000), available at http://www.inmotion-magazine.com/ptinter1.html.

76. Thomas, *Down These Mean Streets,* 191.

77. Ibid., 193.

78. Ibid., 246.

79. Kenneth Mostern, *Autobiography and Black Identity Politics: Racialization in Twentieth-Century America* (Cambridge: Cambridge University Press, 1999), 177.

80. Mohr, 52.

81. Thomas, *Down These Mean Streets,* 299.

82. Piri Thomas, *Seven Long Times* (New York: Praeger, 1974).

83. See Andrew Greeley, "The Rediscovery of Cultural Pluralism," *Antioch Review* 31 (1971): 343–367; Michael Novak, *The Rise of Unmeltable Ethnics: Politics and Culture in the Seventies* (New York: Macmillan, 1973); Nathan Glazer and

Daniel Patrick Moynihan, eds., *Ethnicity: Theory and Experience* (Cambridge, MA: Harvard University Press, 1975); and Herbert Gans, "Symbolic Ethnicity: The Future of Ethnic Groups and Cultures in America," in *Theories of Ethnicity: A Classical Reader,* ed. Werner Sollors (New York: New York University Press, 1996), 425–459. In education, where leaders in multicultural discourses were often located, see Manuel Ramirez and Alfredo Casañeda, *Cultural Democracy, Bicognitive Development, and Education* (New York: Academic Press, 1974).

84. ASCD Multicultural Education Commission, "Encouraging Multicultural Education," in *Multicultural Education: Commitments, Issues, and Applications,* ed. Carl A. Grant (Washington, DC: Association for Supervision and Curriculum Development, 1977), 3.

85. The same tropes of the self-made, self-educated man are evidenced in other autobiographical works of black men such as Malcolm X, Brown, and Cleaver as well in the 1960s. For example, black male autobiographers, especially Cleaver and Malcolm X, tended to use their stay in prison as a time to educate themselves through reading and engaging world affairs. Prison and education become sites for contemplation and self-growth.

86. Thomas, *Seven Long Times,* 77.

87. Ibid., 195.

88. In *Seven Long Times,* Piri begins to assert seriously the distinctions between Puerto Ricans (of all racial backgrounds) and African Americans and even white Americans. In a candid example, he states, "I got to know guys like Bayamón, Pancho, Zorro, Gordo, who were Puerto Ricans *like me,* and L'il Henry and Karl, who were black, and Johnny Lee and Checkers, who were white" (Thomas, *Seven Long Times,* 70; emphasis mine).

89. Ibid., 145.

90. Ibid., 144.

91. Ibid., 196.

92. Reid-Pharr, 354.

93. Ibid., 360.

94. Thomas, *Seven Long Times,* 140, 67.

95. Thomas, *Down These Mean Streets,* 263.

96. Thomas, *Seven Long Times,* 155. Surprisingly, in this passage, the Spanish words are not italicized, although most Spanish words are italicized in *Down These Mean Streets* and *Seven Long Times.* For the sake of consistency, I have italicized Spanish words in this passage. See *Seven Long Times* for the nonitalicized words in the passage.

97. As an adolescent, Piri participates in same-sex activities in the gay men's apartment to show that he has "heart" when with his Puerto Rican gang. He does not want to participate, as Thomas suggests, but participating falls under

his ethos of "standing together with your boys." His response to the scene reads: "I felt both good and bad. I felt strong and drained. I hadn't liked the scene, but if a guy gotta live, he gotta do it from the bottom of his heart; he has to want it, to feel it. It's no easy shake to hold off the pressure with one hand while you hold up your sagging pants with the other. But the game is made up as you go along, and you got to pick up what you have or dive out the top-floor window" (Thomas, *Down These Mean Streets*, 58, 61–62).

98. Ibid., 323.

99. Ibid., 322.

100. Ibid., 330.

101. Ibid., 331.

102. Binder, 72.

103. A notable precursor to Thomas's autobiography by a black Latino is Jesús Colón, *A Puerto Rican in New York and Other Sketches* (New York: International Publishers, 1961). Colón, a first-generation immigrant, identifies his racial identity as peripheral to his larger political consciousness, however.

104. Spanish terms include:

*adios*—good-bye

*aguacates*—avocados

*alma*—soul

*(el) barrio*—(the) neighborhood

*bendito*—blessed

*blancos*—whites

*chevere*—wonderful

*chica*—girl

*coquís*—cricket

*corazón*—heart

*finca*—farm

*frutas*—fruits

*grande*—big

*hombre*—man

*latinidad*—[L]atino identity

*loco*—crazy

*(mi) madre*—(my) mother

*moyetos*—blacks

*mucho*—a lot; much

*nada*—nothing

*negrito*—black man

*(un) numero*—a number

*pajaritos*—little birds

*(la) pobreza*—(the) poverty

*puertorriquenidad*—Puerto Ricanness

*(no) quiero morir*—I don't want to die

*te vamos a perder*—[W]e are going to lose you

## NOTES TO CHAPTER 5

1. Translations for Spanish lyrics in songs are mine unless otherwise indicated; *Proyecto Uno, "El tiburón," In Da House,* J & N Records, CD, H2 7243 B 28857 2 6, 1994.

2. I have decided to use the Spanish language format for song titles. Spanish words within the English prose will be italicized. However, lyrics in block quotations (with accompanying translations) will not be italicized.

3. George Lipsitz, *Dangerous Crossroads: Popular Music, Postmodernism, and the Poetics of Place* (London: Verso, 1994), 8.

4. See Hazel Carby, "'It Jus Be's Dat Way Sometime': The Sexual Politics of Women's Blues," in *Unequal Sisters: A Multicultural Reader in U.S. Women's History,* ed. Ellen Carol DuBois and Vicki L. Ruiz (New York: Routledge, 1990), 238–249; Farah Jasmine Griffin, *"Who Set You Flowin'?" The African-American Migration Narrative* (New York: Oxford University Press, 1995); and Frances Aparicio, *Listening to Salsa: Gender, Latin Popular Music, and Puerto Rican Cultures* (Hanover, NH: Wesleyan University Press, 1998).

5. See Press Release: *Proyecto Uno,* J & N Records, circa 1994, 1; Press Release: *Proyecto Uno,* H.O.L.A. Recordings, 1996, 1–2. Author's personal file. Both press releases provide the following information: In 1992, *Proyecto Uno* won the *"Premio estrella del merengue"* in New York for "Merenrap." Other awards include the "Premio Too Much" (1992) for the single *"Brinca"* and the *"Premio Ronda"* (1993) in Venezuela for single of the year for *"Brinca."* The group's 1993 album *In Da House* went platinum in Latin America. Most of H.O.L.A.'s artists were R&B or hip-hop singers of Spanish Caribbean descent. The record company is now defunct, but it did have a huge impact on the emergence of Latino artists in the 1990s. Its artists included Veronica, Reign, *Proyecto Uno,* and Voices of Theory. I want to thank Al McLean, director of the Artist and Repertoire Department at H.O.L.A. Recordings, for meeting with me regarding my research for this chapter.

6. Scholars such as Juan Flores and Dick Hebdige discuss the importance of understanding the role of Caribbean immigrants in hip-hop culture, a role often negated by the commercialization of rap music as an African American musical genre. Their studies are noticeable exceptions to the lack of scholarship on the subject. See Juan Flores, "Puerto Rican and Proud, Boyee! Rap, Roots and Am-

nesia," in *Microphone Fiends,* ed. Andrew Ross and Tricia Rose (New York: Rout-
ledge, 1994), 89–97; and Juan Flores, "'It's a Street Thing!': An Interview with
Charlie Chase," *Callaloo* 15.4 (1992): 999–1021. Also see Dick Hebdige, *Cut 'n'
Mix* (London: Comedia, 1987). Juan Flores is one of the best documenters of the
Puerto Rican presence in the emergence of hip hop. In "Puerto Rican and Proud,
Boyee! Rap, Roots and Amnesia," he explores the development of black and
Latino interchange in the Bronx during the 1970s. Dick Hebdige's *Cut 'n' Mix* is
also helpful in mapping the participation of West Indians in American hip hop.
In *Cut 'n' Mix,* see the chapter "Rap and Hip Hop: The New York Connection,"
pp. 136–148 in particular.

7. For an understanding of the debates over rap music and hip-hop culture,
see George Lipsitz, "The Hip Hop Hearings: Censorship, Social Memory, and In-
tergenerational Tensions among African Americans," in *Generations of Youth:
Youth Cultures and History in Twentieth-Century America,* ed. Joe Austin and
Michael Nevin Willard (New York: New York University Press, 1998), 395–411.

8. A research grant from the Yale Center of International Area Studies
afforded me the opportunity of interviewing Dominican teenagers in New York
and Connecticut. Part of my interview project was completed in 1997. I did a second set of interviews in the summer of 2000. Interviews included second generationers affiliated with several social organizations, including Dominicans
2000 and *La Alianza Dominicana.* The interviews were informal and were done
to provide background contextualization for this chapter. Most of my respon-
dents reported that their parents were not fond of hip-hop music or their children's "hip-hop" cultural practices. One respondent, "Juan," a thirteen-year-
old, for example, responded that part of the reason for his mother's reaction to
hip hop was that "[his] mother just didn't understand the words," and, by implication, his mother didn't understand why something so "different" from Dominican culture was his music of choice. "Margo," an eighteen-year-old from
Washington Heights, remarked that her parents referred to hip hop in the following manner: "That's garbage. That's for drug dealers. That's for black people"; personal interviews, 2000. These comments by "Juan" and "Margo" reflect the tenor of the remarks made by other teenagers interviewed. Most asserted
that their parents felt that their hip-hop practices were antithetical to their participation in Dominican culture. Most also noted that their parents perceived hip
hop as part of African American culture only. The names of interviewees quoted
have been changed.

9. Portes and Zhou, 81.

10. Waters, 296.

11. Both Tricia Rose and Robin Kelley offer excellent analyses of hip-hop culture in the United States. See Tricia Rose, *Black Noise: Rap Music and Black Cul-*

*ture in Contemporary America* (Hanover, NH: Wesleyan University Press); also see Kelley, 183–227.

12. Portes and Zhou, 81, 84.

13. Paul Gilroy, "Cultural Studies and Ethnic Absolutism," in *Cultural Studies,* ed. Lawrence Grossberg, Cary Nelson, and Paula Treichler (New York: Routledge), 193; see also Paul Gilroy, *There Ain't No Black in the Union Jack: The Cultural Politics of Race and Nation* (Chicago: University of Chicago Press, 1991). Interestingly, Gilroy seems to depart from his understanding of "diasporic intimacy" in a more recent book, *Against Race: Imagining Political Culture Beyond the Color Line* (Cambridge, MA: Harvard University Press, 2000). I find his chapter on hip hop a particular departure, especially considering his previous work on the subject. For example, in the chapter, "'After the Love Has Gone': Biopolitics and the Decay of the Black Public Sphere," he observes, "Though it has won wide acceptance, the idea that vernacular forms embody a special 'ethnic' essence has been most regularly articulated by critics who are comfortable with the absolutist definitions of culture I have criticized" (Gilroy, *Against Race,* 179). See pp. 177–206 in *Against Race* for a detailed discussion.

14. Paul Gilroy, *The Black Atlantic: Modernity and Double Consciousness* (Cambridge, MA: Harvard University Press, 1993), 102.

15. "*La voz dominicana*" can be translated as "the Dominican voice."

16. Gilroy, *The Black Atlantic: Modernity and Double Consciousness,* 101.

17. Christopher Smalls, *Music of the Common Tongue: Survival and Celebration in Afro-American Music* (London: John Calder, 1987), 50. I find Smalls's analysis helpful because of the term "musicking," which I use throughout the chapter. It is useful to my discussion because it refers to the *making* of music. When defining the term, Smalls writes, "I define the word to include not only performing and composing . . . but also listening and even dancing to music; all those involved in any way in a musical performance can be thought of as musicking."

18. Perla Perez, liner notes, Angel Viloria, *Merengues Vol. 2,* Belton Recording Studios, CD, HGCD1207, converted 1991; translation and emphasis mine: "Probablemente unto [*sic*] de los grandes acontecimientos en la historia de la música grabada en discos fue el transplante del Merengue, de origen espannol [*sic*], traido a las Colonias del Nuevo Mundo."

19. Luis Alberti, *De música y orquestas bailables dominicanas, 1910–1959* (Santo Domingo, DR: Editora Taller, 1975), 71. Original excerpt reads: "tenga nada que ver con los ritmos negroides o africanistas"; translation mine.

20. Alberti, 71. Original excerpt reads: "una mezcla de lo español y nuestras tonadas campesinas de tierra adentro"; translation mine.

21. The term "Hispanization" throughout this chapter connotes "of Spanish

origin, that is, from the Iberian peninsula." I use "Hispanic," on the other hand, interchangeably with "Latino."

22. Paul Austerlitz, *Merengue: Dominican Music and Dominican Identity* (Philadelphia: Temple University Press, 1997), 5.

23. Deborah Pacini Hernández, *Bachata: A Social History of a Dominican Popular Music* (Philadelphia: Temple University Press, 1995), 42.

24. Austerlitz, 60.

25. Etienne Balibar, "The Nation Form: History and Ideology," in *Race, Nation, Class: Ambiguous Identities,* ed. Etienne Balibar and Immanuel Wallerstein (London: Verso, 1991), 96. Balibar observes, "Fictive ethnicity is not purely and simply identical with the *ideal nation* which is the object of patriotism, but it is indispensable to it, for, without it, the nation would appear precisely only as an idea or an arbitrary abstraction; patriotism's appeal would be addressed to no one."

26. Merengue was a means by which Trujillo challenged the resistance of the cultural elite in particular. As Hernández writes in *Bachata,* "He [Trujillo] transformed merengue's social position by literally forcing it upon the elite. . . . As Miniño observed, 'The merengue was one of the means that the tyrant used to break the resistance of the social elite, who had previously rejected him, this being a subtle way of imposing one class upon another.'" (Hernández, 40).

27. Quoted in Austerlitz, 64. Austerlitz cites it from Martha Ellen Davis, "Afro-Dominican Religious Brotherhoods," Ph.D. diss., University of Illinois, 1976, 22.

28. Grasmuck and Pessar, 31–33.

29. Ibid., 33.

30. The revision of the Immigration Act in 1965 overturned discriminatory policies against postcolonial nations that hindered immigration from Caribbean countries in particular. The Immigration Act of 1965 (revised in 1986) put in place measures for family reunification, replacing restrictions on Caribbean immigration by setting quotas that were evenly distributed among foreign countries. For more information, see Grasmuck and Pessar, 10–11; and see Kasinitz, 26–27.

31. Grasmuck and Pessar, 33–43; Silvio Torres-Saillant and Ramona Hernández, *The Dominican Americans* (Westport, CT: Greenwood Press, 1998), 34.

32. Torres-Saillant and Hernández point out that as early as 1844, "Secretary of State John C. Calhoun suggested to the Spanish minister in Washington that the United States, France, and Spain should proceed to 'recognize the new Republic, as a means of preventing the further spread of Negro influence in the West Indies'" (Torres-Saillant and Hernández, 14). See pp. 9–27 for a succinct discussion of U.S.-Dominican relations.

33. Ibid., 63.

34. See Grasmuck and Pessar; also see Eugene Georges, *The Making of a Transnational Community: Migration, Development, and Cultural Change in the Dominican Republic* (New York: Columbia University Press, 1990).

35. Rose, 22.

36. Gilroy, "Cultural Studies and Ethnic Absolutism," 193.

37. For more information on West Indian participation in hip-hop culture, see Lipsitz, *Dangerous Crossroads,* 25–48; Hebdige, *Cut 'n' Mix,* 136–148; and William Eric Perkins, "The Rap Attack: An Introduction," in *Droppin' Science: Critical Essays on Rap Music and Hip Hop Culture,* ed. William Eric Perkins (Philadelphia: Temple University Press, 1996), 1–45.

38. Flores, "Puerto Rican and Proud, Boyee!" 93.

39. Mandalite del Barco, "Rap's Latino Sabor," in *Droppin' Science: Critical Essays on Rap Music and Hip Hop Culture,* ed. William Eric Perkins (Philadelphia: Temple University Press, 1996), 87.

40. See Benedict Anderson, *Imagined Communities: Reflections on the Origin and Spread of Nationalism* (London: Verso, rpt. 1991), 6. Anderson observes, "Communities are to be distinguished not by their falsity/genuineness, but by the style in which they are imagined."

41. Gustavo Pérez Firmat, *Life on the Hyphen: The Cuban-American Way* (Austin: University of Texas Press, 1994), 7.

42. Quoted in Luis Guarnizo, "Los Dominicanyorks: The Making of a Binational Society," *Annals of the American Academy of Political and Social Sciences* 533 (May 1994): 80.

43. Patricia Pessar, *Visa for a Dream: Dominicans in the United States* (Boston: Allyn and Bacon, 1995), 29.

44. Torres-Saillant, 142.

45. Jorge Duany, "Reconstructing Racial Identity: Ethnicity, Color, and Class among Dominicans in the United States and Puerto Rico," *Latin American Perspectives* (Issue 100) 25, no. 3 (May 1998): 166.

46. Firmat, 7.

47. Ibid.

48. "Press Release: *Proyecto Uno,*" H.O.L.A. Recordings, 1996, 2.

49. *Sandy y Papo* is a group from the Dominican Republic (Sandy died in a car accident in 1999). The group was produced by Pavel de Jesús, Nelson Zapata's friend who helped him start *Proyecto Uno. Los Ilegales,* in some ways, is a more manufactured group. The creator, Vladimir Dotel, had auditions to find other members of the group. Again, he was assisted by Pavel de Jesús.

50. Alisa Valdés, "How *Proyecto Uno* Is Working to Be the Next Big Thing," *Boston Globe* (February 25, 1996): B27.

51. Juan Flores, "'Qué assimilated, brother, yo so asimilao': The Structuring of Puerto Rican Identity," in *Divided Borders: Essays on Puerto Rican Identity,* ed. Juan Flores (Houston: Arte Público Press, 1993), 182–195.

52. Ibid., 184.

53. Ibid., 186. Flores uses his theoretical framework for exploring the identities of Puerto Ricans in New York. However, his framework can be extended to consider the assimilation processes of other Caribbean immigrants in the United States. Thus, I adopt and adapt his framework in my discussion of Dominican second-generation youth.

54. Ibid., 190.

55. See Ramiro Burr, "*Proyecto Uno* Embraces Adventure," *Houston Chronicle* (May 7, 1997): 18; Eamon Dolan, "New Era," *Wired* 5.04 (April 1997), available at http://www.wired.com/wired/archive/5.04/music_reviews.html?pg=4; and Valdés, B27.

56. Quoted in Mario Castro, "Los tiburones del merengue hip hop," *Variedades,* Edición 291 (30 Octubre 1999): 2, available at http://www.ipcdigital .com/espanol/variedade/291/index.shtml; translation mine. (In expanding this project from a dissertation to a book, I learned that this link no longer houses the referenced article.)

57. Valdés, B27.

58. When I identify the name of the singer or rapper from the group, I will refer to his "character" when analyzing the songs. However, I will refer to the anonymous singer in all other cases.

59. *Proyecto Uno,* "Another Night," *In Da House,* J & N Records, CD, H2 7243 8 28857 2 6, 1994.

60. Aparicio, 130.

61. Carolyn Cooper offers a fine example of the relationships between women and sites in Caribbean songs. See her discussion of Babylon in Bob Marley's songs especially; Carolyn Cooper, *Noises in the Blood: Orality, Gender, and the "Vulgar" Body of Jamaican Popular Culture* (Durham, NC: Duke University Press, 1995), 117–135.

62. See discussion in Hernández, *Bachata,* 153–184.

63. See Grasmuck and Pessar, 133–161, 186–195.

64. Quoted in Jennifer Parris, "Original Ones: *Proyecto 1,*" *Urban Latino* (Issue 16): 5, available at http://www.urbanlatino.com/magazine/features/originalones/originalones.html. (In expanding this project from a dissertation to a book, I learned that this link no longer houses the referenced article.)

65. Gilroy, "Cultural Studies and Ethnic Absolutism," 193.

66. *Ando* really translates more as "in the process of."

67. *Proyecto Uno, "No hay nada," In Da House,* J & N Records, CD, H2 7243 8 28857 2 6, 1994.

68. *Interesada* often suggests the existence of an ulterior motive.

69. Quoted in Austerlitz, 130.

70. Portes and Zhou, 86.

71. M. Patricia Fernández Kelly and Richard Schauffler, "Divided Fates: Immigrant Children and the New Assimilation," in *The New Second Generation,* ed. Alejandro Portes (New York: Russell Sage Foundation, 1996), 52–53.

72. Gilroy, "Cultural Studies and Ethnic Absolutism," 193.

73. *Proyecto Uno, "Latinos," New Era,* H.O.L.A. Recordings, CD, 119-341-006-2, 1996; *"Empujando al cielo," 4,* H.O.L.A. Recordings, LLC, CD, 153373-2, 1999.

74. *Proyecto Uno,* liner notes, *New Era,* H.O.L.A. Recordings, CD, 119-341-006-2, 1996.

75. Lipsitz, *Dangerous Crossroads,* 71.

76. Flores, "'Qué assimilated, brother, yo soy asimilao,'" 187.

77. Valdés, B27.

78. Austerlitz, 93.

79. *Proyecto Uno, "Merengue con letra"* [Merengue with Lyrics], *Proyecto 1: Mega Mix Hits,* J & N Records, CDZ-82581, 1997.

80. See "The Riddle of the Zoot: Malcolm Little and Black Cultural Politics during World War II" in Kelley, *Race Rebels,* 161–181.

81. Flores, "'Qué assimilated, brother, yo soy asimilao,'" 189.

82. Quoted in Castro, 2; translation mine.

83. Ibid., translation mine.

84. *Proyecto Uno, "¿Qué sabes tú?"* [What do you know?] *New Era,* H.O.L.A. Recordings, CD, 119-341-006-2, 1996.

85. Philip Brasor, *"Proyecto Uno*—Viva Zapata!" *Japan Times* (November 26, 1999), available on nexis/lexis, unpaginated.

86. *Proyecto Uno, "El grillero," New Era,* H.O.L.A. Recordings, CD, 119-341-006-2, 1996. See *"El tiburón."*

87. Lipsitz, *Dangerous Crossroads,* 37.

88. Gilroy, "Cultural Studies and Ethnic Absolutism," 193.

89. Flores, "'Qué assimilated, brother, yo soy asimilao,'" 191.

90. *Proyecto Uno, "Ven y te enseñaré," In Da House,* J & N Records, CD, H2 7243 B 28857 2 6, 1994.

91. See Linda Basch et al., *Nations Unbound: Transnational Projects, Postcolonial Predicaments, and Deterritorialized Nation-States* (Langhorne, PA: Gordon and Breach Science Publishers, 1994), 7–8, for definitions of transnationalism.

92. Quoted in Peggy Levitt, "Variations in Transnational Belonging: Lessons from Brazil and the Dominican Republic," in *Dual Nationality, Social Rights and Federal Citizenship in the U.S. and Europe,* ed. Randall Hansen and Patrick Weil (New York: Berghahn Books, 2002), 269.

93. Press Release: *Proyecto Uno,* H.O.L.A. Recordings, 1996.

94. *Proyecto Uno,* liner notes, *New Era,* H.O.L.A. Recordings, CD, 119-341-006-2, 1996.

95. See Guarnizo, 80–82.

## NOTES TO THE POSTSCRIPT

1. Stuart Hall, "Cultural Identity and Diaspora," in *Identity, Community, Culture, Difference,* ed. Jonathan Rutherford (London: Lawrence and Wishart, 1990), 222.

2. Daryl Cumber Dance, "An Interview with Paule Marshall," *Southern Review* 28, no. 1 (January 1992): 7.

3. Lisa D. McGill, "A Conversation with Piri Thomas," *The Bilingual Review/La Revista Bilingüe* 25, no. 2 (May–August 2001): 179–184.

# SELECTED BIBLIOGRAPHY

## BOOKS, ARTICLES, AND ESSAYS

Ackah, William B. *Pan-Africanism: Exploring the Contractions.* Brookfield, VT: Ashgate, 1999.

Alberti, Luis. *De música y orquestas bailables dominicanas, 1910–1959.* Santo Domingo, DR: Editora Taller, 1975.

Alexander, Elizabeth. "'Coming Out Blackened and Whole': Fragmentation and Reintegration in Audre Lorde's *Zami* and *The Cancer Journals.*" *American Literary History* 6, no. 4 (Winter 1994): 695–715.

Algarín, Miguel, and Miguel Piñero. *Nuyorican Poetry.* New York: Morrow, 1975.

Allen, Robert. *Black Awakening in Capitalist America.* Garden City, NY: Doubleday, 1970.

Alpern, Stanley B. *Amazons of Black Sparta: The Women Warriors of Dahomey.* London: Hurst, 1998.

Anderson, Benedict. *Imagined Communities: Reflections on the Origin and Spread of Nationalism.* 2nd ed. London: Verso, 1991.

Andrews, William, ed. *African-American Autobiography: A Collection of Critical Essays.* Englewood Cliff, NJ: Prentice Hall, 1993.

Aparicio, Frances. *Listening to Salsa: Gender, Latin Popular Music, and Puerto Rican Cultures.* Hanover, NH: Wesleyan University Press, 1998.

Appadurai, Arjun. *Modernity at Large: Cultural Dimensions of Globalization.* Minneapolis: University of Minnesota Press, 1996.

ASCD Multicultural Education Commission. "Encouraging Multicultural Education." *Multicultural Education: Commitments, Issues, and Applications.* Ed. Carl A. Grant. Washington, DC: Association for Supervision and Curriculum Development, 1977.

Austerlitz, Paul. *Merengue: Dominican Music and Dominican Identity.* Philadelphia: Temple University Press, 1997.

Ayala, César J. "The Decline of the Plantation Economy and the Puerto Rican Migration in the 1950s." *Latino Studies Journal* 7, no. 1 (Winter 1996): 61–90.

Balibar, Etienne, and Immanuel Wallerstein. *Race, Nation, Class: Ambiguous Identities.* London: Verso, 1991.

Baraka, Amiri. *The Autobiography of LeRoi Jones.* New York: Freundlich, 1984.

———. *Black Art.* New York: Quill, 1967.

———. *Black Music.* New York: Quill, 1967.

Barbour, Floyd. *The Black Seventies.* Boston: Porter Sargent, 1970.

Barbour, Floyd, ed. *The Black Power Revolt: A Collection of Essays*. Boston: Porter Sargent, 1968.

Barlow, William. *From Swing to Soul. An Illustrated History of African-American Popular Music from 1930–1960*. Washington, DC: Elliot and Clark, 1994.

Basch, Linda. "The Politics of Caribbeanization: Vincentians and Grenadians in New York." *Caribbean Life in New York City: Sociocultural Dimensions*. Ed. C. R. Sutton and E. M. Chaney. New York: Center for Migration Studies, 1992. 147–166.

Basch, Linda, Cristina Blanc Szanton, and Nina Glick Schiller. *Nations Unbound: Transnational Projects, Post-Colonial Predicaments, and De-Territorialized Nation-States*. Langhorne, PA: Gordon and Breach Science Publishers, 1994.

Béhague, Gerard H., ed. *Music and Black Ethnicity: The Caribbean and South America*. New Brunswick, NJ: Transaction, 1992.

Belafonte, Harry. Black History Month Keynote Address, Quinnipiac University, Hamden, CT. 21 February 2000.

Bell, Roseann, Bettye Parker, and Beverly Guy-Sheftall, eds. *Sturdy Black Bridges*. New York: Doubleday, 1979.

Bhabha, Homi, ed. *Nation and Narration*. London: Routledge, 1990.

Binder, Wolfgang. "An Interview with Piri Thomas." *Minority Voices* 4, no. 1 (Spring 1980): 63–78.

Black, Gregory. *The Catholic Crusade against the Movies, 1940–1975*. Cambridge: Cambridge University Press, 1997.

Blocton, Lula Mae. *Heresies: Third World Women*. New York: Heresies Collective, 1979.

Boelhower, William. *Through a Glass Darkly: Ethnic Semiosis in American Literature*. New York: Oxford University Press, 1987.

Bogle, Donald. *Dorothy Dandridge: A Biography*. New York: Amistad, 1997.

———. *Toms, Coons, Mulattoes, Mammies and Bucks*. New York: Bantam, 1974.

Bourne, Randolph S. "Trans-national America." *Atlantic Monthly* 118 (July 1916): 86–97.

Bowen, Angela. "Who Said It Was Simple: Audre Lorde's Complex Connections to Three U.S. Liberation Movements, 1952–1992." Ph.D. diss., Clark University, 1998.

Bracks, Lean'tin L. *Writings on Black Women of the Diaspora*. New York: Garland, 1998.

Brady, Tom P. *Black Monday*. Winona, MI: Association of Citizens' Councils, 1955.

Branch, Taylor. *Parting the Waters: America in the King Years, 1954–63*. New York: Simon and Schuster, 1988.

Brasor, Philip. "*Proyecto Uno*—Viva Zapata!" *Japan Times*, November 26, 1999.

Breitman, George, ed. *Malcolm X Speaks: Selected Speeches and Statements*. New York: Pathfinder, 1989.

——. *By Any Means Necessary: Speeches, Interviews, and a Letter by Malcolm X*. New York: Pathfinder Press, 1970.

Brock, Sabine. "Transcending the 'Loophole of Retreat': Paule Marshall's Placing of Female Generations." *Callaloo* 10, no. 1 (Winter 1987): 79–90.

——. "'Talk as a Form of Action': An Interview with Paule Marshall." *History and Tradition in Afro-American Culture*, Ed. Günter H. Lenz. New York: Campus Verlag, 1984. 194–206.

Brodzki, Bella, and Celeste Schenk, eds. *Life/Lines: Theorizing Women's Autobiography*. Ithaca: Cornell University Press, 1988.

Brown, Claude. *Manchild in the Promised Land*. New York: Macmillan, 1965.

Brownley, Martine Watson. *Deferrals of Domain: Contemporary Women Novelists and the State*. New York: St. Martin's Press, 2000.

Burr, Ramiro. "*Proyecto Uno* Embraces Adventure." *Houston Chronicle* (May 7, 1997): 18.

Burns, Stewart. *Social Movements of the 1960s*. Boston: Twayne, 1990.

Butterfield, Stephen. *Black Autobiography in America*. Amherst: University of Massachusetts Press, 1974.

Carby, Hazel. *Race Men*. Cambridge, MA: Harvard University Press, 1998.

——. "'It Jus Be's Dat Way Sometime': The Sexual Politics of Women's Blues." *Unequal Sisters: A Multicultural Reader in US Women's History*. Ed. Ellen Carol DuBois and Vicki L. Ruiz. New York: Routledge, 1990. 238–249.

——. *Reconstructing Womanhood: The Emergence of the Afro-American Woman Novelist*. New York: Oxford University Press, 1987.

Carew, Jan. *Ghosts in Our Blood with Malcolm X in Africa, England, and the Caribbean*. Chicago: Lawrence Hill Books, 1994.

Carmichael, Stokely. *Stokely Speaks: Back to Pan-Africanism*. New York: Random House, 1971.

Carmichael, Stokely, and C. Hamilton. *Black Power: The Politics of Liberation in America*. New York: Random House, 1967.

Castro, Mario. "Los tiburones del merengue hip hop." *Variedades*, Edición 291 (30 Octubre 1999): 2.

Chafe, William H. *The Unfinished Journey: America since World War II*. 2nd ed. New York: Oxford University Press, 1991.

Chambers, Iain. *Migrancy, Culture, Identity*. New York: Routledge, 1994.

Chávez-Silverman, Susana, and Frances R. Aparicio. *Tropicalizations: Transcultural Representations of Latinidad*. Hanover, NH: University Press of New England, 1997.

Chenault, Lawrence. *The Puerto Rican Migrant in New York City.* New York: Columbia University Press, 1938.

Childress, Alice. "The Negro Woman in American Literature." *Freedomways* 6, no. 1 (Winter 1966): 14–19.

Chilton, John. *Let the Good Times Roll: The Story of Louis Jordan and His Music.* London: Quartet Books, 1992.

Chinosole. "Audre Lorde and the Matrilineal Diaspora: Moving History beyond Nightmare into Structures for the Future." *Wild Women in the Whirlwind.* Ed. Joanne Braxton and Andrée McLaughlins. New Brunswick, NJ: Rutgers University Press, 1990. 379–394.

———. "Black Autobiographical Writing: A Comparative Approach." Ph.D. diss., University of Oregon, 1986.

Christian, Barbara. *Black Feminist Criticism: Perspectives on Black Women Writers.* New York: Pergamon Press, 1985.

Cleaver, Eldridge. *Soul on Ice.* New York: McGraw-Hill, 1968.

Cliff, Michelle. *Abeng.* Trumansburg, NY: Crossing Press, 1984.

Cohan, Steven. *Masked Men: Masculinity and the Movies in the Fifties.* Bloomington: Indiana University Press, 1997.

Coleman, Emily. "Organization Man Named Belafonte." *New York Times Magazine* (December 13, 1959): 35, 37–38, 40, 42.

Colón, Jesús. *A Puerto Rican in New York and Other Sketches.* New York: International Publishers, 1961.

Condé, Maryse. "Return of a Native Daughter: An Interview with Paule Marshall and Maryse Condé." Trans. John Williams. *SAGE* 3, no. 2 (Fall 1986): 52–53.

Cooper, Carolyn. *Noises in the Blood: Orality, Gender, and the "Vulgar" Body of Jamaican Popular Culture.* Durham, NC: Duke University Press, 1995.

Coser, Stelamaris. *Bridging the Americas: The Literature of Paule Marshall, Toni Morrison, and Gayle Jones.* Philadelphia: Temple University Press, 1995.

Cripps, Thomas. *Black Film as Genre.* Bloomington: Indiana University Press, 1978.

———. *Making Movies Black: The Hollywood Message Movie from World War II to the Civil Rights Era.* New York: Oxford University Press, 1993.

Cross, Brian. *It's Not about a Salary: Rap, Race, and Resistance in Los Angeles.* New York: Verso, 1993.

Cruse, Harold. *The Crisis of the Negro Intellectual.* New York: Morrow, 1967.

Cubberley, Ellwood P. *Changing Conceptions of Education.* Boston: Houghton Mifflin, 1909.

D., Chuck, and Yusaf Jah. *Fight the Power: Rap, Race, and Reality.* New York: Delacorte Press, 1997.

Daly, Mary. *Gyn/Ecology: The Metaethics of Radical Feminism*. Boston: Beacon Press, 1978.

———. *Beyond the Father: Toward a Philosophy of Women's Liberation*. Boston: Beacon Press, 1973.

Dance, Daryl Cumber. "An Interview with Paule Marshall." *Southern Review* 28, no. 1 (January 1992): 1–20.

Davenport, Doris. "Four Contemporary Black Women Poets: Lucille Clifton, June Jordan, Audre Lorde, & Sherley Anne Williams." Ph.D. diss., University of Southern California, 1985.

Davies, Carole Boyce. *Black Women, Writing and Identity: Migrations of the Subject*. London: Routledge, 1994.

Davis, Martha Ellen. "Voces del purgatorio: estudio de la salve dominicana." Santo Domingo, DR: Museo del Hombre Dominicana, 1981.

———. "Afro-Dominican Religious Brotherhoods." Ph.D. diss., University of Illinois, 1976.

Dearborn, Mary, ed. *Pocahontas's Daughters: Gender and Ethnicity in American Culture*. New York: Oxford University Press, 1986.

Deckard, Barbara Sinclair. *The Women's Movement: Political, Socioeconomic, and Psychological Issues*. 3rd ed. New York: Harper and Row, 1983.

DeLamotte, Eugenia C. *Places of Silence, Journeys of Freedom: The Fiction of Paule Marshall*. Philadelphia: University of Pennsylvania Press, 1998.

Del Barco, Mandalite. "Rap's Latino Sabor." *Droppin' Science: Critical Essays on Rap Music and Hip Hop Culture*. Ed. William Eric Perkins. Philadelphia: Temple University Press, 1996. 62–84.

Denning, Michael. *The Cultural Front: The Laboring of American Culture in the Twentieth Century*. London: Verso, 1996.

Denniston, Dorothy Hamer. *The Fiction of Paule Marshall: Reconstructions of History, Culture, and Gender*. Knoxville: University of Tennessee Press, 1995.

DeVeaux, Alexis. "Paule Marshall: In Celebration of Our Triumph." *Essence* (May 1979): 70–71, 96, 123–124, 126, 128, 131, 133, 135.

Dhairyam, Sagri. "'Artifacts for Survival': Remapping the Contours of Poetry with Audre Lorde." *Feminist Studies* 18, no. 2 (Summer 1992): 229–256.

Dilworth, Thomas. "Lorde's Power." *Explicator* 57, no. 1 (Fall 1998): 54–57.

Dolan, Eamon. "New Era." *Wired* 5.04 (April 1997). Available at http://www.wired.com/wired/archive/5.04/music_reviews.html?pg=4.

Downey, Pat, George Albert, and Frank Hoffman. *Cash Box: Pop Singles Charts, 1950–1993*. Englewood, CO: Libraries Unlimited, 1994.

Duany, Jorge. "Reconstructing Racial Identity: Ethnicity, Color, and Class among Dominicans in the United States and Puerto Rico." *Latin American Perspectives* (Issue 100) 25, no. 3 (May 1998): 147–172.

Due, Tananarive, and Allison Samuels. "Where Is the Love?" *Essence* 30, no. 10 (February 2000): 84–86, 90, 144–146.

Dyer, Richard. *Heavenly Bodies: Film Stars and Society.* London: Macmillan Education, Ltd., 1986.

Eakin, Paul John. "Malcolm X and the Limits of Autobiography." *African-American Autobiography: A Collection of Critical Essays.* Ed. William L. Andrews. Englewood Cliff, NJ: Prentice Hall, 1993. 151–161.

España-Maram, Linda. "Brown 'Hordes' in McIntosh Suits: Filipinos, Taxi Dance Halls, and Performing the Immigrant Body in Los Angeles, 1930s-1940s." *Generations of Youth: Youth Cultures and History in Twentieth Century America.* Ed. Joe Austin and Michael Willard. New York: New York University Press, 1998. 118–135.

Estades, Rosa. *Patterns of Political Participation of Puerto Ricans in New York.* San Juan: University of Puerto Rico, 1978.

Evans, Mari. *Black Women Writers (1950–1980): A Critical Evaluation.* New York: Anchor Press, 1984.

Faderman, Lillian. *Odd Girls and Twilight Lovers: A History of Lesbian Life in Twentieth-Century America.* New York: Penguin, 1992.

Favor, J. Martin. *Authentic Blackness: The Folk in the New Negro Renaissance.* Durham, NC: Duke University Press, 1999.

Featherstone, Mike. *Global Culture: Nationalism, Globalization, and Modernity.* London: Sage, 1990.

Fernando, S. H. *The New Beats: Exploring the Music, Culture, and Attitudes of Hip-Hop.* New York: Anchor Books, 1994.

Ferraro, Thomas J. *Ethnic Passages: Literary Immigrants in Twentieth Century America.* Chicago: University of Chicago Press, 1993.

Firmat, Gustavo Pérez. *Life on the Hyphen: The Cuban-American Way.* Austin: University of Texas Press, 1994.

Fischkin, Barbara. *Muddy Cup: A Dominican Family Comes of Age in a New America.* New York: Scribner, 1997.

Fitzpatrick, Joseph. "Attitudes of Puerto Ricans toward Color." *American Catholic Sociological Review* 20, no. 3 (1959): 219–233.

Flores, Juan. "Puerto Rican and Proud, Boyee! Rap, Roots and Amnesia." *Microphone Fiends.* Ed. Andrew Ross and Tricia Rose. New York: Routledge, 1994. 89–97.

———. *Divided Borders: Essays on Puerto Rican Identity.* Houston: Arte Público Press, 1993.

———. "'It's a Street Thing!' An Interview with Charlie Chase," *Callaloo* 15.4 (1992): 999–1021.

Fogelson, Gina. *Belafonte.* Los Angeles: Holloway, 1980.

Fontaine, Joan. *No Bed of Roses*. New York: Morrow, 1978.

Fouron, Georges. "The Black Immigrant Dilemma in the United States: The Haitian Experience." *Journal of Caribbean Studies* 3, no. 3 (1985): 242–265.

Franklin, John Hope. *From Slavery to Freedom: A History of Negro Americans*. 5th ed. New York: Knopf, 1980.

Freedomways (The Editors of). *Paul Robeson: The Great Forerunner*. New York: Dodd, Mead, 1965.

Friedman, Lester, ed. *Unspeakable Images: Ethnicity and the American Cinema*. Urbana: University of Illinois Press, 1991.

Fusco, Coco. *English Is Broken Here: Notes on Cultural Fusion in the Americas*. New York: New Press, 1995.

Gaines, Kevin Kelly. *Uplifting the Race: Black Leadership, Politics and Culture in the 20th Century*. Chapel Hill: University of North Carolina Press, 1996.

Gans, Herbert J. "Symbolic Ethnicity: The Future of Ethnic Groups and Cultures in America." *Theories of Ethnicity*. Ed. Werner Sollors. New York: New York University Press, 1996. 425–459.

———. "Second-Generation Decline: Scenarios for the Economic and Ethnic Futures of the Post-1965 American Immigrants." *Journal of Ethnic and Racial Studies* 15, no. 2 (April 1992): 173–192.

Gates, Henry Louis, Jr. *Thirteen Ways of Looking at a Black Man*. New York: Random House, 1997.

———. *Reading Black, Reading Feminist: A Critical Anthology*. New York: Meridian Books, 1990.

———. *The Signifying Monkey: A Theory of African-American Literary Criticism*. New York: Oxford University Press, 1988.

Gates, Henry Louis, Jr., and Nellie Y. McKay, eds. "Marcus Garvey." *The Norton Anthology: African American Literature*. New York: Norton, 1997. 972–980.

Gayle, Addison. *The Black Aesthetic*. New York: Doubleday, 1971.

Georges, Eugenia. *The Making of a Transnational Community: Migration, Development, and Cultural Change in the Dominican Republic*. New York: Columbia University Press, 1990.

Gibbs, Joan, and Sara Bennett, eds. *Top Ranking: A Collection of Articles on Racism and Classism in the Lesbian Community*. Brooklyn, NY: February 3rd Press, 1980.

Gibson, Richard. *African Liberation Movements: Contemporary Struggles Against White Minority Rule*. London: Oxford University Press, 1972.

Gilroy, Paul. *Against Race: Imagining Political Culture beyond the Color Line*. Cambridge MA: Harvard University Press, 2000.

———. *The Black Atlantic: Modernity and Double Consciousness*. Cambridge, MA: Harvard University Press, 1993.

————. *Small Acts: Thoughts on the Politics of Black Cultures.* London: Serpent's Tail, 1993.

————. "Cultural Studies and Ethnic Absolutism." *Cultural Studies.* Ed. Lawrence Grossberg, Cary Nelson, and Paula Treichler. New York: Routledge, 1992. 187–198.

————. *There Ain't No Black in the Union Jack: The Cultural Politics of Race and Nation.* Chicago: University of Chicago Press, 1991.

Glazer, Nathan, and Daniel Patrick Moynihan. *Beyond the Melting Pot: The Negroes, Puerto Ricans, Jews, and Italians of New York City.* Cambridge, MA: MIT Press, 1963.

————, eds. *Ethnicity: Theory and Experience.* Cambridge, MA: Harvard University Press, 1975.

Gmelch, George. *Double Passage: The Lives of Caribbean Migrants Abroad and Back Home.* Ann Arbor: University of Michigan Press, 1992.

Gordon, Avery F., and Christopher Newfield, eds. *Mapping Multiculturalism.* Minneapolis: University of Minnesota Press, 1996.

Gordon, Max. *Live at the Village Vanguard.* New York: Da Capo Press, 1980.

Gourse, Leslie. *Unforgettable: The Life and Mystique of Nat King Cole.* New York: St. Martin's Press, 1991.

Grahn, Judy. *Another Mother Tongue: Gay Words, Gay Worlds.* Boston: Beacon Press, 1984.

Grant, Madison. *The Passing of the Great Race: or, The Racial Basis of European History.* New York: Charles Scribner's Sons, 1916.

Grasmuck, Sherri, and Patricia Pessar. *Between Two Islands: Dominican International Migration.* Berkeley: University of California Press, 1991.

Graulich, Melody, and Lisa Sisco. "Meditations on Language and the Self: A Conversation with Paule Marshall." *NWSA Journal* 4, no. 3 (Fall 1992): 282–302.

Gray, Obika. *Radicalism and Social Change in Jamaica, 1960–1972.* Knoxville: University of Tennessee Press, 1991.

Greenbaum, Susan. *More Than Black: Afro-Cubans in Tampa.* Gainesville: University Press of Florida, 2002.

Greeley, Andrew. "The Rediscovery of Cultural Pluralism." *Antioch Review* 31 (1971): 343–367.

Griffin, Farah Jasmine. *"Who Set You Flowin'?" The African-American Migration Narrative.* New York: Oxford University Press, 1995.

Grillo, Evelio. *Black Cuban, Black American: A Memoir.* Houston: Arte Público Press, 2000.

Guarnizo, Luis. "Los Dominicanyorks: The Making of a Binational Society." *An-*

*nals of the American Academy of Political and Social Sciences* 533 (May 1994): 70–86.

Guerrero, Edward. *Framing Blackness: The African-American Image in Film.* Philadelphia: Temple University Press, 1993.

Hall, James C. *Mercy, Mercy Me: African-American Culture and the American Sixties.* Oxford: Oxford University Press, 2001.

Hall, Stuart. "What Is This 'Black' in Black Popular Culture?" *Stuart Hall: Critical Dialogues in Cultural Studies.* Ed. David Morely and Kuan-Hsing Chen. London: Routledge, 1996.

———. "Cultural Identity and Diaspora." *Identity, Community, Culture, Difference.* Ed. Jonathan Rutherford. London: Lawrence and Wishart, 1990. 222–237.

Hall, Stuart, and James Donald, eds. *Politics and Ideology: A Reader.* Philadelphia: Open University Press, 1985.

Hall, Stuart, and Tony Jefferson, eds. *Resistance through Rituals: Youth Subcultures in Post-War Britain.* London: Hutchinson, 1976.

Hamilton, Jack. "The Storm over Belafonte." *Look* 21, no. 13 (June 25, 1957): 138–142.

Handlin, Oscar, ed. *Children of the Uprooted.* New York: G. Braziller, 1966.

Hannerz, Ulf. "Some Comments on the Anthropology of Ethnicity in the United States." *Ethnicity in the Americas.* Ed. Frances Henry. The Hague and Paris: Mouton, 1976. 429–438.

Hansberry, Lorraine. "Black Revolution and White Backlash." *National Guardian* 16, no. 39 (July 4, 1964): 5–9.

Hansen, Marcus Lee. *The Problem of the Third Generation Immigrant.* Rock Island, IL: Augustana Historical Society, 1938.

Hansen, Randall, and Patrick Weil, eds. *Dual Nationality, Social Rights and Federal Citizenship in the U.S. and Europe: The Reinvention of Citizenship.* New York: Berghahn Books, 2002.

Harlem Writers' Guild. *Harlem Writers' Guild Page.* October 15, 2000. Available at http://members.aol.com/HWG1950.

Harris, Leonard, ed. *The Philosophy of Alain Locke: Harlem Renaissance and Beyond.* Philadelphia: Temple University Press, 1989.

Harris, Norman. *Connecting Times: The Sixties in Afro-American Fiction.* Jackson: University Press of Mississippi, 1988.

Harvey, David. *The Condition of Postmodernity: An Enquiry into the Origins of Cultural Change.* Oxford: Blackwell, 1989.

Haskins, James, and Kathleen Benson. *Lena.* New York: Stein and Day, 1984.

Hathaway, Heather. *Caribbean Waves: Relocating Claude McKay and Paule Marshall.* Bloomington: Indiana University Press, 1999.

Hebdige, Dick. *Cut 'n' Mix: Culture, Identity, and Caribbean Music*. New York: Methuen, 1987.

Heinl, Robert, Nancy Heinl, and Michael Heinl. *Written in Blood: The Story of the Haitian People, 1492–1995*. Lanham, MD: University Press of America, 1996.

Henderson, Stephen. *Understanding the New Black Poetry: Black Speech and Black Music as Poetic References*. New York: Morrow, 1973.

Henry, Paget, and Carl Stone. *The Newer Caribbean: Decolonization, Democracy, and Development*. Philadelphia: Institute for the Study of Human Issues, 1983.

Hernández, Carmen Dolores. *Puerto Rican Voices in English: Interviews with Writers*. Westport, CT: Praeger, 1997.

Hernández, Deborah Pacini. *Bachata: A Social History of a Dominican Popular Music*. Philadelphia: Temple University Press, 1995.

Hill, Donald. *Calypso Calaloo: Early Carnival Music in Trinidad*. Gainesville: University Press of Florida, 1993.

Hill, Errol. *The Trinidad Carnival: Mandate for a National Theatre*. Austin: University of Texas, 1972.

Hirsch, Marianne. *The Mother/Daughter Plot: Narrative, Psychoanalysis, Feminism*. Bloomington: Indiana University Press, 1989.

Hirshey, Gerri. *Nowhere to Run: The Story of Soul Music*. New York: Times Books, 1984.

Hogan, William. "Review of *Down These Mean Streets*." *San Francisco Chronicle* (December 31, 1967).

Holden, Stephen. "The Pop Life." *New York Times* (May 8, 1991): C18.

hooks, bell. *Black Looks: Race and Representation*. Boston: South End Press, 1992.

Horne, Lena, and Richard Schickel. *Lena*. Garden City, NY: Doubleday, 1965.

Hull, Gloria, Patricia Bell Scott, and Barbara Smith, eds. *All the Women Are White, All the Blacks Are Men, But Some of Us Are Brave*. New York: Feminist Press, 1982.

Hutchinson, Earl Ofari. *Blacks and Reds: Race and Class in Conflict, 1919–1990*. East Lansing: Michigan State University Press, 1995.

Jacobson, Matthew. *Whiteness of a Different Color: European Immigrants and the Alchemy of Race*. Cambridge, MA: Harvard University Press, 1998.

Jacoby, Tamar, ed. *Reinventing the Melting Pot: The New Immigrants and What It Means to Be American*. New York: Basic Books, 2004.

Jaworski, Irene D. *Becoming American: The Problems of Immigrants and Their Children*. New York: Harper and Brothers, 1950.

Johnson, Abby, and Ronald Johnson. *Propaganda and Aesthetics: The Literary*

*Politics of African-American Magazines in the Twentieth Century.* Amherst: University of Massachusetts Press, 1979.

Jones, LeRoi, and Larry Neal, eds. *Black Fire: An Anthology of Afro-American Writing.* New York: Morrow, 1968.

Jordan, June. *Naming Our Destinies.* New York: Thunder's Mouth Press, 1989.

———. *Civil Wars.* Boston: Beacon Press, 1981.

———. *Passion: New Poems, 1977–1980.* Boston: Beacon Press, 1980.

———. *Things That I Do in the Dark.* New York: Random House, 1977.

———. *His Own Where.* New York: Crowell, 1971.

———. *Some Changes.* New York: Dutton, 1971.

———. *New Days.* New York: Emerson Hall, 1970.

Joseph, Gloria, and Jill Lewis. *Common Differences: Conflicts in Black and White Feminist Perspectives.* New York: Anchor Press, 1981.

Kader, Cheryl. "'The Very House of Difference': *Zami,* Audre Lorde's Lesbian-Centered Text." *Journal of Homosexuality* 26, nos. 2, 3 (1993): 181–194.

Kaiser, Ernest. "Five Years of FREEDOMWAYS: An Evaluation." *Freedomways* 6, no. 2 (Spring 1966): 103–117.

Kallen, Horace M. "Democracy Versus the Melting-Pot: A Study of American Nationality." *Nation* 100, no. 2591 (February 25, 1915): 212–220.

———. "Democracy Versus the Melting-Pot: A Study of American Nationality." *Nation* 100, no. 2590 (February 18, 1951): 190–194.

Kasinitz, Philip. *Caribbean New York: Black Immigrants and the Politics of Race.* Ithaca: Cornell University Press, 1992.

Keating, AnaLouise. *Women Reading Women Writing: Self-Invention in Paula Gunn Allen, Gloria Anzaldúa, and Audre Lorde.* Philadelphia: Temple University Press, 1996.

———. "Myth Smashers, Myth Makers: (Re)Visionary Techniques in the Works of Paula Gunn Allen, Gloria Anzaldúa, and Audre Lorde." *Journal of Homosexuality* 26, nos. 2, 3 (1993): 73–95.

———. "Making 'Our Shattered Faces Whole': The Black Goddess and Audre Lorde's Revision of Patriarchal Myth." *Frontiers* 13, no. 1 (1992): 20–33.

Kelly, M. Patricia Fernández, and Richard Schauffler. "Divided Fates: Immigrant Children and the New Assimilation." *The New Second Generation.* Ed. Alejandro Portes. New York: Russell Sage Foundation, 1996. 30–53.

Kelley, Robin. *Race Rebels: Culture, Politics, and the Black Working Class.* New York: Free Press, 1996.

Kennedy, Randall. *Interracial Intimacies: Sex, Marriage, Identity, and Adoption.* New York: Pantheon Books, 2003.

Killens, John O. "On *El Barrio* and Piri Thomas." *Negro Digest* 17 (January 1968): 94–97.

Kincaid, Jamaica. *Annie John*. New York: Farrar, Straus and Giroux, 1985.

King, Anthony. *Culture, Globalization, and the World-System: Contemporary Conditions for the Representation of Identity*. Binghamton, NY: Department of Art and Art History, State University of New York at Binghamton, 1991.

Kirk, John A. *Redefining the Color Line: Black Activism in Little Rock, Arkansas, 1940–1970*. Gainesville: University Press of Florida, 2002.

Kisch, John, and Edward Mapp. *A Separate Cinema: Fifty Years of Black-Cast Posters*. New York: Farrar, Straus and Giroux, 1992.

Knobel, David T. "America for the Americans": The Nativist Movement in the United States. New York: Twayne, 1996.

Kofsky, Frank. *Black Nationalism and the Revolution in Black Music*. New York: Pathfinder Press, 1970.

Kritz, Mary M., ed. *U.S. Immigration and Refugee Policy: Global and Domestic Issues*. Lexington, MA: Lexington Books, 1983.

Lamming, George. *In the Castle of My Skin*. New York: McGraw-Hill, 1953.

Larsen, Nella. *Passing*. New York: Knopf, 1929.

———. *Quicksand*. New York: Knopf, 1928.

Lasch, Christopher. *The Agony of the American Left*. New York: Random House, 1968.

Laughlin, Harry H. *Analysis of America's Modern Melting Pot: Hearings Before the Committee on Immigration and Naturalization, House of Representatives, November 21, 1922*. Washington, DC: Government Printing Office, 1923.

Leab, Daniel. *From Sambo to Superspade: The Black Experience in Motion Pictures*. Boston: Houghton Mifflin, 1976.

Leadbeater, Bonnie, and Niobe Way, eds. *Urban Girls: Resisting Stereotypes, Creating Identities*. New York: New York University Press, 1996.

Leff, Leonard, and Jerold L. Simmons. *The Dame in the Kimono: Hollywood, Censorship, and the Production Code from the 1920s to the 1960s*. New York: Grove Weidenfeld, 1990.

Levine, Barry B, ed. *The Caribbean Exodus*. New York: Praeger, 1987.

Levine, Lawrence. *Black Culture and Black Consciousness: Afro-American Folk Thought from Slavery to Freedom*. New York: Oxford University Press, 1977.

Levitt, Peggy. "Variations in Transnational Belonging: Lessons from Brazil and the Dominican Republic." *Dual Nationality, Social Rights and Federal Citizenship in the U.S. and Europe*. Ed. Randall Hansen and Patrick Weil. New York: Berghahn Books, 2002. 264–289.

Lincoln, Abbey. "The Negro Woman in American Literature." *Freedomways* 6, no.1 (Winter 1966): 11–13.

Lipsitz, George. "The Hip Hop Hearings." *Generations of Youth: Youth Cultures and History in Twentieth Century America.* Ed. Joe Austin and Michael Willard. New York: New York University Press, 1998. 395–411.

————. *Dangerous Crossroads: Popular Music, Postmodernism, and the Poetics of Place.* London: Verso, 1994.

————. *Time Passages: Collective Memory and American Popular Culture.* Minneapolis: University of Minnesota Press, 1990.

Locke, Alain, ed. *The New Negro: An Interpretation.* New York: Albert and Charles Boni, 1925.

López, Adalberto, and James Petras, eds. *Puerto Rico and Puerto Ricans: Studies in History and Society.* Cambridge, MA: Schenkman, 1974.

Lorde, Audre. *The Collected Poems of Audre Lorde.* New York: Norton, 1997.

————. *Audre Lorde Compendium: Essays, Speeches, and Journals.* London: Pandora, 1996.

————. "Of Generators and Survival—Hugo Letter." *Callaloo* 14.1 (1991): 72–82.

————. "Showing Our True Colors." *Callaloo* 14.1 (1991): 67–71.

————. "What Is at Stake in Lesbian and Gay Publishing Today: The Bill Whitehead Memorial Award Ceremony—1990." *Callaloo* 14.1 (1991): 65–66.

————. *A Burst of Light: Essays by Audre Lorde.* Ithaca, NY: Firebrand Books, 1988.

————. "I Am Your Sister: Black Women Organizing Across Sexualities." *Freedom Organizing Series, No. 3.* Albany, NY: Women of Color Press (Kitchen Table), 1985.

————. *Sister Outsider: Essays and Speeches.* Freedom: Crossing Press, 1984.

————. *Zami: A New Spelling of My Name.* Watertown, MA: Persephone Press, 1982.

————. *The Cancer Journals.* Argyle, NY: Spinsters, 1980.

————. "Feminism & Black Liberation: The Great American Disease." *The Black Scholar* 10, nos. 8, 9 (May–June 1979): 17–20.

————. *The Black Unicorn.* New York: Norton, 1978.

————. *Coal.* New York: Norton, 1976.

————. *New York Head Shop and Museum.* Detroit: Broadside, 1974.

————. *From a Land Where Other People Live.* Detroit: Broadside, 1973.

————. *Cables to Rage.* London: Paul Breman, 1970.

————. *The First Cities.* New York: Poets Press, 1968.

Lott, Eric. *Love and Theft: Blackface Minstrelsy and the American Working Class.* New York: Oxford University Press, 1993.

Lovejoy, Paul E., and Jan S. Hogendorn. "Slave Marketing in West Africa." *The Uncommon Market: Essays in the Economic History of the Atlantic Slave Trade.*

Ed. Henry A. Gemery and Jan S. Hogendorn. New York: Academic Press, 1979. 213–235.

Luis, Robert. *Authentic Calypso: The Song, the Music, the Dance.* New York: Latin American Press, 1957.

Luis, William. *Dance between Two Cultures: Latino Caribbean Literature Written in the United States.* Nashville: Vanderbilt University Press, 1997.

Madsen, Catherine. "The Thin Thread of Conversation: An Interview with Mary Daly." *Cross Currents* 50, no. 3 (Fall 2000): 332–348.

Magida, Arthur. *Prophet of Rage: A Life of Louis Farrakhan and His Nation.* New York: Basic Books, 1996.

Major, Clarence. *The New Black Poetry.* New York: International Publishers, 1969.

Malcolm X. *By Any Means Necessary.* 2nd ed. New York: Pathfinder, 1992.

———. *The Last Speeches.* New York: Pathfinder, 1989.

———. *The End of White World Supremacy: Four Speeches.* New York: Merlin House, 1971.

———. *The Autobiography of Malcolm X.* New York: Grove Press, 1965.

———. *Malcolm X Speaks.* New York: Merit, 1965.

Manuel, Peter Lamarche, Kenneth Bilby, and Michael Largey. *Caribbean Currents: Caribbean Music from Rumba to Reggae.* Philadelphia: Temple University Press, 1995.

Mapp, Edward. *Blacks in American Films: Today and Yesterday.* Metuchen, NJ: Scarecrow Press, 1972.

Marshall, Paule. *Daughters.* New York: Atheneum, 1991.

———. *Praisesong for the Widow.* New York: Putnam, 1983.

———. *Reena and Other Stories.* Old Westbury, NY: Feminist Press, 1983.

———. "Shaping the World of My Art." *New Letters* 40 (Autumn 1973): 97–112.

———. *Soul Clap Hands and Sing.* Chatham, NJ: Chatham Bookseller, 1971.

———. *The Chosen Place, The Timeless People.* New York: Harcourt, Brace, and World, 1969.

———. "The Negro Woman in American Literature." *Freedomways* 6, no. 1 (Winter 1966): 20–25.

———. "Reena." *Harper's* 225, no. 1349 (October 1962): 154–163.

———. *Brown Girl, Brownstones.* New York: Random House, 1959.

Matthew, Thomas. "Color in Puerto Rico." *Slavery and Race Relations in Latin America.* Ed. Robert Toplin. Westport, CT: Greenwood Press, 1974. 299–323.

Matusow, Allen J. *The Unraveling of America: A History of Liberalism in the 1960s.* New York: Harper and Row, 1986.

Mayfield, Julian. *The Hit* and *The Long Night*. Foreword by Phillip M. Richards. Boston: Northeastern University Press, 1989.

Mazón, Mauricio. *The Zoot-Suit Riots: The Psychology of Symbolic Annihilation*. Austin: University of Texas Press, 1984.

McGill, Lisa D. "A Conversation with Piri Thomas." *The Bilingual Review/La Revista Bilingüe* 25, no. 2, (May–August 2001): 179–184.

McKay, Claude. *Harlem: Negro Metropolis*. New York: Dutton, 1940.

————. *A Long Way from Home*. New York: L. Furman, 1937.

————. *Banana Bottom*. New York: Harper and Brothers, 1933.

————. *Home to Harlem*. New York: Harper and Brothers, 1928.

McRobbie, Angela. *Postmodernism and Popular Culture*. London: Routledge, 1994.

Mellen, Joan. *Big Bad Wolves: Masculinity in the American Film*. New York: Pantheon Books, 1977.

Miller, E. Willard, and Ruby M. Miler. *United States Immigration: A Reference Handbook*. Santa Barbara: ABC-CLIO, 1996.

Mills, C. Wright, Clarence Senior, and Rose Kohn Goldsen. *The Puerto Rican Journey: New York's Newest Migrants*. New York: Harper and Row, 1950.

Minority Rights Group, ed. *No Longer Invisible: Afro-Latin Americans Today*. London: Minority Rights Publications, 1995.

Mirel, Jeffrey. "Civic Education and Changing Definitions of American Identity, 1900–1950." *Educational Review* 54, no. 2 (2002): 143—152.

Mirikitani, Janice, et al. "Against Apartheid." *Feminist Studies* 14, no. 3 (Fall 1988): 417–452.

Mohanty, Chandra Talpade, Ann Russo, and Lourdes Torres, eds. *Third World Women and the Politics of Feminism*. Bloomington: Indiana University Press, 1991.

Mohr, Eugene. *The Nuyorican Experience*. Westport, CT: Greenwood Press, 1982.

Mostern, Kenneth. *Autobiography and Black Identity Politics: Racialization in Twentieth-Century America*. Cambridge: Cambridge University Press, 1999.

Muller, Gilbert H. *New Strangers in Paradise: The Immigrant Experience and Contemporary American Fiction*. Lexington: University of Kentucky Press, 1999.

Naison, Mark. *Communists in Harlem during the Depression*. Urbana: University of Illinois Press, 1983.

Neal, Larry. "The Black Arts Movement." *The Black Aesthetic*. Ed. Addison Gayle Jr. Garden City, NY: Doubleday, 1971. 272–290.

————. *Black Boogaloo: Notes of Black Liberation*. San Francisco: Journal of Black Poetry Press, 1969.

————. *Visions of a Liberated Future: Black Arts Movement Writing*. New York: Thunder's Mouth Press, 1989.

Neal, Larry, and Amiri Baraka, eds. *Black Fire: An Anthology of Afro-American Writing*. New York: Morrow, 1968.

Nettleford, Rex. *Caribbean Cultural Identity: The Case of Jamaica*. Kingston: Institute of Jamaica, 1978.

————. *Mirror Mirror: Identity, Race and Protest in Jamaica*. New York: Morrow, 1970.

Nicholls, David. *From Dessalines to Duvalier: Race, Colour and National Independence in Haiti*. Cambridge: Cambridge University Press, 1979.

Noble, Peter. *The Negro in Films*. London: S. Robinson, 1948.

Norris, Jerrie. *Presenting Rosa Guy*. Boston: Twayne, 1988.

Novak, Michael. *The Rise of Unmeltable Ethnics: Politics and Culture in the Seventies*. New York: Macmillan, 1973.

Null, Gary. *Black Hollywood: The Negro in Motion Pictures*. Secaucus, NJ: Citadel Press, 1975.

Ogundipe-Leslie, Omolara. "Re-creating Ourselves All Over the World: Interview with Paule Marshall." *Matatu* 6.3 (Jahrgang 1989): 25–38.

Osofsky, Gilbert. *Harlem: The Making of a Ghetto, Negro New York, 1890–1930*. New York: Harper and Row, 1963.

Padilla, Elena. *Up from Puerto Rico*. New York: Columbia University Press, 1958.

Palmer, Ransford W., ed. *In Search of a Better Life: Perspectives on Migration from the Caribbean*. New York: Praeger, 1990.

Patterson, James T. *America in the Twentieth Century: A History*. San Diego: Harcourt Brace Jovanovich, 1989.

Parris, Jennifer. "Original Ones: *Proyecto 1*." *Urban Latino* (Issue 16) (June 8, 2000): 1–5.

Pedraza, Silvia, and Rubén Rumbaut, eds. *Origins and Destinies: Immigration, Race, and Ethnicity in America*. Belmont, CA: Wadsworth, 1996.

Perkins, William Eric. *Droppin' Science: Critical Essays on Rap Music and Hip Hop Culture*. Philadelphia: Temple University Press, 1996.

Perreault, Jeanne. *Writing Selves: Contemporary Feminist Autography*. Minneapolis: University of Minnesota Press, 1995.

————. "'That the Pain Not Be Wasted': Audre Lorde and the Written Self." *Auto/Biography Studies* 4, no. 1 (Fall 1988): 1–16.

Pessar, Patricia, ed. *Caribbean Circuits: New Directions in the Study of Caribbean Migration*. New York: Center for Migration Studies, 1997.

————. *Visa for a Dream: Dominicans in the United States*. Boston: Allyn and Bacon, 1995.

Pettis, Joyce. *Toward Wholeness in Paule Marshall's Fiction*. Charlottesville: University of Virginia Press, 1995.

——. "A MELUS Interview: Paule Marshall." *MELUS* 17, no. 4 (Winter 1991–1992): 117–129.

Pichaske, David. *A Generation in Motion: Popular Music and Culture in the Sixties*. New York: Schirmer Books, 1979.

Poitier, Sidney. *This Life*. New York: Knopf, 1980.

Pons, Frank Moya. *The Dominican Republic: A National History*. Princeton: First Markus Wiener, 1998.

Portes, Alejandro, ed. *The New Second Generation*. New York: Russell Sage Foundation, 1996.

Portes, Alejandro, and Alex Stepick. *City on the Edge: The Transformation of Miami*. Berkeley: University of California Press, 1993.

Portes, Alejandro, and Rubén G. Rumbaut, eds. *Ethnicities: Children of Immigrants in America*. Berkeley: University of California Press, 2001.

——. *Legacies: The Story of the Immigrant Second Generation*. Berkeley: University of California Press, 2001.

Portes, Alejandro, and Min Zhou. "The New Second Generation: Segmented Assimilation and Its Variants." *Annals of the American Academy of Political and Social Sciences* 530 (November 1993): 74–91.

Potter, Russell. *Spectacular Vernaculars: Hip-Hop and the Politics of Postmodernism*. Albany: State University of New York Press, 1995.

Provost, Kara. "Becoming Afrekete: The Trickster in the Work of Audre Lorde." *MELUS* 20 (Winter 1995): 45–59.

Pryse, Marjorie, and Hortense J. Spiller, eds. *Conjuring: Black Women, Fiction, and Literary Tradition*. Bloomington: Indiana University Press, 1985.

Quevedo, Raymond. *Atilla's Kaiso: A Short History of Trinidad Calypso*. St. Augustine, Trinidad and Tobago: University of the West Indies, Department of Extra Mural Studies, 1983.

Rahming, Melvin. *The Evolution of the West Indian's Image in the Afro-American Novel*. Millwood, NY: Associated Faculty Press, 1986.

Ramírez, Manuel, and Alfredo Casañeda. *Cultural Democracy, Bicognitive Development, and Education*. New York: Academic Press, 1974.

Raynaud, Claudine. "'A Nutmeg Nestled Inside Its Covering of Mace': Audre Lorde's *Zami*." *Life/Lines: Theorizing Women's Autobiography*. Ed. Bella Brodzki and Celeste Schenck. Ithaca: Cornell University Press, 1988. 221–242.

Reid, Ira De Augustine. *The Negro Immigrant: His Background, Characteristics and Social Adjustment, 1899–1937*. New York: Columbia University Press, 1939.

Reid-Pharr, Robert. "Tearing the Goat's Flesh: Homosexuality, Abjection, and the Production of a Late-Twentieth-Century Black Masculinity." *Novel Gazing: Queer Readings in Fiction.* Ed. Eve Kosofsky Sedgwick. Durham, NC: Duke University Press, 1997. 353–376.

Reimers, David M. *Still the Golden Door: The Third World Comes to America.* New York: Columbia University Press, 1985.

Ro, Ronin. *Gangsta: Merchandizing the Rhymes of Violence.* New York: St. Martin's Press, 1996.

Roaring Lion. *Calypso from France to Trinidad: 800 Years of History.* San Juan: Latin American Press, 1987.

Robeson, Paul. *Here I Stand.* Boston: Beacon Press, 1958.

Robinson, Cedric J. *Black Movements in America.* New York: Routledge, 1997.

Rodney, Walter. *West Africa and the Atlantic Slave-Trade.* Historical Association of Tanzania, Paper No. 2. Dar-es-Salaam: East African Publishing House, 1969.

Romano, Renee. "Crossing the Line: Black-White Interracial Marriage in the United States, 1945–1990." Ph.D. diss., Stanford University, 1996.

Rose, Tricia. *Black Noise: Rap Music and Black Culture in Contemporary America.* Hanover, NH: Wesleyan University Press, 1994.

Rosen, Craig. *The Billboard Book of Number One Albums.* New York: Watson-Guptill, 1996.

Ross, Andrew, and Tricia Rose, eds. *Microphone Fiends.* New York: Routledge, 1994.

Ruoff, A. LaVonne Brown, and Jerry W. Ward, Jr. *Redefining American Literary History.* New York: Modern Language Association of America, 1990.

Rowell, Charles H. "Above the Wind: An Interview with Audre Lorde." *Callaloo* 14.1 (1991): 83–95.

Ryan, Thomas. *American Hit Radio: A History of Popular Singles from 1955 to the Present.* Rocklin, CA: Prima, 1996.

Sanchez, Marta. "La Malinche at the Intersection: Race and Gender in *Down These Mean Streets.*" *PMLA* 113 (January 1998): 117–128.

Said, Edward. "Reflections on Exile." *Out There, Marginalization and Contemporary Cultures.* Ed. Russell Ferguson, Martha Gever, Trinh T. Minh-ha, and Cornel West. Cambridge, MA: MIT Press, 1990. 357–363.

Sandiford, Lloyd Erskine. *Politics and Society in Barbados and the Caribbean.* Barbados: Cassia, 2000.

Schiller, Nina Glick, and Georges Fouron. "Everywhere We Go We Are in Danger: Ti Manno and the Emergence of a Haitian Transnational Identity." *American Ethnologist* 17, no. 2 (1990): 329–347.

Schiller, Nina Glick, Linda Basch, and Cristina Blanc Szanton. *Towards a*

*Transnational Perspective on Migration: Race, Class, Ethnicity and Nationalism Reconsidered.* New York: New York Academy of Sciences, 1992.

Schlesinger, Arthur M., Jr. *The Disuniting of America: Reflections on a Multicultural Society.* New York: Norton, 1993.

Schoener, Allon, ed. *Harlem on My Mind: Cultural Capital of Black America, 1900–1968.* New York: Random House, 1968.

Shaw, Arnold. *Belafonte: An Unauthorized Biography.* Philadelphia: Chilton, 1960.

Simone, Roberta. *The Immigrant Experience in American Fiction: An Annotated Bibliography.* Metuchen, NJ: Scarecrow Press, 1995.

Smalls, Christopher. *Music of the Common Tongue: Survival and Celebration in Afro-American Music.* New York: Riverrun Press, 1987.

Smethurst, James. *The New Red Negro: The Literary Left and African-American Poetry, 1930–1946.* New York: Oxford University Press, 1999.

Smith, Robert. *Kingdoms of the Yoruba.* Madison: University of Wisconsin Press, 1988.

Sollors, Werner. *Theories of Ethnicity: A Classical Reader.* New York: New York University Press, 1996.

———. *Beyond Ethnicity: Consent and Descent in American Literature.* New York: Oxford University Press, 1986.

Solomon, Mark. *The Cry Was Unity: Communists and African Americans, 1917–36.* Jackson: University Press of Mississippi, 1998.

Sowell, Thomas. *Ethnic America: A History.* New York: Basic Books, 1981.

Spretnak, Charlene, ed. *The Politics of Women's Spirituality: Essays on the Rise of Spiritual Power Within the Feminist Movement.* Garden City, NY: Anchor Books, 1982.

Staples, Robert. "The Myth of Black Macho: A Response to Angry Black Feminists." *The Black Scholar* 10, nos. 6, 7 (March–April 1979): 24–33.

Steirman, Hy, ed. *Harry Belafonte: His Complete Life Story.* New York: Hillman Periodicals, 1957.

Stepto, Robert. *From Behind the Veil: A Study of Afro-American Narrative.* 2nd ed. Urbana: University of Illinois Press, 1991.

Stern, Daniel. "One Who Got Away." *New York Times Book Review* 72 (May 21, 1967): 1, 44.

Stone, Merlin. *When God Was a Woman.* New York: Dial Press, 1976.

Stowe, David W. *Swing Changes: Big-Band Jazz in New Deal America.* Cambridge, MA: Harvard University Press, 1994.

Sutton, Constance, and Elsa Chaney, eds. *Caribbean Life in New York City.* New York: Center for Migration Studies of New York, 1987.

Tate, Claudia. "Audre Lorde." *Black Women Writers at Work*. New York: Continuum, 1983. 100–116.

Teubig, Klaus. *Straighten Up and Fly Right: A Chronology and Discography of Nat "King" Cole*. Westport, CT: Greenwood Press, 1994.

Thadious, Davis. *Nella Larsen, a Novelist of the Harlem Renaissance: A Woman's Life Unveiled*. Baton Rouge: Louisiana State University Press, 1994.

Thomas, Piri. "The Inspiration to Write *Down These Mean Streets*." *In Motion* magazine. April 2, 2000. Available at http://www.inmotionmagazine.com/pt-inter1.html.

———. *Seven Long Times*. New York: Praeger, 1974.

———. *Savior, Savior, Hold My Hand*. Garden City, NY: Doubleday, 1972.

———. *Down These Mean Streets*. New York: Knopf, 1967.

Thomas, Piri, and Carmen Dolores Hernández. "They Have Forced Us to Be Universal." March 5–6, 1995. Available at http://www.cheverote.com/reviews/hernandezinterview.html.

Thomas-Hope, Elizabeth. *Explanation in Caribbean Migration: Perception and the Image: Jamaica, Barbados, St. Vincent*. London: Macmillan Caribbean, 1992.

Toop, David. *The Rap Attack: African Jive to New York Hip Hop*. Boston: South End Press, 1984.

Torres-Saillant, Silvio. "The Tribulations of Blackness: Stages in Dominican Racial Identity." *Latin American Perspectives* (Issue 100) 25, no. 3 (May 1998): 127–145.

Torres-Saillant, Silvio, and Ramona Hernández. *The Dominican Americans*. Westport, CT: Greenwood Press, 1998.

Tumin, Melvin, ed. *Social Class and Social Change in Puerto Rico*. Princeton: Princeton University Press, 1961.

Turner, Victor. *The Ritual Process: Structure and Anti-Structure*. Chicago: Aldine, 1969.

Tyack, David. "Preserving the Republic by Educating Republicans." *Diversity and Its Discontents: Cultural Conflict and Common Ground in Contemporary American Society*. Ed. Neil Smelser and Jeffrey Alexander. Princeton: Princeton University Press, 1999. 63–84.

Ugwu, Catherine, ed. *Let's Get It On: The Politics of Performance*. Seattle: Bay Press, 1995.

United Nations Centre against Apartheid. "The Effects of Apartheid on the Status of Women in South Africa." *The Black Scholar* 10, no. 1 (September 1978): 11–19.

U.S. Department of Justice and U.S. Department of Immigration Service. *1998 Statistical Yearbook of the Immigration and Naturalization Service*. Washington, DC: U.S. Department of Justice and U.S. Department of Immigration Service, 1998.

Valdés, Alisa. "How *Proyecto Uno* Is Working to Be the Next Big Thing." *Boston Globe* (February 25, 1996): B27.

Van Deburg, William. *New Day in Babylon: The Black Power Movement and American Culture, 1965–1975*. Chicago: University of Chicago Press, 1992.

Van Holmes, Jean. "Belafonte Gives It All He's Got." *Saturday Evening Post* 229, no. 42 (April 20, 1957): 28, 69, 73, 75–77.

Vickerman, Milton. *Crosscurrents: West Indian Immigrants and Race*. New York: Oxford University Press, 1999.

Wald, Alan. "African Americans, Culture and Communism (Part 1)." *Against the Current* 84 (January–February 2000): 23–29.

———. "African Americans, Culture and Communism (Part 2)." *Against the Current* 86 (May–June 2000): 27–34.

———. *Writing from the Left: New Essays on Radical Culture and Politics*. London: Verso, 1994.

Waldrep, Shelton. "'Being Bridges': Cleaver/Baldwin/Lorde and African-American Sexism and Sexuality." *Journal of Homosexuality* 26, nos. 2–3 (1993): 167–180.

Wallace, Elisabeth. *The British Caribbean: From the Decline of Colonialism to the End of Federation*. Toronto: University of Toronto Press, 1977.

Wallerstein, Immanuel. *Africa: The Politics of Unity*. New York: Random House, 1967.

———. *Africa: The Politics of Independence*. New York: Vintage Books, 1961.

Walrond, Eric. *Tropic Death*. New York: Boni and Liveright, 1926.

Walters, Ronald W. *Pan Africanism in the African Diaspora: An Analysis of Modern Afrocentric Political Movements*. Detroit: Wayne State University Press, 1993.

Warner, William Lloyd, and Leo Srole. *The Social Systems of American Ethnic Groups*. New Haven: Yale University Press, 1945.

Waters, Mary C. *Black Identities: West Indian Immigrant Dreams and American Realities*. Cambridge, MA: Harvard University Press, 1999.

———. "Ethnic and Racial Identities of Second-Generation Black Immigrants in New York City." *The New Second Generation*. Ed. Alejandro Portes. New York: Russell Sage Foundation, 1996. 171–196.

———. *Ethnic Options: Choosing Identities in America*. Berkeley: University of California Press, 1990.

Watkins, S. Craig. *Representing: Hip Hop Culture and the Production of Black Cinema*. London: University of Chicago Press, 1998.

Watkins-Owens, Irma. *Blood Relations: Caribbean Immigrants and the Harlem Community, 1900–1930*. Bloomington: Indiana University Press, 1996.

Waugh, Alec. *Island in the Sun*. New York: Farrar, Straus, and Cudahy, 1955.

Wechsler, James A. "Sound Barrier." *New York Post* (June 22, 1964): 26.

———. "Sound Barrier II." *New York Post* (June 23, 1964): 26.

West, Hollie. "Sexual Politics and the Afro-American Writer." *Washington Post* (May 8, 1978): B5.

Whitburn, Joel. *The Billboard Book of Top 40 Albums*. 3rd ed. New York: Billboard Books, 1995.

Whitcomb, Jon. "Backstage at the Birth of a Hit." *Cosmopolitan* 136, no. 3 (March 1954): 54–59.

Woldemikael, Tekle Mariam. *Becoming Black American: Haitians and American Institutions in Evanston, Illinois*. New York: AMS Press, 1989.

Wright, Sarah. "The Negro Woman in American Literature." *Freedomways* 6, no.1 (Winter 1966): 8–10.

Yang, Philip Q. *Post-1965 Immigration to the United States: Structural Determinants*. Westport, CT: Praeger, 1995.

Zanuck, Darryl. "Controversy Is Box Office." *International Film Annual*. Ed. Dixon Campbell. London: John Calder, 1957. 78–80.

## ARCHIVES AND COLLECTIONS

Harry Belafonte Photograph Collection
Photographs and Prints Division
Schomburg Center for Research in Black Culture
New York Public Library
New York

Harry Belafonte Scores
Manuscripts, Archives, and Rare Books Division
Schomburg Center for Research in Black Culture
New York Public Library
New York

Harry Belafonte Television Archives
Television and Radio Library
Museum of Television and Radio
New York

Black Films Collection, 1939–1984
Manuscripts, Archives, and Rare Books Division
Schomburg Center for Research in Black Culture
New York Public Library
New York

Piri Thomas Papers
Manuscripts, Archives, and Rare Books Division
Schomburg Center for Research in Black Culture
New York Public Library
Astor, Lenox, and Tilden Foundations
New York


SELECTED NEWSPAPERS, JOURNALS, AND MAGAZINES

*The Black Scholar*
*Business Week*
*Crisis*
*Cosmopolitan*
*Essence Magazine*
*Freedomways*
*Life Magazine*
*Look Magazine*
*Negro Digest/Black World*
*The New York Times*
*Newsweek*
*Opportunity: A Journal of Negro Life*
*The Saturday Evening Post*
*Time Magazine*
*U.S. News and World Report*
*Vibe*
*Vogue*


SELECTED DISCOGRAPHY

Banton, Buju. *Voice of Jamaica*. PolyGram Records, CD, 314 518 013-2, 1993.
Belafonte, Harry. *Harry Belafonte—Calypso*. RCA, CD, 07863 53801-2, 1992.
———. *Island in the Sun*. CD, RCA, PDC2-1295, 1991.
———. *Belafonte at Carnegie Hall*. RCA, CD, 6006-2-R, 1989.

————. *Belafonte*. RCA Victor, LP, LSP-1150(e), 1956.

————. *Harry Belafonte—Calypso*. RCA Victor, LP, LPM-1248, 1956.

————. *Mark Twain and Other Folk Favorites*. RCA Victor, LP, LPM-1022, 1954.

Born Jamericans. *Yardcore*. Delicious Vinyl, CD, DV5018-2, 1997.

————. *Kids from Foreign*. Delicious Vinyl, CD, 92349-2, 1994.

Dark Latin Groove. *Gotcha!* Sony Discos, CD, TRK82924/2-475033, 1999.

The Fugees. *The Score*. Ruffhouse/Columbia, CD, CK 67147, 1996.

Heavy D & the Boyz. *Blue Funk*. Uptown Records, CD, UPTD-10734, 1992.

Jean, Wyclef. *The Carnival, Featuring Refugee All-Stars*. Columbia, CD, CK 67974, 1997.

Latinos. *Pa' la calle*. Copacabana Records, CD, 44003-2, 1999.

Lopez, Jennifer. *On the 6*. Work/Sony, CD, OK 69351, 1999.

Marley, Bob. *Chant Down Babylon*. Island Def Jam Music Group, CD, 314 546 404-2, 1999.

Maxwell. *Embrya*. Columbia, CD, CK 68968, 1998.

————. *Maxwell's Urban Hang Suite*. Columbia, CD, CK 66434, 1996.

Mighty Sparrow. *Sixteen Carnival Hits*. Ice (import), CD, 92090, 1992.

Notorious B.I.G. *Life after Death*. Bad Boy Records, CD, 78612-73011-2, 1997.

————. *Ready to Die*. Bad Boy Entertainment, CD, 78612-73000-2, 1994.

Pras. *Ghetto Supastar*. Ruffhouse/Columbia, CD, CK69516, 1998.

*Proyecto Uno. 4*. H.O.L.A. Recordings, LLC, CD, 153373-2, 1999.

————. *Mega Mix Hits*. J & N Records, CD, CDZ-82581, 1997.

————. *Todo el mundo*. J & N Records, CDZ-82311, 1997.

————. *New Era*. H.O.L.A. Recordings, LLC, CD, 119-341-006-2, 1996.

————. *In Da House*. J & N Records, CD, H2 7243 B 28857 2 6, 1994.

*Rap: Hall of Fame*. K-Tel International, CD, 2275 30412, 1992.

Roaring Lion, King Radio, et al. *Calypso Carnival, 1936–1941*. Rounder Records, C 1077, 1993.

Santana, Carlos. "Maria Maria." Arista, CD Single, 7822-13773-2, 2000.

Viloria, Angel. *Merengues: Volume 2*. Beltone/Ansonia, CD, HGCD1207, 1991.

SELECTED FILMOGRAPHY

*Beware!* Dir. Bud Pollard. Perf. Louis Jordan, June Richmond, and Lorenzo Tucker. Astor, 1946.

*Big Phat Ones of Hip-Hop, Volume I*. Dir. Jon Baum. Perf. Notorious B.I.G., Warren G, Rappin' 4-Tay, Patra, K7, Scarface, the 69 Boyz, Coolio, Craig Mack, Method Man, Salt 'N' Pepa, R. Kelly. Videocassette. Polygram, 1995.

*The Birth of a Nation*. Dir. D. W. Griffith. Perf. Henry Walthall, Miriam Cooper, and Mae Marsh. Epoch, 1915.

*The Body of a Poet: A Tribute to Audre Lorde: Warrior Poet, 1934–1992/a Film by Sonali Fernando*. Dir. Sonali Fernando. Videocassette. Women Make Movies, 1995.

*Bright Road*. Dir. Gerald Mayer. Perf. Harry Belafonte, Dorothy Dandridge, and Robert Horton. MGM, 1953.

*Carmen Jones*. Dir. Otto Preminger. Perf. Harry Belafonte, Dorothy Dandridge, and Pearl Bailey. Twentieth Century Fox, 1954.

*The Emperor Jones*. Dir. Dudley Murphy. Perf. Paul Robeson, Dudley Diggs, and Ruby Elzi. United Artists, 1933.

*An Evening with Harry Belafonte and Friends*. Dir. Jim Brown. Perf. Harry Belafonte. Videocassette. Polygram, 1997.

*Gentlemen's Agreement*. Dir. Elia Kazan. Perf. Gregory Peck, Dorothy McGuire, and John Garfield. Twentieth Century Fox, 1947.

*Hip-Hop + R&B Music Videos*. "Busta Rhymes vs. Redman." Videocassette. Make It or Break It Videos, 1999.

*I Walked with a Zombie*. Dir. Jacques Tourneur. Perf. Sir Lancelot, Tom Conway, and Frances Dee. RKO, 1943.

*Island in the Sun*. Dir. Robert Rossen. Perf. Joan Fontaine, James Mason, Dorothy Dandridge, Joan Collins, and Harry Belafonte. Darryl Zanuck Productions, 1957.

*A Litany for Survival: The Life and Work of Audre Lorde*. Dirs. Ada Gray Griffin and Michelle Parkerson. Perfs. Barbara Smith, Audre Lorde, Sonia Sanchez. Videocassette. Third World Newsreel, 1996.

*No Way Out*. Dir. Joseph L. Mankiewicz. Perf. Sidney Poitier, Richard Widmark, and Linda Darnell. Twentieth Century Fox, 1950.

*Odds against Tomorrow*. Dir. Robert Wise. Perf. Harry Belafonte, Ed Begley, Sr., and Robert Ryan. United Artists, 1959.

*Pinky*. Dir. Elia Kazan. Perf. Jeanne Crain, Ethel Waters, and Ethel Barrymore. Twentieth Century Fox, 1949.

*Rap and R&B Music Videos*. "The Best of Wyclef Jean." Videocassette. Make It or Break It Videos, 1999.

*Rap and R&B Music Videos*. "Wyclef Jean #2." Videocassette. Make It or Break It Videos, 1999.

*Reet, Petite, and Gone*. Dir. William Forest Crouch. Perf. Louis Jordan, June Richmond, and Lorenzo Tucker. Astor, 1947.

*Scandalize My Name: Stories from the Blacklist*. Dir. Alexandra Isles. Perf. Harry Belafonte, Morgan Freeman, and Ossie Davis. BET Movies, 1999.

*Showboat*. Dir. James Whale. Perf. Irene Dunn, Allan Jones, Charles Winninger, and Paul Robeson. Universal, 1936.

*The Trial.* Dir. Mark Robson. Perf. Juano Hernandez, Glenn Ford, and Dorothy McGuire. MGM, 1955.

*Two Yanks in Trinidad.* Dir. Gregory Ratoff. Perf. Sir Lancelot, Pat O'Brien, and Brian Donlevy. Columbia, 1942.

*The World, the Flesh, and the Devil.* Dir. Ranald MacDougall. Perf. Harry Belafonte, Inger Stevens, and Mel Ferrer. MGM, 1959.

# INDEX

Africa. *See* Lorde, Audre; Marshall, Paule; Pan-Africanism

Afrika Bambaataa, and hip hop, 211

Alberti, Luis, and merengue, 208–209

American Left. *See* Marshall, Paule; Communism

American Negro Theater (ANT), and Harry Belafonte, 33

Anderson, Benedict, imagined communities, 212

Aparicio, Frances, music and gender, 17–18, 203, 219–220

Association of Artists for Freedom, 76–85

Austerlitz, Paul, 207, 228

*Autobiography of Malcolm X. See* X, Malcolm (Little)

Bachata, 207, 220

Balaguer, Joaquín: and the Dominican Republic, 208

Baraka, Amiri (LeRoi Jones), political and artistic affiliations, 77–98

Basch, Linda, and transnationalism, 12, 75

*Belafonte* (album) 40, 42–44. *See also* Belafonte, Harry

Belafonte, Harry, 20; as King of Calypso, 24–72, 238–241

Benitez, "Jelly Bean." *See* Home of Latino Artists (HOLA) Recordings

Big Punisher, and hip hop, 215

*Birth of a Nation, The* (movie), use of racial stereotypes, 34–35, 46, 248n. 26

Black Arts Movement: and Paule Marshall, 88–98; and Audre Lorde, 118–160, 262n. 3

Black Cultural Nationalism. *See* Black Panther (Party); Lorde, Audre; Marshall, Paule; Nation of Islam (Black Muslims); Pan-Africanism; X, Malcolm (Little)

Black Muslims. *See* Nation of Islam (Black Muslims); X, Malcolm (Little)

Black Panther (Party), 87–88, 164–165

Black Power, 85. *See also* Carmichael, Stokely

*Black Scholar, The*, and Audre Lorde, 119–121, 124–125, 128–131

*Black Unicorn, The*, 21, 118–119, 133–142. *See also* Lorde, Audre

*Black World. See Negro Digest/Black World*

"Blackness," use of, 246n. 25

Blanc, Cristina Szanton, and transnationalism, 12, 75

Bogle, Donald, 64

Born Jamericans, and hip hop, 215

Bowen, Angela, 148, 269n. 95

Bracks, Lean'tin, 74

Brady, Tom P., and *Black Monday*, 50

Brasor, Philip, 233

Brock, Sabine, 74

Brown, Claude, and black male autobiography, 163, 167, 172

*Brown Girls, Brownstone*, 74–77, 83, 107. *See also* Marshall, Paule

*Brown v. Board of Education of Topeka*, 26, 49–50. *See also* Civil Rights Movement

Calypso, 24–59. *See also* Belafonte, Harry; Mighty Sparrow, and calypso; Roaring Lion, and calypso; Sir Lancelot, and calypso; Wilmoth Houdini, and calypso

Carby, Hazel, 17–18, 34, 203

Carmichael, Stokely, 87,131, 265n. 42. *See also* Student Nonviolent Coordinating Committee; Black Power

Charlie Chase, and hip hop, 211

Chenault, Lawrence, 8, 166

# ABOUT THE AUTHOR

Lisa D. McGill is the principal of LM Strategies Consulting, a diversity and equity consulting group in Chicago, Illinois. She works primarily to bridge theory and practice in her concentration on helping institutions build better relationships with urban and ethnic communities. She graduated from Yale University in 2001 with a Ph.D. in American Studies. Her undergraduate degree, in English modified with Latin American and Caribbean Studies, is from Dartmouth College.